Hillier's
Fundamentals of Motor Vehicle Technology

Book 3

Chassis and Body Electronics

Hillier's
Fundamentals of Motor Vehicle Technology

5th Edition

Book 3

Chassis and Body Electronics

V.A.W. Hillier & David R. Rodgers

Nelson Thornes

First published in 1966 by:
Hutchinson Education
Second edition 1972
Third edition 1981 (ISBN 0 09 143161 1)
Reprinted in 1990 (ISBN 0 7487 0317 9) by Stanley Thornes (Publishers) Ltd
Fourth edition 1991

Fifth edition published in 2007 by:
Nelson Thornes Ltd
Delta Place
27 Bath Road
CHELTENHAM
GL53 7TH
United Kingdom

10 11 12 13 14 15 / 10 9 8 7 6 5

A catalogue record for this book is available from the British Library

ISBN 978 0 7487 8435 6

Cover photograph:

New illustrations Peters & Zabransky and GreenGate Publishing Services

Page make-up by GreenGate Publishing Services, Tonbridge, Kent

Printed in China by 1010 Printing International Ltd

CONTENTS

ACKNOWLEDGEMENTS

We should like to thank the following companies for permission to make use of copyright and other material:

Audi
Blaupunkt
Fluke
Hellas
Crypton
Daimler-Chrysler
DENSO
Lucas
Robert Bosch Ltd
Pioneer
Porsche
Sun Electric (UK) Ltd
Tektronix
Valeo
Volkswagen UK Ltd

Every effort has been made to trace the copyright holders, but if any have been inadvertently overlooked, the publishers will be pleased to make the necessary arrangements at the first opportunity.

Although many of the drawings are based on commercial components, they are mainly intended to illustrate principles of motor vehicle technology. For this reason, and because component design changes so rapidly, no drawing is claimed to be up to date. Students should refer to manufacturers' publications for the latest information.

PREFACE

The *Hillier's Fundamentals* books are well-established textbooks for students studying Motor Vehicle Engineering Technology at Vocational level. In addition, there are many other readers in the academic and practical world of the automotive industry. As technology has evolved, so have these books in order to keep today's automotive student up to date in a logical and appropriate way.

Many of the chassis and body systems discussed in previous editions of *Fundamentals of Motor Vehicle Technology* have now become standard equipment on modern vehicles or have evolved considerably over time. It is important that anyone wanting to understand these systems has a clear overview of the technology used, right from the first principles!

The *Fundamentals* series now consists of three volumes. Volume one is similar to the previous editions of *FMVT* but has been updated appropriately. It covers most of the topics that students will need in the early part of their studies.

Volume two explores more advanced areas of technology employed in the modern vehicle powertrain, including all of the appropriate electronic control systems with supporting background information. This volume also includes insights into future developments in powertrain systems that are being explored by manufacturers in order to achieve compliance with forthcoming emissions legislation.

Volume three focuses on the body and chassis electronic systems. It covers in detail all of the systems that support the driver in the use and operation of the vehicle. First it introduces the basic principles of electricity and electronics, followed by information on sensor and actuator technology. This equips the reader with the prerequisite knowledge to understand the subsequent sections that are logically split into the relevant topic areas. Finally, a section on diagnostics suggests tools and techniques that can be employed whilst fault finding. This section also includes information to help the reader when faced with typical problems or scenarios whilst attempting diagnostic work on electronic chassis and body systems.

It is interesting to note that most of the current developments that aim to make us safer and more comfortable whilst we drive are due to the massive growth in the availability (due to reducing cost) and performance of electronic control systems and microcontrollers. These offer the vehicle system designer a high degree of freedom to implement features that provide added value and function with respect to comfort and safety.

The complexity of vehicle electronic and control systems will continue to grow exponentially in response to the requirement for technologies to achieve low-pollutant emissions and in order to meet the high expectations of the modern vehicle driver. It is important that today's automotive technician is equipped with the correct skills and knowledge to be able to efficiently maintain and repair modern vehicle systems. I hope that this book will be useful in providing some of this knowledge, either during studies or as a reference source.

Dave Rogers, 2007
www.autoelex.co.uk

LIST OF ABBREVIATIONS

ABS	anti-lock braking system
AC	alternating current
ACC	adaptive cruise control
ADC	analogue to digital converter
AFS	adaptive front-lighting system
AGM	absorbent glass mat
Ah	ampere hours
ALU	or arithmetic logic unit
AVO	amps, volts, ohms
BSI	British Standards Institution
CAN	controller area network
CARB	California Air Resources Board
CCFL	cold cathode fluorescence
cd	candela
CDI	capacitor discharge ignition
CMOS	complementary metal oxide semiconductor
CO	carbon monoxide
CPU	central processing unit
CRC	cyclic redundancy check
DAB	digital audio broadcast
DAC	digital to analogue converter
DC	direct current
DCEL	direct current electroluminescent
DSTN	double-layer supertwist nematic
DTC	body and chassis diagnostic trouble code
EBS	electronic battery sensor
ECL	emitter-coupled logic
ECU	electronic control unit
EGAS	electronic gas
EGR	exhaust gas recirculation
EMC	electromagnetic compatibility
emf	electromotive force
EPROM	erasable programmable read only memory
ESP	electronic stability program
FET	field effect transistor
FSC	function-system-connection
FWD	front-wheel drive
$GaPO_4$	gallium orthophosphate
GB	gigabyte
GPRS	general packet radio service
GPS	global positioning system
GSM	global system for mobile communication
HC	hydrocarbon
h_{fe}	current gain in a transistor
HIL	hardware-in-the-loop method
HT	high tension
HUD	head-up display
Hz	hertz
I/O	input/output

IC	integrated circuit
IEC	International Electrotechnical Commission
ISG	integrated starter–generator
JFET	junction field effect transistor
Kbps	kilobits per second
kHz	kilohertz
LAN	local area network
LDR	light-dependent resistor
LED	light-emitting diode
LIN	local interconnect network
Mbps	megabits per second
MHz	megahertz
MMS	multimedia messaging service
MOSFET	metal oxide semiconductor field effect transistor
ms	milliseconds
NTC	negative temperature coefficient
OBD	on-board diagnostics
OBD2	on-board diagnostics generation two
PAN	personal area network
PCB	printed circuit board
pd	potential difference
PES	poly-ellipsoidal system
PID	proportional-integral-derivative
ppm	parts per million
PSU	power supply unit
PTC	positive temperature coefficient
PVC	polyvinyl chloride
PWM	pulse width modulated
RAM	random access memory
R–C	resistance–capacitance
RDS	radio data system
RF	radio frequency
rms	root mean square
ROM	read-only memory
SC	segment conductor
SI	System International
SIM	subscriber identity module
SMS	short messaging service
SRS	supplementary restraint system
SSI	small-scale integration device
STN	super-twisted nematic
TCS	traction control system
TFT	thin film transistor
TN-LCD	twisted nematic-liquid crystal display
TTL	transistor-transistor logic
UART	universal asynchronous receiver transmitter
VFD	vacuum fluorescent display
VLSI	very-large-scale integration

Chapter 1

BASIC PRINCIPLES AND TECHNIQUES

what is covered in this chapter ...

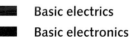 Basic electrics

■ Basic electronics

1.1 BASIC ELECTRICS

1.1.1 Fundamental principles of electricity

Basic electricity and circuits

This is a book about the fundamentals, hence we will start at a very fundamental level to introduce some simple concepts about electricity, electronics and the way circuits behave. This will be the underpinning knowledge for the more sophisticated topics within this book.

All matter around us consists of complex arrangements of particles made up of protons (positively charged) and electrons (negatively charged). These are known as atoms. For example, a hydrogen atom consists of a proton at the centre (or nucleus) and one electron which orbits the proton (nucleus) at high speed. The nucleus can be regarded as a fixed point and the mobility of the electrons dictates the behaviour of that material with respect to electrical current flow.

Conductors and insulators, electron flow, conventional flow

In certain materials, the electrons are not bonded tightly to their nucleus and they drift randomly from atom to atom. Electrical current flow is the movement of electrons within a material, so a substance in which the electrons are not bonded tightly together will make a good conductor. This is because little effort is needed to push the electrons through the atomic structure.

Conversely, insulators have no loosely bound electrons so this impedes the movement of electrons and therefore prevents the flow of electrical current. One point to note though is that no material is a perfect insulator; all materials will allow some electron movement if the force (i.e. voltage) is high enough.

The conduction of electricity in a material is due to electron movement from a low to high potential (often described as potential difference). As the electrons move

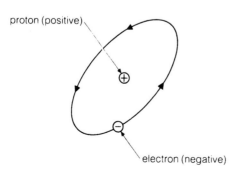

Figure 1.1 Hydrogen atom

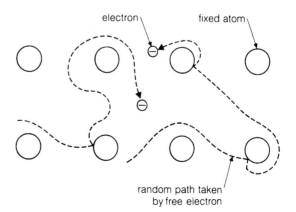

Figure 1.2 Copper atom

they collide with atoms in their path and this raises the temperature of the conductor. This electron flow gives rise to an energy flow called 'current'. An important point to note is that electron flow works in the opposite direction to current flow, i.e. conventional current flow is from positive to negative whereas electrons flow from negative to positive. For all practical purposes we can consider that electricity flows from positive to negative – as this is an agreed convention!

Electric circuit – hydraulic analogy

Electrons moving in a circuit can be difficult to visualise. The easiest way to think about an electrical circuit and its behaviour is with an analogy of hydraulics. Picture the movement of electrons in a circuit as water flowing in a hosepipe. In order for the water to flow in the pipe a pressure difference must occur between two points. This then forces the water along the pipe. The pressure in such a hosepipe system can be likened to the voltage of an electrical system (see Figure 1.4).

This pressure has to be generated, and in a hydraulic system, for example, this would be via a pump. This pump can be compared directly with a generator (mechanical to electrical energy converter) or a battery (chemical to electrical energy converter) as a pressure source. Note though that just as the pump does not 'make' the fluid, the generator or battery does not 'make' electricity. These components just impart energy to the electrons that already exist. The rate at which the water flows can be measured and this would be measured in volume (litres, gallons) per unit of time (hours/minutes/seconds). In an electrical circuit, this flow rate of electrons is expressed in a unit called amps (amperes).

Further parallels can be drawn to assist in understanding. For example, to control the flow in a hydraulic circuit, a tap can be installed (see Figure 1.5). This can be used to enable or disable flow of water. In an electric circuit this would be a switch. Also, the tap can be used to restrict or control the flow rate. In an electric circuit, this function is carried out by a variable resistor which would control the flow of electrons into a circuit. A fixed resistor would be a flow restrictor or restriction in the hydraulic circuit.

Potential difference

The potential, with respect to electrical circuits, indicates that the capability to do some work via the movement of electrons exists. Just as the pressure gauge of an air compressor storage vessel shows that pressure exists and hence some work can be done via the stored 'potential' energy in the compressed air when required.

In an electric circuit, the amount of work done depends on the flow rate of electrons and this depends on the potential difference (or pressure drop) between the two points in a circuit. Therefore it is the potential difference in an electrical circuit that gives rise to electron or current flow. For example, the voltage difference across a battery is a potential difference.

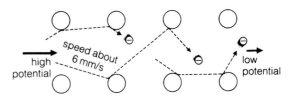

Figure 1.3 Electron flow from high to low potential

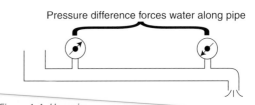

Figure 1.4 Hosepipe

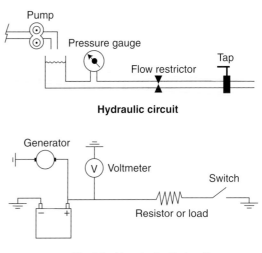

Figure 1.5 Hydraulic and electric circuit

Electromotive force

A battery or generator is capable of creating a difference in potential. The electrical force that gives this potential difference is called the electromotive force. This is again a pressure difference that drives electrons around a circuit. As mentioned previously, the unit of electrical pressure and electromotive force is the volt. The terminal connections of a battery or generator are marked as positive and negative and these relate to the higher and lower potential respectively.

Amps, volts, ohms, Ohm's law, power

A certain quantity of electrons set in motion by a potential difference is known as a coulomb. This is a unit which represents the quantity of electrons or charge. In a hydraulic system, a similar unit of measure would be the litre (i.e. volume).

More useful than the volume of charge is the flow rate as this represents the rate of energy flow. This flow rate is expressed in electrical terms by the unit amps (amperes). When one coulomb of charge passes a given point in a circuit in one second, then the current flow is defined as one amp.

In order that a current can flow in a circuit, a difference in pressure must exist created by an electromotive force (as mentioned previously). This pressure is measured and expressed in volts. Of course, circuits and circuit components can resist the flow of electrons. This is known as resistance and can be measured and expressed in units of ohms. Voltage, current and resistance are all related and this was discovered by the scientist called Ohm in 1827. He discovered that at a constant temperature, the current in a conductor is directly proportional to the potential difference across its ends. Also, the current is inversely proportional to resistance. This is known as Ohm's law and the relationship is:

$$\frac{V}{I} = R$$

where V = pd (potential difference); I = Current; and R = Resistance.

The resistance of any conductor is determined by the material properties with respect to electron flow, its length and cross-sectional area, and the temperature. A normalised measure of the resistance of a material, i.e. its ability to resist electrical current flow, can be gained by knowing its resistivity (units are ohm metre). This is the resistance (in ohms) measured across a one-metre length of the material which has a cross-section of one square metre. Some typical values for common materials are shown in Table 1.1.

The most commonly used material for electrical components and wiring is copper as this has a low resistance at a moderate cost. Precious metals have lower resistivity but of course are more expensive. Irrespective of this fact, it is not uncommon to see gold or silver connectors or contacts in switches or relays due to the lower resistance of the material. It is also important to note that most materials increase their resistance as temperature increases. This is known as a positive temperature coefficient and is a factor that

must be taken into account where cables run in areas of elevated temperatures (e.g. in the engine compartment) or where there is limited circulating air for cooling (e.g. under a carpet or trim panel).

The watt is the SI (System International) unit of power and is universally applied in mechanical and electrical engineering. It expresses the rate of doing work or energy release. The unit of energy is the joule and this is the amount of work required to apply a force of one newton for a distance of one metre. Work expended at the rate of one joule per second is a watt (named after James Watt). In electrical terms, a current flowing in a circuit of one amp under an electromotive force (emf) of one volt will dissipate one watt.

This can be expressed as:

$$P = VI$$

where P = Power, V = Voltage, I = Current.

Also, combining the above equations we can say that:

$$P = I^2R \quad \text{or} \quad P = \frac{V^2}{R}$$

where R = Resistance.

An important point to note from the above is that if the current is doubled then the power (heating effect) is increased by a factor of four. This is used to great effect in fuses where any increase in current produces a significant increase in heat which is used to intentionally melt the fuse conductor and break the circuit.

Earthing arrangements

The simple circuit shown in Figure 1.6 connects the lamp to the battery and uses a switch to control the supply from the battery via the feed wire. To complete the circuit a return path to the battery must exist and in Figure 1.6 it is via a return wire.

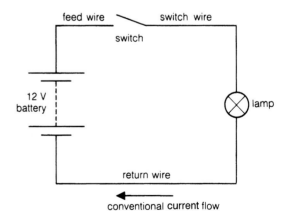

Figure 1.6 Insulated return circuit for a supply current

For vehicle wiring systems this is generally not the case! Feed wires supply the current to components via switches etc., but the return path is normally completed through the vehicle frame or bodywork (assuming it is metallic, a conductor). The reasons for this are:

Table 1.1 Resistivity of some materials used for electrical conductors

Substance	Approximate resistivity (ohm m at 20°C)
Silver	1.62×10^{-8} (or 0.000 000 0162)
Copper	1.72×10^{-8}
Aluminium	2.82×10^{-8}
Tungsten	5.50×10^{-8}
Brass	8.00×10^{-8}
Iron	9.80×10^{-8}
Manganin	44.00×10^{-8}
Constantin	49.00×10^{-8}

- The amount of cabling required is theoretically halved. This reduces cost and saves weight.
- The complexity of the wiring harness and connections is also greatly reduced; this creates a more reliable wiring system.

One important point though is that the wiring system must be protected from abrasion against the bodywork. This abrasion can occur due to vibrations and it will reduce the integrity of the cable insulation (i.e. by rubbing through it). Under these circumstances a 'short' circuit could occur (i.e. the current flows directly back to the battery via a low-resistance path through the metallic bodywork, high current can flow due to this low resistance and this in turn can overheat the cable). There is a risk of fire if the circuit is not suitably protected via a fuse.

For certain vehicle types, separate earth return cables are used to optimise safety by reducing the risk of short circuits due to the above scenario. This technique is generally used for fuel tankers for example and is known as an insulated return system (see Figure 1.8).

An important point with respect to earth connections is the polarity. That is, which of the two battery connections will be connected to the vehicle frame as described above. Generally, all modern cars have the battery 'negative' connected to earth. This means that live cables are at the same potential as the battery (12 volts for a car) and the earth connection is at 0 volts. Hence a potential difference between the live cable and the frame exists (i.e. 12 volts; see Figure 1.9).

This method has been common since the 1970s, but prior to this some vehicles were positive earth, i.e. a 12 volt positive connection to the frame and zero volts at the live cables. The potential difference was the same and it was thought that positive earth systems would produce better ignition performance as the spark polarity at the plug was negative (the spark jumps from earth to centre electrode with respect to conventional flow). This meant that the electron flow (opposite to conventional flow) was from centre to earth electrode, i.e. from a hotter to colder surface. This temperature difference worked in favour of the electron flow and marginally improved ignition performance. Due to the lack of sophistication in the electrical system at that time, the polarity of the vehicle could be changed quite easily. In a modern vehicle with electronic systems reverse polarity would be catastrophic; also, the high performance of modern ignition systems is such that the advantage of a positive earth system is now irrelevant.

Circuit faults – open and short circuit

The two most common faults in a simple circuit are an open circuit and a short circuit. One point that is clear by now is that a complete circuit is needed if current is to flow. To control a circuit we can install a switch and this device intentionally breaks the circuit to prevent current flow when required. An open circuit has the same effect. It prevents current flow, but it is an unintentional break in the circuit due to a wiring or component fault (e.g. an unintentionally disconnected terminal; see Figure 1.10).

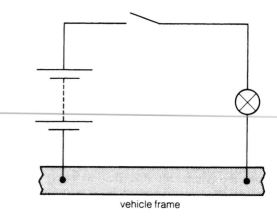

Figure 1.7 Earth return circuit

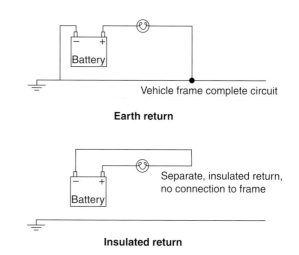

Figure 1.8 Simple earth and insulated return circuit

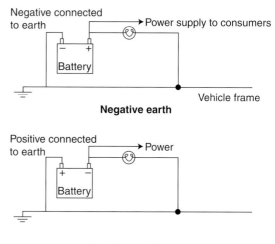

Figure 1.9 Positive and negative earth systems

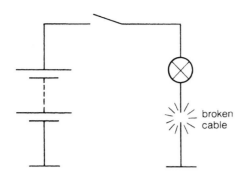

Figure 1.10 Open circuit

As mentioned previously, if the insulation of a live wire is damaged and the conductor is allowed to touch the metal bodywork, then a very low-resistance return path for current will exist. Some or all of the current will flow along this path thus taking a short cut back to the battery (i.e. without passing through the intended consumer). Hence the term 'short circuit' (see Figure 1.11).

In these circumstances very high current levels can flow due to the fact that a vehicle battery has very high current density. This has a damaging and dangerous effect on the vehicle wiring as these large currents can heat the cables such that they glow red hot. This then melts the insulation on the cable and causes further shorts to surrounding cables. Worse than this, the insulation can combust and cause a fire. Normally if this occurs the wiring harness and possibly the vehicle is damaged beyond repair! For these reasons a circuit is normally protected by a current-limiting device such as a fuse or circuit breaker and this protects the wiring system from over current caused by a short circuit.

Key Points

Electrical energy flow through a conductor can be likened to water flowing through a hosepipe. Bearing this analogy in mind, voltage is the pressure and current is the flow rate in the system. The more pressure the more flow!

Conductors allow the free movement of electrons through them and hence electrical current flow. Insulators do not

Key Points

The direction of current flow and electron flow are opposite

Multiply amps and volts in a circuit and this gives power in watts. This is an SI unit to measure the rate at which work is done

Generally, in an automotive electrical circuit, one of the battery terminals is connected to the vehicle frame and this is used as a return path for the current. The terminal connected to the frame dictates the earthing arrangement, i.e. positive or negative earth. Modern vehicles are negative earth

A short circuit is an unintentional low-resistance path in a circuit causing excessive current to flow. An open circuit is an unintentional high-resistance path which reduces or prevents current flow. Both of them, if they occur, are fault conditions

1.1.2 Electromagnetics

Magnetism
A magnet (permanent or electromagnet) is surrounded by a magnetic field. This is an invisible region around the magnet which produces an external force on ferromagnetic objects. The two ends of a magnet are known as 'poles', north and south. Figure 1.12 shows the lines of force around a bar magnet.

An important property of a magnet is that these poles attract and repel each other, i.e. like poles repel and unlike poles attract.

Magnetic flux and flux density
The lines of force around a magnet are known as magnetic flux and indicate a region of magnetic activity. Certain materials will concentrate the field due to an effect called permeability which concentrates the path of the flux. For example, Figure 1.14 shows how the iron frame (which has high permeability) concentrates the flux.

The unit of magnetic flux is the weber. Note that a change in flux of one weber per second will induce an electromotive force of one volt.

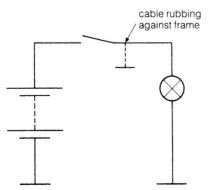

Figure 1.11 Short circuit

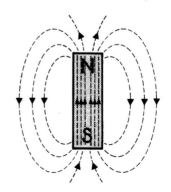

Figure 1.12 Lines of force around a bar magnet

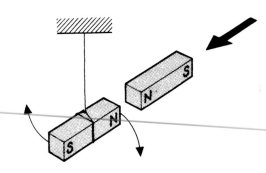

Figure 1.13 *Action when two opposing poles are brought together*

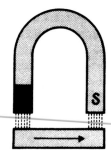

Figure 1.15 *Reluctance*

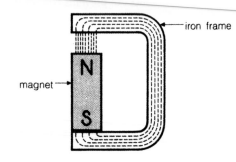

Figure 1.14 *Iron frame concentrates the flux*

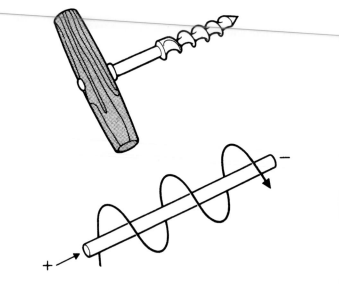

Figure 1.16 *Maxwell's corkscrew rule*

The unit of flux density is the tesla and is expressed as a ratio of the magnetic flux relative to the area.

Reluctance

This property is can be compared to resistance in electrical terms, except of course it applies to a magnetic circuit. It is the resistance of a material to a magnetic field. Figure 1.15 shows how the reluctance of an air gap is reduced when two poles of a magnet are bridged by a piece of iron.

The unit of reluctance is the henry and is defined as the reluctance of a circuit where the rate of change of current is one ampere per second and the resulting electromotive force is one volt.

Electromagnetism

One effect of a current flowing in a conductor is to create a magnetic field around that conductor. The direction of this magnetic field depends on the direction in which current flows through the conductor. This can be visualised by using Maxwell's corkscrew rule (see Figure 1.16). It has a number of practical applications as discussed below.

Electromagnets

When current flows through a wire conductor that has been wound into a coil, the flux produced around this coil can be concentrated by using a soft iron core (as discussed above). The windings are placed close to each other and the flux blends to form a common pattern around the iron core similar to a bar magnet.

The polarity of the magnet depends on the direction of current flow through the coil. The strength of the magnet depends on two factors:

- the amount of current flowing through the winding
- the number of turns in the winding.

Laws of magnetism

During the 19th century many scientists researched electricity and magnetism. Their experimental work produced a number of fundamental principles which form a basis of understanding of how electrical and electromagnetic systems behave. This is useful knowledge for anyone working on automotive electrical and electronic systems.

Faraday – electromagnetic induction

One of the most important experiments is shown in Figure 1.17.

Faraday noticed that when he inserted the magnet into the coil the galvanometer needle moved. He also noted that on removal, the galvanometer needle flicked in the

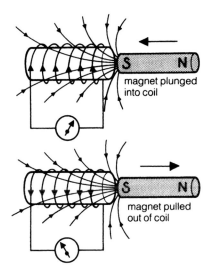

Figure 1.17 Electromagnetic induction

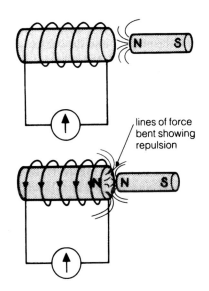

Figure 1.18 Apparatus for showing Lenz's law

opposite direction. This behaviour showed that current was being generated but only when the magnet was moving. It also showed that the direction of the current depended on the direction of movement of the magnet.

This characteristic is known as *electromagnetic induction* and can be described as follows:

An electromotive force (emf) is induced in a coil whenever there is a change in the magnetic flux adjacent to that coil.

The magnitude of this emf depends on:

- the number of turns in the coil
- the strength of the magnetic flux
- the speed of relative movement between the flux and coil.

Lenz – direction of induced current

This law relates to the direction of the induced current resulting from electromagnetic induction. Figure 1.18 shows experimental apparatus to demonstrate the principle.

When the magnet enters the coil an induced current is generated. This current sets up a magnetic field the polarity of which opposes the magnet itself. In other words, the induced current sets up a north pole to repel the magnet.

In practical terms, this law explains 'back emf' which is a well-known phenomenon in motors and coils.

Faraday – mutual and self-induction

Faraday conducted experiments with an iron ring to show that a coil could be used instead of a magnet to induce a current in another coil. Figure 1.19 shows the apparatus.

The primary circuit is connected to a battery, the secondary circuit to a galvanometer. The galvanometer needle responds every time the circuit is completed or broken but in opposite directions. The induced current in the secondary winding depends on:

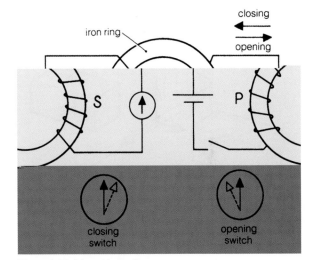

Figure 1.19 Mutual induction

- the magnitude of the primary current
- the turns ratio between primary and secondary coils
- the speed at which the magnetic field collapses.

This is property is known as *mutual induction* and forms the basic principle of operation behind transformers and ignition coils.

In the above experiment, when closing the switch, the growing magnetic field produces an emf in the primary circuit itself that opposes the current flowing into that circuit (according to Lenz's law). This slows down the growth of the current in the primary circuit.

Conversely, when opening the switch, the collapsing magnetic field will induce current in the primary circuit (in the opposite direction to that described above), which causes arcing at the switch contacts. This is due to *self-induction* and is the reason why capacitors were connected across contact breaker points (standard coil ignition systems) to absorb this emf and reduce arcing, thus extending service life and increasing performance.

Faraday – induction in a straight conductor

Another experiment carried out by Faraday involves the movement of a straight conductor through a magnetic field as shown in Figure 1.20.

An emf is generated when the conductor is moved through the magnetic field. This was developed further by Fleming to show the relationship between the direction of the field, the current and the conductor.

Fleming – right-hand rule (generators), left-hand rule (motors)

The right-hand rule applies to generators and is shown in Figure 1.21.

This can be described as follows:

When the thumb and first two fingers of the right hand are all at right angles to each other, the forefinger points in the direction of the field, the thumb in the direction of motion and the second finger in the direction of current.

This can be summarised as:

thuMb	Motion
foreFinger	Field
seCond finger	Current

The left-hand rule gives the relationship between field, current and motion for a motor.

Just use the left hand instead!

Direct current circuit theorems

These circuit theorems are used in electrical engineering to evaluate the current flows in more complicated direct current (DC) networks containing emf sources and load resistances. It is not the intention to study the application of these in detail as they are less likely to be used by the automotive technician or engineer. However, they are worthy of mention as they highlight important basic principles and knowledge of them means that they can be explored and researched in more detail should you wish to do so.

- *Kirchhoff's current law*: this states that at any junction in a electrical circuit the total current flowing towards that junction is equal to the total current flowing away (see Figure 1.23).

  i.e. $I_1 + I_2 - I_3 - I_4 - I_5 = 0$

- *Kirchhoff's voltage law*: this states that in any closed loop network, the sum of the voltage drops taken around the loop is equal to the resulting emf acting in that loop (see Figure 1.24).

  i.e. $E_1 - E_2 = IR_1 + IR_2 + IR_3$

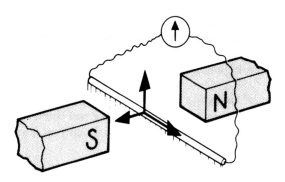

Figure 1.20 Induction in a straight conductor

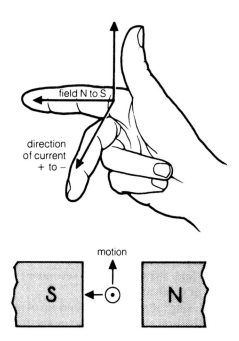

Figure 1.21 Fleming's right-hand rule

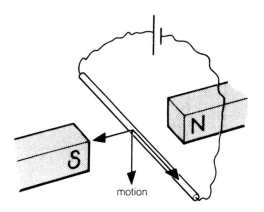

Figure 1.22 Fleming's left-hand rule

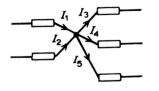

Figure 1.23 Kirchhoff's current law

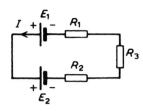

Figure 1.24 Kirchhoff's voltage law

Simple AC generator

This consists of apparatus as shown in Figure 1.25.

Basically there are two magnetic poles either side of a field magnet and a loop conductor which is rotated in the magnetic field. Each end of the loop is connected to a slip ring which makes contact with a carbon brush. When the conductor loop rotates in the magnetic field an emf is generated in it and this drives current around the circuit formed by the loop, slip rings, carbon brushes and connecting wires to the resistor, which forms the electrical load. The slip rings and brushes allow the loop to rotate freely whilst passing current to the static (non-rotating) part of the circuit.

When the loop is at position 1 (in Figure 1.26) the direction of current can be found using Fleming's right-hand rule (above) and is indicated by the arrows and symbols in the figure.

As the loop rotates, the output emf falls until it reaches position 2. Since at this point no flux is 'cut' by the conductors, the output will be zero.

The loop rotates further until it reaches position 3 (effectively 180 degrees from position 1). At this point dense flux is cut by the conductors and emf will be induced in the loop again, but the emf will be the opposite polarity to position 1 and hence the current will flow in the opposite direction (refer to position 3

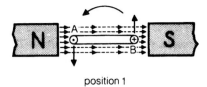

position 1

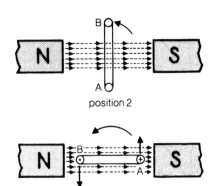

position 2

position 3

Figure 1.26 Coil position and current flow

above and use Fleming's left-hand rule to check your understanding).

The emf generated in the coil is shown below as a plot of emf versus angular movement. The current flow reverses continually as the generator rotates at a frequency directly proportional to speed. This type of current flow is commonly used in many electrical circuits of all kinds and is known as alternating current.

AC circuits, single and three phase

When alternating current (AC) is plotted as a graph of emf versus angle (as above and shown in Figure 1.28), the resulting curve forms a characteristic shape known as a *sine* wave (short for sinusoidal). Using this example, each complete turn gives a repeating, cyclic pattern and this is known as a *cycle*. The time required for this cycle is known as the *periodic time*. The maximum peak in either direction on the y-axis (positive or negative) is known as the *amplitude* and the total distance from the positive peak to the negative peak is the *peak-to-peak* value.

The number of complete cycles that occur per second is known as the *frequency* and the SI unit of frequency is *hertz*. Note that:

$$\text{Frequency} = \frac{1}{\text{Periodic time } (T)}$$

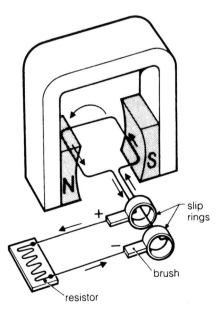

Figure 1.25 Simple dynamo

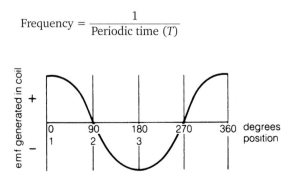

Figure 1.27 Emf generated in a coil

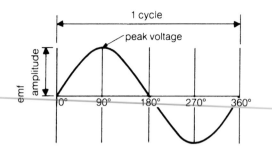

Figure 1.28 Sine wave

Example: A sine-wave cycle repeats in 0.1 seconds, therefore $f = \dfrac{1}{T}$ where f = Frequency and T = Periodic time:

$$f = \frac{1}{0.1} = 10$$

i.e. 10 Hz

Alternating current is widely used in power transmission networks where transformers can be used to step up or down voltages to reduce current flow and losses. In the home, AC is standard at 230 volts 50 Hz (in Europe) but for motor vehicles, current flow must be unidirectional, particularly important for charging batteries! Alternating current can be converted to unidirectional or DC via a process called rectification. Rectifiers are discussed in detail in section 1.2.2. Basically the alternating wave-forms are converted electronically so that the generated emf is always in the same direction. This is known as full-wave rectification, see Figure 1.29.

The instantaneous emf gives a proportional current flow in a connected circuit with a given resistance (R). The power dissipated in this circuit as heat will be given by:

Power (Watts) = VI or I^2R (as discussed above)

An important point with respect to a sine wave is the amount of energy or work that the alternating current flow can do. Power is converted to heat in a resistance and this is not a polarity conscious effect. That is, the direction of the current flow is not important in a resistor, just its magnitude.

If the peak value of an AC sine wave is, say, 12 volts, this means that in one cycle, the emf is at its peak value only twice (once in each direction of current flow). At this point, only, does the maximum current flow. Compared to a DC emf of 12 volts (where this voltage is continuously existing), less energy will be dissipated. In order to compare AC sine-wave voltages with DC

values directly in terms of power output, we can use the root mean square (rms) values of a sine wave and this is directly comparable to a DC voltage value with respect to power. The rms value of a sine wave can be calculated from:

rms = Peak voltage × 0.707

Also note the mean (average) value of a sine wave:

Mean = Peak voltage × 0.637

Most modern measurement devices, for example multimeters, will display the true rms value of a sine-wave voltage. Rms values are used because the normal average voltage value of a pure sine wave is zero no matter how high the peak voltage.

Sine wave, plus more complex wave-forms (i.e. from an analogue crank angle pick-up for an engine management system) can be viewed, measured, stored and analysed using a digital oscilloscope.

Another factor important in AC circuit analysis is the *impedance*. This is the opposition in a circuit to the flow of an AC. Apart from resistance, in an AC circuit the back emf caused by self-induction opposes the build-up current due to the continually reversing voltage. In a DC circuit this phenomenon only occurs at switch-on. Impedance is expressed in ohms and is calculated as follows for an AC circuit:

$$\text{Impedance} = \frac{\text{Voltage}}{\text{Current}}$$

The output delivered by the simple AC generator consists of a single sine-wave emf that produces a simple, reversing current flow. This is known as single-phase alternating current. In practice, as higher power is needed, single-phase alternating current becomes less efficient at transferring power and where higher power requirements exist a multi-phase supply is used. In most cases this will be three phase. If three conductor coils, each with a single-phase emf, are connected together with the peak voltage spaced equidistantly (at 120 degrees) then this produces a smoother output emf with less ripple and much higher current density than a single-phase supply. The connections of the coils and the resulting output graph are shown in Figures 1.30 and 1.31.

There are two configurations in which the three phases can be connected together according to the requirement of the application. These are known as *star* and *delta* windings and are discussed in more detail in Chapter 4.

Eddy currents

In any electrical machine, in addition to current being induced in windings, currents are also induced in the electrical frames or component parts. These induced emfs cause circulating currents which, due to the low resistance of these parts (generally iron), can be quite considerable and cause excessive heat to build up, as well as causing significant power loss. These are known as 'eddy currents'. Another effect seen in rotating

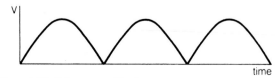

Figure 1.29 Full-wave rectification

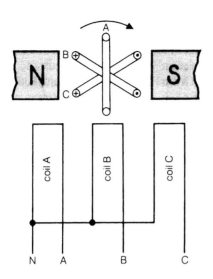

Figure 1.30 Three coils connected

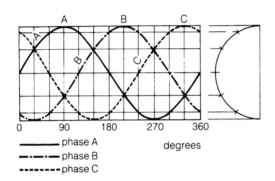

Figure 1.31 Three-phase output

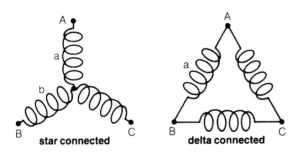

Figure 1.32 Stator windings

machines (such as generators and motors) is that these eddy currents set up a magnetic field which tends to oppose rotation.

Electric machines must have high efficiency and the resistance of these core parts can be increased by laminating the construction, i.e. making the part from thin iron stampings which are insulated from each other with layers of varnish. This increases the resistance of the eddy current path and improves the efficiency of the machine considerably. Figure 1.33 shows the laminated construction of the armature of a DC machine.

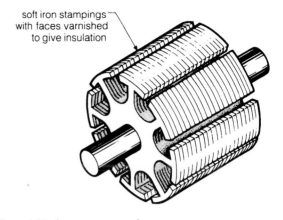

Figure 1.33 Armature construction

Transformer

A transformer is a device which utilises the phenomenon of mutual inductance (as discussed above) to change the voltages of ACs, i.e. to step up or down the magnitude of the supply voltage according to the requirements of the application. The basic schematic is shown in Figure 1.34.

It consists of two windings, a primary and secondary. These are wound around a common ferromagnetic core (which is laminated to reduce eddy currents). The voltage increase or decrease depends on the turns ratio of the windings, i.e.

$$\frac{\text{Secondary voltage}}{\text{primary voltage}} = \frac{\text{Secondary turns}}{\text{primary turns}}$$

The transformer must be supplied with AC in the primary winding to set up a continuously reversing magnetic flux in the core. This flux then induces an emf into the secondary winding. A transformer is a very efficient machine with no moving parts but it cannot create power (i.e. the total amount of energy in an isolated system remains constant). An increase in voltage from primary to secondary gives a proportional decrease in

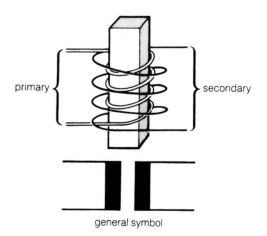

Figure 1.34 Transformer

current (discounting efficiency losses). The losses in a transformer are mainly due to:

- iron losses due to eddy currents
- copper losses due to heating from internal resistance.

Simple DC motor

When current from a battery is applied to a conductor in a magnetic field, then according to Fleming's left-hand rule, a force is produced which will move the conductor.

The cause of this deflecting force can be seen when the lines of magnetic force are mapped. Figure 1.35 shows a current being passed through a conductor and the formation of the magnetic field around it. This field causes the main field to deflect and the repulsion of the two fields produces a force that gives motion to the conductor.

The force acting on this conductor is proportional to the flux density, the current flowing and the length of the conductor exposed in the field.

This effect is used in a DC motor to create a rotating torque. Figure 1.36 shows the construction of a simple DC electric motor.

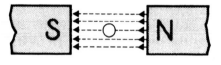

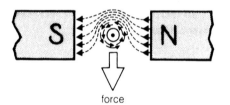

force

Figure 1.35 Bending of main field

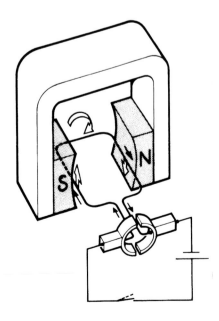

Figure 1.36 DC motor

The conductor coil is formed in a loop and the ends of this are connected to a *commutator*. This device reverses the current in the coil each cycle. In the simple machine shown, the arrangement is a two-segment commutator. The current to the motor coil is applied via the commutator from carbon brushes which slide against it as it rotates. In practice, commutators used in real DC machines are far more complex and consist of many commutator segments.

There are some important general characteristics of DC motors worthy of note:

- Torque is proportional to armature current.
- As speed increases, a back emf is produced (Lenz's law) and this opposes the current flowing into the machine. Therefore, as speed increases, torque decreases (and vice versa).

Hall effect devices

In 1879 Edward Hall discovered that when a magnet is placed perpendicular to the face of a flat current-carrying conductor, a difference in potential appeared across the opposite edges of that conductor. This is known as the 'Hall effect' and the potential difference (pd) produced across the edges is known as the *Hall voltage*.

Figure 1.37 shows the basic principle. The vertical edges of the plate have equal potential so the voltmeter registers zero.

When the plate is placed in a magnetic field (as shown in Figure 1.38) a pd across the edges is shown as a reading on the voltmeter.

The magnitude of the Hall voltage depends upon the current flowing through the plate and the strength of the magnetic field. When the current is constant, the Hall voltage is proportional to the field strength. Similarly, if the field strength is constant, the Hall voltage is proportional to the current flowing through the plate.

With common conductive materials the Hall voltage is relatively low. With the use of semiconductor materials, a much higher voltage can be achieved. Note though that the magnetic field does not generate energy but acts effectively as a switch or controller. Hall effect devices are

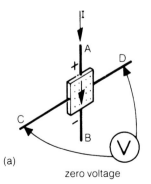

(a)

zero voltage

Figure 1.37 Hall effect – zero voltage

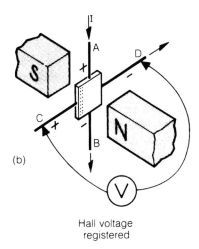

Hall voltage
registered

Figure 1.38 Hall effect – Hall voltage registered

commonly used in sensor technology in combination with magnets or magnetic fields with interrupters to activate the Hall switching. Another application is to use the Hall effect device for measuring current via strength of the magnetic field around a conductor.

Piezoelectrical effect

The piezoelectric effect was discovered by Pierre and Jacques Curie in 1880. It remained a curiosity until the 1940s. The property of certain crystals to exhibit electrical charges under mechanical loading was of no practical use until very high-input impedance amplifiers enabled engineers to amplify these signals. In the 1950s, electronic components of sufficient quality became available and the piezoelectric effect was commercialised.

The charge amplifier principle was patented by the Kistler company in the 1950s and gained practical significance in the 1960s. The introduction of MOSFET (metal oxide semiconductor field effect transistor) solid state circuitry and the development of highly insulating materials such as Teflon and Kapton greatly improved performance and propelled the use of piezoelectric sensors into virtually all areas of modern technology and industry.

During experimentation, Pierre and Jacques Curie discovered the piezoelectric effect using a tourmaline crystal. They found that pressure applied in certain directions to opposing crystal faces produced a reverse poled electric charge on the surface proportional to the applied pressure. During these experiments they found that this effect also applied to other asymmetric crystals like quartz. This is known as the direct piezoelectric effect and is generally employed in sensors measuring mechanical forces like pressure and acceleration.

The reciprocal effect should also be noted. In this phenomenon, an external electrical field causes mechanical stresses in the crystal which alter its physical size proportionally to the strength of this field. This effect is commonly utilised in ultrasonic and communications engineering.

Piezoelectricity, in general terms, can be described as an interaction between the mechanical and electrical state in certain type of crystals. The phenomenon of the direct piezoelectric effect can be described for the electrically free state of a piezo crystal by the following equation:

$$\text{Flow density} = aT$$

Where
a = piezoelectric coefficient
T = mechanical stresses in crystal structure

$$\text{Charge output} = ADn$$

Where
A = face area of crystal
D = flow density
n = components of measuring face

When subjected to mechanical strain/stress caused by an external force, charges are generated on the surface of a piezoelectric material and this can be accessed via electrodes and used in a measurement chain. The generated charges do not remain the whole time that a force is applied, they tend to leak away and for this reason piezoelectric elements are suitable only for measuring dynamic (changing) forces.

	Direct piezoelectric effect	Reciprocal piezoelectric effect
Description	A mechanical deformation of a piezoelectric body causes a charge in the electric polarisation that is proportional to the deformation.	An external electric Field E causes mechanical stresses proportional to the field, which alter the size of the piezo-crystal.
	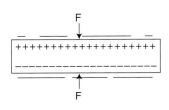	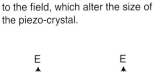
Application	For measuring mechanical parameters, especially of forces, pressures and accelerations.	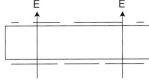In ultrasonic and telecommunications engineering.

Figure 1.39 Piezoelectric effects

For current automotive electronic applications, piezoelectric principles are used within sensors as a technique to measure force or stress in a material as a part of the sensor technology or measurement chain (e.g. yaw sensors), i.e. to indirectly determine the measured phenomenon. There are examples where piezoelectric measuring principles are used directly to measure the phenomenon of interest. Common applications are for measuring vibration forces, for example a combustion knock sensor which measures the structure-borne vibrations caused when a gasoline engine runs into detonation. In the future it is likely that combustion pressure sensors will be fitted to engines. These generally employ piezoelectric measuring elements due to their resistance to high temperature, pressures and forces in the combustion chamber and also due to the high natural frequency of piezoelectric measuring elements.

Key Points

A magnet has two poles, north and south. Between them run magnetic lines of force. With respect to these poles, like poles repel, unlike poles attract

Electromagnets are effectively magnets that can be switched on and off as required. Permanent magnets always have a magnetic field present around them

If a conductor passes through the magnetic lines of force of a magnet, then a current will be induced into that conductor

Basic principles of electromagnetism are used in generators and motors. These can be classified as energy convertors, i.e. they convert mechanical to electrical energy (generator) or vice versa (motor)

Direct current (DC) flows in one direction in a circuit. Alternating current (AC) continuously reverses direction. The rate at which the reversal takes place is known as the frequency and is expressed in hertz (Hz)

Transformers are used to change the voltage/current relationship in a circuit as required. This is a factor of the turns ratio

1.1.3 Test and measurement

There is a large selection of general purpose and dedicated test equipment available to the automotive technician or electrician. For basic fault finding on simple vehicle electrical circuits a home-made test lamp can suffice. When fitted with a bright (21 watt) bulb, in skilled hands this tool can pinpoint many common faults. The wattage of the bulb draws significant current at 12 volts (nearly 2 amps) and this is sufficient to test the quality of the supply to components, highlighting poor connections etc. which can be seen clearly as a reduction in filament brightness.

A test light like this has to be used carefully. Modern cars with sophisticated electronic controllers and systems

can easily be damaged or overloaded by the current that this lamp draws. Printed circuit tracks (on dash inserts) will burn through like fuses when using a lamp such as this. Therefore, for most modern vehicles, unless you are very familiar with that particular vehicle wiring system, the safest bet is to use a voltmeter or multimeter.

Multimeters are very common and are used extensively in industry. Hence, the price of quality units is now quite reasonable. It is also possible to get multimeters with extended features useful for vehicle diagnostic use, for example:

- thermocouple input for temperature measurement
- frequency measurement for speed and pulse-width evaluation
- dwell angle measurement
- rev counter with spark high tension (HT) lead pick up
- shunt for high current measurement
- inductive clamp for current measurement.

Oscilloscopes are useful for analysis of complex waveforms found on vehicle electronic systems and can significantly aid diagnostics. In the past they were generally scientific laboratory instruments, but special version oscilloscopes combined with large multimeters and exhaust gas analysers became commonplace in the vehicle repair and diagnostics industry (known as engine tuning and diagnostic analysers). These were manufactured by companies such as Sun, Crypton and Bosch but due to their size were restricted to workshop use.

As electronic systems have developed, hand-held digital storage oscilloscopes have become common and feature useful additional functions such as data storage, event trigger measurement and freeze frame. These units can be bought as standalone units or combined with diagnostic interface capability to form hand-held analysers.

With the advent of on-board diagnostics on all modern cars, a notebook computer is now a workshop tool. PC-based scan tools programs that can access fault code information and display live data from the engine electronic control system are easily affordable and very useful. Oscilloscope interfaces for PCs allow sophisticated digital storage scope functions to be available for the automotive technician (e.g. www.picotech.com) and these can make life much easier when searching for that elusive fault.

In this section we will concentrate on the basics of measurement equipment, how it works and how it can be used.

Moving coil meters

These are analogue electrical indicating devices. They display the magnitude of the measured quantity by a pointer moving over a graduated scale to give a visible induction. All analogue indicating meters require three attributes:

- a deflection mechanism to move the pointer from rest

- a controlling mechanism to provide a balancing force against the above deflection
- a damping mechanism to ensure that the pointer comes to rest at an appropriate position quickly and without oscillation.

The principle of operation is similar to an electric motor. Figure 1.40 shows the construction.

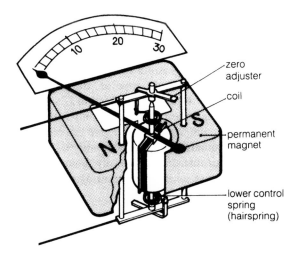

Figure 1.40 Moving-coil meter

There is a permanent magnet with shaped pole pieces and between these there is a fixed iron cylinder. This concentrates the magnetic field and makes the lines of force radiate from the cylinder centre. A coil is wound on an aluminium former and this pivots on jewelled bearings; it is attached to a pointer that registers on the scale. This aluminium former provides the damping effect due to the eddy currents induced in it from the main field.

When current is passed through the coil, the flux distortion causes the coil to move (the deflection mechanism). The angle of movement is controlled by two hairsprings which are also used to supply current to the coil (the controlling mechanism). They are wound in opposite directions to compensate for changes in temperature. This basic meter measures

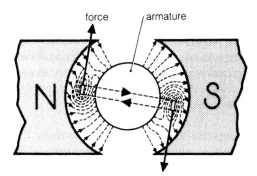

Figure 1.41 Bending of magnetic flux by current

amps (actually milliamps). It is highly sensitive but can be adapted/extended by adding external circuits (shunts and multipliers).

Ammeters

The moving coil device cannot read amps in full due to its size and sensitivity. In order to do this a 'shunt' can be fitted. This is a very low-resistance resistor that is placed in series with the circuit under test which bypasses the meter movement. The meter then just measures a small but proportional amount of the current flow. Different shunts can be selected for different ranges and these can be fitted inside the meter case (for lower values) or externally (for high-value amp range).

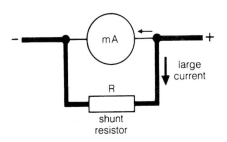

Figure 1.42 Moving-coil ammeter

Voltmeters

The moving-coil meter basically measures current but this flows due to the applied potential difference (voltage). By fitting an external resistance in the circuit (known as a multiplier) higher voltages can be indicated by the device. These resistances are normally fitted inside the meter case and can be selected according to range requirements (multi range).

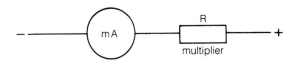

Figure 1.43 Multiplier resistor for measuring voltage

Ohmeters

For measuring resistance, the moving-coil meter can be connected to a circuit with its own power source (battery) and a calibration resistor. The resistance scale has opposite direction to volts and amps as zero is at full-scale deflection. The principle of operation uses Ohm's law, i.e. for a given voltage (supplied by the battery) the resistance is inversely proportional to the current. Therefore, the meter responds to current in the circuit which increases as the resistance decreases. By adding appropriate multiplying resistors in the circuit, multiple ranges can be selected.

Before measuring a resistance, the test leads are connected together and the calibration resistor (potentiometer) is adjusted until the pointer is at zero.

Then the test leads can be connected to the target for measurement.

Other types of resistance measurement devices are a continuity tester (for low-resistance measurement) and a insulation tester (also known as a 'megger') for high-resistance values.

Multimeters

It is clear that the above mechanism is appropriate for measuring volts, amps and ohms and each of these can be configured multi-range. It is less common to see these instruments on their own; normally they are combined in a single measuring instrument called a multimeter (also known as a AVO (amps, volts, ohms)). The single, moving-coil measuring element is housed in a case that also contains all the necessary shunts, multipliers and a battery. On the front side of the case a dial is fitted which acts as a selector switch to provide a means to select what to measure and in what range. Additionally, the front normally houses socket connections for the test leads. Normally the return lead is common, but the input (red) lead must be connected to different input jacks depending on which unit will be measured (current, emf or resistance). Most multimeters also incorporate internal fuse protection to prevent damage to the sensitive components inside.

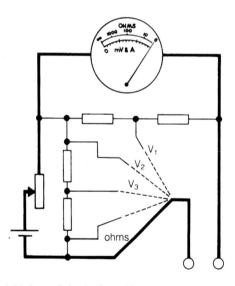

Figure 1.44 Internal circuit of a multimeter

Digital multimeters

Digital multimeters are now universally adopted as a standard measurement device replacing moving-coil multimeters completely. They are easy to use and the display is very clear and unambiguous. Analogue meters can suffer from errors due to the viewing angle (most meters have a mirrored scale to reduce this effect); this is known as parallax error. Additionally, digital meters can be bought as auto-ranging meters. This means that the user only selects the input type (volts, ohms etc.). The meter then intelligently selects the appropriate range and also, if required, switches between ranges whilst in use.

Another advantage of the digital multimeter is that it possesses a very high internal resistance (typically $10\,M\Omega$ (megohms)). This means it has very little effect on the circuit from which the measurement is being taken in terms of placing additional loading on that circuit. This additional circuit load can affect the measured value or the operation of the circuit itself. This is particularly important in sensitive electronic circuits found on modern vehicles.

Figure 1.45 Digital multimeter (Fluke)

Oscilloscopes

Oscilloscopes (also known as scopes) are basically laboratory instruments used in electrical and electronics engineering as a development tool for detailed analysis of the dynamic behaviour of circuits, as well as the analysis of complex signal wave-forms. Originally these units were analogue devices, similar in construction and operating principle to an old-fashioned television screen (cathode ray tube)(see Figure 1.47). Units of this type were rarely seen in the automotive repair industry as they were expensive and not very user friendly.

Analogue-type scopes were more common, and these were built into engine diagnostic systems in combination with an exhaust gas analyser (as supplied by Sun, Crypton, Bear etc., see Figure 1.46). These were used for analysis of faults in ignition low- and high-tension circuits. The problem with these units was that they were expensive and not at all portable.

As developments in digital electronics evolved, digital storage scopes became cheaper, more common and much more useful. For most applications (apart from very high-frequency signal analysis) they were far superior. Screen display was much clearer and the ability to freeze the screen display and store it

Figure 1.46 Computer analyser (Sun Electric (UK) Ltd)

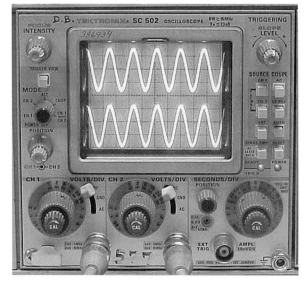

Figure 1.47 Typical analogue scope (Tektronix)

for further analysis, as well as carry out real-time calculations on the raw data curves (like peak values or difference curves) are powerful additional features. In addition, the user interface and ease-of-operation could be improved, for example via auto set-up functions for wave-form capture.

The problem with these laboratory-type instruments is that they are not really designed for use in an automotive environment. They generally need mains power so they are not portable. Also, they are not rugged enough. On a modern vehicle a scope is becoming an essential piece of test equipment. Most engine management actuators and sensors cannot be evaluated properly for correct function under dynamic conditions without one (i.e. connected to the system, in operation with a running engine). Generally the signal to be measured is a complex wave-form that needs to be analysed carefully. This has promoted a new generation of hand-held units specifically designed for use on automotive systems (see Figure 1.48).

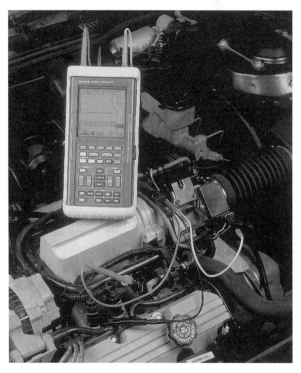

Figure 1.48 Hand-held oscilloscope (Fluke)

The new hand-held units include features such as:

- rugged, portable design
- in-built battery operation or from vehicle, 12 volts
- sturdy input jacks and wiring connectors for daily use
- dedicated harnesses and adaptors for vehicle systems
- dedicated clamps for high tension and current measurement
- interface to PC for storage and analysis.

A good example of current technology in this field is the Bosch FSA 450 shown in Figure 1.49.

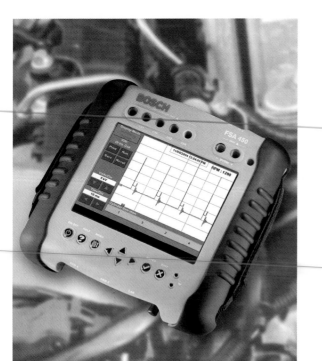

Figure 1.49 Bosch FSA 450

Logic probes

These are tools generally used in the electronics industry, but they have found application in the automotive repair industry due to the high proportion of electronic components in modern vehicles. The logic probe is a simple tool that senses pulses (even of short duration) and also determines whether they are high (logic 1) or low (logic 0). Normally indication is given via LEDs or an audible signal (bleep). The probe can be used at special voltage levels known as CMOS (complementary metal oxide semiconductor) or TTL (transistor-transistor logic) and is ideal for checking signals from a number of vehicles and engine electronics systems and sensors.

The logic probe is ideal for detecting pulses from AC and DC speed sensors (for example distributor ignition trigger, ABS wheel speed, camshaft position sensor), optical sensors (ignition trigger) and frequency

signals (certain types of air flow and manifold pressure sensors). It can also be used to confirm trigger signals at fuel injectors.

It is important to note that because the logic probe has very high internal resistance, it is safe to use on even the most sensitive electronic circuits and components and it will not damage these parts.

Fault code readers and scan tools

These devices consist generally of hand-held units that can connect to the engine electronic diagnostic interface to provide a portal into the system for:

- Interrogating the fault memory to access stored fault codes and to erase stored faults once the cause has been rectified.
- Allowing data transfer during engine operation. This allows the technician access to live data from the sensors and also internal electronic control unit (ECU) data. This can be extremely useful for fault finding. Some scan tools allow event-based data capture for isolating the cause of intermittent faults.
- Resetting of factory conditions and programming of replacement parts, for example resetting the immobiliser for use with a new ignition key transponder, resetting of the air bag control unit etc.

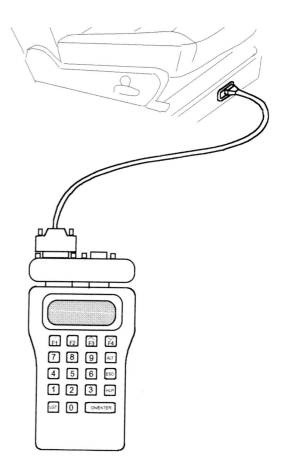

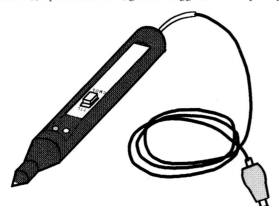

Figure 1.50 TTL/CMOS logis probe

Figure 1.51 Scan tool

In the past each vehicle manufacturer had a specific standard for data transfer protocol and interface hardware. This meant that generally the diagnostic unit supplied by the manufacturer had to be used for the above tasks. Certain manufacturers of diagnostic equipment, who worked closely with automotive manufacturers, produced tools that were multi-application. That is, by exchanging a software memory cartridge, a diagnostic unit could be used on a number of vehicles from different manufacturers. The amount of data and functions available varied considerably according to the manufacturer and so these units could never really be considered universally applicable (i.e. for use on any vehicle).

However, this situation changed with the introduction of OBD (on-board diagnostics) for vehicles. This legislation was driven by the CARB (California Air Resources Board) in an attempt to reduce emissions. With the introduction of on-board diagnostics generation two (OBD2), the first steps were taken to introduce a standard for data protocols and connection interfaces. This allowed diagnostic system manufacturers to create fully generic scan tools that could interrogate the fault memory of any vehicle ECU to access and reset fault codes. Under OBD2 legislation, these fault codes follow a standard convention, hence anybody with the appropriate diagnostic unit can access the fault memory, understand the codes and, when required, reset the ECU. In addition (and depending on the manufacturer), extra information can be made available via this interface. Typical data availability comparison is shown in Table 1.2.

Table 1.2 Data via OBD2 comparison

Typical data values via EOBD	Typical additional data values – manufacturer specific
Throttle position	Alternator load
Engine load	Ambient temperaure
Engine coolant temperature	Battery voltage
Ignition advance	Cam signal
Intake air temperature	Coil charge
Intake mass air pressure	Engine bay temperature
Fuel trim	Fuel pump
Oxygen sensor	Fuel rich/lean status
Engine speed	Fuelling correction
Vehicle speed	Idle speed control
	Idle speed error
	Injector signals
	Injector relay status
	Malfunction indicator lamp (MIL) status
	Cyinder specific misfire signal
	Oxygen sensor heater status
	Oil temperature
	Purge valve duty cycle
	Radiator fan status
	Throttle status
	Throttle voltage

In addition, PC-based software for OBD2 interfacing is now fairly cheap and can be sourced via the internet. This turns the average PC into a powerful diagnostic tool for the automotive technician at a reasonable price.

Key Points

Voltmeters measure system voltage, potential difference or electromotive force and are connected in parallel. An ammeter measures the current flowing and must be connected in series

Ohmeters have an internal power source and use this to measure the resistance of a circuit or component. Normally, the circuit or component must be disconnected first and hence live readings cannot be taken

A multimeter combines the voltmeter, ammeter and ohmmeter plus other useful functions in a single instrument (e.g. diode check, frequency etc.)

Oscilloscopes can be used to analyse the complex wave-forms and dynamic changes in an electronic circuit that cannot be seen with a meter due to the 'averaging' effect (this is true of analogue or digital meters)

Fault-code readers and scan tools interface with the ECU to provide access to stored or live data directly from the electronic control system. For engine and powertrain ECUs this interface is standardised under OBD (on-board diagnostics)

1.1.4 Electrical symbols and units

Symbols

Diagrams of electrical systems are shown in pictorial or theoretical form. In the latter, graphical symbols are used to indicate the various items in an electrical circuit.

There are many separate component parts in an automotive electrical system. Therefore a convention is needed to enable a clear understanding of the graphical symbols and to avoid any confusion. In the past each country had its own set of standards, but now most countries have adopted the recommendations made by the International Electrotechnical Commission (IEC). In the UK the British Standards Institution (BSI) recommends that the symbols shown in BS 3939:1985 should be adopted. A selection of the symbols is shown in Table 1.3.

Circuit diagrams are discussed in more detail in Chapter 6.

Units

The system of units used in engineering and science is the *System Internationale d'Units*, known as SI units and based on the metric system. There are a number of basic units such as:

Length = Metre (m)
Mass = Kilogram (kg)
Time = Seconds (s)

Table 1.3 Electrical symbols (BS 3939:1985)

Description	Symbol
Direct current Alternating current	
Positive polarity Negative polarity	+ −
Current approaching Current receding	⊙ ⊕
Battery 12V (Long line is positive)	
Earth, chassis frame Earth, general	

Description	Symbol
Conductor (permanent) Thickness denotes importance Conductor (temporary)	
Conductors crossing without connecting	
Conductors joining	
Junction, separable Junction, inseparable Plug and socket	

Description	Symbol
Variability: applied to other symbols	
Resistor (fixed value)	
Resistor (variable)	
General winding (inductor, coil)	
Winding with core	
Transformer	

Description	Symbol
Diode, rectifying junction	
Light emitting diode	
Diode, breakdown: Zener and avalanche	
Reverse blocking triode thyristor	
pnp Transformer npn	

Description	Symbol
Lamp	⊗
Fuse	
Switch ('make' contact, normally open)	
Switch ('break' contact, normally closed)	
Switch (maunally operated)	
Switch (two-way)	
Relay (single winding)	
Relay (thermal)	
Spark gap	
Generator ac and dc	Ⓖ Ⓖ
Motor dc	Ⓜ
Meters: ammeter, voltmeter, galvanometer	Ⓐ Ⓥ ⊕

Description	Symbol
Capacitor, general symbol	
Capacitor, polarised	
Amplifier	

Description		Symbol
Junction FET	N-type channel	
	P-type channel	
Photodiode		
Thyristor		

These basic units are made larger or smaller by using prefixes to denote multiplication or division by a particular amount. For example:

Mega = Multiply by 1 000 000 (10^6): megawatt is a million watts

Milli = Divide by 1000 (10^3): millisecond is one-thousandth of a second

Table 1.4 Electrical units

Unit	Symbol	Electrical property
Ampere	A	Current
Ampere-hour	Ah	Battery capacity
Coulomb	C	Electrical charge
Farad	F	Capacitance
Hertz	Hz	Frequency (1 Hz = 1 cycle per second)
Volt	V	Potential difference or electromotive force
Watt	W	Power (watt = volt × ampere)

Electrical units are derived from these basic units. For example:

Volt = 1 joule per coulomb

where joules are the unit of energy or work and coulombs are the unit of electrical charge.

The main electrical units used in this book are shown in Table 1.4.

> **Key Points**
>
> SI units are coherent and comparable. Hence, for example, power in watts can be expressed as electrical power or mechanical power
>
> In the SI system there are a number of basic physical units covering all standard dimensions (e.g. mass, force etc.). From these, further units can be derived (e.g. work = force × distance moved; therefore work in joules is force (newtons) multiplied by distance (metres); J = N m)
>
> Electrical symbols for components in a circuit diagram generally conform to an international or British standard

1.2   **BASIC ELECTRONICS**

1.2.1 Resistance and capacitance

Fixed resistors

Resistors are used in various electronic systems and applications for the purpose of voltage dividing and changing and for current limiting. The main types of resistor encountered in automotive electrical and electronic systems are fixed and variable.

The lowest cost, general-purpose fixed-value resistors are made from moulded carbon. Where high stability and compact size is required, one of the following types of resistor is used:

- wirewound
- carbon film
- metal oxide.

Fixed resistors are available in a wide range of values from about 10 ohms up to 1 megohm. Generally a code is used (according to British Standards) to identify the resistance value and the tolerance. Typical example values are shown in Table 1.5.

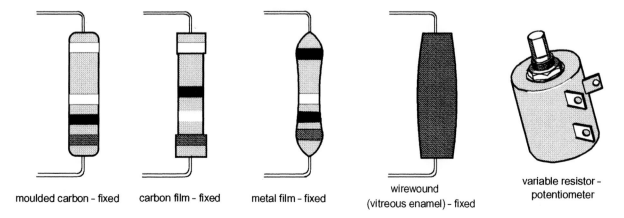

moulded carbon – fixed   carbon film – fixed   metal film – fixed   wirewound (vitreous enamel) – fixed   variable resistor – potentiometer

Figure 1.52 Types of resistor

Table 1.5 Commonly used resistor values

Resistance value	Code marking
0.47 Ω	R47
1 Ω	1R0
4.7 Ω	4R7
47 Ω	47R
100 Ω	100R
1 kΩ	1K0
10 kΩ	10K0
1 MΩ	1M0

A letter after the resistance value indicates the tolerance:

F = ±1%
G = ±2%
J = ±5%
K = ±10%
M = ±20%

For example, a resistance marked 6K8F has a resistance value of 6.8 kohms and a tolerance of ±1%.

Resistors are identified by a code consisting of four coloured bands. To identify the value and tolerance the resistor should be placed with the three bands to the left, as shown in Figure 1.53.

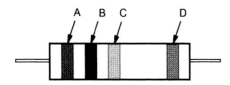

Figure 1.53 Resistor code markings

Reading from left to right, the colour of the first three bands indicates the resistance value and the fourth band the tolerance. Table 1.6 shows the colour coding.

Table 1.6 Resistor colour code

Colour	A 1st digit	B 2nd digit	C No. of 0's	D tolerance
BLACK	0	0	NONE	–
BROWN	1	1	1	1%
RED	2	2	2	2%
ORANGE	3	3	3	–
YELLOW	4	4	4	–
GREEN	5	5	5	–
BLUE	6	6	6	–
VIOLET	7	7	7	–
GREY	8	8	8	–
WHITE	9	9	–	–
GOLD	–	–	–10	5%
SILVER	–	–	–100	10%
NONE	–	–	–	20%

Variable resistors, potentiometers

Variable resistors or potentiometers can be adjusted so that their resistance value can be varied from a low value up to its full rated value. These units are normally carbon track or wire wound. They can be designed such that the variation can be made in service (via a knob on a control panel for example; Figure 1.56) or alternatively they can be pre-set to a certain value and adjusted to the application (using a screwdriver for example). They are normally rated by their maximum resistance and power, e.g. 100 ohms, 3 watts.

A typical automotive application for a potentiometer is for a throttle position, pedal position sensor or fuel-level sensor unit (see Figure 1.55).

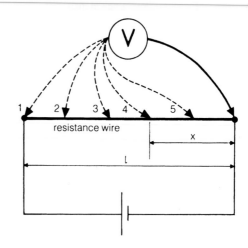

Figure 1.54 Potentiometer

Resistors in series and parallel

Electrical circuits normally consist of complex networks of components which generally behave like resistors. In some parts of a circuit, resistance is undesirable as it causes voltage drops and power losses. In other parts, resistance is desirable to control the flow of current into a component or circuit. Alternatively, the resistance in a component may achieve the desired function (e.g. a bulb, where the resistance in the filament causes the heating to illuminate the bulb). A basic understanding of resistances in simple circuits is desirable for electrical analysis and diagnostics, for example understanding the configuration of resistances in circuits, how these affect the circuit and the electron or current flow. Resistors can be connected in series, parallel or a combination of both.

Resistors in series

Placing resistors in series means that the full current must pass through each resistor in turn (see Figure 1.57). The total resistance in the circuit is therefore the sum of the resistances.

$$R = R_1 + R_2 = 2 + 4 = 6 \text{ ohms}$$

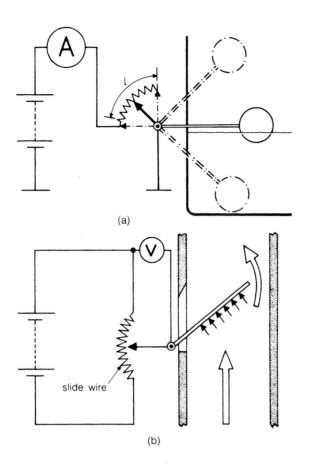

(a)

(b)

Figure 1.55 Use of potentiometers

Figure 1.56 Types of resistor (variable resistor – potentiometer)

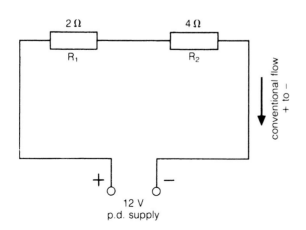

Figure 1.57 Resistors in series

Assuming the resistance of the cables is negligible, by applying Ohm's law we can calculate the current flow in the circuit:

$$V = IR \longrightarrow I = \frac{V}{R} \longrightarrow \frac{12}{6} = 2$$

Therefore 2 amps will flow in the circuit.

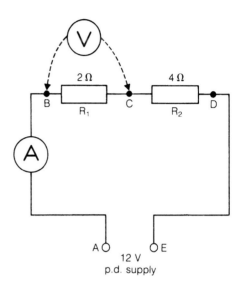

Figure 1.58 Voltage distribution

Consider the same circuit with an ammeter and voltmeter connected as shown in Figure 1.58. Energy is expended driving current through the resistances and this causes a volt drop across them. This is measured by the voltmeter across R_1 at 4 volts, hence the voltage across R_2 must be the supply voltage, less the volt drop across R_1:

$$R_2 = 12\,V - 4\,V = 8\,V$$

There are two main observations:

- the current is the same in any part of the circuit
- the sum of the voltage drops is equal to the total applied voltage.

Measuring voltages around the circuit allows the voltage distribution to be established. This is a useful method in practice to find unintentional resistances in circuits under working conditions and is a useful technique to adopt when fault-finding vehicle electrical circuits.

Resistors in parallel

Connecting resistors in parallel ensures that the applied voltage to each resistor is the same (see Figure 1.59). Current flowing through the ammeter is shared between the two resistors and the amount of current flowing through each resistor will depend on the resistance in that branch of the circuit. Using Ohm's law, the current in each branch can be found as follows:

$$\text{Current } R_1 = \frac{V}{R} = \frac{12}{2} = 6 \text{ amps}$$

$$\text{Current } R_2 = \frac{V}{R} = \frac{12}{6} = 2 \text{ amps}$$

The equivalent resistance, i.e. a single resistance that has the same value as the two resistances in parallel, can be found by using Ohm's law again:

$$\text{Equivalent } R = \frac{V}{I} = \frac{12}{8} = 1.5 \text{ ohms}$$

This can also be found via:

$$\frac{1}{R} = \frac{1}{R_1} + \frac{1}{R_2} \ldots$$

The main observations are:

- the sum of the currents in each branch is equal to the total circuit current
- the applied voltage across each resistor is the same as the source voltage.

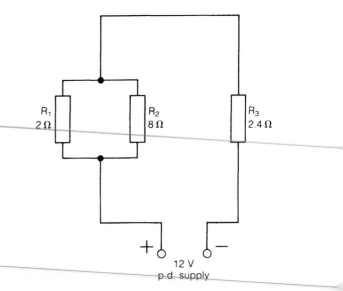

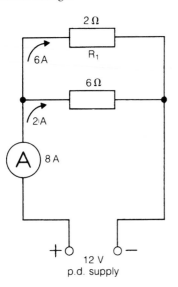

Figure 1.59 Resistors in parallel

Series-parallel or compound circuit

This is a combination of both of the above types in a single network. When calculating the current flow in these circuits, imagine that the parallel resistors are replaced by a single resistor of equivalent value. This then produces a series circuit that is easy to deal with (see Figure 1.60).

Equivalent resistance of R_1 and R_2:

$$\frac{1}{R} = \frac{1}{R_1} + \frac{1}{R_2}$$

therefore

$$R = \frac{R_1 \times R_2}{R_1 + R_2} = \frac{16}{10} = 1.6 \text{ ohms}$$

Total resistance of circuit:

$$\text{Total } R = 1.6 + R_3 = 1.6 + 2.4 = 4 \text{ ohms}$$

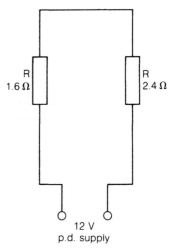

Figure 1.60 Compound circuit

Current flow via Ohm's law:

$$I = \frac{V}{R} = \frac{12}{4} = 3 \text{ amps}$$

The 3 amp current is shared by R_1 and R_2:

$$R_1 = \frac{R_2 \times I}{R_1 + R_2} = \frac{24}{10} = 2.4 \text{ amps}$$

Therefore, current flow through $R_2 = 0.6$ amps

This simple method of dissecting circuits for evaluation is a powerful technique when analysing more complex circuit networks.

Potential divider

The circuit shown in Figure 1.61 consists of two resistors in series and is commonly known as a potential divider. A circuit of this kind can consist of a number of elements with the voltages being taken from the connections in between the elements. In the circuit shown in Figure 1.61 the voltage output can be given by:

$$V_{out} = \frac{R_2 \times V_{in}}{R_1 + R_2}$$

Practical applications of this circuit include using it to provide a varying voltage signal due to a change in resistance. It is commonly used with potentiometers (throttle pedal position sensor circuit) and thermistors (coolant temperature sensor circuit).

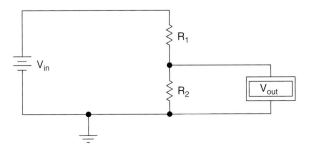

Figure 1.61 Simple potential divider

Bridge circuit

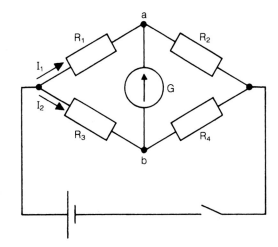

Figure 1.62 Wheatstone bridge

A simple bridge circuit, as shown in Figure 1.62, can be used for finding the value of an unknown resistor and this is the principle used by some accurate ohmmeters. It can also be used for detecting a change in resistance in part of an electronic circuit. The four resistors form the four arms of the bridge. Current is supplied across the bridge (I_1 and I_2) and a centre zero voltmeter measures the voltage across the bridge circuit (i.e. from a to b). The currents in the two paths I_1 and I_2 are governed by the resistance of the relative section compared to the alternative section. If all the resistors in the bridge are the same then the voltage at a–b is zero and the bridge is in balance. This means that:

$$\frac{R_1}{R_2} = \frac{R_3}{R_4}$$

Therefore, any slight change in resistance values of any resistor is shown as a voltage change across the bridge. This technique is used in sensor and measurement

technology. Bridge circuits are commonly used with strain gauges to measure stress in materials during testing or monitoring. Also, a practical application in an automotive electrical system is a hot wire air mass flow meter. The bridge circuit is used in this device as part of the measurement and compensation circuitry, with the hot wire forming one resistance on the bridge.

Capacitors (basics, types and characteristics)

A capacitor is an electronic component that is capable of storing electrical charge. The amount of charge that a capacitor can store is measured in capacitance (units: farads) but more commonly expressed in microfarads (μF) or nanofarads (nF) as these units are more appropriate to the volume or quantity of charge that can be stored by common capacitors used in electronics.

Figure 1.63 shows the construction of a very simple capacitor. Basically, it is constructed of two parallel conducting plates separated by a layer of insulating material (this is known as the dielectric). Connecting leads are attached to each plate and the whole assembly is encapsulated in a small container. When a voltage is applied across the plates, a charge accumulates on them and this gives rise to a potential difference that builds up across them. When the capacitor voltage is equal to the applied voltage, no more charge builds on the plates and hence no more current flows into the capacitor. In this state the capacitor is 'charged' and will retain this pd even after the charging voltage has been removed. In effect, the capacitor becomes a miniature battery. When connected to a circuit load the pd across the plates will drive a current in the circuit but only momentarily as the voltage across the plates falls quickly due to the charge depletion. The amount of energy stored by a capacitor is dependent on the area of the plates. This is normally a tiny amount compared with a battery.

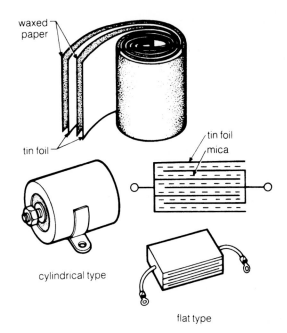

Figure 1.63 Capacitor construction

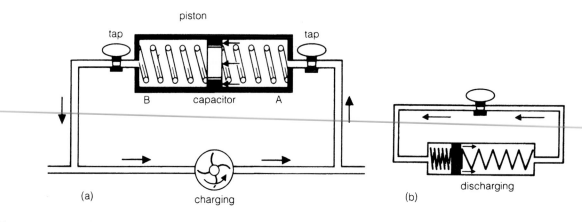

Figure 1.64 Action of the capacitor

The amount of charge (Q) stored by a capacitor is given by:

$$Q = C \times V$$

where V is the applied voltage and C is the capacitance in farads.

Capacitance therefore equals Q/V. Note that a one farad capacitor will store one coulomb of charge when one volt is applied across the plates.

The amount of energy (W) stored by a capacitor is given by:

$$W = \frac{Q \times V}{2}$$

High-voltage energy can be stored in a capacitor. An example of this is capacitor discharge ignition (CDI) where charge stored in a capacitor is used to generate the spark.

R–C time constant

When a capacitor is connected in a circuit, the current flowing in or out is not constant. Figure 1.65 shows the charge voltage (in %) versus time (in time constants) when charging and discharging. This

characteristic profile follows the natural law of growth and decay and can be expressed mathematically as an exponential function (e^x).

The time taken in seconds (t) to charge a capacitor to 63% of its capacity (established via the voltage across the plates or the decaying current as the charge builds up) is known as the *time constant*. This can be expressed as:

$$t = C \times R$$

where C is the capacitance (farads) and R is the resistance (ohms) in the circuit.

It takes approximately five time constants ($5t$) to completely charge or discharge a capacitor. Resistance–capacitance (R–C) networks are very commonly used to provide timing functions in electronic circuits. A good example in an automotive system would be a courtesy light delay timer or an intermittent wipe delay circuit for the windscreen wipers. Connecting a potentiometer in the R–C network of the wiper delay circuit would provide the possibility to change the R–C time constant of the circuit and thus provide variable, adjustable delay. This is very common on modern vehicles.

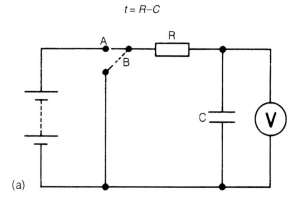
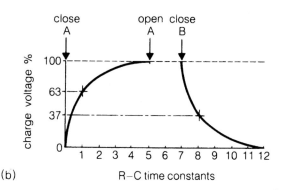

Figure 1.65 Charging and discharging a capacitor

Construction

Many materials are used to construct capacitors for automotive electronic circuits, including tantalum, ceramics and polyester. Common types of capacitor are shown in Figure 1.66.

Capacitors are generally colour coded, numbered or lettered to show their capacitance value. In addition, polarity conscious types (e.g. electrolytic) have the polarity marked.

Series and parallel connection of capacitors

When two or more capacitors are connected in series the total capacitance will decrease. For example, when a 1.1 µF and a 3.3 µF capacitor are connected in series, the total capacitance can be calculated thus:

$$\text{Total capacitance (series connection)} = \frac{C_1 \times C_2}{C_1 + C_2}$$

$$\frac{1.1 \times 3.3}{1.1 + 3.3} = \frac{3.63}{4.4} = 0.825\,\mu F$$

If these two same capacitors are connected in parallel then the capacitance increases. They are simply added together as shown:

$$\text{Total capacitance (parallel connection)} = C_1 + C_2$$

$$1.1 + 3.3 = 4.4\,\mu F$$

The above is exactly to opposite behaviour of resistors in series and parallel.

Key Points

Resistors are used to control or limit the current flowing in a circuit. They can be fixed or variable in nature and are the only simple circuit component that can truly dissipate power as heat (this is compared to capacitors or inductors which just store energy)

Resistors in series add together and increase the total resistance of the network. When connected in parallel the total resistance of the network decreases

Parallel and series connection of resistor networks form the basis of other commonly used resistor configurations like potential dividers and bridge circuits

Capacitors can store energy like miniature batteries; the amount of energy depends upon the size of the capacitor plates and the charging voltage

Capacitors are commonly used in timer circuits due to the predictable and repeatable nature of the time taken to charge or discharge a capacitor when connected in a circuit with a resistor

In a capacitor network, when multiple capacitors are connected in series, the total capacitance reduces. When connected in parallel, the total capacitance increases. This is the opposite of a resistor network

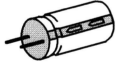

radial

axial

sub-miniature

ELECTROLYTIC TUBULAR

tantalum bead

cylindrical ceramic

resin dipped ceramic

TANTALUM AND CERAMIC

dipped case

encapsulated

sub-miniature

POLYESTER

Figure 1.66 Common types of capacitor

1.2.2 Transistors and diodes

Semiconductors

A semiconductor is a material which has an electrical resistance value lower than an insulator but higher than a conductor. To be more specific, a conductor must have a resistivity value lower than 0.000 000 01 ohm metres and an insulator must have a resistivity greater than 10 000 ohm metres. To summarise, it is a material which can act as a conductor or an insulator.

Silicon and germanium are generally used for construction of semiconductor components. The conductivity of these materials can be varied in a predictable way by adding impurity atoms to the pure semiconductor crystal. Boron, phosphorous or arsenic are used for this purpose. This process is called doping, and it alters the behaviour of the semiconductor by changing the number of charge carriers (electrons and holes) in the material.

PN junctions

Diodes and transistors form the building blocks of modern electronic systems. Two main types of semiconductor material are used together in constructing these components:

- N-type: this has a surplus of negatively charged electrons. It is produced by adding a small trace of arsenic to silicon or germanium crystal. The name N-type is short for negative as the arsenic gives extra (negatively charged) electrons to the semiconductor.
- P-type: this is made by adding boron to the semiconductor base material which creates a shortfall of electrons and thus a positive charge is produced. Hence the name 'p-type', indicating positive.

PN junctions are formed when p-type and n-type semiconductor materials are joined together. At the point where the surfaces diffuse together, a thin area is formed where electrons and holes penetrate the P and N semiconductors respectively. After initial electron and hole transfer has taken place, the negative charges on the P side and the positive charges on the N side build up to produce a barrier potential difference which opposes further diffusion. This narrow region at the junction is called the depletion layer.

Diodes, characteristics, forward and reverse bias

Diodes are two terminal electronic devices (anode and cathode) formed by a PN junction. Diodes can be likened to a check valve or one-way valve in a hydraulic circuit. That is, they allow current to flow in one direction only. Figure 1.67 shows a PN junction diode.

When the diode is connected in such a way that it will conduct and allow current to flow, this is known as *forward bias* condition. When the diode is blocking current flow, this is known as *reverse bias*. This property of the diode means it is universally adopted where conversion from AC to DC current is required. Components called

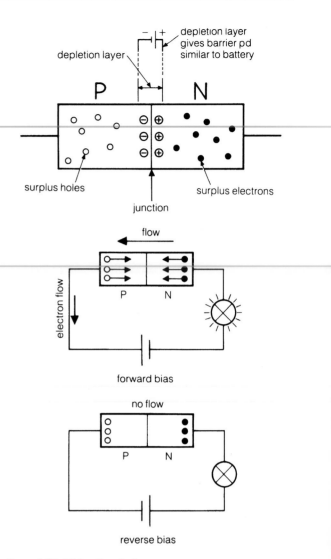

Figure 1.67 PN junction diode

rectifiers are used for this and are constructed from diode networks. Figure 1.68 shows current and voltage curves of a silicon diode in a circuit.

An important characteristic of a diode is that under forward bias conditions, the diode does not start to conduct until a certain voltage has been applied across it. The magnitude of this voltage depends on the semiconductor material but is generally around 0.5 volts. Once this threshold is reached, the diode begins to conduct and it can be seen from the graph (see Figure 1.68) that small increases in voltage result in large increases in the current.

Under reverse bias, the diode opposes current flow apart from a very small leakage current. As the applied reverse voltage increases, a point can be reached where the diode begins to conduct again as it effectively breaks down thus allowing current to flow in reverse. This causes overheating of the junction and is a failure mode which normally destroys the diode. This voltage level is known as the breakdown or peak-inverse voltage and is normally stated clearly in the specifications of the diode. Generally this voltage can vary from a few volts to hundreds of volts.

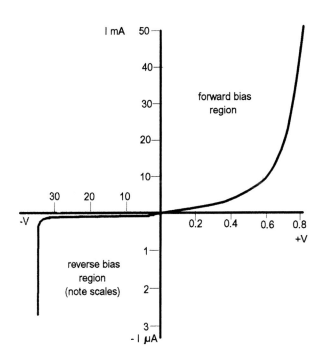

Figure 1.68 Silicon diode characteristics

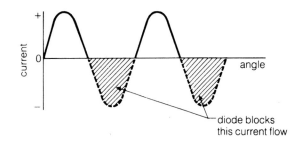

Figure 1.70 Half-wave rectification of AC

Another important feature of a diode is the volt drop across it. This is constant irrespective of the current flowing through it and this property effectively defies Ohm's law! This is different to a resistor which complies with Ohm's laws such that the volt drop varies with current flow for a fixed resistance value (as discussed above). The actual volt drop across a diode varies according to the semiconductor material, but it is generally constant at about 0.5 volts.

Rectifiers

As mentioned above, diodes are very commonly used in rectifier equipment for converting AC electricity to DC. A single diode in a circuit (see Figure 1.69) is known as a half-wave rectifier and gives a pulsating, unidirectional DC current (see Figure 1.70). It allows only one half of the AC sine wave to pass through and is clearly not the most efficient method as half of the energy is lost.

In order to avoid this loss and to provide full rectification of the AC sine wave, a network of four diodes must be used connected in a bridge arrangement as shown in Figure 1.71.

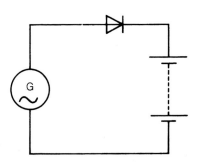

Figure 1.69 Rectifier action of junction diode

This converts the AC current to unidirectional DC current with minimal losses and is a commonly used configuration seen in many electronic circuits. It also forms the basis of the rectifier pack used on modern automotive alternators.

Zener and avalanche diodes

A zener diode uses the previously mentioned general property of diode that under reverse bias conditions a point is reached were the diode breaks down and begins to conduct. In this case though, this is due to the zener effect which is caused by the high electrical field pressure which acts at the PN junction (see Figure 1.72). This effect is reversible and zener diodes are designed to operate under this condition. This makes them particularly suited for use as a voltage-conscious switch in a charging system regulator or as a 'dump device' (i.e. hydraulic analogy; pressure relief valve) in a circuit subjected to voltage surge.

Generally, a diode with a reverse breakdown voltage below 4.5 volts is a zener diode, whereas a diode with a breakdown voltage above 4.5 volts is an avalanche diode. These diodes can be employed in voltage stabilisation circuits as shown in Figure 1.73.

As the volt drop across the diode in the circuit is constant (Figure 1.74), the diode acts as a voltage regulator. When the input voltage exceeds the diode's breakdown voltage, the diode conducts and absorbs the excess voltage. During this phase the output voltage remains constant because it represents the volt drop across the diode. This arrangement is commonly used in the permanent magnet alternator charging systems employed on small motorcycles.

LEDs

Light-emitting diodes (LEDs) were discovered in the mid-1950s when it was found that a diode made of gallium phosphide (GaP) emitted a red light when it was forward biased. Since that time further development has meant that LEDs are now available in many colours and intensities, including white LEDs. In addition, infrared LEDs are commonly used for photoelectric applications (for example trigger circuits in electronic ignition systems). LEDs are now also being employed in many vehicle external lighting and signalling applications due to their low current draw relative to light output, high reliability and durability. This technology is discussed in more detail in Chapter 8.

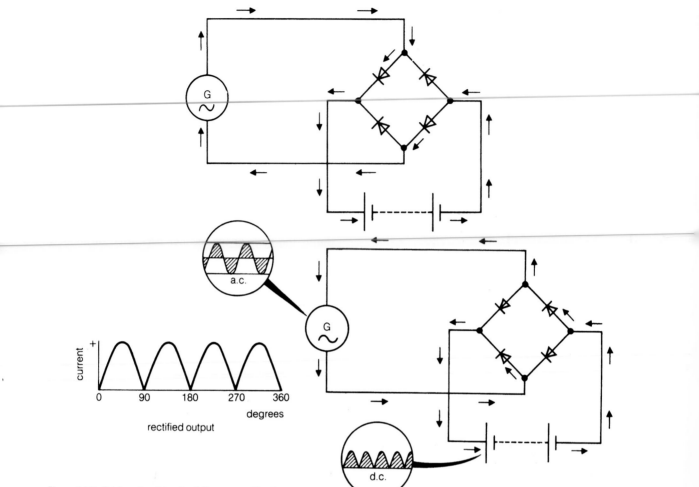

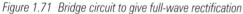

Figure 1.71 *Bridge circuit to give full-wave rectification*

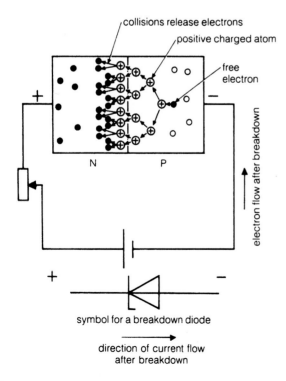

Figure 1.72 *Zener-type diode*

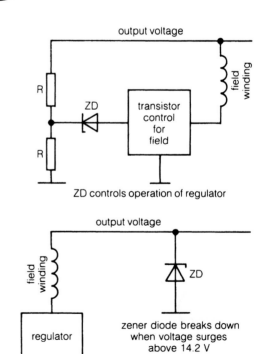

ZD controls operation of regulator

zener diode breaks down
when voltage surges
above 14.2 V

ZD acts as a surge protection diode

Figure 1.73 *Zener-type diode applications*

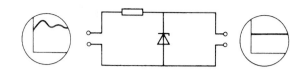

Figure 1.74 Zener-type diode used as a regulator to stabilise voltage

The characteristic of an LED is the same as any PN junction diode. A typical red LED requires approximately 2 volts and a current of 10 mA in order to illuminate. Typically other colours require a slightly larger current of approximately 20 mA. LEDs are also commonly used in instrument panels as indicator lamps. Note that in order to determine the polarity of an LED, the cathode (negative) has a shorter connection lead; in addition, a 'flat' is made on the casing of the LED on the cathode side.

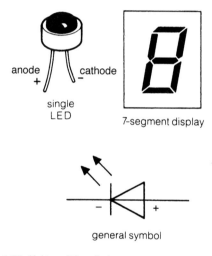

Figure 1.75 Light-emitting diode

Note that when testing an LED a series resistor must be used to limit the supply voltage to 2 volts. This can be calculated thus:

$$R = \frac{V_{supply} - V_{led}}{I_{led}}$$

where:

R = Series resistance
V_{supply} = Supply voltage
V_{led} = Voltage across LED required (~2 V)
I_{led} = LED current (~10 mA).

Optoelectronics

This subsection covers light-sensing or light-sensitive electronic components, although strictly speaking the LED is also an optoelectronic component.

Photoresistor or LDR (light-dependent resistor)

These are resistors whose resistance decreases as they are exposed to light. They are generally made of cadmium sulphide but can also be made from other

materials according to the light wavelength that the unit is designed to be sensitive to. The general appearance and circuit symbol are shown in Figure 1.76.

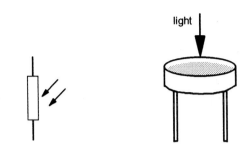

Figure 1.76 LDR symbol and appearance

Photodiode

This is a light-sensitive diode that behaves in a similar manner to the LDR except that it is capable of switching at much higher frequencies. In operation, it is connected reverse bias and the leakage current under this condition increases as a function of the incident light (i.e. light increases, resistance decreases). The general construction and symbol are shown in Figure 1.77.

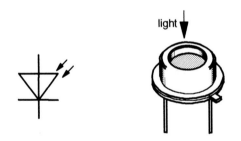

Figure 1.77 Photodiode symbol and appearance

These units have many applications in industry, e.g. light meters, photoelectric beams etc. For automotive applications they can be found in security systems and automatic switching systems for headlights and panel light dimming. They are also used in optical sensors for engine speed/rotation as well as steering wheel rotation/position sensors.

Thermistors

A thermistor is a resistor whose resistance value changes when the temperature it is exposed to changes. This makes thermistors ideal for temperature sensing applications. For most common conductors their resistance increases with temperature. Therefore they have a positive temperature coefficient (PTC). Conversely, semiconductor material reduces its resistance as the temperature increases and thus has a negative temperature coefficient (NTC). Figure 1.78 shows PTC and NTC as functions of temperature.

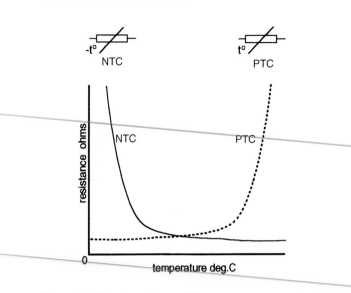

Figure 1.78 Thermistor characteristics

Generally thermistors are made from semiconductor material irrespective of whether they are PTC or NTC as these semiconductor materials have the best temperature coefficients for the application.

For automotive applications, temperature sensors are nearly always NTC type and are found sensing engine and atmospheric temperatures for control systems and driver information systems.

Transistors

Transistors are formed when the P- and N-type semiconductor material is arranged in layers according to type. They have three connections: collector (c), base (b) and emitter (e).

Figure 1.79 shows some transistors and their respective symbols. Note that in the symbol of each respective type, the arrow points either to or from the base and is placed on the emitter side. That is, it shows the direction of current flow (from P to N). A transistor can be used to control a relatively large current with a small current and it can act as a switch or amplifier. Transistors are widely used as switches or amplifiers. Note that because they can amplify signals, they are termed as *active* components (compared to diodes, resistors or capacitors, which are known as *passive* components).

Two main types of transistors are commonly in use:

- bipolar: operation depends upon the flow of electrons and holes
- unipolar (field effect transistors (FET)): depends on the flow of holes or electrons, not both!

Bipolar transistors

This type of transistor is consists of three semiconductor regions to form a PNP or NPN configuration. It is effectively two junctions (diodes) back-to-back. It makes use of charge carriers of both polarities (holes and electrons) and the emitter–collector current can be many times the base current that controls the flow (approximately 100 times). Figure 1.80 shows a simple NPN transistor circuit.

In operation, when the circuit has no current flowing into the base (i.e. the transistor is off), no current will pass through the transistor due to the

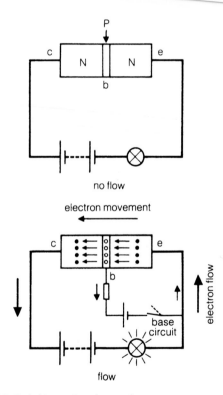

Figure 1.80 Switching action of a transistor

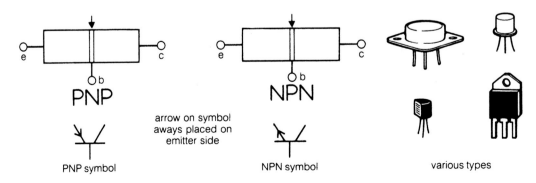

Figure 1.79 Transistor construction and symbols

reverse bias PN junction between the collector and the base. The base circuit is used to influence and control the flow of electrons and this gives the switching action. When current flows into the base emitter, this causes a disturbance in the PN junction and reduces its potential which then allows the electron charge carriers to bridge this junction and thus allows current to flow freely from collector to emitter. In this state the transistor conducts and the current flowing in the main circuit is proportional to the base current (by the transistor gain factor – hfe).

An alternative to the NPN is the PNP transistor. The circuit is shown in Figure 1.81.

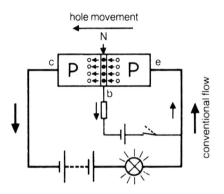

Figure 1.81 PNP transistor

A PNP transistor must have its emitter connected to a positive supply. The current flow is opposite to an NPN transistor. Note that the NPN type is faster in operation and is therefore more suitable for high-speed switching applications.

Field effect transistors (unipolar) – J and MOSFET

Unipolar transistors involve only one type of charge carrier (either electrons or holes). They can be subdivided into:

- JFET (junction field effect transistor)
- MOSFET (metal oxide semiconductor transistor).

Both types operate as voltage-controlled current sources. The JFET is constructed of a single element of either P- or N-type semiconductor. Across this the connections for the main circuit are made, which are known as drain and source. On the sides of this element a third electrode is attached called the gate which consists of a thin layer of conductor that is electrically insulated for the main semiconductor element. The construction and symbol for a JFET is shown in Figure 1.82.

In operation, electrons (hence current) flow from the source to the drain and this flow rate is controlled by the voltage applied to the gate. As the gate voltage (relative to the source) increases, the electron (current) flow in the source-drain circuit decreases to a point where it ceases altogether. This is due to the fact that raising the gate voltage increases the depletion region and this reduces the width of the channel through which the current can flow from drain to source, effectively using an electrical field to control the current (hence the term 'field effect') and acting as a voltage-controlled current source (see Figure 1.83).

The MOSFET is formed by diffusing two P+ to the side of an N-type silicon crystal as shown in Figure 1.84.

When a negative charge is applied to the gate, positive charges (i.e. holes) are attracted to the N region. This builds up an inversion layer which forms a P-type channel between the two P+ regions and thus provides a path for the electrons to flow from source to drain. As the gate voltage increases, the channel gets deeper and this allows a larger current to flow. The device thus acts as a voltage-controlled current amplifier.

Compared to bipolar transistors, FETs are superior due to:

- lower switching current
- lower power requirement
- higher input impedance
- better frequency response.

FETs are very suited to highly integrated circuits. Their superior thermal characteristics allow many thousands of FETs to be located on a single chip.

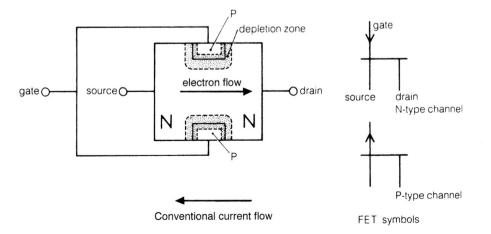

Figure 1.82 Junction field effect transistor (JFET)

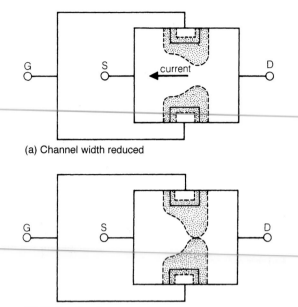

(a) Channel width reduced

(b) Pinch–off action

Figure 1.83 JFET action

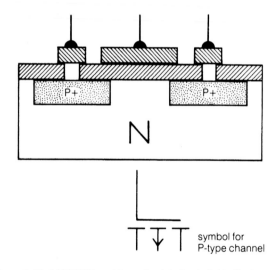

symbol for P-type channel

Figure 1.84 MOSFET transistor or insulated gate field effect transistor (IGFET)

Thyristors

Thyristors are semiconductors which possess at least three PN junctions. They are a development of the transistor and basically consist of two interconnected transistors as shown in Figure 1.85.

The main feature is the characteristic switching action, applying a small current to the gate switches on the thyristor, and this causes current to flow from anode to cathode. Once this current is flowing, interruption of the gate current only has an effect when the anode-cathode current reduces to zero (or changes polarity) as the unit switched off.

Referring to Figure 1.85, the operation is as follows. When voltage is applied to the anode, no current will flow to the cathode because both T_1 and T_2 are switched off. Applying a voltage of similar polarity to the gate will switch on T_2 and as a result T_1 will also switch on. Current flow from the collector of T_1 to the base of T_2 will now keep T_2 switched on even if the gate current is discontinued.

Thyristors are commonly used in power electronic switching applications like electric motor speed controllers, rectifiers, inverters and converters. In automotive applications, an example of their use is in switching circuits for capacitor discharge ignition (CDI) systems where a small trigger current of short duration is needed to start a large current flow.

Example transistor circuit applications

Transistors are used as the building blocks of amplifier and signal conditioning circuits. The following are examples of transistors commonly used and relevant to automotive electronic circuits:

- Darlington pair: a limited current gain can be achieved with a single transistor and, where this is insufficient, transistors can be cascaded to multiply the available gain. This is known as a Darlington pair (see Figure 1.86).

  The transistors are mounted in a single package with three terminals marked e, b and c, and they look similar to a single transistor. The gain of the two transducers is multiplied together to give the overall gain, but the advantage is that a high gain, low power transistor can be packaged with a low gain, high power transistor to form a unit which has high gain and power and is very suitable for switching low voltage, high current as found in automotive electrical circuit applications.

- Schmitt trigger: this can be used in circuits where rapid switching and clear signal edges are required which rely on positive feedback. The circuit is shown in Figure 1.87.

  The Schmitt trigger uses a higher base voltage to switch on the input transistor T_1 than that required to switch it off. This voltage difference provides hysteresis and overcomes the problem of repeated switching between two states when the base voltage is varied slightly around its operating value. The basic principle is that when T_1 is off, T_2 is switched on and the collector–emitter current of T_2 passes through resistor R_4 which forms part of the base circuit of T_1. This means that T_1 base–emitter voltage must be higher than normal to overcome the voltage at R_4 before T_1 can switch on. The operation of the circuit is summarised in Table 1.7.

  The circuit can be used to provide a sharp switching action or to condition and convert analogue signals (see Figure 1.88).

  In an automotive electronics example, it could be used to convert the signal from a crankshaft position sensor, from an analogue sine wave, to a clear digital signal with defined edges, suitable for processing in an ECU timer circuit to determine engine speed.

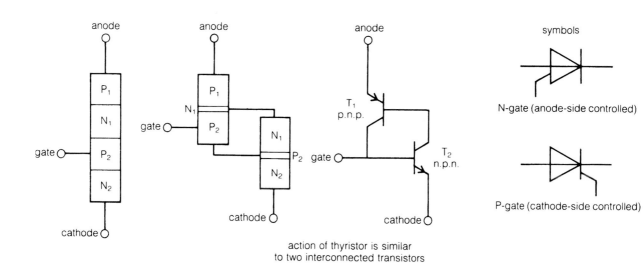

Figure 1.85 Thyristor construction and symbols

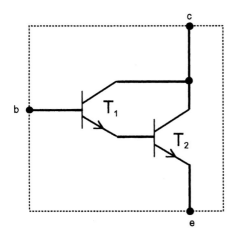

Figure 1.86 Darlington pair

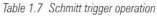

Table 1.7 Schmitt trigger operation

Input voltage	T_1	T_2	Output voltage
Above 3.5 V	switches on	off	high
Below 2.5 V	switches off	on	low

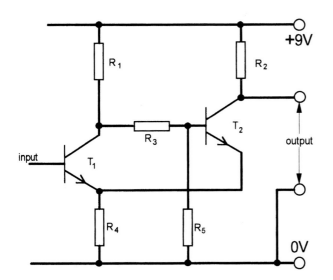

Figure 1.87 Schmitt trigger

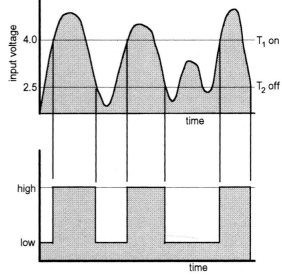

Figure 1.88 Conversion of an analogue signal to a digital signal

All active electronic components are composed of semiconductor materials such as silicon and germanium. Impurities are added to this material to change the basic properties. This is known as 'doping'

Electronic components are formed by fusing together this doped semiconductor material to form junctions. The two materials used are known as P- and N-type semiconductors. A diode consists of one PN junction, a transistor consists of two junctions, either NPN or PNP

A diode is an electrical one-way valve. It is a component commonly used in rectifiers which convert AC to DC current flow. Light-emitting diodes glow when forward biased. They are available in different colours and are used in instrumentation applications to replace bulbs as they have long life and low power consumption. Zener diodes allow current to flow when a certain voltage threshold is reached. They are used in voltage regulator or overload protection circuits

Transistors are used as electronic switches as a very small control current or voltage can be used to switch a very large power current (similar to a relay). They are also used as amplifiers as they have a gain property such that the output current is a fixed multiple of the control voltage or current. There are two main types of transistor: bipolar and unipolar (the latter are also known as FETs (field effect transistors))

Thyristors are three-junction devices. Once they are activated via a small control current they remain conductive even if the control current is removed. They are commonly used in high-power switching applications for rectifiers and inverters

1.2.3 Digital circuits

Binary number systems

Many of the electronic systems in motor vehicles process signals or communicate via digital signals. Most electrical signals from sensors around the vehicle are analogue signals. This means that they are continuous with respect to time. A digital signal is expressed at fixed levels or increments (see Figure 1.89).

A simple example is a clock – think of the minute display. For an analogue clock the minute hands sweeps around the face of the clock and shows a continuous display of the advancing minutes via its position at any given point. A digital display shows the minute value in single steps as each minute passes. This means that the digital display can only show discrete steps (45 minutes, then 46 minutes for example) whereas the analogue display can indicate a value anywhere between 45 and 46 minutes (or any other value). In modern electronic controllers analogue signals have to be converted to digital in order to be processed by the signal processor. This is discussed below.

The advantage of digital signal processing is that once a value is converted into digital form it can be stored easily in a computer memory for processing. It can then be manipulated, complex calculations can be executed and the results can be stored again for further use by the system. Digital processors to carry out these functions are cheap and widely available.

Digital circuits rely on the use of a binary number system which involves signals at only two levels, known as 0 (zero) and 1 (one). These are very easy to represent electrically or optically by switching signals between defined thresholds. All numbers are represented by a series of 0s or 1s arranged in the form of a place position number system or code.

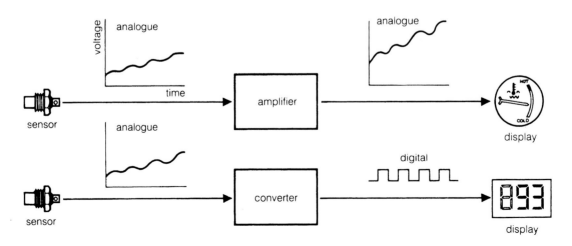

Figure 1.89 Temperature measuring systems: analogue and digital

Binary and denary numbers

Numbers generally in everyday use are in denary notation. As you know, this uses 10 digits between zero and nine. As mentioned, a binary number system has only two digits (0 and 1). These digits are arranged in a position such that each extra digit represents a 'power of two' moving from right to left. For example, the binary number 1111 is:

$$(1 \times 2^3) + (1 \times 2^2) + (1 \times 2^1) + (1 \times 2^0)$$

That is:

$$8 + 4 + 2 + 1 = 15$$

Table 1.8 shows denary numbers represented in binary form.

In summary, to convert from binary to decimal, multiply each number by its relative place value and then add the products.

Logic circuits

Binary notation allows any denary number to be represented as a string formed by 1s and 0s. Systems which respond to these signals are called logic (or binary) circuits. In an electronic system, the binary digits (or bits) are represented electrically via voltage signals at defined levels. The voltage needed to operate at these two levels is called the logic level. Commonly, these levels are:

Logic zero (0) 0 to 0.8 volts (low)
Logic one (1) 2.4 to 5.0 volts (high)

As mentioned previously, analogue signals have to be converted to digital prior to processing via a digital processor. An analogue-to-digital converter performs this function. Figure 1.90 shows an analogue signal from a sensor converted and represented in digital form.

Table 1.8 Binary and denary tables

128	64	32	16	8	4	2	1	Denary digit (base 10)
2^7	2^6	2^5	2^4	2^3	2^2	2^1	2^0	Binary digit (base 2)
8	7	6	5	4	3	2	1	Bit sequence

Denary number				Binary number or code				
0	0	0	0	0	0	0	0	0
1	0	0	0	0	0	0	0	1
2	0	0	0	0	0	0	1	0
3	0	0	0	0	0	0	1	1
4	0	0	0	0	0	1	0	0
5	0	0	0	0	0	1	0	1
6	0	0	0	0	0	1	1	0
7	0	0	0	0	0	1	1	1
8	0	0	0	0	1	0	0	0
9	0	0	0	0	1	0	0	1
10	0	0	0	0	1	0	1	0
11	0	0	0	0	1	0	1	1
12	0	0	0	0	1	1	0	0
13	0	0	0	0	1	1	0	1
14	0	0	0	0	1	1	1	0
15	0	0	0	0	1	1	1	1
16	0	0	0	1	0	0	0	0
17	0	0	0	1	0	0	0	1
18	0	0	0	1	0	0	1	0
19	0	0	0	1	0	0	1	1
20	0	0	0	1	0	1	0	0
21	0	0	0	1	0	1	0	1
22	0	0	0	1	0	1	1	0
23	0	0	0	1	0	1	1	1
24	0	0	0	1	1	0	0	0
25	0	0	0	1	1	0	0	1
26	0	0	0	1	1	0	1	0
27	0	0	0	1	1	0	1	1
255	1	1	1	1	1	1	1	1

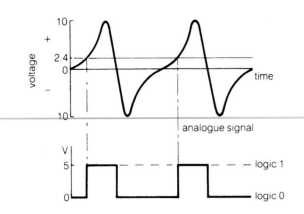

Figure 1.90 Analogue and digital signals

When the analogue voltage exceeds 2.4 volts, the high digital state is reached and this is held until the voltage drops below the logic level required to return to the low state. As a digital signal has only two states it is much easier to transmit, process and store than an analogue signal.

Combinational logic circuits

Logic gates are simple elements which when networked together form a logic circuit that can process and respond to digital signal inputs. They give a binary output signal in response to one or more input signals. Each element (or gate) operates in a different way.

Digital processors consist of thousands of logic gates and can perform bit manipulation easily and quickly using three basic logic gates: the AND gate, OR gate and NOT gate. From these basic gate structures, more complex gates NAND (not and) and NOR (not or) are constructed.

AND gate

The AND gate is shown in Figure 1.91. It has two inputs (A and B) and one output (X). It produces an output of logic 1 only when all the inputs are at logic 1. Otherwise the output remains at logic 0. Operation of the AND gate is similar to an electrical circuit with switches in series, i.e. the lamp only illuminates when both of the switches are closed. The operation of the AND gate can be clearly understood by studying the truth table shown in Figure 1.91.

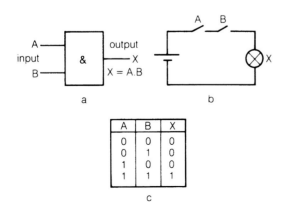

Figure 1.91 AND gate

Another method of expressing the behaviour of logic gates is via Boolean algebra. The AND gate is expressed in this notation as:

$$X = AB$$

OR gate

This gate also has two inputs and one output. In this case though either one or both of the inputs can be at logic 1 to return a logic 1 value at the output. This can be compared to an electrical circuit (as above) but with the switches arranged in parallel (Figure 1.92). The truth table is as shown in Figure 1.92.

The Boolean expression for an OR gate is:

$$X = A + B$$

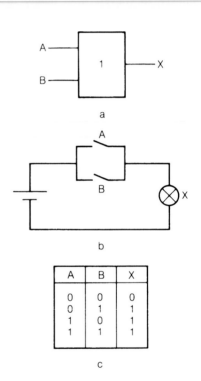

Figure 1.92 2-input OR gate

NOT gate

This gate has a single input and a single output. The device converts the input signal to the opposite state and then sends it to the output. Hence it switches the logic level and acts as an inverter. That is, a 0 input gives a 1 output. The truth table and diagram for this gate are shown in Figure 1.93.

The logic symbol is $\bar{A}$ and is known as 'Not A'.

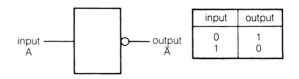

Figure 1.93 NOT gate

NAND and NOR gates

Other logic functions can be achieved by combining AND and OR gates with NOT gates. The symbols and truth tables are shown in Figure 1.94.

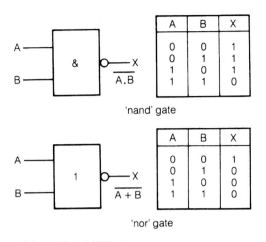

'nand' gate

'nor' gate

Figure 1.94 NAND and NOR gates

Note that the small circle on the output terminal in Figure 1.94 represents the schematic symbol for the NOT function. The NOT gate basically provides an output that is an inverted version of the AND or OR gate respectively.

These gates are normally combined in integrated circuit form. There are various quantities of gates in a package with various numbers of inputs per gate available.

Logic symbols used for vehicle components or circuits can be shown using American-based symbols or British Standard symbols. Figure 1.95 compares the two types.

Sequential logic circuits

The above logic circuits (combinational) are formed by interconnecting the various logic elements, the output from a network of logic gates being a function of the inputs at any given time. A more sophisticated logic circuit with a memory of previously applied inputs can be configured using bi-stable elements (i.e. those which are stable in two states, like a 'toggle' switch, see Figure 1.96), and these circuits are known as sequential logic circuits. Effectively these circuits can hold or store information and therefore, in practical terms, form the basis of computer memory circuits.

R-S flip flop

The reset-set (hence R-S) bi-stable is constructed of two NOR gates and two NAND gates as shown in Figure 1.97.

The truth table for the NAND gates show that when logic 1 is applied to S (the set input), the output at Q is logic 1 also and it will remain in that state even after S changes to logic 0. This demonstrates that the high state of S is effectively 'latched' into the same state as Q.

Only when R changes state to logic 1 and S returns to logic 0 is Q released or 'unlatched'. This resets the

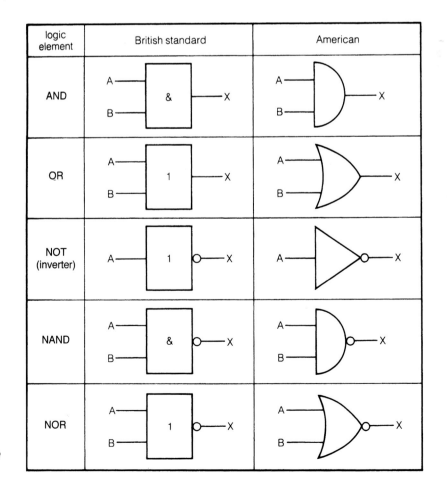

Figure 1.95 Gate symbols

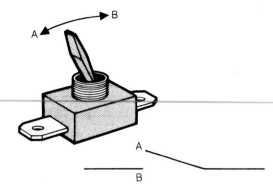

Figure 1.96 Toggle switch is a bi-stable device

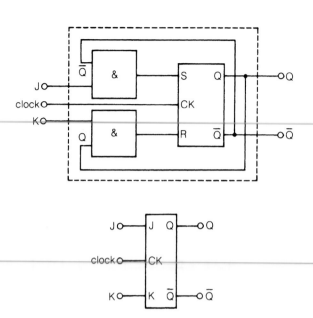

symbol for J.K bi-stable

Figure 1.98 J-K flip flop

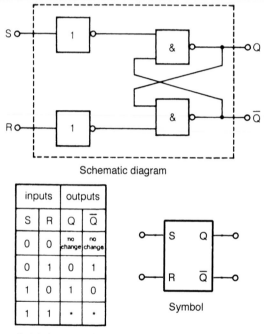

Schematic diagram

inputs		outputs	
S	R	Q	$\overline{Q}$
0	0	no change	no change
0	1	0	1
1	0	1	0
1	1	*	*

* state is uncertain

Symbol

Figure 1.97 R-S flip flop and truth table

The type shown is a clocked version and gives a synchronised action, i.e. the flip flop can only change state when a clock pulse change of state is sensed at the CK (clock) terminal.

Integrated circuits

Logic gates may be constructed from discrete switching transistors, diodes, resistors and capacitors. An integrated circuit consists of a number of gates that are formed on a single piece of silicon. The techniques used to create these integrated circuits include photolithography (a process similar to photographic printing) and diffusion (modifying one material by combining it with another under high temperature). These techniques allow the creation of extremely small, high-performance circuits with high reliability and low power consumption. The first integrated circuits were created around 1960 when a transistor and resistor were formed on a single silicon chip.

Integrated circuits have evolved from relatively simple devices with approximately 10 to 12 gates (known as small-scale integration devices (SSIs)) through to very large-scale integrated devices (VLSIs) and beyond! These circuits have thousands of gate elements.

The types of logic circuits commonly encountered are:

- Transistor-transistor logic (TTL): these are widely used in low-cost integrated circuits (ICs) and cover a large range of functions. They are highly resistant to spurious switching caused by interference.
- Emitter-coupled logic (ECL): these have a faster switching time than TTL circuits but consume more power and are relatively expensive.
- Complementary metal oxide semiconductor (CMOS): these can provide a large number of gates/chip area due to the low power consumption. Switching speed

latch and returns the gate to its original state. When both inputs are at logic 1, the two gates oppose or *buck* each other and the final state of the flip flop is uncertain. This state has no practical use as it is indeterminate so normally the circuit is designed such that this condition never occurs.

J-K flip flop

A J-K flip flop is another bi-stable device which operates in a similar manner to the R-S type but incorporates two extra AND gates to overcome the indeterminate state produced when the two inputs are at logic 1 as mentioned above. This means it is stable in one of two different states.

When either input changes state to create logic 1 simultaneously at both inputs, the flip flop changes its output to a state opposite to that which existed before the input change. The J-K flip flop is shown in Figure 1.98.

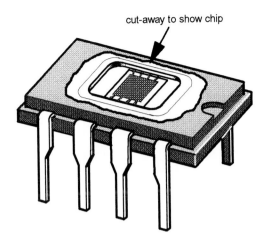

cut-away to show chip

Figure 1.99 Eight-pin integrated circuit

is low compared to TTL circuits and CMOS circuits are susceptible to damage from static charges, hence care must be exercised when handling and antistatic precautions should be taken.

An important development of this technology is the fact that digital circuits became available in IC form and the functional capability of these digital ICs has increased exponentially over the years.

Microprocessors, microcomputers and microcontrollers

Many vehicle control systems require sophisticated functionality and interfacing capability. Simple analogue electronic circuits are insufficient to provide the level of performance and integration which is expected by the end user and they have mostly been replaced by some form of microelectronic or computer control.

A good example of this is an electric window lift system. In the past an electric motor driving the window regulator mechanism, controlled via a motor reversing switch for the operator, was sufficient. Now, the motor is controlled via a digital control chip. This chip will monitor the motor speed and window position for safety and system protection reasons (e.g. trapping of body parts in the window mechanism, switching off the motor at the window travel limit to prevent overheating). This optimises system operation and safety but also allows interaction of the window controller with other systems (e.g. central locking for total closure operation of doors and windows). This system is now fitted to many vehicles and shows how electronic control of even simple functions enhances the vehicle as a whole.

Digital electronics and microprocessing technology have made this possible. The complexity of a microelectronic system depends upon the application, but at the heart of the system is the microprocessor itself.

Microprocessors

The microprocessor concept was introduced in the early 1970s by Intel. The company developed a philosophy to divide the hardware circuit into two parts. One part processed the data, the other part stored data (i.e. memory). These two parts together required an instruction routine or program (i.e. software) and this would be stored in the memory. The program was application specific which meant that hardware could be used for different applications just by changing the software program. The microprocessor acts as a central processing unit (CPU) and its duty is to initiate and control all the actions that take place in the computer or controller in which the microprocessor is located.

The microprocessor operates on a digital system using high and low voltage levels to transmit information from one part to another. These are binary signals (as discussed above) and hence the information must be encoded in that format (binary notation). Each binary digit is called a *bit* and a group of eight bits is known as a *byte*. Early generation microprocessors could sample the instructions eight bits at a time. Therefore programs were developed in this format. Now processors can handle 16 or 32 bits at a time; hence they can execute programs much more quickly. Another point to bear in mind is that the CPU works in a sequential manner, hence each cycle of the CPU operation (sampling data, executing a calculation, returning the result) takes place in a synchronised way but also very quickly. This is achieved by supplying pulses from an oscillator; the speed of the oscillator dictates the CPU processing speed and is expressed in megahertz (MHz).

The CPU has the facility to store instructions temporarily whilst processing other information. The instructions are held in special memory locations called *registers*. Instructions are stored in an appropriate register until they are required by the processor. Figure 1.100 shows the registers typically incorporated in a CPU. The program counter is the main register and its duty is to record the location, in the memory store, of the instructions that the CPU has to follow. At a given time, when the instruction is required, the CPU fetches the data from the memory and executes the instruction according to the information given to it in the form of the program (software).

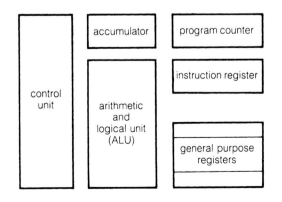

Figure 1.100 Parts of a microprocessor

The ALU or arithmetic logic unit processes information relating to any arithmetic or logic functions that are needed. All data supplied to the CPU requiring addition or subtraction of binary data is directed to the ALU. Storage of data that is being used by the ALU during the processing operation is retained in a temporary store called an *accumulator*.

The command unit that directs the processing operation is performed by the *control unit*. This arranges the movement of data between the sections of the computer and provides the appropriate control signals to activate the parts that process the data.

Microcomputers and microcontrollers

In automotive electronics, microprocessors are generally combined with other components to form an application-specific computer or embedded system. A typical system would consist of:

- a microprocessor or CPU
- memory (for program and data)
- input/output (I/O) system and peripherals (often consisting of switching devices such as transistors).

These are connected via a bus system which forms a highway between these components for data transmission. These sub-systems can be combined on a single chip to form a microcomputer. A unit of this type has the capacity to monitor and control many vehicle components or systems and due to the relatively low cost and high performance of these units, they have found many applications in the control systems of modern motor vehicles.

Most microcomputers operate according to a set of instructions programmed into the unit during the manufacturing process. Unlike a personal computer, an embedded system receives its inputs from various sensors rather than a keyboard or mouse. The main components and their bus interfaces are shown in Figure 1.101.

Bus systems

As mentioned above, these are data highways and are multi-lane but in some cases they are arranged to give one-way flow. A microcomputer bus is divided into three sections which are named according to the information they carry:

- The data bus: this carries data in both directions between the computer parts.
- The address bus: this carries the data address in the form of a binary code from the CPU to the memory. The information carried by this bus identifies the actual place in the memory where a given item of information is stored. The signals on this bus are normally unidirectional.
- The control bus: data on this bus controls the functions of the computer, selecting units required and determining the direction of data movement at any given time. The terms 'reading' and 'writing' apply to the direction of data movement. Reading

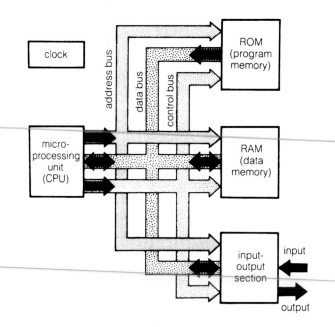

Figure 1.101 Sections of a microcomputer

means that data is passing to the CPU for processing, writing means data is coming from the CPU for storage.

Clock pulse generator

Movement of data between the various sections of the microcomputer is controlled via a timing pulse which is generated by an oscillator (or system clock). When this clock pulse is applied simultaneously to two parts of the microcomputer, then data is free to pass between them. Other parts of the microcomputer will be inactive unless their contents are unlocked at the same time by a similar pulse. This system of data control and movement allows the various computer sections to be interconnected in a simple manner by a bus.

Operating memory

A memory is a number of separate cells which store bits in binary form so they can be read by the CPU as and when required. To enable the microprocessor to perform the required function, it has to be given the information in the form of a program. This is basically a list of instructions in binary form that is held in the memory.

The memory unit is separated into two parts, one part stores the programs for the CPU and the other holds information either as an input to the CPU or as an output from the microcomputer.

Dedicated memory

If the microprocessor is dedicated to a single task, then the operating system and program will be held in memory that is not generally rewritten. This is known as ROM or read-only memory. ROM is non-volatile which means that any information in the memory remains even after a complete power down of the microprocessor. A common type of ROM is EPROM (erasable programmable read-only memory). This type of memory can be rewritten externally (not by the microprocessor itself) and hence can be programmed to suit the application. This means that standard chips can be purchased and programmed by the vehicle manufacturers and this reduces production costs.

Temporary memory

Where larger amount of data have to be stored but fast access is less critical, additional memory known as RAM (random access memory) is used. This is normally volatile memory and hence any data in this memory will be lost on power down. Occasionally a back-up battery will be fitted to keep the information in this memory for short periods.

Peripheral devices

The CPU and memory need a link to the operating environment so that the microprocessor can receive and send signals and information. The peripheral devices form the basis of this interface. Each peripheral module has a connection to the microprocessor via a bus connection and an external connection via an actuator, sensor or other microprocessor. A schematic diagram is shown in Figure 1.102.

The main tasks of the peripheral module can be defined as:

- communication with the internal bus
- communication with the application environment
- data storage
- monitoring and timing
- fault detection.

Analogue input

Monitoring of the vehicle component functions is carried out by sensors or transducers. These convert physical quantities into electrical voltages, and where the output is in analogue form the signal must be converted to a digital form in order to be processed by the CPU in the ECU. Normally this task is carried out by a small peripheral module called an analogue to digital converter (ADC). Analogue signals change continuously

with respect to time. The principle of analogue-to-digital conversion is that the continuously changing signal is sampled regularly and at high speed. Each sample is digitised and stored as a single value in the memory complete with a time stamp.

Even though the signal is not continuously sampled, the sampling frequency (if sufficiently high) means the 'string' of digital numbers in memory accurately represent the original signal when reconnected together (with some interpolation between the missing points).

Of course this principle relies strongly on sufficient sampling quality, with respect to frequency and bit resolution. Well-known theorems on digital sampling state that the signal must be sampled at least twice as fast as the highest-frequency component of the signal in order to accurately capture the signal and all of its frequency components. In addition, the bit resolution, i.e. the number of digital steps available, must also be chosen appropriately in order that the signal does not lose definition in digital conversion.

Typically bit resolution is quoted as a power of 2. For example, an 8-bit ADC has 2^8 steps, i.e. 256 steps across its full voltage range. Therefore, assuming the range of an ADC is 0 to +10 volts, the smallest change detectable by this ADC is $10/256 = 0.039$ or $39\,mV$. For a slowly changing signal (e.g. temperature sensor), sampling rate and bit resolution can be minimised to an appropriate level, whereas for a more dynamic signal (e.g. knock sensor), the sampling frequency and analogue–digital resolution must be much greater. This is necessary so that the signal can be converted into digital form without losing the high-frequency detail from it (thus filtering it in an effect known as 'aliasing').

Analogue outputs

Once data has been processed by the CPU, calculations are made that result in decisions which must be implemented in the hardware (i.e. actuators). In general, this is the output from the microcontroller system and is handled by peripheral modules of various types. For an actuator which is driven by a varying voltage, a DAC or digital to analogue converter is used.

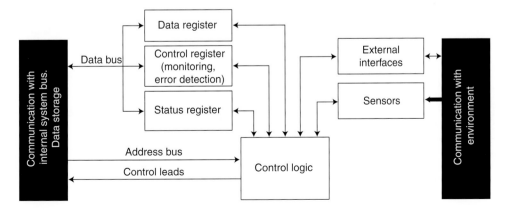

Figure 1.102 CPU communication with external environment

This is an interface module which accepts a digital input from the CPU at a low switching level and then by using a power-switching network of transistors can provide a varying analogue voltage output as required to drive an actuator. An example would be an idle-speed control valve. Generally a DAC is specified for the application via bit resolution. In general though this is not required to be as high as it would be for an ADC (12 bit maximum is typical, i.e. 4096 steps).

Other I/O peripheral modules

Additional driver modules will be available according to the requirements to interface with actuators and components. These will all interface to the microcontroller bus system. Typical examples would be:

- on-off switching outputs for solenoid valves (e.g. exhaust gas recirculation (EGR))
- stepper motor driver modules (e.g. idle speed control)
- modulated pulse width/frequency driver circuit modules.

In addition, counter-timer input modules will be available to count external pulses and time differences between pulses. These are commonly used for rotary encoder signals for speed and position sensing as well as misfire detection via engine acceleration and deceleration.

Intelligent digital interfaces

Modern microcontrollers will have interface capability and this is realised via an appropriate peripheral module according to the interface technology. This allows the CPU to send and receive data to and from other control units via an external bus, for example controller area network (CAN) or local area network (LIN) vehicle bus

technology (discussed in Chapter 6). The CPU can then be programmed to take into account information from other controllers (e.g. ABS, traction control etc.) and can also send information out to other control systems (e.g. engine load signal, torque demand etc.).

Operating mode of peripheral modules

These can be distinguished as:

- Polled I/O: when there are a number of inputs to the system, the microprocessor *polls* each one in turn. This means that the I/O peripheral acts independently and stores its data in a buffer. The CPU checks the module regularly and transfers data as required. Each signal is monitored, processed and then stored before moving on to the next signal. This is carried out in sequence known as a *polling order*.
- Interrupt driven I/O: an alternative method to the above allows the CPU to perform routine tasks until an input signals a change; this state then *interrupts* the processor. In this mode the I/O peripheral processes all I/O operations independently and then signals the CPU (via the interrupt line) when new information is received or when an action by the CPU is required. The advantage is that the CPU and peripherals can operate in parallel.

Programming and development technology

The main operations of the microcontroller are:

- data manipulation
- data storage
- data exchange
- data event monitoring.

The structure of a microcontroller with respect to these activities is shown in Figure 1.103.

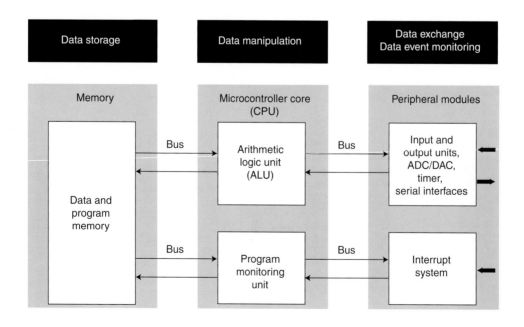

Figure 1.103 Main functional operation areas of a microcontroller

In order for the microcontroller to operate in its environment, it needs to have an operating sequence to follow, and this is known as a program. Unfortunately the microcontroller only follows a program written in binary notation (machine code) and this is difficult to understand and work with, especially for large programs. To resolve this, most programs are written and developed using an appropriate higher-level language as an interface between the programmer and the hardware. The program when created in this form (known as source code) is much easier to understand, develop and work with.

The microcontroller is equipped with an instruction set (optimised commands) that the programmer can address and use. These enable the microcontroller to carry out any expression of a higher-level language by a sequence of simple instructions that can be executed quickly. They can be accessed via the programming language and used by the programmer to optimise the program for the microcontroller. The main classifications of these instructions are:

- data processing (mathematical operations)
- control instructions (jumping to specific points in the program)
- input/output instructions
- memory instructions (reading and writing).

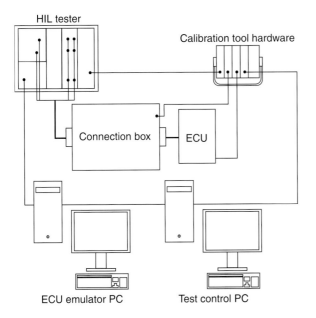

HIL tester

Calibration tool hardware

Connection box

ECU

ECU emulator PC   Test control PC

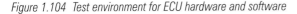

Figure 1.104 Test environment for ECU hardware and software

Using these instruction sets increases the overall speed and efficiency of program execution in the microcontroller especially for repetitive tasks (e.g. mathematical operations). When the program is ready to be tested or run on the microcontroller, it is converted from source code (the program text) to machine code (binary form) in a process known as compiling. This creates an executable program which can be uploaded from the developer's PC directly to the microcontroller hardware for testing.

Testing of the complete system, hardware and software, is done at a test bench. Modern development methods use hardware-in-the-loop methods (HIL). This test technology originates from the aerospace industry and creates a simulation environment where test conditions can be created in a very repeatable way. Durability and longevity of the microcontroller-based system can be established with great accuracy using original hardware connected to a simulation hardware/ software environment. In addition, these methods allow accelerated testing techniques that shorten component development times and thus reduce development costs for the manufacturer.

Key Points

In order to process numbers or values in a digital system, they must first be converted to digital (binary) form

Combinational logic circuits give outputs that are a direct function of the input status at any given time. Sequential logic circuits have a latching or bi-stable property which means they can remain in a given state even if the input is removed. Due to this property, these circuits can effectively remember states and this forms the basis of computer memory circuits

A microprocessor is a central processing unit (CPU) complete with memory on a single chip

Microcontrollers and microcomputers integrate a microprocessor with other components (memory, I/O peripherals etc.) required to build up a complete, digital, computer-controlled system. Microcontrollers often integrate all of these components on a single chip

Program instructions can only be interpreted by a microprocessor in the form of a bit pattern (i.e. binary form). This is difficult to work with, so programs are normally written in a higher-level language. A program in this form is known as source code and is converted to binary form (machine code) in a process known as compiling

An embedded system is designed specifically for a particular application or task. The entire program is permanently stored in the hardware in read-only memory (ROM) and cannot be altered by the user

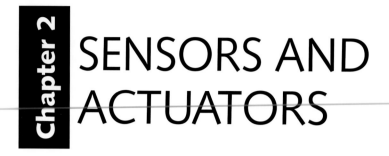

Chapter 2

SENSORS AND ACTUATORS

what is covered in this chapter ...

■ Sensors for chassis and body systems
■ Actuators for chassis and body systems
■ Control systems

2.1   SENSORS FOR CHASSIS AND BODY SYSTEMS

2.1.1 Basic function

Electronic control systems are increasingly important in the modern motor vehicle system architecture and are very commonly used for controlling and monitoring even the most basic functions around the vehicle chassis and body system (as well as the powertrain). In order for these systems to perform their functions they need inputs from the physical environment and these are provided via a sensor.

Sensors perform an information-gathering function to feed the electronic control system with information which relates to some physical, chemical or thermal effect. In general terms, the sensors convert the input quantity into an electrical output quantity or signal. Sensors are also known as transducers if the output signal is proportional to the measured quantity.

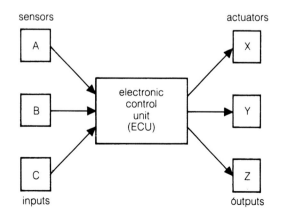

Figure 2.1 Electronic system

Automotive sensors are commonly used to measure:

- pressure
- position and level
- flow
- temperature
- gas composition
- vibration (knock)
- acceleration
- speed
- rotation (position).

The number of sensors required in a system depends on the application and complexity of that system and can vary widely. The output from a sensor can be a simple digital signal (for example a switch) or it can be far more complex and convey more detailed information. Typical output signal types produced by automotive sensor systems are:

- analogue voltage or current
- resistance
- frequency, phases, pulse width.

Sensors can be divided into two main classes:

- active (self-generating)
- passive.

Passive sensors need an external energy source and hence act as energy controllers to produce the required output signal.

Cost normally influences the accuracy and reliability of a sensor, so a typical general-purpose sensor used for a vehicle system has an accuracy of about 2–5% and a moderate life span. In cases where this level of performance would be unacceptable, such as the on-board diagnostic system, more accurate sensors must be used. Signal output to the electronic control system must relate closely to the physical quantity that the sensor is intended to measure. Once the output signal is created, no amount of signal processing can improve the original raw data quality. So if precision is required, the sensor quality must be appropriately high.

2.1.2 Sensor developments

Current and future trends are towards 'smart sensor' technology (also known as intelligent sensors). This term relates to sensors that are equipped with additional intelligence via an on-board microprocessor which allows functionality beyond simple conversion of measured value to electrical signal.

These sensors have become available due to the development of highly integrated micro-electronic circuit technology. The sensor itself is capable of signal conditioning and linearisation and this means that a high-quality signal can be transmitted directly to the ECU. Using this technology, this signal can be transmitted in digital bit form via a bus connection. This improves the quality of the measurement chain considerably as the signal conditioning occurs close to the source, then the signal is transmitted in a form that is highly immune to interference and it can be received easily and handled via a microprocessor equipped with an appropriate interface.

This technique distributes the intelligence around the system components, relieving the ECU of the signal conditioning task and allowing intelligent interfaces between sensors and with the ECU. The sensor itself can perform self-check and monitoring functions and can report a fault or implausible signal via an intelligent bus system (e.g. CAN (controller area network), see Chapter 6).

The various levels of technology integration at the sensor itself are shown in Figure 2.4.

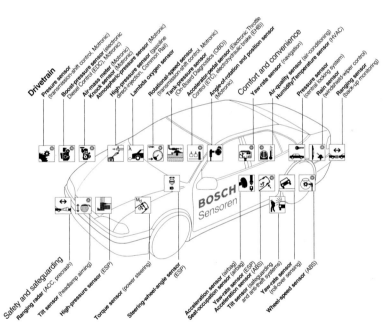

Figure 2.2 Vehicle sensor applications

Automotive sensors	
Requirements	**Development measures**
High reliability	Rugged, well-proven technology
Low manufacturing costs	Efficient mass production
Severe operating conditions	Highly resistant packaging
Low volume	Minaturisation techniques
High accuracy	Local fault compensation

Figure 2.3 Requirements for automotive sensor technology with resulting development targets

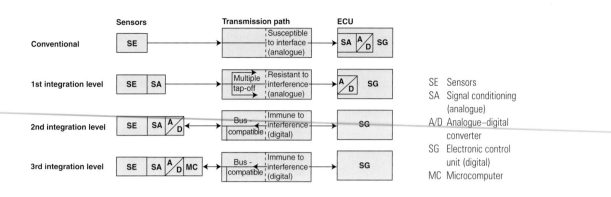

Figure 2.4 Technology integration in sensors

2.1.3 Signal conditioning and processing

Analogue sensors are connected to the analogue inputs of an electronic control unit. These inputs are generally protected against voltage surges and include a hardware filter to help reduce noise and improve signal quality. If necessary the input stage of the ECU will include an amplifier to increase the amplitude of the signal from the sensor to an appropriate level for digital conversion. In the case of a thermistor (commonly seen for temperature measurement in automotive systems), an appropriate resistor bridge network will form part of the input signal conditioning.

If the sensor signal is in digital bit form (i.e. an intelligent sensor), the microcontroller may already be equipped with a proprietary interface which allows direct connection to the bus system on which the sensor is connected. If not, a suitable peripheral I/O module will be installed in the control unit to handle this interface and communicate the data to the CPU in the control unit. No active signal conditioning is required as this is done at the sensor. Typically a CAN interface is used on automotive systems due to the inherent robustness and reliability of this protocol which was developed specifically for automotive applications.

Crankshaft or camshaft position sensor signals will be connected to digital counter-timer inputs at the ECU. These would typically be rotation sensors and could be seen in any application where speed and position information is needed (e.g. window lift or sunroof motors). Rotation speed can be derived by counting the time difference between edges of the incoming pulse train. Position can be established by counting the number of edges one after another from a fixed reference point (for example, a missing tooth).

2.1.4 Sensors for chassis and body systems

This section considers sensors specifically used for chassis and body systems in order to understand their operating principle with respect to specific application. Examples are provided in order to fully understand the technology involved. Note that sensors used for engine and powertrain control systems are not included as they are covered fully in *Hillier's Fundamentals of Motor Vehicle Technology 5th edition: Book 2 Powertrain Electronics*.

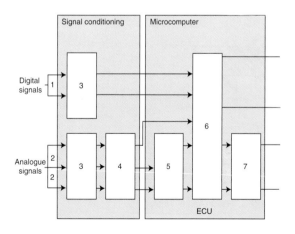

1 Digital input signals
2 Analogue input signals
3 Protective circuit
4 Amplifier, filter
5 A/D converter
6 Digital signal processing
7 D/A converter

Figure 2.5 Signal processing path between source and ECU

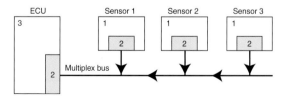

Figure 2.6 Data flow between intelligent sensors and ECU via a bus system (for example, CAN)

Position sensors

These are generally used to register travel and angular position and are commonly found in the modern automotive environment.

Generally the trend is towards non-contact measurement techniques as these technologies produce sensors that are very reliable and have a long service life. In general terms, these sensors are used to measure distances > 1 mm and angles > 1 degree. Some examples of chassis and body applications are as follows.

Pedal position sensor

This sensor application is necessary where drive-by-wire systems have been adopted, i.e. there is no direct mechanical connection between the throttle pedal and the fuel metering (diesel) or throttle plate (gasoline). In addition, latest developments in clutch control systems (i.e. clutch-by-wire systems) will also require a signal from the clutch pedal to establish pedal position, movement and rate of change. These pedal position signals are fundamental driver demand inputs and they require high reliability. More importantly though, a sensing mechanism in this application requires a high degree of redundancy (i.e. safety) so that the likelihood of complete failure, or even worse, a failure mode that could create a dangerous condition (i.e. throttle position fails in wide-open position) is avoided at all costs, and this must be considered as essential in the design specification for the sensor.

For a pedal position sensor, typical maximum angular deviation will be approximately 30 degrees. A commonly used principle for this application is the potentiometer as a potential divider. (The working principle is discussed in Chapter 1.) For a pedal sensor the potentiometer is constructed from a film-type resistor which is contacted by a wiper contact. From this contact, the output signal voltage is connected. This voltage is a function of the pedal position and hence the pedal travel and position can be derived in the connected control unit. The typical construction of the wiper track is shown in Figure 2.7.

The advantage of this design is simplicity and low cost. Disadvantages are wear and size (they cannot be miniaturised). For this application, in order to achieve the required system safety, a second wiper track is available which operates in parallel but at a different voltage level. This signal can be also be used for diagnostics and cross-checking. The voltage curves are shown at Figure 2.8.

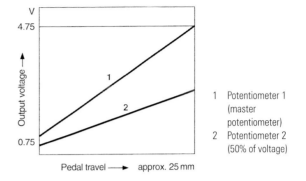

Figure 2.8 Twin track throttle position sensor output voltages

An alternative technology is the Hall effect angle-of-rotation sensor. The Hall effect principle is described in Chapter 1. In this sensor a semicircular permanent-magnet disc rotor generates a magnetic flux which is returned back to the rotor via the pole shoe and shaft. In the process, the amount of flux returned through these conductive elements is a function of the rotation angle, and the Hall effect sensor located in the magnetic path generates an output signal that is linear to pedal position. The Hall effect chip includes signal conditioning so that an appropriate voltage signal is output from the sensor unit. The sensor components are shown in Figure 2.9.

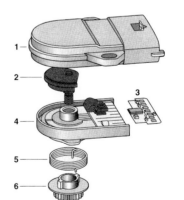

Figure 2.9 Hall-type position sensor components

Steering-wheel angle sensor

Vehicle dynamic control systems (electronic stability program (ESP), anti-lock braking system (ABS) etc.) rely on a number of inputs relating to vehicle position and status, as well as driver demand. An important sensor for this technology detects the steering wheel position and hence the intended vehicle direction as dictated by the driver. In addition, modern power-steering systems that incorporate electronic control as

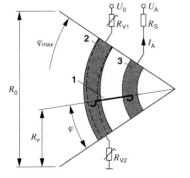

Figure 2.7 Wiper track

well as electric actuation need steering-wheel position information as a fundamental input. In response to this, steering angle sensors have been developed. These sensors must provide absolute steering angle in addition to incremental angular movement and this is particularly challenging as the steering wheel will rotate through more than one revolution from lock to lock. In addition to this, the sensor must have a high degree of redundancy and self-plausibility checking.

There are three main types of sensor commonly in use:

- Hall effect: this sensor uses the Hall effect principle (explained in Chapter 1). A number of Hall effect vane switches mounted around the steering shaft measure the magnetic flux from adjacent magnets. A magnetic slotted disc rotates with the shaft and as the shutters formed on the disc pass between the magnet and the hall switch, the magnetic field is reduced or shielded from the switch. In this way, a number of switches (nine altogether) can output the steering wheel angle in digital form. Figure 2.10 shows the construction of such a unit. The printed circuit board (PCB) shown below the disc contains the Hall effect switches and a microprocessor which decodes the information from the switches and sends this information to the vehicle systems via the CAN bus. The microprocessor also performs safety and plausibility checks.
- Magneto-resistive: this depends upon magneto-resistive sensors for its operation. The sensing elements change electrical resistance according to the direction of an external magnetic field. The sensor

elements are used in conjunction with magnets mounted on small gearwheels in the steering-angle sensor assembly. The angular position information is provided across a range of four complete steering-wheel rotations by measuring the respective angles of two gearwheels which are connected and driven by a mating gearwheel on the steering shaft. These measuring gearwheels have a different number of teeth, and hence a definite pair of angular values of these gearwheels is associated with every possible steering-wheel position. An integrated microprocessor in the sensor assembly calculates the output value, performs self-checks and compensates for inaccuracies due to wear. The construction of the sensor unit is shown at Figure 2.11.

- Optical: the optical-type sensor consists of a code plate with two code rings and seven photoelectric transmitters and receivers as shown in Figure 2.12.

The increment ring is separated into five segments each of 72 degree increments and is read by a single photoelectric beam pair. Within each segment the ring is split and the gap of the segments is equal within that segment, but all the segments have different gaps. This provides the necessary code to differentiate between the segments.

The absolute ring determines the angle and is read by the remaining six photoelectric beam pairs.

With this configuration, the optical steering angle sender can detect a total of 1044 degrees movement.

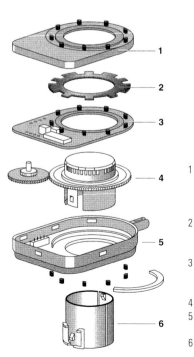

1	Housing cover with nine equidistantly spaced permanent magnets
2	Code disc (magnetically soft material)
3	PCB with 9 Hall-effect switches and microprocessor
4	Step-down gearing
5	Remaining 5 Hall-effect vane switches
6	Fastening sleeve for steering column

Figure 2.10 Hall effect steering angle sensor

1	Steering-column shaft
2	AMR sensor elements
3	Gearwheel with m teeth
4	Evaluation electronics
5	Magnets
6	Gearwheel with n > m teeth
7	Gearwheel with m + 1 teeth

Figure 2.11 Magneto-resistive steering angle sensor

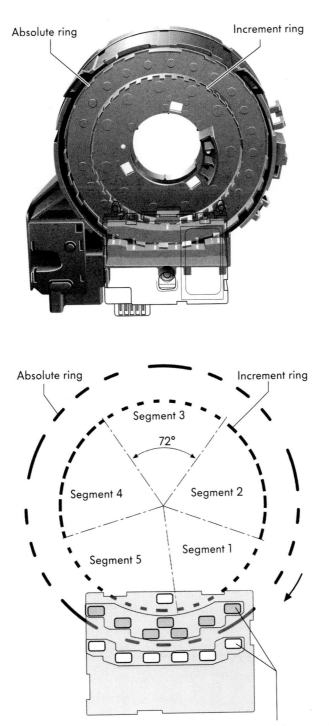

Figure 2.12 Optical-type steering angle sensor

It accumulates the degrees after each turn of the steering wheel and can detect each full turn of the wheel.

The principle of the photoelectric beam measurement is shown in Figure 2.13.

This shows the increment ring only for clarity. The photo transmitter and receiver are mounted on opposite sides of the code plate. When the light passes through a slot a voltage is generated by the photo receiver. If the code plate blocks the light signal passing from transmitter to receiver then the voltage at the receiver drops to a low level. As the wheel turns, a sequence of voltage pulses is created. These can be evaluated to calculate how far the wheel has rotated and this can then be used to calculate absolute movement and position.

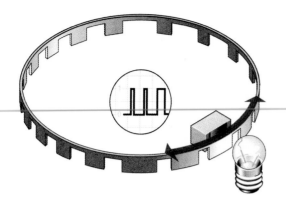

Figure 2.13 Photoelectric beam measurement

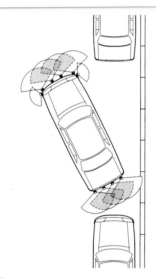

Figure 2.14 Front and rear parking sensors

Parking sensor

These sensors are mounted in the vehicle bumper. They are a driver aid when reversing to prevent collision with fixed obstacles that may not be visible. Normally 4–6 of these sensors are fitted. They have a wide sensing angle and can sense obstacles in the range of 1.5–0.25 m.

The sensor uses an ultrasonic pulse/echo measurement principle. The sensors transmit ultrasonic pulses and receive the echo pulses reflected back from an obstacle. The distance of the vehicle to the nearest obstacle is calculated by the ECU from the propagation time of the first echo pulse to be received back. This is described by the following equation:

$$\text{Distance} = \frac{1}{2}\, t_e c$$

where t_e = Propagation time of ultrasonic signal (s) and c = Speed of sound in air (m/s).

A pulse repetition rate of about 15 Hz is used. The sensor itself contains electronic circuitry to transmit an ultrasound frequency signal via a piezo-ceramic diaphragm element. An obstruction will reflect this signal back to the sensor diaphragm. In the meantime, during this process, the sensor electronics switch to a receive

mode. The reflected sound waves from the obstruction cause the diaphragm to oscillate at resonance (i.e. close to its own frequency) and generate an analogue signal which is processed in the sensor itself and sent back to the control electronics in digital form. This transmit and receive process repeats in a cyclic way so that the changes in distance to an object can be monitored continuously. The sensor element and block diagram of the electronic circuit is shown in Figure 2.15.

Fluid sensors

Traditionally simple sensor technology (potentiometers, float switches) has been employed in the past for condition monitoring of the vehicle fluid levels to inform the driver of any abnormally low level of essential fluids. In addition, essential to any vehicle, is a fuel gauge to measure the quantity of fuel left. In the future, more sophisticated sensing technology will be employed to evaluate not only quantity but quality of essential fluids. This will be important for self-diagnostics on vehicle systems and also for predictive maintenance scheduling. A good example is the oil quality sensor and this is discussed below.

Fuel level

This sensor is used to monitor the remaining fuel quantity in the tank. The value can then be displayed to the driver via the instrumentation and also used to calculate vehicle range via a trip computer system. Commonly the fuel tank sensor is combined with the electric fuel lift pump to form a single in-tank module (see Figure 2.17). The most common technology

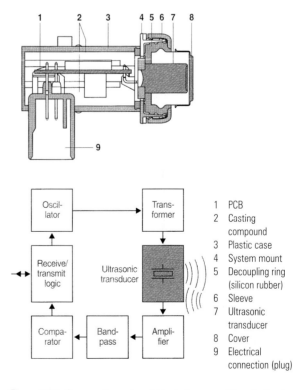

Figure 2.15 Sensor element and block diagram of the electronic circuit in a parking sensor

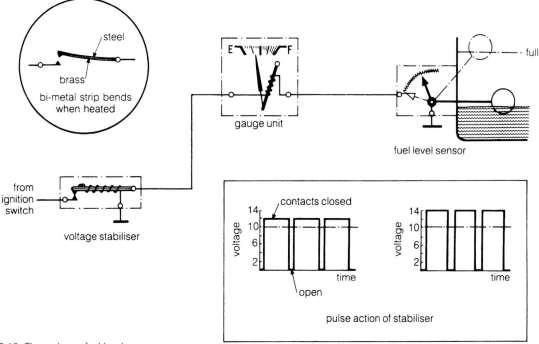

Figure 2.16 Thermal-type fuel level gauge

used in these units is the potentiometer (the working principle is discussed in Chapter 1). The wiper contact is connected to an arm and float arrangement (see Figure 2.18). The float rests at the surface of the fuel level and as the fuel quantity changes, the fuel level changes and this moves the wiper arm position. The potentiometer track can be designed with a non-linear characteristic to match the fuel tank profile so that the actual gauge reading is relatively linear. Generally the instrumentation incorporates a damping characteristic so that small, brief changes in fuel level (as the vehicle moves) are not seen on the display. An overview of a typical fuel measuring system is shown in Figure 2.16.

Engine oil sensors

Engine oil level is a slightly more complex measurement task. The engine oil level must be measured under certain conditions, i.e. level vehicle, hot (or cold) engine, etc. Most applications for oil-level measurement simplify the task by just monitoring the level to ensure that the minimum amount of oil is maintained in the sump. In the past, an instrumented dipstick has been used in conjunction with an evaluation circuit that checks that the minimum oil level is present before the engine is started. Generally this technique uses a heated sensing element in the dipstick that, if immersed in oil, dissipates heat (when heated with a current) and thus temperature and resistance remains within defined limits. If the oil level is low, the sensing element heats up (due to the lack of surrounding oil to dissipate the heat) and the resistance change is detected by an electronic circuit (see Figure 2.19).

This system has reliability problems due to the connector at the dipstick which needs to be disconnected regularly and this causes wear and tear on the connector and increased resistance, thus giving false readings.

Current developments use more sophisticated electronic sensing technology to evaluate oil level. Thermal-type sensors, using a constant current principle, can detect maximum and minimum oil levels. The voltage drop across the sensing element depends on the amount of heat that is dissipated from the wire to the surrounding medium (similar to the dipstick

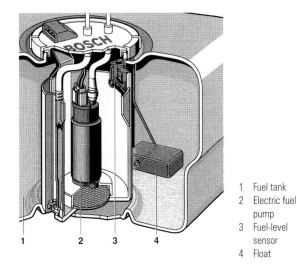

1 Fuel tank
2 Electric fuel
   pump
3 Fuel-level
   sensor
4 Float

Figure 2.17 In-tank pump and sensor assembly

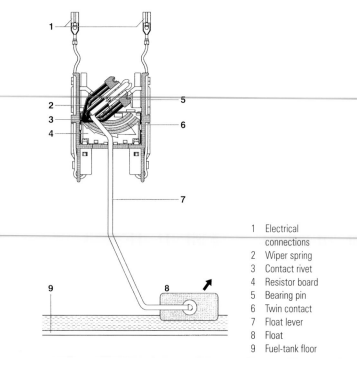

1	Electrical connections
2	Wiper spring
3	Contact rivet
4	Resistor board
5	Bearing pin
6	Twin contact
7	Float lever
8	Float
9	Fuel-tank floor

Figure 2.18 Fuel level sensor

above). Thus the oil level is known, as oil conducts the heat away better than air. The voltage drop value is compared to values in a look-up table where voltage-drop versus temperature is listed, and this information is used in the evaluation circuit to calculate oil level.

These sensors are available for permanent installation in the sump. Hence connector problems associated with the dipstick sensor are reduced considerably. More sophisticated heating elements in conjunction with a microprocessor-based evaluation system can monitor oil temperature as well as oil level.

Future developments for oil-level detection will involve the use of an ultrasonic-type detector for fluid level. This technique is being used in industrial applications and has the advantage that levels can be detected beyond the sensor housing. Excess and minimum oil levels plus any value in between can be measured, and the adoption of this technology will effectively make the dipstick redundant as oil level will be available for display directly to the driver via the instrument panel.

The requirement for flexible maintenance intervals drives the need for development of a reliable oil-quality sensor. Knowledge of oil condition helps to:

- allow appropriate maintenance intervals taking into account oil condition
- maximise service life of the oil
- prevent the possibility of engine damage due to oil deterioration.

The following parameters can be monitored by a sensor to establish oil condition:

- viscosity
- density
- permittivity (the ability of a material to polarise in response to a magnetic field).

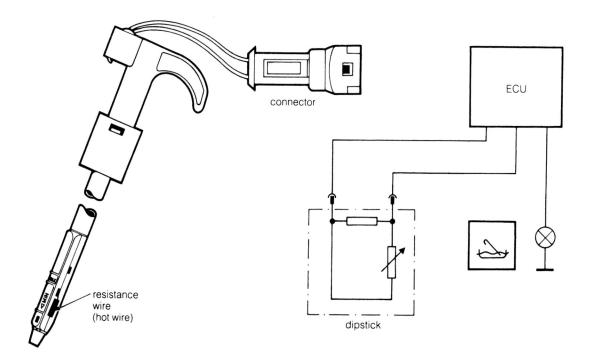

resistance wire (hot wire)

connector

ECU

dipstick

Figure 2.19 Engine oil-level sensor

One current design of sensor uses a tuning fork principle. This tuning fork element is excited over a specific frequency range and its is response monitored. The mechanical-electrical behaviour of this tuning fork can be represented in an electrical equivalent circuit, the equivalent variables of which correspond to the above parameters.

These electrical equivalent variables are varied with the aid of a complex algorithm until a defined correlation with the measured response is achieved. This way it is possible to determine the permittivity, viscosity and density as mutually independent variables.

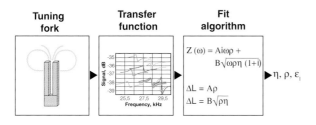

Figure 2.20 Principle of oil condition sensor

Future developments will involve smart oil sensors. The trend of current developments to integrate sensor technologies will mean that in the near future smart oil sensors will be single-sensor units that monitor oil pressure, temperature and condition. All the required processing is done at the sensor via inbuilt electronics and the connection to the vehicle system will be via a communication bus (e.g. local interconnect network (LIN)).

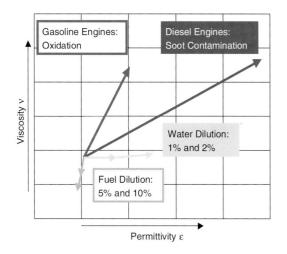

Figure 2.21 Correlation of oil condition with sensor measurements

Pressure sensors

Pressure-sensing applications are mainly used around the engine and powertrain systems and these applications are covered in *FMVT: Book 2 Powertrain Electronics*. However, there are some interesting pressure-sensing applications around the vehicle chassis and body system.

Tyre pressure monitoring

Correct tyre pressure has a dramatic effect on the safety and stability of a vehicle as well as its economy. Therefore, the ability to monitor tyre pressures is important as increased tread wear will lead to:

- a greater chance of aquaplaning in the wet
- reduced handling characteristics and reduced control of the vehicle
- longer stopping distances
- a greater chance of sudden tyre failure.

Two main methods are currently adopted to measure tyre pressure – direct and indirect. Indirect systems use existing wheel-speed sensors to monitor relative wheel speeds. A tyre with significant deflation will have a smaller rolling radius and hence will rotate faster. This can be detected via the ABS ECU microcontroller and an appropriate warning given to the driver via the instruments. This system is limited due to the indirect method of tyre pressure monitoring and is hence for indication only.

Most interesting with respect to sensor technology is the direct method of tyre pressure sensing. This relies on a pressure sensor permanently installed inside the tyre which can communicate to the body electrical system via telemetry. This remote sensing module comprises a pressure and temperature sensor, signal processor and radio frequency (RF) transmitter. The power supply is provided by a long-life battery and the signal processor manages power consumption of the sensor so effectively that the battery life can be up to 10 years.

The receiver unit is mounted close to the wheel and receives the data transmitted by the tyre sensor which includes pressure, temperature and wheel ID. This can then be transmitted via the vehicle network to the instrument panel where detailed information can be processed and displayed to the driver about the tyre pressure status.

Figure 2.22 Tyre pressure sensor

Fluid pressure monitoring

There are a number of systems around the chassis and body where fluid pressure sensing is required for monitoring and control purposes. Generally the applications involve higher pressure measurements. For example:

- Brake fluid pressure: installed in the hydraulic brake system modulator, this pressure measurement is needed for correct operation of ABS and ESP. The sensor element is required to measure pressures up to 350 bar. Monitoring of this brake pressure into and out of the modulator allows the ABS/ESP ECU to establish driver brake demand and to assess the brake pressure in individual brake hydraulic circuits.
- Air conditioning: these systems use pressure sensors to detect correct fluid pressure at various parts of the systems in order to protect the system components from damage should a leak occur (loss of fluid/lubricant) or system over-pressure.
- Steering and suspension: pressure sensors are used in these applications to provide feedback to the control systems so the pressure can be kept within acceptable limits or for correct operation of the system.

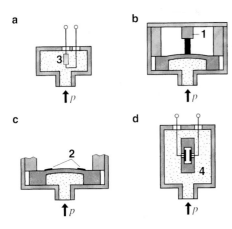

a Direct measurement, pressure-dependent resistor (3)
b Measurement using a force sensor (1)
c Measuring the diaphragm deformation/DMS (2)
d Capacitative measurement using the deformation of a diaphragm cell

Figure 2.23 Pressure measurement sensing techniques

The basic sensor technology for these applications is similar and consists of an active pressure sensor which includes the sensing element and evaluation/signal conditioning microprocessor in a single unit. The sensing element consists of a steel diaphragm which converts the pressure into a force/stress. This is monitored via resistive/capacitive or piezoelectric means in the measuring element which then creates a low-level signal that is conditioned and amplified by the microprocessor such that the measured pressure value can be transmitted to the required monitoring system. The microprocessor

inside the unit will perform linearisation of the signal in addition to temperature correction. In simple applications, the signal will be transmitted in analogue form, generally in the range 0–5 volts. For more sophisticated applications, the pulse width modulated (PWM) signal or databus signal transmission will be used (this is a typical smart sensor application).

Temperature sensors

Temperature sensors are located at various points around the vehicle but are mainly used for providing temperature information to the engine control unit. This allows optimisation of control parameters to prevent any perceivable change in performance or drivability due to temperature changes in the environment. This would include:

- engine and coolant temperature
- intake air temperature
- fuel temperature
- oil temperature.

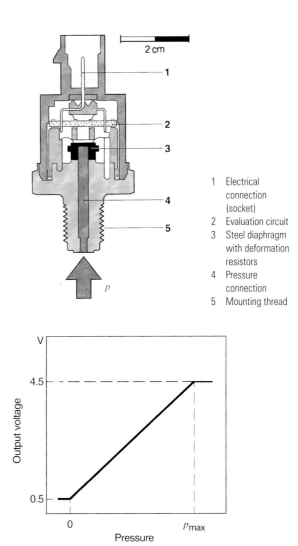

1 Electrical connection (socket)
2 Evaluation circuit
3 Steel diaphragm with deformation resistors
4 Pressure connection
5 Mounting thread

Figure 2.24 Internal view of sensor and graph of sensor output voltage

These sensor technologies are covered in *FMVT: Book 2 Powertrain Electronics*. Additional applications around the chassis and body system include:

- cabin air temperature
- outside air
- air-conditioning control (fan outlet temperature, evaporator temperature)
- battery
- brakes
- exhaust temperature.

Measurement technology

- Thermistor: in most cases the temperature range is –40 to 200 degrees Celsius and for this application negative (negative temperature coefficient (NTC)) or positive (positive temperature coefficient (PTC)) resistance technology is used almost exclusively (also known as thermistors).

  Most materials change resistance in direct or indirect proportion to temperature and this is exploited in the sensing element of the thermistor. Generally the thermistor is used in conjunction with other circuit components (temperature neutral or inversely sensitive) to provide an analogue voltage (via a potential divider circuit) which can then be monitored via electronics. The response of the thermistor is non linear and hence linearisation of the signal is necessary during the signal conditioning stage (normally via a look-up table). Figure 2.25 shows the construction and resistance variation with temperature of a typical sensor as fitted to an engine block to measure coolant temperature.

  Another application of temperature measurement for the thermistor is for component temperature monitoring, i.e. to protect electrical components (processors and circuit boards) from damage, and also to compensate for deviation due to temperature change.

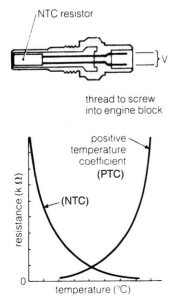

Figure 2.25 Thermistor sensor characteristics

- Thermocouple: exhaust temperatures need a wider range (up to 1000 degrees Celsius) and for this application a resistance-type sensor (in which the sensing element of platinum is normally used) can be employed. Another alternative for measuring wider temperature ranges is the thermocouple. The principle of the thermocouple is shown in Figure 2.26.

  The thermocouple consists of two dissimilar metals joined together as shown and connected to a galvanometer. When the junction is heated an electromotive force (emf) is generated that is registered by the galvanometer. This voltage is generated due to the fact that thermoelectric currents are obtained from a pair of metals when their junctions are maintained at different temperatures. A thermocouple can be made of a number of different metals according to the temperature range required. The chrome/aluminium type commonly used is suitable for a temperature range of 0 to 1000 degrees Celsius.

  In practice, thermocouples are used in conjunction with reference junctions in order to accurately measure absolute temperature values at a specific point where the junction is placed. Also, they are normally connected to a conditioning circuit and/or a microcontroller which amplifies the voltage, linearises it (this means that the output signal changes in the same proportion as the input temperature), and then converts the signal to temperature value for display to a user. In vehicle applications measurement of exhaust gas temperature is necessary when an oxygen sensor is used.

- Pyrometer: this is a non-contact method which measures temperature by using the radiation emitted by a body. The radiation emitted is in the infrared range and can be detected easily by an appropriate sensor, as shown in Figure 2.27.

  The measurement point is projected onto a heat-sensing element which, as a result, heats up very slightly compared to its surroundings. The element's temperature therefore reflects the temperature of the body being measured (but in the ratio of 1:1000). Nevertheless this minute change can be detected and temperature of the body can be accurately established to within 0.5 degrees Celsius. Typical applications for non-contact temperature sensing in the vehicle include passenger compartment temperature, occupant detection, exhaust gas temperature and image sensing.

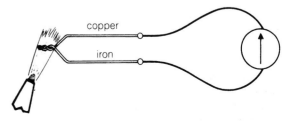

Figure 2.26 Thermocouple

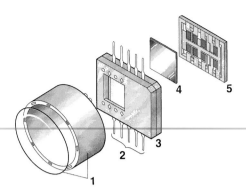

1   Lens housing with lens
2   Connections
3   Infra-red-detector housing
4   Infra-red window
5   Detector

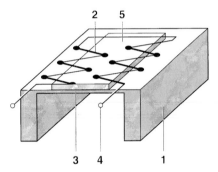

Principle of the measuring element
1   Si chip
2   Thermocouples connected in series (i.e. Al/Poly-Si)
3   SiN diaphragm
4   Thermopile junctions
5   Absorber layer

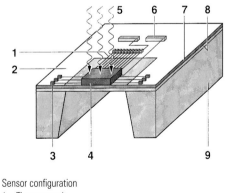

Sensor configuration
1   Thermocouple
2   'Cold' junction
3   Diaphragm
4   Absorber
5   Heat radiation
6   Electrical connection
7   Si_3N_4 layer
8   SiO_2 layer
9   Heat sink

Figure 2.27 Pyrometer based sensor unit

Dynamic speed and position sensors

This section considers sensors for speed and position, either of the vehicle body itself or the wheels in contact with the ground. Note that there are a large number of speed/position sensing requirements in the powertrain system, for example engine speed, throttle position, gearbox shaft speed etc., but these sensors and applications are covered in *FMVT: Book 2 Powertrain Electronics.*

Many of the applications for these sensors in the chassis and body system are the result of significant developments in safety systems relating to the moving vehicle itself, for example anti-lock brakes, brake force distribution, stability control systems etc. These sophisticated systems need as much information as possible about the dynamic state of the vehicle so that fast, real-time calculations and decisions can be made by the electronic control system to protect the driver in the event of a critical state of the vehicle occurring (e.g. a skid or slide). Hence the requirements for not only wheel speed, but vehicle speed and direction, in addition to acceleration. The following sensor types are typical of those employed in such systems.

Wheel/vehicle speed

This application is commonly seen for anti-lock braking systems, and in modern vehicles this is appended by additional functions such as traction control and stability control utilising the same sensors at the wheel. The most commonly used technology in this application is the inductive-type sensor. This is a passive-type sensor installed at the wheel hub which senses the passing of teeth of an installed sensor ring on the rotating hub, as shown in Figure 2.28.

The sensor's pole pin is surrounded by a coil winding and is installed directly at the sensor ring. The soft magnetic pole pin is connected to a permanent magnet which projects a magnetic field towards the trigger wheel. As the wheel and hub rotates, the alternating sequence of teeth/gap induces fluctuations in the magnetic field in the pole pin and winding and hence an alternating current in the coil. The frequency of this alternating current is directly proportional to the wheel speed and can be easily monitored by the ECU to detect rapid deceleration of the wheel which would indicate the onset of a skid (loss of frictional contact between the wheel and the road surface). An important point to note with this type of sensor is that correct installation (with respect to air gap) is a critical factor.

A more recent development is the active wheel-speed sensor. In place of the toothed wheel, a magnetic sensor ring is fitted comprising magnets installed with alternating poles. The sensor element is placed adjacent to this. The general arrangement is shown in Figure 2.29.

Rotation of the wheel (and sensor ring) induces a continuously alternating magnetic flux through the sensor element. This sensing technique can be packaged within the wheel-bearing assembly itself to form an extremely compact unit (see Figure 2.30). In this case, the bearing seal contains magnetic powder to form the

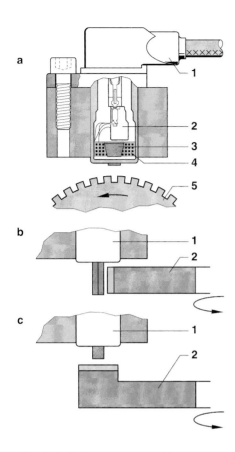

Figure 2.30 Compact wheel-speed sensor

a   Chisel pole pin: Radial installation, radial scan
b   Rhombus pole pin: Axial installation, radial scan
c   Round pole pin: Radial installation, axial scan
1   Sensor case with electrical connections
2   Permanent magnet
3   Soft-iron core (pole pin)
4   Winding
5   Trigger wheel

Figure 2.28 Inductive wheel-speed sensor

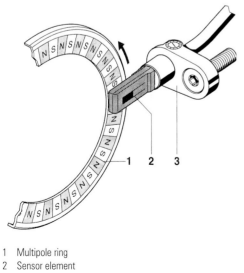

1   Multipole ring
2   Sensor element
3   Sensor case

Figure 2.29 Active wheel-speed sensor

magnetic poles and this then effectively replaces the need for a separate magnetic sensor ring, the bearing seal effectively becomes the sensor ring.

The sensor itself contains Hall effect or magneto-resistive elements which, as part of the signal conditioning chain, convert the changing flux into an analogue signal which can be processed by an ECU. The output signal amplitude does not depend on speed and thus sensing of wheel speed down to near stationary conditions can be achieved.

Another notable development with this sensor type is that, in line with current trends, the sensor itself can have built-in signal conditioning electronics in addition to the sensor element. The sensor requires a power supply and this is provided by the connected ECU over a two-wire connection. Interestingly though, the signal is also transmitted along the same wires as an alternating, load-independent current, the frequency of which is proportional to wheel speed. This current signal is far less prone to interference than the voltage signal from an inductive sensor. The following additional features can also be available with this integrated intelligence:

- direction of travel – used for hill-holding feature of electronic handbrakes and for navigation systems
- plausibility check – self-monitoring in the sensor for correct function.

Vehicle yaw angle

When the vehicle is moving, a complex set of dynamic forces are acting upon it. One of these forces is known as 'yaw'. This is a moment or turning force acting on the vehicle trying to rotate it about its vertical axis. For normal steering manoeuvres, these forces are necessary, but under critical conditions (braking on surfaces where the wheels have different coefficients of friction) undesirable yaw moments can occur that create an unstable vehicle state.

With the advent and availability of sophisticated systems to control and manage the vehicle stability (e.g. ESP, TCS), measurement of yaw becomes necessary in order to manage and control these situations with the body electronics system. In addition, vehicle navigation systems can use a yaw signal as an input for calculating direction of the vehicle. A number of sensors with differing technologies are available:

- Tuning fork sensor: the main sensing element consists of a tuning fork complete with attached piezo element sensors (see Figure 2.31). In operation, the two lower piezo elements oscillate and excite the upper section of the assembly which then starts a resonant, counter-phase oscillation. The oscillations cause the upper part of the fork assembly to react more slowly to an application of force. This means that as the vehicle turns, the upper part lags behind and the fork effectively twists. This causes changes in the charge distribution of the fork which is sensed by the upper two piezo elements and interpreted by the sensor electronics to give an output signal of turn direction and amplitude.

- Oscillating drum sensor: the general arrangement of this sensor is shown in Figure 2.32.

  The main sensing element consists of a metallic, hollow cylinder with four pairs of opposed piezo elements (see Figure 2.33). Two pairs of the elements generate and control resonant oscillations in the cylinder. The remaining two pairs observe the vibration nodes in the cylinder. When the vehicle turns, the vibration nodes shift (due to Coriolis acceleration; the Coriolis effect is an apparent deflection of a moving object in a rotating frame of reference). The result is that these nodes generate forces which are proportional to rotational speed. The forces are sensed by the piezo elements and used in the sensor's built-in electronics to establish the yaw angle.

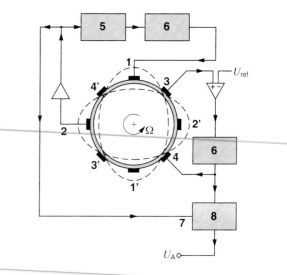

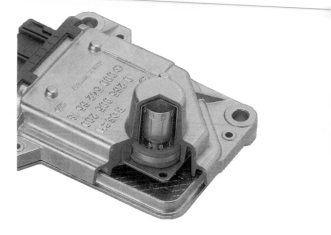

1–4	Piezo elements	8	Rectifier (phase-selective)
5	Circuit	U_A	Output voltage
6	Bandpass filter (phase-locked)	Ω	Yaw rate
7	Phase reference	$U_{ref} = 0$	(normal operation)
		$U_{ref} \neq 0$	('built- in' test)

Figure 2.32 Oscillating drum sensor

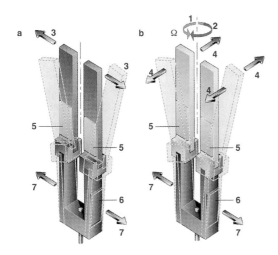

1 Tuning-fork direction of oscillation resulting from cornering
2 Direction of rotation of the vehicle
3 Direction of oscillation resulting from straight-ahead driving
4 Coriolis force
5 Upper piezo elements (sensing)
6 Bottom piezo elements (drive)
7 Excitation oscillation direction
Ω Yaw

Figure 2.31 Tuning fork yaw angle sensor

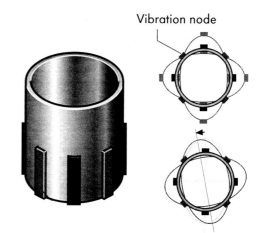

Vibration node

Figure 2.33 Operating principle – oscillating drum

Vehicle acceleration

Acceleration sensors are used to detect vehicle acceleration or deceleration for a number of safety-related vehicle applications, for example:

- airbag trigger
- seatbelt tensioners
- roll-bar activation
- electronic dynamic safety systems, e.g. ABS, ESP, TCS
- 4WD vehicles (certain critical conditions preclude the use of wheel-speed data where a four-wheel-drive system is fitted).

Numerous technologies are available and in use:

- Capacitive effect: this sensing technique uses two differential capacitors to determine acceleration forces. The sensor basically consists of two series connected capacitors (see Figure 2.34). The common central plate is moved under acceleration/deceleration force. Each capacitor then has a certain capacity. As long as no acceleration occurs, the dielectric gap remains constant and equal and therefore the capacity of the two capacitors is the same. Under acceleration, the central plate moves and this changes the relative capacity of the two capacitors. The sensor electronics can detect this and use it to determine the magnitude of the acceleration force. This technology can be built in a very compact micro-mechanical form using a comb-like structure that is commonly seen in airbag and impact detection accelerometers where the accelerations are quite high (i.e. 50–100 g (note that acceleration is expressed in units 'g'. This represents acceleration due to gravitational force and is generally about 9.81 m/s^2)).

- Hall effect: used to measure longitudinal and transversal acceleration depending on installation position. The sensing element consists of a permanent magnet seismic mass mounted on a spring strip that is clamped at one end (see Figure 2.36). The

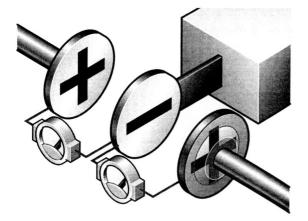

Figure 2.34 Operating principle – capacitive sensor for acceleration

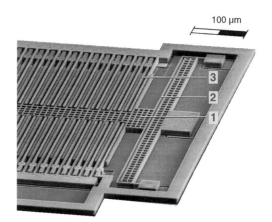

1 Spring-mounted seismic mass with electrode
2 Spring
3 Fixed electrodes

C_2 C_M C_1

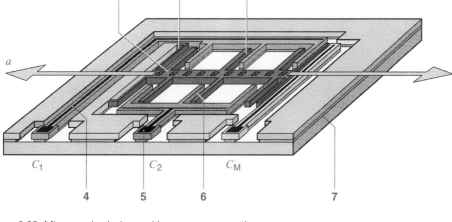

Figure 2.35 Micro-mechanical capacitive sensor construction

1 Spring-mounted seismic mass with electrodes
2 Spring
3 Fixed electrodes with capacity C_1
4 Printed Al conductor
5 Bond pad
6 Fixed electrodes with capacity C_2
7 Silicone oxide
a Acceleration in sensing direction
C_M Measuring capacity

movement of this mass is monitored by a Hall effect sensor located above, which is in turn connected to evaluation electronics inside the sensor. When the vehicle accelerates, the spring-mass element changes its position accordingly and the deflection is proportional to the acceleration. This deflection generates a corresponding Hall voltage in the sensing element and this is conditioned electronically for an output signal.

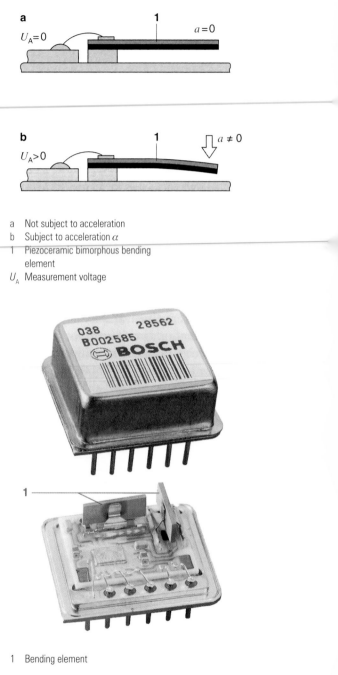

a   Not subject to acceleration
b   Subject to acceleration α
1   Piezoceramic bimorphous bending element
U_A Measurement voltage

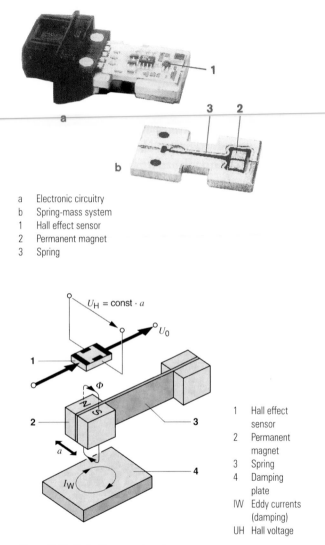

a   Electronic circuitry
b   Spring-mass system
1   Hall effect sensor
2   Permanent magnet
3   Spring

1   Hall effect sensor
2   Permanent magnet
3   Spring
4   Damping plate
IW   Eddy currents (damping)
UH   Hall voltage

Figure 2.36 Hall effect acceleration sensor

1   Bending element

Figure 2.37 Piezoelectric acceleration sensor

- Piezoelectric: a piezo bending element is used in this sensor type. It is a bonded structure comprising two piezoelectric layers of opposite polarities (see Figure 2.37). Under acceleration, one half of the structure bends and the other compresses such that a stress occurs and this creates a charge disturbance which is monitored by the integrated signal conditioning circuit via attached electrodes. The integrated signal conditioning includes a charge amplifier and filter and these components define the useful frequency range which is typically up to 10 Hz. The complete assembly

is housed in a single, hermetically sealed unit. Single and dual sensors are available for monitoring longitudinal and lateral acceleration of the vehicle.

Current and future developments of this sensor technology include packaging the yaw and acceleration sensor in a single micro-mechanical unit (see Figure 2.38), which can perform both functions. This reduces the number of individual components and signal lines, as well as reducing installation space in the vehicle.

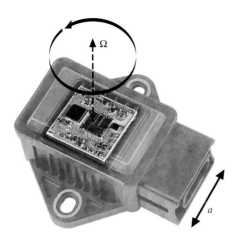

α acceleration in sensing direction Ω Yaw rate

Figure 2.38 Combined yaw and acceleration sensor

New sensor technologies and applications

Sensor technology is constantly emerging due to the demands on modern vehicles for more sophisticated and automated comfort and control systems. This means that new techniques for measuring the required variables around the vehicle are constantly being developed and applied. Below is a summary of some of the more recent innovations seen on current vehicles in the market.

- Rain sensor: this sensor is used to automatically trigger the windscreen wipers and also for automatic setting of intermittent wipe interval according to weather (i.e. rain) conditions. The adoption of this feature in a vehicle reduces the required interaction from the driver and hence increases the level of driver concentration on the driving task. The sensor comprises an optical transmit/receive path. An LED emits light which is coupled into the windscreen

at a given angle. The dry windscreen reflects the light back to a photodiode in the sensor which is also aligned at an angle to the screen. If water droplets are on the screen, the amount of reflected light is considerably reduced due to refraction and this forms the basis of the measurement principle to control whether wiper operation is needed and at what speed. The rain sensor can be used in conjunction with central locking/closure system to close the windows/sunroof if rain is detected.

- Dirt: similar in technology to the above, but the application is for headlamp cleaning. Headlamp wash systems are commonplace but normally they are activated when the screen washer and headlamps are both on. The problem is that under this activation mode these systems can waste screen-wash fluid as they will be activated unnecessarily. Also, the headlamp lens may not always be clean when the headlamps are switched on. A better solution is to clean the headlamp lenses when necessary and this can be achieved if a sensor is used to monitor the dirt on the lens. The sensor, consisting of a transmitter-receiver unit, is mounted on the inner surface of the lens but not in the lamp beam path. When the lens is clean the transmitted infrared light from the sensor passes through it unhindered. If this light hits dirt particles on the surface of the lens, it is scattered and reflected back to the opto-receiver in the sensor unit. The degree of scatter is a function of the dirt on the lens and hence can trigger the cleaning mechanism once a predefined threshold is reached.

- Radar: for certain vehicle applications the wheel speed can be misleading to determine vehicle speed. This is particularly true with off-road/special-purpose vehicles due to the fact that they may operate in conditions where considerable wheel slip occurs. For these applications a Doppler radar system can be used effectively. This system consists of a transceiver probe which directs a radar beam onto the ground at an oblique angle and with a certain frequency. This beam is reflected back from the ground to the transceiver,

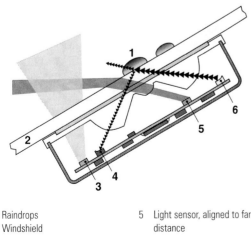

1	Raindrops	5	Light sensor, aligned to far
2	Windshield		distance
3	Ambient-light sensor	6	LED
4	Photodiode		

Figure 2.39 Rain sensor

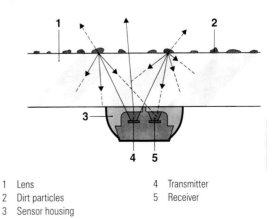
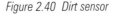

1	Lens	4	Transmitter
2	Dirt particles	5	Receiver
3	Sensor housing		

Figure 2.40 Dirt sensor

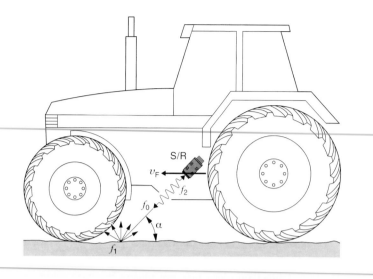

S/R   Transmitter/receiver
vF   Vehicle speed
f_0 Transmit-signal frequency
f_1 Frequency of signal arriving at the ground
f_2 Frequency of signal arriving at the receiver
α Alignment angle of the measuring system

Figure 2.41 Radar type speed sensor

and due to the fact that the vehicle is moving forward, towards the reflected signal, a frequency shift occurs due to the Doppler effect. This frequency shift is directly proportional to the speed and can be used to accurately evaluate vehicle speed over ground.

Other applications for radar sensors include obstruction detection (using ultrasonics, discussed above), collision avoidance (using RF technology) and distance to ground for ride control, navigation, dynamic safety systems.

More sophisticated radar sensors are used in collision avoidance systems and form part of active cruise control systems (ACC).

An interesting development from Bosch is the ranging radar. This sensor combines several radar elements with an additional processing capability to determine range to preceding vehicles, their relative speed and position (side offset). When the vehicle is in cruise mode this information is processed in the sensor and provides commands for all of the relative actuators in the powertrain and braking systems to maximise safety.

- Battery: due to the increased loading and complexity of vehicle electrical systems, a battery sensor which monitors battery charging state and condition is a useful and perhaps necessary development. This means that the vehicle electronics control system can actually establish if the battery is being charged and by how much. With the addition of a microprocessor evaluation unit incorporating sophisticated algorithms, the sensor can itself calculate the condition of the car battery at any given time. It can even predict the future state of charge based on a given set of existing conditions.

This allows for the adoption of a complete vehicle energy management system that guarantees sufficient energy will always be available to start the vehicle at any time. In addition, this system can assist in the efficient usage of energy within the vehicle in order to contribute to emission reduction. It is also possible that a system like this can increase battery life as a reduced charge-discharge cycle of the battery can be achieved.

An example is the electronic battery sensor (EBS) from Bosch. This consists of a microprocessor comprising the electronics and a shunt for current measurement. These components are integrated into a single unit that can be fitted between the battery terminal and the connector on the main power cable. The arrangement is shown in Figure 2.43.

Figure 2.42 Radar sensor for active cruise control

Figure 2.43 Electronic battery sensor

The battery state detection software for the sensor is completely integrated into the microprocessor chip. The sensor directly measures the temperature, voltage and current of the battery and on this basis it calculates capacity and state of charge as well as present and future performance capability. The information is transmitted through a vehicle network interface to the higher-ranking energy management of the vehicle. Note that the battery sensor can also be used by the manufacturer during the vehicle's assembly to test electrical components and quiescent current levels.

- Air quality: these sensors monitor the quality of the air as it enters the vehicle. In particular, they respond to toxic exhaust components (carbon monoxide (CO) and nitrogen oxide (NO_x)). They can also include a humidity sensor to assist in the demisting function. The sensor elements used are thick film resistors. As soon as the measured medium collects on them, the resistors change resistance and this is monitored by the internal evaluation electronics. The sensors are mounted on a heated substrate (330 degrees Celsius). The CO sensor measures concentrations of 10 to 100 parts per million (ppm) and the NO_x sensor 0.5 to 5 ppm. As soon as a high level of pollutants is detected the ventilation into the vehicle can be suppressed to prevent the driver from breathing these gases. The humidity sensor includes a temperature sensor so that the dew point can be calculated and the ventilation control system can prevent misting of the vehicle's windows.

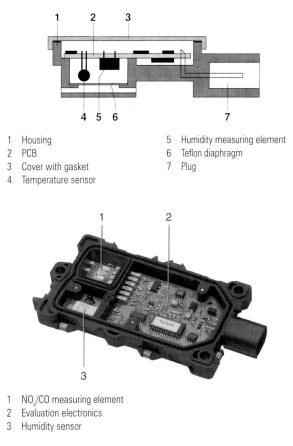

1 Housing	5 Humidity measuring element
2 PCB	6 Teflon diaphragm
3 Cover with gasket	7 Plug
4 Temperature sensor	

1   NO_x/CO measuring element
2   Evaluation electronics
3   Humidity sensor

Figure 2.44 Air quality sensor

Key Points

Sensors perform an information-gathering function for the engine and powertrain control system

They convert physical quantities into electrical signals

Smart sensors have on-board intelligence and can communicate to a control unit in digital form via a bus system

Key Points

Commonly used sensors measure pressures, temperature and flows. More sophisticated types of sensor are found in modern cars with advanced control systems that measure more sophisticated data such as vehicle yaw angle

The number of sensors in modern vehicles has increased due to advances in vehicle safety and emission control systems which require more data. This trend is likely to continue

2.2   ACTUATORS FOR CHASSIS AND BODY SYSTEMS

2.2.1 Overview

There are a large number of open- and closed-loop systems in the chassis and body control system that need an actuator to convert a control signal into a physical movement or action. Basically the actuator is an energy converter, converting electrical energy into mechanical force, a simple example being a solenoid. In modern electronic systems the conversion chain is slightly more complicated than simple electrical to mechanical conversion. Most electronic signals from a microprocessor are at a very low power and voltage level. This signal is normally interpreted by

an additional element known commonly as a driver or output module. It converts the low-level digital signal to an appropriate level and type to drive the output actuator, for example a stepper motor. During this process additional power is needed and this is sourced from the vehicle power system. The general arrangement is shown diagrammatically in Figure 2.45. An important point to note is that in modern systems the distribution of the components in the chain can vary. Often the actuator driver circuit may be incorporated inside an ECU as part of the output signal conditioning system. It is also possible that the driver could be combined in the actuator itself.

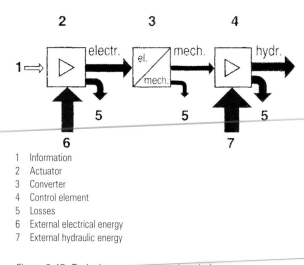

1   Information
2   Actuator
3   Converter
4   Control element
5   Losses
6   External electrical energy
7   External hydraulic energy

Figure 2.45 Typical actuator conversion chains

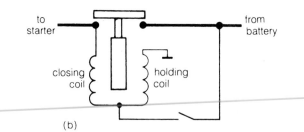

(b)

Figure 2.46 Solenoid

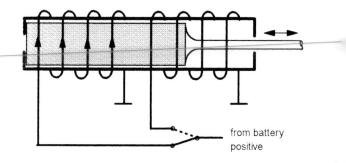

Figure 2.47 Double-acting solenoid

Actuators fall into two main categories for most common applications where a force is needed (linear and rotary). In addition to this, pyrotechnic actuators for passenger safety systems need to create a large amount of energy (as pressure) in a short time for operation of such systems. These are discussed in Chapter 9.

2.2.2 Linear actuators

Linear solenoids

A simple solenoid consists of a bobbin that holds a coil of thin copper wire which is enamelled for insulation purposes. A soft iron armature or plunger, of sufficient diameter to permit axial movement, slides into the bobbin when the coil is energised. A spring returns the plunger to a rest position when the solenoid is not powered.

An alternative winding arrangement reduces current consumption and prevents overheating of the solenoid (see Figure 2.46). This utilises separate closing and holding coils. On initial activation, both coils are energised and this provides sufficient energy to move the armature rapidly from its rest position. Once the armature reaches its final energised position the closing coil is switched off (mechanically or electrically) and sufficient energy is provided by the holding coil to overcome the return spring force and maintain position until the solenoid is de-energised (i.e. switched off) completely. This arrangement is used to great effect in most vehicle starter solenoids and pre-engaged type starters. In the latter, the solenoid performs two functions – engaging the drive pinion and closing the starter switch contacts.

If bi-directional linear movement is required, two separate coils can be used in the same assembly, as shown in Figure 2.47. The armature can rest in either position at the limit of its travel and the appropriate solenoid is momentarily energised in order to move the armature to the required position. Solenoids of this type were employed in very early central-locking systems.

In operation the solenoid actuator depends on the forces which occur at the interfaces in the magnetic field generated by the coil when it is energised. The actuation force follows the relationship:

$$\text{Actuator force} = A \times \frac{B^2}{2} \times \mu_0$$

where A = Pole face area, B = Magnetic induction and μ_0 = Permeability constant.

A solenoid can produce large forces and rapid operation, but the stroke is very limited. This is due to the fact that the force on the armature is proportional to the square of the distance between the armature and pole piece (i.e. the air gap). Thus the force reduces considerably as the armature moves further. To compensate for this, in certain applications a lever arrangement is used to reduce the force but increase the stroke.

Linear motors

These are very similar in construction to the solenoid, but in place of the soft, iron core a powerful permanent magnet is used. This gives the advantage of a longer stroke with near constant force. The two main types commonly in use are:

- moving winding
- moving field.

As shown in Figure 2.48, the moving winding type has a fixed magnet around which is fitted a hollow armature and a coil winding. When direct current is supplied to the coil, the armature is displaced in or out depending on the direction of current flow through the coil.

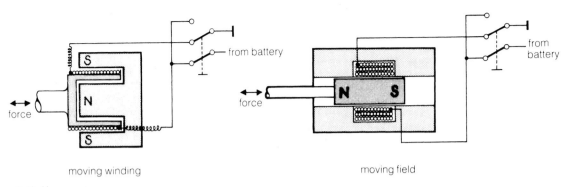

Figure 2.48 Linear motors

The moving field type has a static field winding and a moveable, permanent magnet core which provides the actuating force output. As above, the direction of motion is governed by the polarity of the supply. The stroke is limited to half the length of the magnet and the optimal construction form is that the width of the coil winding should equal the stroke. An alternative design is to include two overlaid windings of opposite direction and in this case current reversal is not necessary, just activation of the appropriate winding to give force in the required direction.

The most common vehicle application for linear solenoids and motors is for door locking systems and remote opening systems for vehicle load space areas, fuel filler flaps etc. They are less common now. Linear servo actuators incorporating DC motors are nearly exclusively used now in new vehicles for the above applications. A typical door lock servo actuator is shown in Figure 2.49.

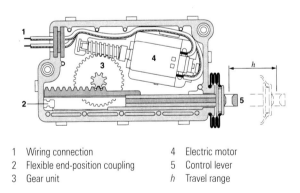

1	Wiring connection	4	Electric motor
2	Flexible end-position coupling	5	Control lever
3	Gear unit	*h*	Travel range

Figure 2.49 Typical door lock servo actuator

The unit consists of a small DC motor combined with reduction gears (to increase force/torque) and a rack mechanism (to convert rotary to linear motion). Small, high-speed DC motors are very common and cheap to produce. When combined with plastic components in the gearbox/rack mechanism a very compact and light actuator can be produced cheaply and it has a long stroke with constant force over the entire travel.

2.2.3 Rotary actuators

Rotary actuators/DC motors

The conventional permanent magnet DC motor is still commonly used in vehicle actuation systems such as washer pumps, fuel pumps, window and sunroof open and closure, seat adjustment etc. This type of motor is very compact but high speed is needed to generate sufficient usable power. This tends to compromise the reliability and also means that for most applications a gearbox is needed to adapt speed and torque for the application. Cost and weight are important and the gearbox is generally constructed of plastic for cost reasons, although this also has a negative effect on durability.

Many applications now require high-precision, durable motor actuator systems and for these the brushless or electronically commutated DC motor is becoming more widespread. Typical applications are where high reliability is important, such as:

- gear shift actuators
- electrical power-steering systems
- electrical clutch actuators.

The basic construction of this motor incorporates a permanent magnet rotor that rotates inside a static stator winding. This consists of a number of separate field windings. Note that this is the opposite arrangement to a classically commutated DC motor where the field is static and the winding rotates. The field windings are energised in sequence by the motor drive electronics and this creates a rotating magnetic field. The permanent magnet rotor is locked by magnetism to this rotating field and hence drives an output shaft onto which it is mounted.

EC motor
1 Electrical machine with rotor-position sensor, 2 Control and power electronics, 3 Input.

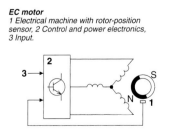

Figure 2.50 Basic principle – electronically commutated DC motor

The frequency with which the field winding is energised dictates the motor speed, and the current in the windings dictates the torque that the motor produces. This is monitored and controlled in the drive electronics according to the application requirements. An important factor is that the drive electronics must know the position of the rotor in order to energise the windings in the correct sequence. This can be achieved by fitting a rotor position sensor which feeds rotor position information back to the electronic drive system. Alternatively, where lower precision/reduced cost is required, the rotor position can be inferred from the emf that is induced in the non-energised windings whilst the motor rotates.

The main advantage is that this motor dispenses with the commutator and carbon brush arrangement. This means a reduction in noise and also an increase in reliability. These motors are basically maintenance free for the whole of their service life. The only moving parts are the bearings. The electronic drive system can incorporate a high degree of built-in intelligence for enhanced operation, for example:

- infinitely variable speed/torque control
- direction reversal
- motor protection – soft starting, protection against overload and locking
- in-built diagnostic capability.

Stepper motors

The introduction of digital electronics in vehicles has been accompanied by the adoption of stepper motors in numerous actuator applications. These respond to electrical pulses provided by an electronic driver circuit, normally built into an ECU. For precise control applications a stepper motor can move small angles in either direction in response to signals from the controller via the drive circuit. The type of motor governs the smallest step angle. Typical applications use step angles of 1.8, 2.5, 3.75, 7.5, 25 and 30 degrees. There are three main types of stepper motor.

Permanent magnet

In this type of motor the active rotor is a two-pole permanent magnet. The stator has two pairs of independent windings AA1 and BB1, through which current from the driver circuit may pass in either direction and this will turn the rotor by 90 degree steps. When current passes through BB1 the magnetic laws of attraction and repulsion align the rotor with the active poles of the stator (see Figure 2.51).

Complete rotation is obtained by applying to the motor four electrical pulses of suitable polarity. Direction of rotation depends on the polarity of the stator during the first pulse, e.g. if the current direction in Figure 2.51(b) is reversed, the rotor will move clockwise. The frequency of the step pulses will dictate the speed of rotation. By increasing the number of rotor/stator poles the step angle can be reduced. This can be calculated as follows:

$$\text{Step angle} = \frac{360}{\text{number of step positions}}$$

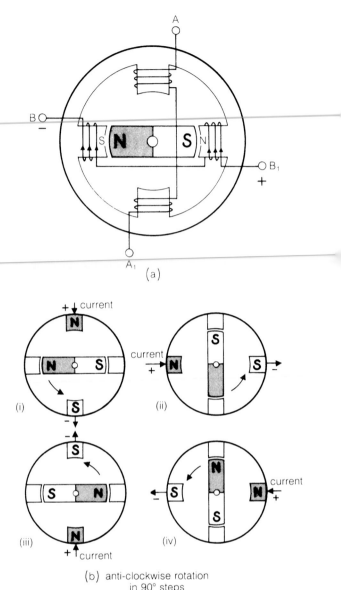

Figure 2.51 Permanent-magnet stepper motor

Each winding has two directions of current flow so the number of step positions will always be an even number. Motors of this type normally have step angles of 7.5–120 degrees.

The main advantage for these motors is that the permanent magnet holds the rotor in position even when the windings are de-energised. This is known as detent torque and not all stepper motors have this feature. The disadvantage is they have relatively high inertia.

Variable reluctance

This type of motor has a soft iron rotor with radial teeth and a wound stator equipped with more poles than the rotor. Figure 2.52 shows a simplified layout of a three-phase, 15 degree step angle motor. This has eight rotor teeth and 12 stator poles around which the current flows in one direction only.

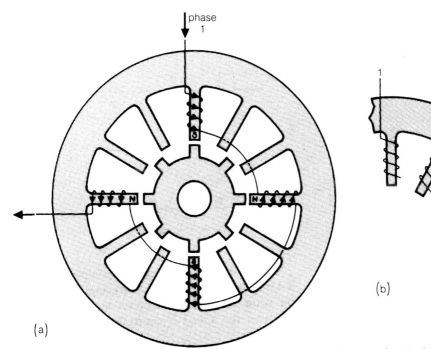

phase 1

1
2
3

(a)

(b)

Figure 2.52 Variable-reluctance stepper motor

The number of step positions (N) is calculated via:

$$N = \frac{SR}{(S - R)}$$

where S = Slots in stator and R = Slots in rotor.

For example, in this case:

$$N = \frac{(8 \times 12)}{(12 - 8)} = \frac{96}{4} = 24$$

Therefore:

$$\text{Step angle} = \frac{360}{24} = 15 \text{ degrees}$$

In Figure 2.52, (b) shows the winding arrangement for phase 1. When a current flows through one phase of the stator windings, the rotor aligns itself to give the shortest magnetic path, i.e. the path of minimum reluctance. In each step position, the rotor aligns with four stator poles and this gives the motor greater power.

An angular movement of one step from the position shown in Figure 2.52 (a) above is obtained by energising either phase 2 or phase 3 depending on the required direction. For a clockwise motion, the phases would be energised in the order 3–2–1–3–2–1. The angle turned by the rotor by these six current pulses is 90 degrees and the time taken for the total movement is governed by the time taken by the control circuit to energise the windings sufficient to move the rotor to the next step.

This type of motor is available with step angles between 1.8 and 15 degrees and has a fast response due to low rotor inertia. The motor can have a fast stepping rate but it does not have any detent torque and hence it has to be damped externally to prevent unwanted oscillation.

Hybrid type

As the name suggests, this type is a combination of the above two types. Figure 2.53 shows that the rotor is constructed in a similar manner to a vehicle alternator rotor. A permanent magnet with its poles coaxial to the rotor shaft is sandwiched between two iron claws which have teeth to form the poles.

The stator has eight main poles which are cut to form small teeth on the surface adjacent to the stator. Operation is similar to the permanent magnet type (above). The rotor aligns itself so that the magnetic reluctance is minimum.

The hybrid stepper motor has stepping angles as low as 0.9 degrees. It also has a relatively high torque and can operate at high stepping rates. The disadvantages are high inertia and resonance at some speeds.

Stepper motor control

All three types of stepper motor respond to digital signals. The direction of current flow through the appropriate stator winding governs the direction of rotor movement, and the speed at which the pulse signals are supplied controls the speed of rotor movement.

Taking the permanent-magnet type as an example, Figure 2.54(a) shows the pulses that are applied to turn the rotor. Note that the pulses do not overlap and the speed is controlled by the pulse frequency.

Figure 2.54(b) shows the pulse pattern needed to move the rotor forward through three steps (270 degrees) and then reverse to the original position. The input to the drive circuit, normally from a logic signal source, has low power and this must be amplified in the motor control electronics to a power level sufficient to drive the motor.

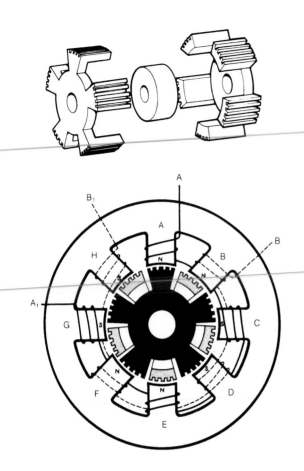

Figure 2.53 Hybrid stepper motor

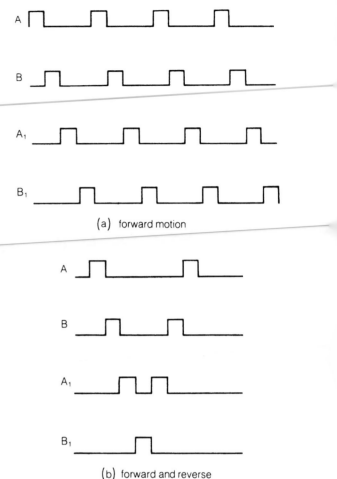

(a) forward motion

(b) forward and reverse

Figure 2.54 Pulse signals to control stepper motor

> **Key Points**
>
> An actuator acts as an energy converter to convert electrical (or other) energy into physical movement or force
>
> Actuators used in automotive systems are generally the linear or rotary type
>
> A solenoid has a coil of wire around a former into which is fitted a soft iron plunger
>
> A linear motor is similar to a solenoid but has a powerful magnetic plunger

> **Key Points**
>
> A rotary actuator is typically a DC motor and can be used with a mechanical arrangement to give linear motion
>
> A stepper motor moves a given angle in response to a digital signal. It can rotate or move a set amount in either direction

2.3   CONTROL SYSTEMS

2.3.1 Introduction

A control system is an arrangement or sub-system which directs the operation of a main system. The commands given by the control system should ensure that the main system performs according to a given set of directions or commands, or performs its function within certain tolerances. An example is an engine control system in an ECU. In this case the system must achieve certain standards with respect to performance and economy of the engine and it is the control system's task to achieve this.

The control system must be able to respond quickly and accurately to changes in the operating conditions. It must also maintain stable control and be able to separate valid input signals from those which are induced into sensing lines by electrical disturbance (known as 'noise immunity'). There are two main types of control system.

2.3.2 Open loop

This type of control system sends commands to the main system but does not have the ability to check or monitor the output of the main system (see Figure 2.55).

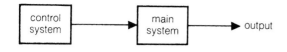

Figure 2.55 Open-loop control

For example, assuming that the main system is an engine, once a control signal has been delivered to the control system (the ECU), the engine will produce its output. However, this output will not always be the same if the engine operating conditions alter. For example, if the control system does not take into account the ambient air temperature, then any change in this condition will affect the power output and will not be corrected by the control system.

Open-loop systems are suitable for many applications, but they cannot be used where there are close tolerances on the performance of the system. For example, an engine emission control system would be unsuitable for open-loop control as it has to operate within legislated tolerances.

2.3.3 Closed loop

This is similar to an open-loop system but with one important addition – it has a means to measure the output and feed back this signal to allow a comparison to be made between the command signal (demand value) and the system's output (actual value). This is shown diagrammatically in Figure 2.56.

The feedback signal from the output sensor is passed back to the input where it is compared using an error amplifier. This intensifies and processes the signal and then compares it to the demand value. If there is a difference between the demand and actual value, the system will respond in such a way as to try to minimise this until the demand value is achieved.

When a control system of this type is applied to an engine, the feedback facility allows any variation in the output to be corrected. This provides a more accurate and stable output than is possible with an open-loop system. Furthermore, the system can be made to respond quickly and correct any changes in the operating conditions. If these conditions are not compensated then the output will be different to that which is intended. In some cases this could lead to damage of the engine or its components.

2.3.4 Theory

It is beyond the scope of this book to discuss control theory in detail, but it is useful to understand the basics in context. A closed-loop system consists of a number of controller parameters/types that can be mathematically modelled or tuned in order to achieve the appropriate overall response for the control system and hence the main system. There are numerous examples of closed-loop systems on a modern vehicle but the most appropriate to illustrate the theory would be a cruise control system which is also discussed in Chapter 7.

In this system the demand value, i.e. the fixed vehicle speed, is set by the driver. The system then operates a throttle actuator and this is controlled via the control system output. The actual value is the actual vehicle speed which is continuously monitored and fed back into the control system. If the vehicle speed deviates from the set value, the control system will adjust the throttle position accordingly to decrease or increase the speed to get closer to the set value. Once the set value is achieved, the control system tries to maintain this irrespective of external conditions. For example, if the vehicle encounters an uphill gradient the control system responds by opening the throttle slightly to re-achieve or maintain the set speed.

The way that the system responds can be adjusted by changing the parameters of the controller. Most closed-loop systems involve one, two or all three of the following parameters and the setting of these define the overall response of the controller. The controller parameters are:

- Proportional: this is a simple feedback system, the difference between the input and output signals is the error signal and this is amplified and fed back as an input. Adjustments to the controller response can be made by adjusting the gain (i.e. the ratio of the amplitude of the output of the controller compared to the input – the input being the error signal). The disadvantage of a simple proportional system is that it would never actually achieve the required set point. It either oscillates, moving back and forth around the set point, or stabilises at a value that is too low or too high. This is because when the error value is zero the controller output is zero and hence there is nothing to remove the error when it overshoots.
- Integral: in this control element the error signal is integrated (added up) over a period of time and then multiplied by a constant which is adjustable

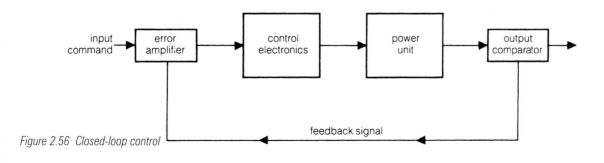

Figure 2.56 Closed-loop control

to define the controller response. By adding a proportion of the average error to the input, the average difference between the output and the set point is continually reduced. Therefore, eventually, a well-tuned controller will settle at the set point within a time defined by the controller settings.

- Derivative: the derivative controller monitors the rate of change of slope of the output. In effect it sees trends in the output signal and can respond accordingly. The first derivative (the slope of the error) is calculated over time and then multiplied by an adjustable constant to define the response of the controller. The larger the derivative term, the more rapidly the controller responds to changes in output. The derivative control element is effectively a predictive controller and is used to dampen the control system response to short-term changes.

It is common to see control systems using all three terms and these are known as PID (proportional-integral-derivative) controllers. Also, it is not uncommon for the P and I elements to be used alone without the D control element. This is dependent on the required response from the control system.

An example application of a PI controller is shown in Figure 2.57 as a vehicle cruise control system. The figure shows that the command signal is the sum of the two outputs from the two blocks A and B. Block A is the proportional part and gives an output that is in proportion to the error signal. Block B is the integral part and gives an output designed to reduce the error to zero within a certain time without oscillation.

Key Points

Control systems can be open or closed loop. Closed-loop systems use feedback to help achieve the required output more accurately and in a more stable way

Open-loop systems can be used in applications where the required tolerance of the output signal is less critical

A common closed-loop control system uses a three-term controller which has three control elements – proportional, integral and derivative. These are used in combination and are adjusted to give the required response and stability of the system under control

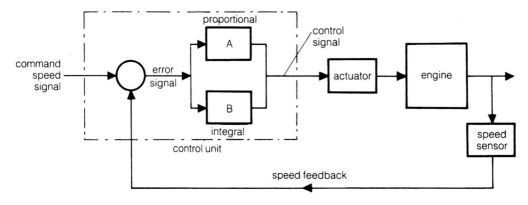

Figure 2.57 Proportional-integral cruise control system

Chapter 3

POWER STORAGE

what is covered in this chapter . . .

- Battery construction and operation
- Starter battery types
- Battery maintenance
- New requirements and developments in power storage

3.1 BATTERY CONSTRUCTION AND OPERATION

3.1.1 Overview

A battery is a chemical accumulator that stores electrical energy generated by the vehicle charging systems, when the engine is running. This stored energy is necessary to start the engine via the starting motor, and the battery acts as a buffer to supply electrical equipment in the vehicle.

Vehicle batteries operate via an electrochemical process. The energy delivered by an electrical current produces a chemical change in the battery materials. Current supplied to a battery is referred to as *charge*. Output from the battery is known as *discharge*.

The two main types of battery are known as primary and secondary cells. In a primary cell, the charging/discharge process is not reversible. This means that the chemical process which produces charge cannot be reversed, the cell cannot be recharged. A simple torch battery (zinc-carbon or alkaline) is an example of a primary cell.

This is clearly not suitable for a vehicle application where the battery must be discharged and charged, so for these purposes secondary cells are used. In secondary cells, the chemical process that produces the energy can be reversed. Secondary cells are characterised by the materials used to construct the plates and the electrolyte. The most common materials for vehicle applications are lead–acid types.

3.1.2 General construction

The starter battery consists of a number of series-connected cells all housed in a polypropylene case. Each cell comprises a cell pack with positive and negative plates and has a nominal voltage of 2V. The plates are connected together internally via lead bars. A typical 12V car battery consists of six cells elements giving a 12V nominal voltage; a 6V battery consists of three cells. The cells are covered and sealed with a one-piece cover which has an opening for filling the cells with electrolyte and servicing. In addition a venting arrangement is provided to allow the cells to breathe. A typical lead–acid battery is shown in Figure 3.1.

The main component parts of the battery are as follows.

Battery case

The battery case is made from an acid-resistant insulating material. It is normally moulded with a small mounting rail or flange arrangement at the bottom edge (on the outside) so that it can be secured in position on the vehicle (via clamps). Internal feet hold the battery plates against moulded rests that run along the floor inside the battery case. Underneath the bottom edges of the plates there are sediment chambers. These catch any material which falls off the plates when in use and prevent it building up to a level at which contact would be made with the bottom of the plates which could cause internal short-circuits of the cells.

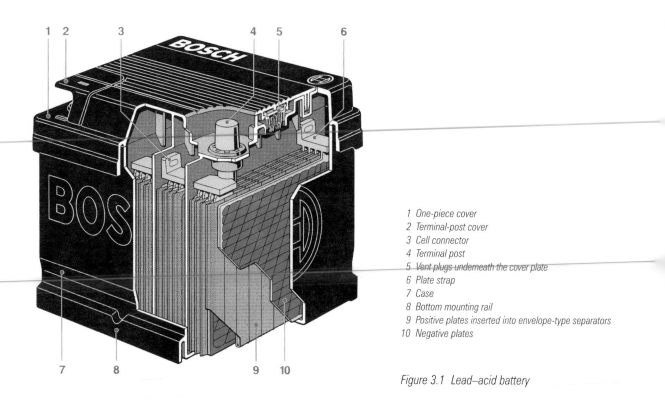

1 One-piece cover
2 Terminal-post cover
3 Cell connector
4 Terminal post
5 Vent plugs underneath the cover plate
6 Plate strap
7 Case
8 Bottom mounting rail
9 Positive plates inserted into envelope-type separators
10 Negative plates

Figure 3.1 Lead–acid battery

Cells (plates and separators)

The cell element is made up of two sets of lead plates – positive and negative (see Figure 3.2). These are placed alternately and separated by an insulating, porous material through which the acid is free to pass (the material is typically made from polythene or glass fibre). Each plate consists of a lattice-type grid of lead–antimony alloy into which the active material is pressed. This is a lead-oxide paste electrically formed into lead peroxide (positive, brown in colour) and spongy lead (negative, grey in colour). The surface area of the plates governs the maximum discharge current that can be supplied for a given time, so in order to give maximum output each cell contains a number of thin plates connected in parallel to increase the surface area. Connection within the cell in this manner does not affect the cell voltage, but the plates are normally welded together with a plate strap. These straps secure the plates in position mechanically. Normally, each cell has one more negative plate than positive.

Electrolyte

The battery plates are immersed in a fluid known generally as electrolyte. In a standard lead–acid battery, the electrolyte is dilute sulphuric acid. In a completely charged state, the acid concentration is approximately 38%. Since the electrolyte is ionised it is capable of conducting electrical current between the cell plates (i.e. the electrodes).

Terminal posts

The plate strap for the positive plates of the first cell is connected to the positive terminal post, and the strap from the negative plates of the last cell is connected to the negative post. The battery terminals are the main interface to the vehicle electrical system (see Figure 3.3) and have to cope with a high current density under operating conditions. The vehicle battery cable is connected to the posts by special cable terminals. These incorporate a number of measures to ensure that the battery cannot be accidentally connected in reverse polarity. In order to achieve this, generally, the positive post is thicker than the negative post, the posts are clearly marked with their polarity, and the positive and negative cable terminals have different opening diameters to fit the respective terminal posts.

3.1.3 Operation and characteristics – charge and discharge process

Cell action

When the battery is fully charged and ready for use the positive plates are comprised of lead peroxide (PbO_2) and the negative plates are spongy lead (Pb). As the battery discharges through an external electrical load, the acid reacts with the plates and this changes both plate materials to lead sulphate ($PbSO_4$). The loss of sulphate from the electrolyte to the plates during the

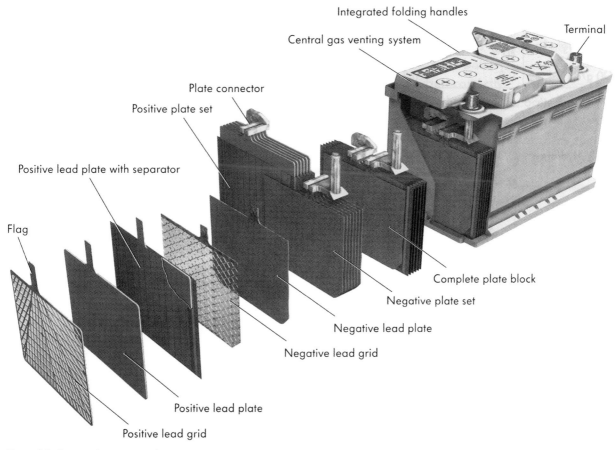

Figure 3.2 Battery plate construction

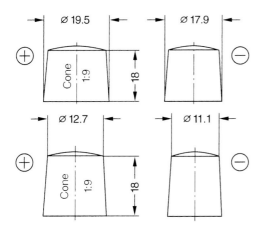

Figure 3.3 Battery posts and clamps

a   Screw-type terminals
b   Solder-type terminals

discharge process decreases the density of the electrolyte (i.e. it reduces its specific gravity). This characteristic enables the state of charge to be assessed by using a hydrometer to measure this property of the electrolyte. The chemical process is shown in a simplified format in Figure 3.4.

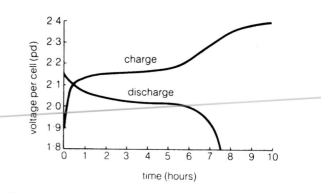

Figure 3.5 Battery cell voltage curve

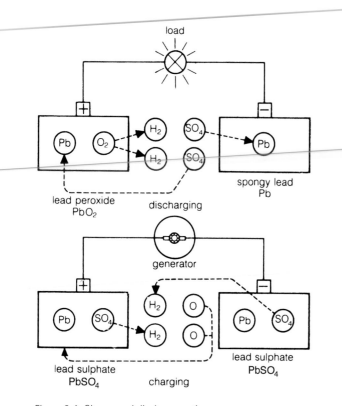

Figure 3.4 Charge and discharge action

To charge a battery it is necessary to have a DC supply at a potential sufficient to force an adequate current through the battery in a direction opposite to the direction of the discharge current. During the charging process plate materials will return to their original forms and the electrolyte density will increase. When the process is completed, i.e. the battery is in a charged state, the continued application of the charging current will lead to excessive gassing of the cell. This gas mixture is composed of hydrogen and oxygen and as such it is highly explosive. Naked flames or electric sparks must not be produced in the vicinity of a battery at any time.

Cell voltage variation

When a battery is taken off charge, the terminal voltage is about 2.4V per cell. This quickly drops to 2.1V as the concentrated acid in the pores of the plates diffuses out into the electrolyte. During discharge at low rate the cell voltage remains around 2.0V for the major part of the discharge period. Towards the end of this period the voltage falls more rapidly until approximately 1.8V is reached, which is the discharged condition. This characteristic voltage curve is shown in Figure 3.5.

This limit should not be exceeded as excessive sulphation causes the growth of large lead sulphate crystals. Once in this condition, the battery will be difficult to reconvert when charging is carried out. The readings shown in Figure 3.5 represent the potential difference and thus the battery must be charging or discharging at the time the measurement is taken.

As mentioned, the terminal voltage during charging rises towards the end of the charging period to approximately 2.4V when the cell is fully charged. Once the charging current has been removed, the cell voltage drops to approximately 2.1V. This characteristic rise in cell voltage when the battery approaches charged condition is used as an indicator to the vehicle charging system. Setting the voltage regulator of the generator (typically an alternator) to 14.2V for six cells ensures that the battery cannot be overcharged. When the cell voltage reaches 2.4V (i.e. 14.2/6), there will be no potential difference between battery and generator and hence no current will flow into the battery.

Electrolyte density

Electrolyte resistance (hence internal resistance) rises outside the relative density limits 1.100–1.300. Therefore, these are the limits within which the battery should operate. In addition, a density higher than 1.300 would cause the plates to suffer attack by the acid. Figure 3.6 shows the electrolyte density as a function of state-of-charge.

Values vary slightly in practice but Figure 3.6 shows typical guidelines. The values represent the strength of the electrolyte, i.e. the mass of a given volume of electrolyte compared with the mass of an equal volume of pure water. This ratio is termed 'specific gravity' and is measured using a hydrometer.

The reading shown in Figure 3.7 is 1.250 and this indicates that the electrolyte is 1.25 times heavier than pure water (often the decimal point is excluded in discussion and this state would be known as 'twelve fifty').

The electrolyte expands as temperature increases and this must be considered when taking readings. A temperature of 15°C is the standard temperature condition, so to obtain a temperature-corrected, true value, a correction factor of 0.002 is deducted from

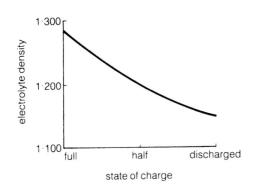

Figure 3.6 *Variation in density of electrolyte*

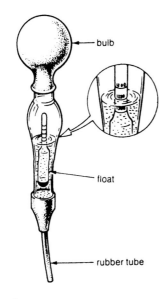

Figure 3.7 *Hydrometer*

the hydrometer reading for every 2°C below 15°C and added for every 3°C above.

An important point for consideration is the freezing point of the electrolyte. Clearly this is dependent on the state of charge due to the fact that it becomes closer to water (less dense) as the charge state decreases. This means it is *more* likely to freeze as the ambient temperature reduces (i.e. at a higher temperature).

3.1.4 Technical properties and specifications

Capacity

The capacity of any battery is expressed in ampere hours (Ah). This is a function of the current that the battery can deliver for a period of time. It is generally based on a time of 10 or 20 hours. For example, a battery capacity of 38 Ah, based on a 10-hour rate should supply a steady current of 3.8 amps for 10 hours at a temperature of 25°C before the cell voltage reduces to 1.8 volts/cell (i.e. a discharged state).

The battery capacity alters slightly depending upon the discharge rate quoted. When the capacity is quoted with a 20-hour rate, the battery capacity is about 10–20% higher. This apparent increase in capacity is due to the fact that the discharge current is lower for a 20-hour rate. This fact highlights an important point, that the actual battery capacity is affected by the discharge current. Figure 3.8 shows a typical performance curve of a battery.

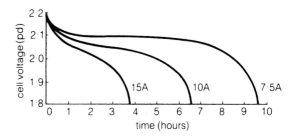

Figure 3.8 *Battery discharge curves*

The graph in Figure 3.8 shows that a lower discharge current extends the battery capacity. This phenomenon can be described with a general equation known as Peukert's formula:

$$C = I^n T$$

where:

C = Battery capacity (Ah)
I = Discharge current (A)
T = Discharge time (h)
n = Peukert's exponent which describes battery characteristic.

This expresses the capacity of a battery in terms of the rate at which it is discharged. The basic formula can be modified to take into account the battery hour rating:

$$T = \frac{C}{\left(\dfrac{I}{C/R}\right)^n} \cdot \frac{R}{C}$$

where:

I = Discharge current (A)
T = Time (h)
C = Capacity of the battery (Ah)
n = Peukert's exponent for that particular battery type
R = The battery hour rating, i.e. 20-hour rating, 10-hour rating etc.

The exponent 'n' describes the characteristic discharge property for that particular battery type. Typical example values would be approximately 1.3 for a standard battery and about 1.1 for an absorbent glass mat (AGM) battery. Hybrid batteries are approximately 1.15. To demonstrate the effect, using the above example of a 38 Ah battery, the calculated discharge time using the Peukert equation when discharged at the 3.8 A is:

$$T = \frac{38}{\left(\frac{3.8}{38/10}\right)^{1.3}} \cdot \frac{10}{38} = 10$$

We know that 10 hours is correct as this is the stated discharge time for the rating of the battery. If we increase the discharge current by a factor of 10 to 38 A, then in theory we would reduce the discharge time by the same factor, giving a discharge time of one hour, but from experience we know this is not true. A typical 38 Ah battery would not supply 38 A for an hour. Using the equation again:

$$T = \frac{38}{\left(\frac{38}{38/10}\right)^{1.3}} \cdot \frac{10}{38} = 0.501$$

the answer is 0.501 hours, i.e. 30.06 minutes. This is considerably less than the value when calculated via a simple amps multiplied by hours relationship. In practical use, under starting conditions, the current used is several hundred amps so that the time that a 38 Ah battery can supply this high current is limited to seconds (e.g. at standard temperature conditions 380 A can be supplied for approximately 90 seconds according to the above equation).

The capacity of a battery is governed by the weight of the active material in the plates, so batteries having many large plates have a corresponding large capacity. A small capacity battery may have only five plates (three negative, two positive) per cell whereas larger units may have more than 30 plates per cell. Capacity of the battery is temperature dependent and this is an important factor when choosing a battery for low-temperature operating conditions.

Reserve capacity

The Ah rating is less popular and most batteries are now specified via a reserve capacity rating. This indicates the time in minutes that a battery will deliver a current of 25 A at 25°C before the cell voltage drops to 1.75 V. This current value is derived from the average discharge on a vehicle battery if the charging system should fail. It therefore indicates the time that a given battery can support the vehicle in operation under normal conditions with a fully charged battery in the first place. A typical value for a 40 Ah battery would be approximately 45 minutes (this can be verified via the Peukert formula).

Cold-test current

The cold-test current indicates the battery's performance under extreme low-temperature conditions. It is the discharge current given by the battery (in fully charged condition) at −18°C assuming that the cell voltage does not fall below 1.25 V per cell measured 10 seconds after commencing the discharge. For automotive applications, the most important factor is the battery's capability to start the engine, and for this reason the cold-start current is a more representative measure of this than the capacity alone. The cold-start performance of the battery is highly dependent on the surface area of the active materials (the number of plates and the surface area).

Internal resistance

When current flows from a battery the resistance of the internal parts within the battery cause the terminal voltage to drop. This internal resistance is the sum of the various resistances including the following:

- Plates: generally an increase in plate area decreases the internal resistance; as the battery ages, the effective plate area reduces and hence internal resistance increases.
- Internal connections: cell connectors and plate straps are sized to minimise resistance.
- Electrolyte: resistance increases as the temperature reduces and also when the acid strength is reduced (i.e. discharged condition).

This internal resistance is a critical factor for the performance of the battery in the starting circuit and is due to the fact that the internal resistance, in combination with the external resistances (starter motor, cabling etc.), determine the cranking speed performance.

The internal resistance can be found by the method shown in Figure 3.9.

A voltmeter of high resistance is connected across the battery and an ammeter is used to measure current (I) that flows through the external resistor (R). The internal resistance (r) is found by applying Ohm's law. V is the open circuit voltage of the battery.

$$V = \frac{I}{R}$$

In this case there are effectively two resistors in series so:

$$V = I(R + r)$$

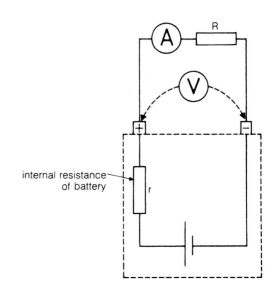

internal resistance of battery

Figure 3.9 Method of finding internal resistance

Therefore:

$$R + r = \frac{V}{I}$$

So, the internal resistance is:

$$r = \frac{V}{I} - R$$

A lead–acid battery has low internal resistance so the comparatively high terminal pd makes it attractive for vehicle use. Nevertheless, the internal resistance causes the battery to become warm in use and the potential to drop from say 12.6 V when a high discharge current has to be supplied. For example, a current of 200 A causes a volt drop of 1 V:

$$V = IR$$
$$11.6 = 200R$$

Therefore:

$$R = 0.058\,\Omega$$

But:

$$r = \frac{V}{I} - R$$

Therefore:

$$r = \frac{12.6}{200} - R$$
$$= 0.063 - 0.058$$
$$= 0.005\,\Omega$$

This is a typical figure for a lead–acid battery in service. Clearly any increase in resistance will proportionally increase the voltage drop.

> **Key Points**
>
> In a charged state a lead–acid battery has lead peroxide positive plates and spongy lead negative plates
>
> The electrolyte is dilute sulphuric acid. When fully charged this has a specific gravity of 1.280, also known as twelve eighty
>
> The voltage of a fully charged cell is 2.4 volts
>
> The battery capacity can be expressed in a number of ways but it is always a function of the discharge current
>
> The battery has internal resistance. This affects its performance under load and tends to increase as the battery ages

---

3.2   STARTER BATTERY TYPES

3.2.1 Standard lead–acid

The lead–acid battery is capable of supplying large currents/power to the starter motor (several hundred amps). Typically it has a working life of three or four years and is relatively inexpensive. The previous drawbacks of weight, size and high maintenance have been minimised over time. Figure 3.10 shows a typical design.

3.2.2 Lead–acid: low maintenance and maintenance free

Low maintenance

Improved materials and construction have reduced or eliminated the need for a battery to be recharged or topped up periodically with distilled water to replace losses due to gassing. Batteries of this type are clearly attractive for the vehicle owner. The factors that have contributed to this battery technology are:

- improved charging system voltage regulation due to developments in alternator and electronics technology
- change of grid material from lead antimony to lead calcium.

Low maintenance means that some maintenance is still required but less than that of a standard battery. Under normal conditions the electrolyte level needs to be checked only once a year (or at service intervals). Figure 3.11 shows a typical design.

Maintenance free

A maintenance-free battery is sealed (apart from venting) and hence requires no maintenance other than being kept clean (see Figure 3.12). Typical designs have eliminated antimony from the plates and this has reduced over-charge, water usage, thermal runaway and self-discharge problems. A small amount of gas is still produced when charging, but this is managed internally via a gas reservoir formed in the container to collect acid spray and return it to the main electrolyte mass. The battery also incorporates a built-in temperature-compensated hydrometer to indicate relative density and level of the electrolyte. The indicator displays various colours to show the states of charge (green – OK; black – recharge; yellow – faulty). Additional design improvements of this battery include:

- strengthened grid supports
- sealed terminal connections
- stronger retention supports
- improved efficiency and weight reduction.

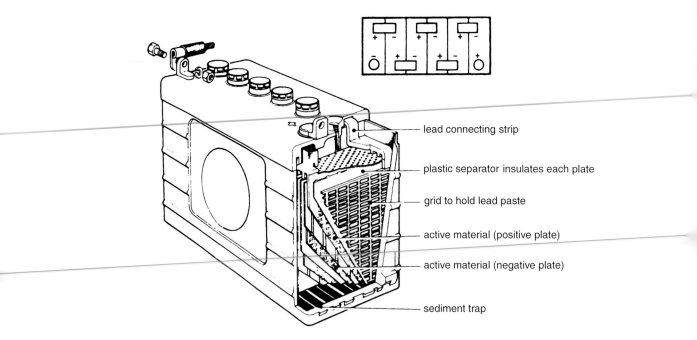

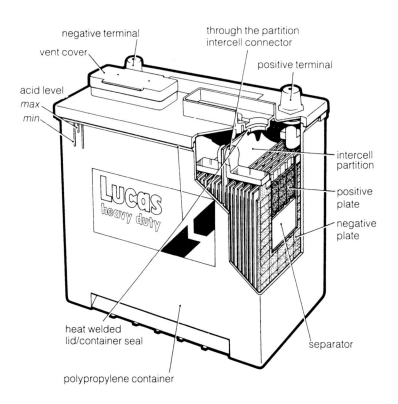

- lead connecting strip
- plastic separator insulates each plate
- grid to hold lead paste
- active material (positive plate)
- active material (negative plate)
- sediment trap

Figure 3.10 12 volt lead–acid battery

negative terminal

vent cover

through the partition intercell connector

positive terminal

acid level
max
min

intercell partition

positive plate

negative plate

heat welded lid/container seal

polypropylene container

separator

Figure 3.11 Low-maintenance battery

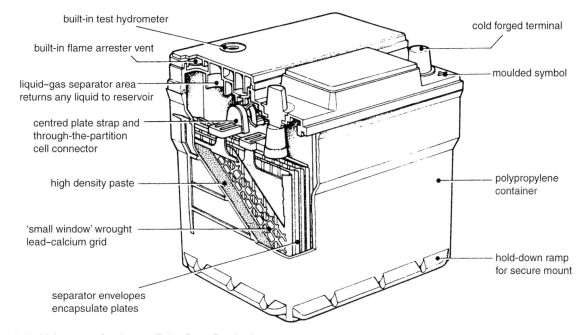

built-in test hydrometer

built-in flame arrester vent

liquid–gas separator area
returns any liquid to reservoir

centred plate strap and
through-the-partition
cell connector

high density paste

'small window' wrought
lead–calcium grid

separator envelopes
encapsulate plates

cold forged terminal

moulded symbol

polypropylene
container

hold-down ramp
for secure mount

Figure 3.12 Maintenance-free battery (Delco-Remy Freedom)

3.2.3 Valve regulated lead–acid

Valve regulated lead–acid (VRLA) batteries are a more recent innovation in maintenance-free batteries. This type uses the recombination principle to reduce the formation of oxygen and hydrogen when the battery is being charged. The main design features of the battery are:

- The plates are wrapped with a glass micro-fibre separator that absorbs in its pores all the liquid electrolyte. There is no free acid in the cell.
- The plate groups are under compression in the cells. There is a slight excess of negative capacity.
- The battery is totally sealed other than a small pressure-release valve.

These features allow electrolytic water loss to be suppressed by the following method. As the battery approaches full charge, the oxygen liberated at the positive plate passes through a separator to the negative plate. In the presence of sulphuric acid, the oxygen reacts with the lead of the negative plate to form lead sulphate. As a consequence, the negative plate never reaches the potential for hydrogen to be released so no water is lost. Since no oxygen or hydrogen is produced it is possible to seal the battery.

Generally this battery is smaller and lighter in weight and can deliver relatively high performance. Due to the absence of dangerous emissions from the battery the vehicle designer has a higher degree of freedom as to where the battery can be located on the vehicle.

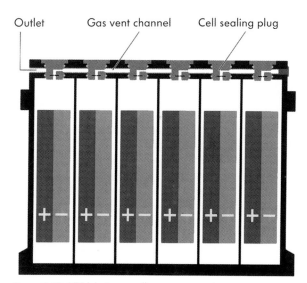

Outlet   Gas vent channel   Cell sealing plug

Figure 3.13 VRLA battery sealing arrangement

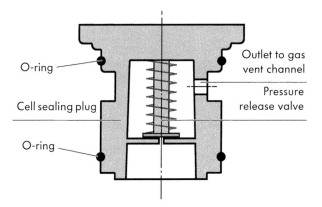

O-ring

Cell sealing plug

O-ring

Outlet to gas
vent channel

Pressure
release valve

Figure 3.14 VRLA battery cell sealing plug

3.2.4 Absorbent glass mat

Absorbent glass mat (AGM) batteries have electrolyte which is solidified by an absorbent glass fleece material made of boron silicate. This acts as a separator between the electrodes and absorbs the free electrolyte (like a sponge). Its purpose is to promote recombination of the hydrogen and oxygen given off during the charging process. The fibreglass matt absorbs and immobilises the acid in the matt but keeps it in a liquid rather than a gel form. In this way the acid is more readily available to the plates so allowing faster reactions between the acid and the plate material and allowing higher charge/discharge rates as well as deep cycling.

This construction is very robust and able to withstand severe shock and vibration and the cells will not leak even if the case is cracked. The battery is sealed with a cover which includes the sealing plugs and the gas vent. Unlike maintenance-free batteries, AGM batteries are not equipped with a built-in condition indicator. AGM batteries generally belong to the VRLA function type and are employed in applications where cycle capacity, cold start and leak protection need to be high. They have a very low self-discharge rate of 1%–3% per month. The disadvantages of the AGM battery are that they are expensive and not suitable for engine compartment mounting due to temperature effects.

3.2.5 Gel

These batteries are similar in operation to the VRLA type in that the gases are recombined during charging. The electrolyte is solidified to a gel mass by the addition of silicic acid to form sulphuric acid. The phosphorus acid contained in the electrolyte increases the charge/discharge cycle capacity and therefore offers favourable conditions for recharging after deep discharge. The battery is sealed by a battery cover which contains non-removable sealing plugs and a gas

vent channel. These batteries are not equipped with a condition indicator.

The advantages of this battery technology are mainly due to the solid electrolyte (which means there is no possibility of acid spillage), the high charge/discharge cycle capability and the fact that they are maintenance free. The disadvantages include poor performance for cold starts, high price and poor suitability for installation in the engine compartment (due to elevated temperatures). Therefore they are normally used in special applications and not for general automotive application.

3.2.6 Hybrid

These batteries were an interim development. The negative plates are made of calcium alloy and the positive from antimony alloy. This substantially reduces gassing and thereby water consumption compared with traditional battery types. However, due to the antimony component that still exists in this battery technology, they cannot meet the extreme demands for low water consumption that are currently a feature of the automotive passenger car sector. Only maintenance-free batteries can achieve this.

Key Points
A number of different battery technologies have been developed over the years. In the future, battery technology is likely to change dramatically with the introduction of hybrid vehicles to meet emission regulations
Modern battery types should not be fast charged and must be handled according to manufacturer instructions
In many batteries there is no access to the cells or electrolyte. Some have built-in hydrometers and condition indicators

3.3   BATTERY MAINTENANCE

3.3.1 Battery testing

There are three basic checks which should be performed in order to establish the condition of the battery for its application. These are:

- visual inspection
- specific gravity check
- load test.

The first indication that a unit is failing is when the starter is operated with a cold engine. Under these severe conditions the output from a healthy battery is well below the potential maximum, so a faulty battery is clearly evident. Assuming that the battery condition

is the source of the problem (after checking cabling, starter motor and switching arrangements), the following checks will confirm the diagnosis.

Visual inspection

The battery should be checked for obvious damage around the external casing (cracks etc.). A white powdery corrosion of metal parts around the battery indicates leakage of acid. This can be removed via washing with ammoniated water. Evidence of bulging of the container suggests that the plates have deformed internally and this results in a reduction of battery capacity. This is normally caused by overcharging. Fluid levels in the cells should be checked (if accessible). If they are not covered by electrolyte then it will be necessary to top up with distilled water before proceeding further. The terminals (see Figure 3.15) are also important as corrosion can cause a high resistance. If the terminal is covered in white powder or green-white paste then the battery should be removed and washed down with ammoniated water. The cable end terminals must be cleaned in the same way, and if there is any doubt about their integrity they should be replaced. On reassembly, the terminals (battery and cable) should be coated with petroleum jelly.

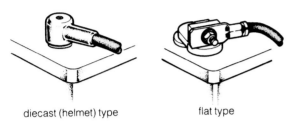

diecast (helmet) type   flat type

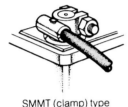

SMMT (clamp) type

Figure 3.15 Battery connectors

Specific gravity check

This check indicates the state of charge of the battery and is done using a battery hydrometer which consists of an acid lifter (glass tube with rubber suction ball) containing an aerometer (a float marked with a scale showing electrolyte relative density) (see Figure 3.16).

A fully serviceable battery should give a reading of 1.280 with a variation between cells of less than 0.050. This result is temperature dependent. Figure 3.17 shows the correction factor which must be applied if the ambient temperature deviates significantly from the standard condition of 15°C.

Typical results of a hydrometer test are shown in Table 3.1.

Table 3.1 Results of hydrometer testing

Reading	Variation	Action
1.270	less than 0.050	Battery in good condition; confirm with drop test
1.190	less than 0.050	Discharged battery; recharge for 10 hours at the battery's bench charge rate and retest
Some cells less than 1.200	more than 0.100	Battery should be scrapped

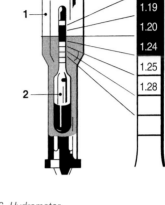

Figure 3.16 Hydrometer

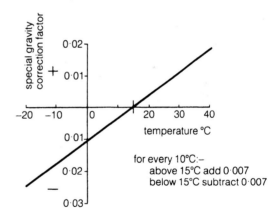

Figure 3.17 Specific gravity correction

Most batteries are now sealed and do not allow access to the electrolyte, but certain types are fitted with built-in hydrometers as shown in Figure 3.18.

Load tests (high rate discharge)

This is a severe test which should only be performed on a charged battery showing at least 1.200 per cell during a specific gravity check. The test simulates the electrical load demanded from the battery under extreme starting conditions. For this reason the test should not be performed for an extended period of time (normally it should be performed for about 15 seconds).

Simple testers of this type consist of a low-resistance strip with a voltmeter connected across it. This is

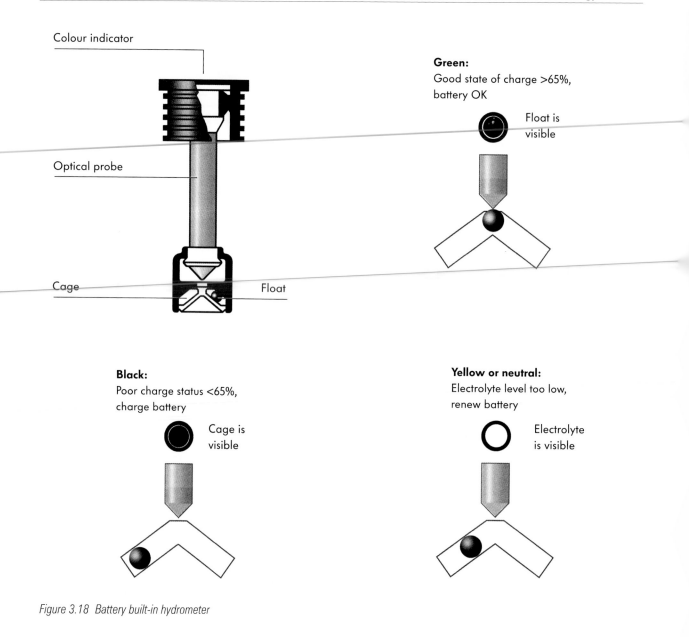

Colour indicator

Optical probe

Cage

Float

Green:
Good state of charge >65%,
battery OK

Float is
visible

Black:
Poor charge status <65%,
charge battery

Cage is
visible

Yellow or neutral:
Electrolyte level too low,
renew battery

Electrolyte
is visible

Figure 3.18 Battery built-in hydrometer

connected to the battery, hence drawing a significant amount of power which is dissipated as heat at the resistor. The voltmeter shows the voltage whilst supplying this current. Generally, a healthy battery should maintain 9.6 V for 15 seconds during this test. A typical hand-held unit is shown in Figure 3.19.

More sophisticated versions of this tester are available and are used in preference to the traditional 'drop' type tester above. These incorporate a carbon pile loading unit that can be adjusted to suit the battery capacity. A load of half the cold-test current for the battery is typically specified. The cold-test current and other information can be found on the battery manufacturer's label.

Note that the performance of the battery is temperature dependent and this must be considered when testing a battery. If the battery does not maintain the voltage for the specified time then it is classified as unserviceable. Removing the vent caps (if possible)

allows visual monitoring of the electrolyte, and if a cell is faulty often the electrolyte can be seen 'boiling' in that cell. This is a vigorous reaction which is due to the cell being faulty and should not be confused with 'gassing' which is a normal cell reaction when the battery approaches full charge.

Modern battery test technology incorporates sophisticated electronics and new test techniques to evaluate the state of the battery. This involves impedance and conductance test modes where the test method involves applying a small AC voltage of known frequency and amplitude across the cell and measuring the in-phase AC current that flows in response to it. The impedance is calculated by Ohm's law and the conductance is similarly calculated as the reciprocal of the impedance.

Note that the impedance increases as the battery deteriorates while the conductance decreases. Thus conductance correlates directly with the battery's ability

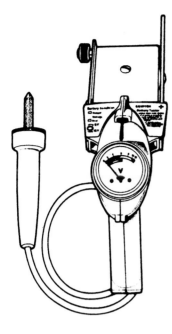

Figure 3.19 High-rate discharge tester

to produce current whereas impedance gives an inverse correlation. The conductance of the cell therefore provides an indirect approximation to the state of health of the cell. This measurement can be refined by taking other factors into account like temperature etc. In addition, impedance and conductance tests will obviously detect cell defects such as shorts and open circuits.

A typical hand-held unit is shown in Figure 3.20.

Figure 3.20 Hand-held impedance and conductance tester

3.3.2 Battery charging

The energy introduced to the battery during charging must always be greater than the energy taken from the battery. This is to compensate for the inefficiency of the electrochemical process which takes place. In order to charge a battery to 100% charge condition, a quantity of energy between 105% and 110% must be reintroduced during charging. This is known as the *current charging factor*. The charging of the battery on the vehicle is performed by an engine-driven generator (see Chapter 4),

but under certain conditions external chargers are needed (i.e. the battery has become completely discharged, the vehicle has been out of use). These off-vehicle chargers can be subdivided as follows.

Bench chargers

Normally used in a workshop environment, these can be standalone units for charging single batteries or larger units that can charge a number of batteries at once in a series-parallel arrangement (see Figure 3.21).

The charger operates from mains voltage and incorporates a transformer (to reduce voltage/increase current) and a rectifier (which converts AC to DC current). A typical simple circuit for a bench battery charger is shown in Figure 3.22.

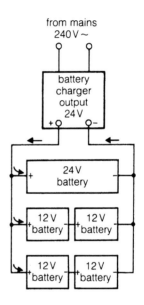

Figure 3.21 Bench charging

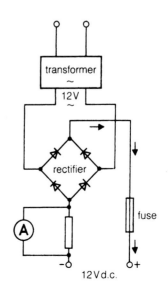

Figure 3.22 Layout of a battery charger

A multi-tapping arrangement on the transformer allows switching of voltage levels (i.e. between 6, 12 and 24V) (see Figure 3.23).

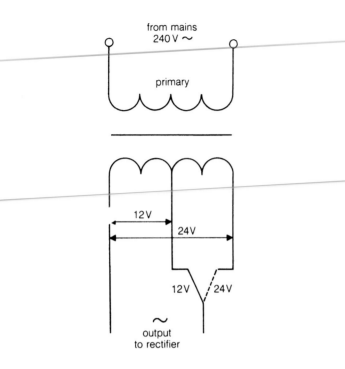

from mains
240 V ~

primary

12V

24V

12V   24V

~
output
to rectifier

Figure 3.23 Battery charger transformer

Generally, normal recharging of the battery should take place using the I_{10} charging current. This is 10% of the battery's nominal Ah capacity:

$$I_{10} = 0.1C \frac{A}{Ah}$$

where:

I_{10} = Charging current required
C = Capacity of battery (Ah).

In order to achieve this the battery charger must incorporate a voltage regulator to adjust the output voltage so that the charging current remains constant (i.e. pd between battery and charger must be a constant value; remember that battery voltage increases as charge state increases). Most simple battery chargers operate on a constant voltage principle where the charger outputs a voltage equivalent to a fully charged battery (e.g. 14.4V for a 12V battery). When a discharged battery is connected to the charger, the initial charge current is high but this gradually falls until it is practically zero. Batteries can be connected in parallel with this charger.

These simple linear-type chargers have been superseded by modern electronic units incorporating switch mode power supply technology. This is an electronic power supply unit (PSU) that incorporates a switching regulator – an internal control circuit that switches power transistors (such as MOSFETs) on and off rapidly in order to stabilise the output voltage or current. This technique is highly efficient and the units are small/lightweight, but they are more complicated and their switching currents can cause noise problems if not carefully suppressed. Chargers of this type have built-in charging intelligence and can adapt the charging current or voltage curve to charge the battery quickly but without excessive gassing or heating. These chargers are ideally suited to charging the battery whilst still installed in the vehicle as it is not necessary to disconnect the battery from the electrical system. The charge voltage from an electronic charger is free from voltage peaks and it is controlled within a close tolerance so the battery cannot be overcharged and all of the electronic systems on the vehicle (airbag, ABS etc.) are fully protected.

The main advantages of these chargers are:

- time-consuming battery disconnection and removal for charging is not required
- data memories in the vehicle are not erased
- electronic systems are fully protected
- there is no danger of damage due to incorrect handling
- reduced possibility of explosion due to less gassing of the battery during charge
- consumers can remain connected if required
- optimised charge curves reduce charging time.

Fast/rapid start/boost battery chargers

These chargers enable the battery (not maintenance-free types) to be recharged in a very short time in order for the engine to be started – typically 30–60 minutes. Initially the current flow is approximately 50A, so special protection devices taper off the charging current during the selected charge period to prevent damage to the battery by overheating. Often a thermostat is fitted to stop the charge when it senses that the electrolyte temperature exceeds 45°C. A charger of this type can bring the battery back up to 80% charge state and boost charging has no negative effect as long as the battery gassing voltage is not reached. High currents can be absorbed by the battery in the vicinity of its Ah rating (i.e. 40A for a 40Ah battery), but once gassing starts, the charge current must be reduced or switched off. A typical portable design is shown in Figure 3.24.

Often chargers of this type incorporate a 'cranking boost' facility. This supports the battery during starter motor operation and provides a very short-time/high-power output to start the engine with a flat battery. Under these conditions a very high current is supplied by the charger. This should be done with caution though as many manufacturers specifically state that this type of start assist should not be used due to sensitive electronics and the possibility of battery explosions.

Figure 3.24 Portable battery charger (Crypton)

3.3.3 General safety requirements

Personal safety is essential when handling, testing or charging vehicle batteries. There are several hazards which exist and must be respected:

- Acid spillage: wet batteries contain acid. Acid splashes to skin and eyes should be treated immediately with clean water and medical attention must be sought.
- Explosion: batteries give off highly flammable fumes whilst charging. Anything which involves a source of ignition (e.g. sparking) must not occur in the vicinity of batteries that are on charge or that have been recently charged.
- Manual handling: batteries are heavy pieces of equipment and appropriate handling with lifting equipment or assistance is essential to avoid physical injury.

When handling batteries, personal protective equipment should be used, for example:

- goggles
- gloves (acid resistant)
- apron
- carrier/handling equipment.

Trickle and home chargers

Most commonly, the trickle charger is intended to ensure that the battery is maintained in a fully charged condition even when the vehicle is not in use. The charging method generally compensates for self-discharge losses in the battery and a charging current of 1 mA/Ah is typical (i.e. 0.04 A for a 40 Ah battery).

Small, home chargers are also commonly used and can provide 2–4 A. These are suitable for slowly recharging the battery but not for maintenance charging. This is due to the fact that they are generally low-cost constant voltage chargers and hence they will overcharge the battery.

Key Points

Batteries can be deadly, they are full of acid and can explode. Always handle them carefully and with respect

Always charge the battery according to the manufacturer's instructions and carry out a visual inspection before any test

High-rate discharge tests must never be performed on a battery which is less than fully charged. This type of test can be dangerous and modern battery testers use different techniques to establish battery condition – they are much safer!

3.4 NEW REQUIREMENTS AND DEVELOPMENTS IN POWER STORAGE

Batteries for automotive applications have evolved from the simple lead–acid type to more sophisticated versions incorporating the latest manufacturing and development techniques. This has allowed optimisation of the construction and operation of the typical vehicle battery, reducing the required amount of maintenance and extending its life. In addition to this, specific power density has been increased whilst weight has been reduced and this is an important factor in the overall target of reducing vehicle emissions.

Batteries are generally considered consumable items, but as mentioned, recent developments have significantly increased the useable lifespan of a standard vehicle battery. Batteries now operate in increasingly

harsh conditions due to elevated operating temperatures caused by high component density under the bonnet of a modern car. More and more frequently batteries are being positioned in other parts of the vehicle (e.g. in the boot), and twin battery solutions are being implemented for luxury cars with a high number of consumers.

An important point is that the basic chemistry of the vehicle starter battery remains unchanged, and for current applications with standard combustion engine types this is appropriate. The future challenges for battery technology will be the adoption of hybrid drive systems in ordinary road vehicles. In order to store the large amounts of power needed for this technology to operate successfully, different battery types are required. The lead–acid type battery is not suitable for this application as even the latest developments do not have the required capacity and are far too heavy. It is important to note though that lead–acid batteries have been/are employed in low-tech traction applications, for example milk floats!

Hybrid powertrain systems (see the appropriate chapter in *FMVT: Book 2 Powertrain Electronics*) employ sophisticated energy-management systems in order to recover energy from the vehicle during braking (known as recuperation) and to provide 'boost' energy during acceleration, such that a smaller capacity engine (with associated reduced emissions) can provide the performance and feel of a larger engine. In order to be able to store and release the required energy, batteries have been developed using alternative technology, for example employing chemistry with nickel and lithium compounds. These are well-proven technologies and are commonly seen in other applications (e.g. small, portable power supplies for notebook computers, power tools etc.). The main properties of these types of batteries are shown in Table 3.2.

The battery for a hybrid drive is formed into a complete energy module comprising a large number of separate cells which can be replaced individually if a fault should occur. These power modules have sophisticated electronic monitoring to prevent damage to the battery elements, or worse, explosion, if a fault should occur. In addition, the power module must be integrated into the vehicle design to ensure complete passenger safety. A typical battery module in current use is shown in Figure 3.25 and is located under the rear seat.

Features of this battery pack include:

- Nickel metal hybrid battery elements, with a weight of approximately 50 kg.
- A thermal well on top of the cell allows approximate measurement of the internal temperature of the electrolyte.
- A hydrogen vent provides for release of hydrogen through a manifold under gassing conditions.
- Sophisticated thermal management – the power capability increases at higher temperatures and decreases at lower temperatures. Active thermal management can improve power capability at lower

Figure 3.25 Battery module for hybrid vehicle applications

temperatures. Forced cabin air system is used for cooling. Heating is required only at temperatures below –20°C.

- Battery control computer – dedicated to keeping the power module at the optimum temperature and optimum charge level. Typically the battery control system ceases discharge at 30% charge level and stops recharging at 40% charge level. This increases the number of charging cycles and extends the battery life considerably.

Nickel-based batteries are most commonly used for current hybrid powertrain applications although they have not provided the breakthrough and the long-term cost benefits that were hoped for hybrid applications. The power of nickel batteries comes from the raw material, which is getting more expensive due to increased demand.

Lithium batteries have very positive attributes for this application. Several automotive manufacturers including Subaru, Nissan and Mitsubishi have produced concept cars that use lithium batteries. Also, they commonly replace the traditional nicad battery in the small power applications mentioned above. The main benefit of these applications is the absence of the well-known 'memory effect' associated with nicad cells which reduces their working life. The lithium-type battery has a high power density and cell voltage (approximately 4 V) and can operate at ambient temperatures or above. Note though that these cells must be monitored closely to avoid overcharging and short-circuiting which will cause destruction or explosion.

Table 3.2 Battery systems

Properties	Lead–acid system open/sealed	Nickel systems Nickel-cadmium (Ni/Cd) Nickel-metal hydride (NiMH)	Lithium systems Lithium-ion Lithium-polymer
Cell voltage	2 V	1.2 V	3…4 V
Energy density	25…30 Wh/kg	35…80 Wh/kg	60…150 Wh/kg
Energy efficiency without heating/cooling	75…80%	60…85%	85…90%
Power density	100…200 W/kg	100…1000 W/kg	300…1500 W\kg
Service life in cycles	600…900	>2000	>
Operating temperature	10…55°C	–20…55°C	–10…50 bzw. 60°C
Maintenance-free	Depending on design	Depending on design	yes

Chapter 4

POWER GENERATION

what is covered in this chapter ...

- Introduction
- Vehicle energy requirements
- Alternators
- Current developments
- Future development in charging systems

4.1 INTRODUCTION

4.1.1 Basic requirement

A large amount of electrical energy is required to operate the numerous electrical systems around the modern motor vehicle. The number of electrical consumers in the vehicle is increasing exponentially and hence the electrical demand becomes greater and greater over time. The battery can supply the energy needed for a specific period of time according to its capacity, but the energy for ongoing requirements whilst the vehicle is being used is supplied via an engine-driven generator system (also known as the charging system).

This generator provides the energy for all of the electrical consumers. It also keeps the battery in a fully charged condition (topping up after starting etc.). This ensures that there is enough energy stored so that when the engine is stopped, electrical loads can be supplied for a short period of time (if required). Most importantly though, the battery must be in a charged condition so that there is enough stored power to start the engine when next required.

Modern vehicles are optimised with respect to weight and packaging of vehicle components. The battery is a heavy unit and hence, in modern vehicles, it is as small as possible. This places extra load on the charging systems due the smaller buffer of stored energy.

The basic requirements of an automotive generator are:

- to supply all the consumers with DC power
- to provide sufficient power, in addition to the above, for recharging the battery
- to maintain a constant system voltage, irrespective of engine speed and electrical loading

- to withstand all likely under-bonnet conditions, e.g. vibration, heat, humidity, dirt etc.
- low weight and compact size
- high power density and efficiency
- long service life, minimal or no maintenance
- low noise output.

4.1.2 History

In most cases, energy is taken from the engine to drive the generator, and the task of the generator is to convert this to electrical energy. Electrical energy can be created by having a current-carrying conductor moving in a magnetic field. The principles behind this are described in detail in Chapter 1. For the vehicle generator the parts that are moving or fixed provide a differentiating factor between two types of generator which have been used:

- Dynamo: fixed magnetic field, conductors rotated in this field driven by the engine.
- Alternator: fixed conductor with a rotating engine-driven field.

Both create an AC current that is rectified to DC and used to supply consumers and charge the battery. The dynamo uses commutation to provide the unidirectional current flow; the alternator uses electronics in the form of rectifier diodes (the underlying principles are discussed in Chapter 1).

Over the years electrical demand in vehicles has increased. Prior to the electronics age, vehicles were fitted with electromechanical charging systems consisting of a dynamo and regulator. The layout of such a system is shown in Figure 4.1.

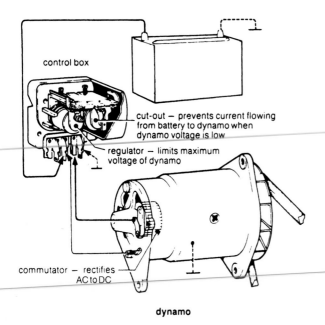

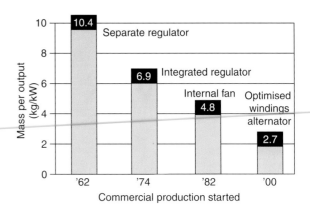

Figure 4.2 Evolution of the alternator

dynamo

Figure 4.1 Dynamo charging system

The dynamo system was used for many years but suffered from the following disadvantages:

- Due to carbon brushes/commutator arrangement, regular servicing and part replacement was needed for the dynamo.
- Rotational speed limit of armature meant that maximum speed was limited to approximately maximum engine speed (at the time 5000 rpm, pulley ratio of 1:1). This meant that the dynamo would start to charge the battery only at higher engine speeds, hence at idling or low engine speeds the battery was not being charged.
- Current regulation in addition to voltage regulation was necessary as the dynamo could be overloaded easily. Current regulation via electromechanical means is imprecise and does not recharge the battery in an optimised way.
- Electromechanical vibrating contact regulators were used and these had moving parts that wore out, which meant that replacement of the regulator was required.
- A cut-out (an isolator relay) was required to ensure that the battery did not discharge through the dynamo (as per a motor) when the output voltage of the dynamo was less than the battery (at low engine speeds).

For these reasons, and due to the decrease in the price of electronic components over time, the alternator has superseded the dynamo and has been universally adopted in road-going vehicles since the mid 1970s.

At first alternators were fitted in up-market/high-end vehicles or as an optional extra. The main points with respect to the evolution of the alternator are shown in Figure 4.2.

First-generation alternators had power outputs slightly greater than the equivalent dynamo. The main advantage came from the fact that they could be driven at higher speed than the engine (via the pulley ratio) due to the fact that the rotating part (the rotor) was lighter and more robust than the rotating part of the dynamo (the armature). Charging 'cut-in' speed was thus lower and the battery could be charging at idle. These units normally incorporated external voltage regulators (sometimes still electromechanical) and warning-light control units (to illuminate/extinguish the dashboard ignition light).

As technology progressed and electronics became more compact, self-contained alternators became standard. These incorporated electronic voltage regulators on board. In addition, the field circuit energy was generated internally via another set of output diodes and thus these units were self-exciting, i.e. no external power supply needed to be connected for the regulator/field circuit (i.e. an ignition supply). The only external connections were battery and warning light (unless external voltage sensing was required to compensate for cable volt drop) and this made installation simple.

As vehicle power requirements increased, alternator specific power output increased. This is important as at the same time more space was being taken up in the engine compartment by the larger number of peripheral components linked to performance, emissions and monitoring (e.g. fuel injections systems etc.). This also created problems with respect to cooling and noise. The latest-generation units are optimised with respect to all of these considerations. Powerful alternators which can generate hundreds of amps are the same physical size as units were 20 years ago and they are more efficient and quieter. In addition, the adoption of smart interfaces between the charging system and the vehicle electrical power system have allowed more intelligent use of the power to optimise the performance and economy of the vehicle as a whole.

The alternator has replaced the dynamo in modern vehicles as it has superior performance with respect to cut-in speed and output

Alternators generate AC current in the windings but this is rectified to DC for battery charging and supplying vehicle power

Alternators only require voltage regulation as their current output is self-limited

4.2   VEHICLE ENERGY REQUIREMENTS

4.2.1 Energy balance

There are a number of electrical loads on the vehicle, but they are not always continuous demands. Certain loads are permanent and always required when the vehicle is being driven, for example the ignition or fuel-injection system. A number of loads can be categorised as long-term loads. These are consumers that have a steady demand and are likely to draw power for a period of time but not continuously whilst the vehicle is in operation, for example the lights, heater blower or heated rear window. In addition, there are electrical consumers that are very short time, like turn signals or brake lights.

The usage of the equipment has an impact on the total loading of the electrical system. It would be impractical to simply add up the power consumption of all the consumers and fit an alternator of that power capability. It would be very expensive, difficult to accommodate and unnecessary. It is possible to apply a factor to de-rate intermittent consumers according to their usage and this is known as a *diversity* factor.

This is a common technique and is used in electrical engineering when designing electrical systems of all kinds. The basic theory is to apply a factor that represents the duty time of the consumer, i.e. the amount of time it is actually switched on in a given period. We can then de-rate the power needed accordingly. This allows a realistic model of the power requirements of the vehicle to be established and hence the alternator can be sized appropriately according to this. Figure 4.3 shows the typical loads in a vehicle.

In modern vehicle design the electrical power requirements of the vehicle are established early in the design stage using sophisticated computer modelling techniques. This allows the requirements for battery, alternator and other components to be considered in the design concept phase of the vehicle and this is an important factor with the accelerated design processes and constraints for modern vehicles. The parameters to be considered when specifying the charging system equipment for a new vehicle are:

- number of consumers and duty factor
- probability of rush-hour driving or long engine idling periods
- operation in extreme climates – heat or cold (air conditioning and heating requirements)
- summer/winter operation
- probability of additional consumers being fitted.

This is a sophisticated algorithm used for designing a system. A simple charge balance calculation can be proposed by adding up all of the permanent and long-time loads, adding this to the short-time loads that have been multiplied by a factor to account for their intermittent duty cycle (normally 1/10). The formula would be:

$$I_{\text{total}} = \Sigma I_{\text{permanent}} + \Sigma I_{\text{long term}} + \Sigma I_{\text{short term}} \times 0.1$$

This would give the average current required by the system. The alternator can be sized based on this figure, but it is also necessary to allow sufficient additional capacity to charge the battery continuously (taking into account the capacity) and to allow for the addition of extra electrical equipment in the future. This factor is generally about 1.5. Alternators are normally produced in a range of standard sizes and hence the unit chosen would be based on the above figure (rounded up to the next available size).

4.2.2 Energy structure

The battery and alternator have to work together and be appropriately harmonised in order to provide sufficient power at the required time in the vehicle. This relationship is known as the energy structure and evolves from the relationship between the battery capacity, the alternator output and the operating conditions of the vehicle.

The battery provides a power source from which the various consumers have to be supplied with energy and therefore must be continuously charged by the alternator. Clearly the alternator has to provide more energy than is required by the consumers (over a given period of time). If this is not the case the energy reserve in that battery will be utilised to a point where the battery becomes discharged or 'flat'. The following points should be noted with respect to the energy structure of a vehicle:

- There must be a well-balanced ratio between energy output (to the consumers) and energy input (from the alternator) taking into account all factors. This provides an optimised energy structure for the vehicle.

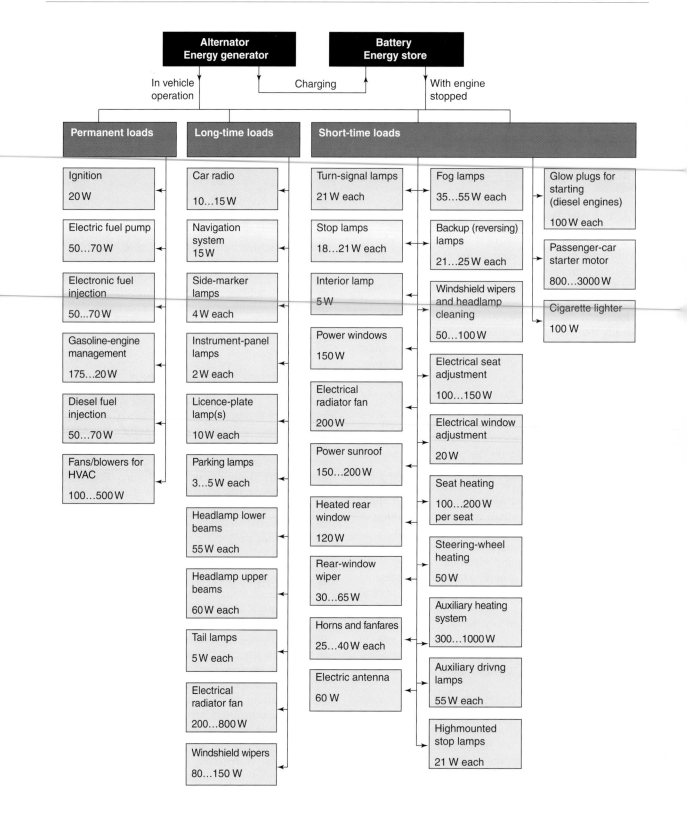

Figure 4.3 Vehicle electrical loads and usage rating

- Additional consumers fitted to the vehicle can affect the balance of the energy structure.
- The sum of the consumption of all the individual consumers, their duty factors and the driving conditions have a considerable affect on the energy structure.

A simple example of the effect of the energy structure can be seen in the following examples:

- *Favourable situation – operation of main beam headlamps.* These are used on open roads where the traffic is less dense and therefore engine speeds are higher. This means the alternator is operating in a preferred speed range and can supply enough energy for all of the consumers. In this case all of the influencing factors are working favourably together (see Figure 4.4).

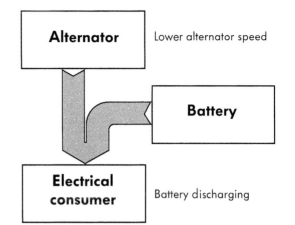

Figure 4.5   Energy structure – unfavourable

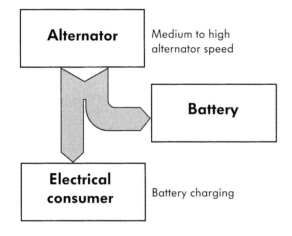

Figure 4.4   Energy structure – favourable

- *Unfavourable situation – operation of fog lamps.* In this case the situation is less favourable. Use of fog lamps is likely to coincide with other consumers due to the ambient conditions (e.g. wipers, heater, heated rear window). Also, the duty factor of the fog lights is such that they are operated for a relatively long period of time (compared with main beam lamps). In addition, during these conditions, the engine/vehicle speed is likely to be lower and thus the influencing factors do not work as well together, with the consequence that the alternator may not be able to provide all of the energy needed (see Figure 4.5).

In modern vehicles the energy structure and power distribution can be managed by an electronic control unit which interfaces between the consumers and the power network of the vehicle (see Figure 4.6). Functions that were previously carried out by distributed control units and relays can be integrated in a single onboard supply control unit. This unit can monitor and control electrical loading and the consumers as well as monitoring the battery and the alternator. The unit can adapt the charging system status if more power is required (for

Figure 4.6   Electronic onboard supply control unit (VW)

example by raising idle speed), and if there is a risk that the vehicle may not start due to excessive loading, then convenience consumers can be switched off to ensure that safety-related consumers have enough power and that the vehicle can be restarted.

Key Points

The alternator and battery are sized carefully according to the vehicle power requirements, which depends upon the equipment fitted

To provide a realistic picture of the vehicle electrical loading, the electrical consumer duty factor (i.e. the amount of time it is switched on) is taken into account as well as the current draw of the consumers

Extra equipment fitted to a vehicle can upset the charge balance of the system and lead to problems such as flat batteries

4.3   ALTERNATORS

4.3.1 General principles and construction

The basic principle of the alternator is that it is a multi-phase AC generator which incorporates a rectifier circuit. This converts the current to DC for supplying the electrical consumers around the vehicle and for charging the battery. This is shown diagrammatically in Figure 4.7.

The unit is engine driven, generally via a composite rubber belt from the non-drive end of the engine (the front pulley end).

The basic principle behind the power generation in an alternator is shown in Figure 4.8.

The figure shows a shaft and four-pole magnet fitted adjacent to a stator (stationary current-carrying conductor). This is connected to form a simple circuit which includes a voltmeter to show the output. Rotation of the magnet generates an emf in the coil. Since the north and south poles present themselves alternately at the stator, the current produced reverses continuously and is hence an alternating current (AC).

The output increases as the speed of rotation increases. In addition the frequency of the AC supply increases proportionally with speed. When the rate of change of current reaches a certain value, self-inductance will retard the growth of current in relation to further increases in speed. This is fortunate as it means that the current output of the alternator will saturate at a certain speed and hence this provides inherent protection against overload (a current regulator is not needed).

Adding another winding in the position shown in (b) gives two independent outputs as shown by the graph of emf versus displacement angle of the rotor. Winding B gives an output which is 45° out-of-phase to winding A. This is known as a two-phase output. Similarly, if another winding is added then a three-phase output is obtained (see Figure 4.9).

Rectification of the current is performed using semiconductor diodes in a rectifier bridge that provides full-wave rectification and a DC output from the alternator. Besides this, the rectifier prevents the battery discharging via the alternator windings due to the one-way valve action of the diodes.

Voltage control is clearly required and this is achieved by using an electromagnet for the field circuit (rather than a permanent magnet). Current in this electromagnetic field circuit is controlled by an electronic regulator which senses the output voltage of the alternator and adjusts the current in the field circuit accordingly to increase or reduce the voltage.

Figure 4.10 shows an exploded view of a typical alternator. This is a three-phase, 12 pole machine that incorporates a rectifier and electronic regulator. The aluminium casing of the alternator contains:

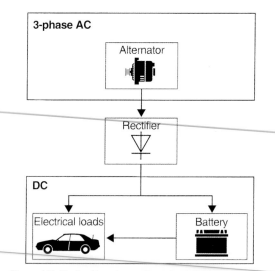

Figure 4.7 Basic alternator system structure

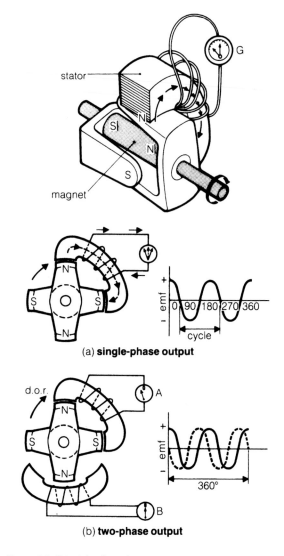

Figure 4.8 Principle of an alternator

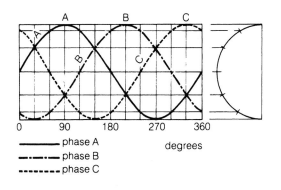

Figure 4.9 Three-phase output

alternators are the latter so that brush wear is even (see Figure 4.12).

The rotor is belt driven from the crankshaft via a pulley/belt. Since the alternator is suitable for speeds up to 15 000 rev/min and also high torque must be transmitted with no belt slip, ball bearings are used to support the rotor. These are prepacked with grease and are maintenance free. Forced ventilation of the machine is essential to cool the windings and the rectifier. Air movement for this is provided by a centrifugal fan fitted adjacent to the pulley, or alternatively incorporated internally in the machine.

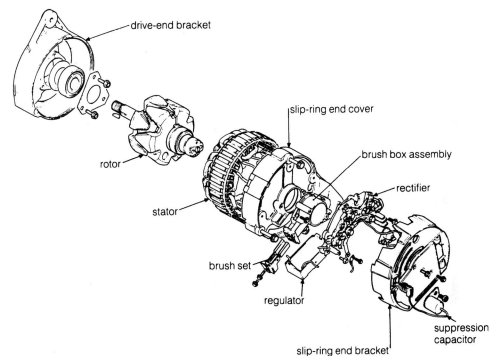

Figure 4.10 Exploded view of an alternator

- the rotor to form the magnetic poles
- the stator to carry the windings in which the current is generated
- the rectifier pack to convert AC to DC current
- the regulator to control the output voltage.

4.3.2 Main components

Rotor

This consists of a field winding that is wound around an iron core and pressed onto a shaft. An iron 'claw' is placed at each end of the core to form the magnetic poles. Generally there are six fingers on each claw which give 12 poles in total (see Figure 4.11).

The current supply to the winding to provide the magnetic field is made via a carbon brush/slip ring arrangement. These can be formed in a face (co-axial) or barrel (axial) arrangement, though most modern

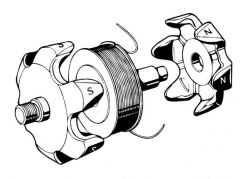

Figure 4.11 Alternator 'claw' pole rotor

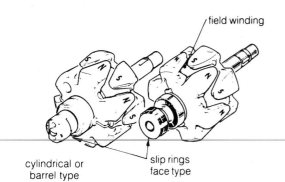

Figure 4.12 Slip ring arrangement

Stator

This is a laminated soft-iron component attached rigidly to the casing that carries the three sets of stator windings as shown in Figure 4.13.

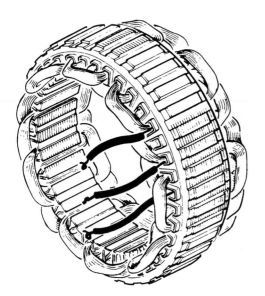

Figure 4.13 Stator construction

The coils of comparatively heavy-gauge enamelled copper wire forming the stator are arranged so that separate AC wave-forms are induced in each winding as they are cut by the changing magnetic flux. There are two methods of interconnecting the three phases.

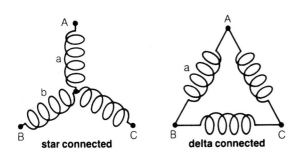

Figure 4.14 Stator windings – connection of phases

Figure 4.14 shows both methods – star and delta. In the star connection, one end of each winding connects to the other two windings and the output current is supplied from ends A, B and C. In the delta connection method, the ends of the windings are connected together as nodes and an output connection is made at node points A, B and C.

The main operational difference between these two arrangements is the magnitude of the voltage and current outputs. In the star arrangement, the output between any two connections (A, B or C) is as follows:

Output voltage = $\sqrt{3} \times$ Phase voltage

Output current = Phase current

This is due to the fact that only one winding can be positioned at the point of maximum induction at any one time. In the delta connected windings:

Output voltage = Phase voltage

Output current = $\sqrt{3} \times$ Phase current

The above arrangements can be considered as similar to a series circuit for the star winding and a parallel circuit for the delta winding. The net power generated by both winding types is the same for any given speed, but the current for a delta-wound machine is clearly greater. For this reason, star windings are commonly used for smaller, light-vehicle applications, whereas delta windings are used in high-current applications (typically commercial vehicles). Certain alternators for special applications allow the possibility to reconfigure the windings according to the application.

Rectifier

Modern alternators employ integrated rectifier packs with the diodes arranged in a bridge network (see Chapter 1 for an explanation). For a three-phase output, six diodes are needed to give full wave rectification, and these are arranged as shown in Figure 4.15.

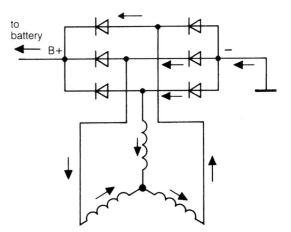

Figure 4.15 Rectifier circuit for three-phase applications

The diodes act as one-way valves, so the generated current will always pass to the battery via the terminal B+. To complete the circuit, an appropriate earth diode is fitted to connect the stator windings to earth as well. The action of the diodes in this application can be verified by inserting two arrows adjacent to any two stator windings. Irrespective of the position and direction of the arrows, it is always possible to trace the circuit between earth and B+.

In addition to the rectifying function, the diodes prevent current flowing backwards from the battery to the alternator and then earth (thus discharging the battery). This feature is necessary when the alternator voltage is less than the battery, and it prevents the need for a cut-out relay as in a dynamo system.

Typical construction of rectifier packs is shown in Figure 4.16.

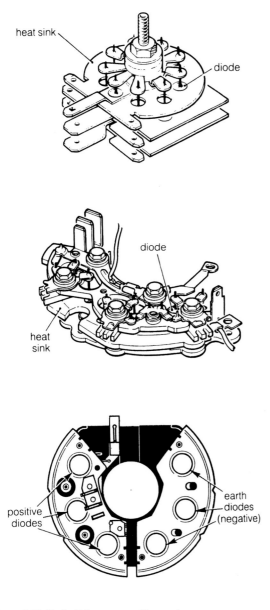

Figure 4.16 Typical alternator rectifier packs

In all designs the most important factor is to keep the rectifier diodes cool. It is usual to mount the diodes in an aluminium alloy block/plate known as a heat sink. This increases the surface area and helps to dissipate the heat to the cooling air passing through the machine.

Field excitation

During the alternator operation a current must be supplied to the field circuit to generate the magnetic field at the rotor so that the required voltage can be induced in the stator. This is known as 'excitation of the field', and the current is supplied to the field windings via brushes and slip rings (see the section on rotors above). Most modern alternators are *self-excited* and these employ an extra three output diodes to feedback a supply, within the machine, to the rotor circuit as shown in Figure 4.17.

Although a self-excited machine supplies the field current when the alternator is charging, it cannot provide the initial current to energise the field to start the charging process. This is due to the fact that there is insufficient residual magnetism in the rotor to initiate the charging process. Self-excitation can only take place when the alternator voltage exceeds the voltage drop across the rectifier diodes (i.e. $2 \times 0.7 = 1.4\,V$). Therefore, the battery must be used to initially excite or activate the build up of flux in the rotor poles. This initial excitation can be provided via:

- A warning lamp circuit. Normally a charge warning lamp is fitted to a vehicle and this can be utilised to provide the initial excitation. The circuit is shown in Figure 4.17 and operates as follows. When the engine is to be started, the ignition is switched on and this connects a supply to the lamp which illuminates as the path to earth is completed via the field circuit. This provides a small current (and hence the flux) in the rotor to start the charging process. As the engine is started and the alternator speed increases, the voltage at the field diodes increases and hence the lamp fades as the voltage difference across it reduces. Once the machine voltage is equal to the battery voltage, the light is extinguished and at this point the field diodes are supplying all of the field current. Now the alternator begins to charge, i.e. it has reached 'cut-in' speed which is generally about 1000 rpm (alternator speed). Note that further increases in voltage are applied on both sides of the warning lamp and hence it remains extinguished whilst the alternator charges.
- A multifunction regulator. Modern alternators are commonly fitted with sophisticated microelectronic regulators and these allow the excitation current to be supplied directly from the battery via the B+ connection. The advantage of this arrangement is that the field diodes can be dispensed with. Figure 4.18 shows a typical circuit.

Operation is as follows: when the ignition is switched on the voltage from the warning lamp is sensed at the connection 'L' at the regulator, which then switches an initial excitation current in the field circuit. Once the rotor is turning, the regulator senses the phase voltage at connection 'V', the frequency of which is used by the regulator to calculate alternator speed. The cut-in speed can be set in the regulator circuitry, and as soon as this speed is reached the regulator switches the field circuit through the final stage so that the alternator starts to deliver current. In this arrangement it is possible that the field circuit can be switched at full battery voltage right from

start-up, and this improves the 'cut-in' performance of the alternator. Note that the terminal numbers or letters can vary between manufacturers but the principle is the same.

Voltage regulator

The voltage regulator maintains the alternator (and hence the electrical system) voltage at a constant level irrespective of electrical load and engine speed. The optimum voltage supplied from the alternator should be

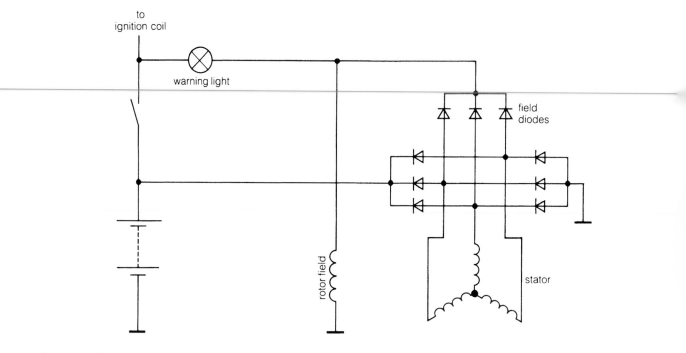

Figure 4.17 Self-excited field system – nine diodes

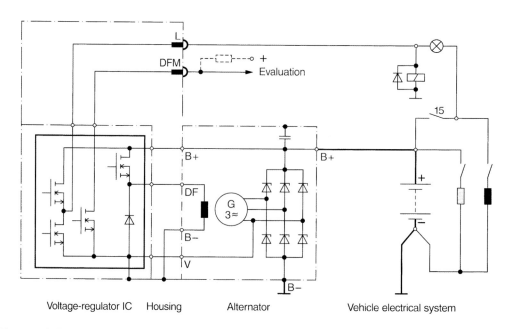

Figure 4.18 Typical circuit – multifunction regulator

that of a fully charged battery (approximately 14.4 V). Therefore the alternator must be capable of varying its output to suit this requirement. In addition the output voltage from the alternator must be limited to prevent overcharging of the battery and damage to electrical consumers There are two main factors that affect the voltage output of the alternator:

- electrical loading of the vehicle system/alternator
- changes in engine speed.

The voltage regulator is connected to the alternator field excitation circuit and controls the current flowing in this circuit. The regulator uses electronic switching with a variable duty-factor to control the rotor field current/flux strength and hence the alternator output according to operating conditions. The switching action of the field circuit can be seen in Figure 4.19.

The operation is as follows. When the alternator voltage is below the control threshold current flows from B+ through resistor R_3 to the base of T_2 and then to earth. Current passing through the base circuit of T_2 switches on the transistor and causes the field F to be connected to earth. At this point, full field current and a strong magnetic flux in the rotor occur. Once the voltage reaches the target level, the zener diode conducts and passes current to the base of T_1 and allows current to flow freely through T_1 from R_3 with the result that the base of T_2 is switched off. T_2 and hence the current in the field winding are also switched off. The sequence is summarised in Table 4.1.

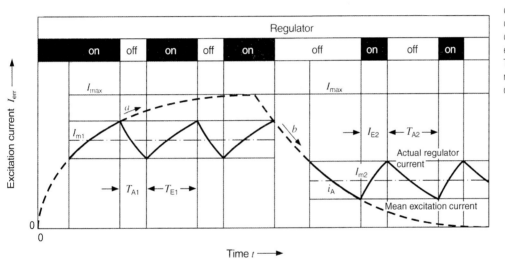

The relationship between on-time T_E and off-time T_A is decisive for the magnitude of the resulting mean excitation current I_m. The excitation current rises along curve a, and decays along curve b.

Figure 4.19 Switching action of the field circuit

The regulator action only takes place when the alternator voltage reaches the target level, below this threshold the regulator is inactive.

Nearly all vehicle alternators utilise microelectronic regulators built into the alternator body itself. The basic principle of operation can be appreciated by looking at Figure 4.20.

The circuit is built around a zener diode (see Chapter 1 for further explanation). This component will not conduct any current until a given voltage is reached, at which point it conducts freely. By using this characteristic, the zener diode senses when output voltage limitation is needed. When the given voltage is reached the diode conducts and activates the field-switching transistor. The zener diode used operates at a voltage less than 14.2 V, so resistors R_1 and R_2 are used as a potential divider and to calibrate the unit to the appropriate voltage level. T_1 and T_2 are switching transistors in a Darlington pair (see Chapter 1) to allow a switching capability of the appropriate power level for the regulator.

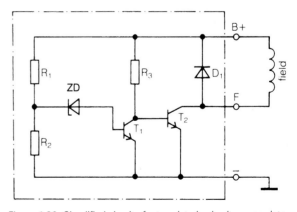

Figure 4.20 Simplified circuit of a transistorised voltage regulator

Table 4.1

ZD	T_1	T_2	Field circuit
No flow	Off	On	Closed
Flow	On	Off	Open

When the output voltage falls below the target, the zener diode switches off and the transistor pair switches back on the field circuit. This cyclic switching action takes place in milliseconds and hence the alternator voltage is regulated to an appropriate mean value.

Note that the diode D_1 is used as a flywheel diode to prevent the induced voltage in the field circuit during switching from damaging the regulator electronics. An additional feature of the regulator circuit is temperature compensation. The regulator includes an ambient temperature sensor which can adjust the target control voltage slightly according to the ambient conditions. This is important for efficient charging of the battery as the electrochemical processes in the battery are temperature sensitive. The temperature-related compensation curve is shown in Figure 4.21.

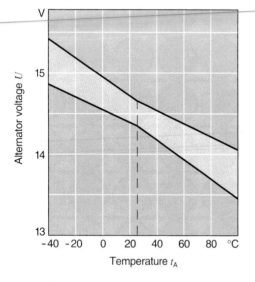

Figure 4.21 Temperature-related compensation curve

The position where the system voltage is sensed and fed back to the alternator regulator can vary. In some cases a separate wire is taken directly from the regulator circuit, via a connection on the alternator, to the battery positive and this allows sensing of the actual battery voltage. This can be useful where the battery is some distance from the alternator, as compensation for cable voltage drop is then taken into account by the regulator circuit. This arrangement is known as *battery-sensed* (see Figure 4.22). If this technique is used, the regulator has a built-in redundancy circuit to prevent overcharging should the sensing wire become disconnected accidentally (i.e. the alternator becomes *machine-sensed*).

Most installations in light vehicles place the battery and alternator close together to minimise the cable length/volt drop, and therefore machine-sensed alternators are the most common (see Figure 4.23).

4.3.3 Alternator characteristics

The performance of the alternator at different speeds can be shown by its characteristic curve. The alternator has to operate at many different speeds, from standstill to maximum, and certain speed points are of particular interest when trying to understand how the alternator performs. Figure 4.24 shows curves of input power and output current versus speed at fixed voltage and temperature conditions.

From these curves specific results of interests are extracted:

- 0 amp speed (n_0). This is the speed at which the alternator reaches its rated voltage before delivering any power. The alternator can only deliver power above this speed.
- Speed at engine idle (n_1).
- Current at engine idle (I_1). At this speed the alternator must deliver enough current for the long-time consumers, the actual speed depends on the drive belt transmission ratio.
- Speed at rated current (n_N).
- Rated current (I_N). The speed at which the alternator generates its rated current. This should be higher than the total vehicle loading.
- Maximum speed (n_{max}).
- Maximum current (I_{max}). The maximum current at the alternator's maximum speed. Limited by the bearings and the slip ring arrangement used.
- Cutting-in speed (n_A). This is the speed at which the alternator starts to deliver current when the speed is increased for the first time from standstill. It is above idle speed and depends on several factors including the pre-excitation power and the battery voltage.
- Power input curve (P_1). This is decisive for belt drive calculations. This curve shows the maximum power to be taken from the engine at a given speed. In addition the efficiency of the alternator at any given speed can be derived.

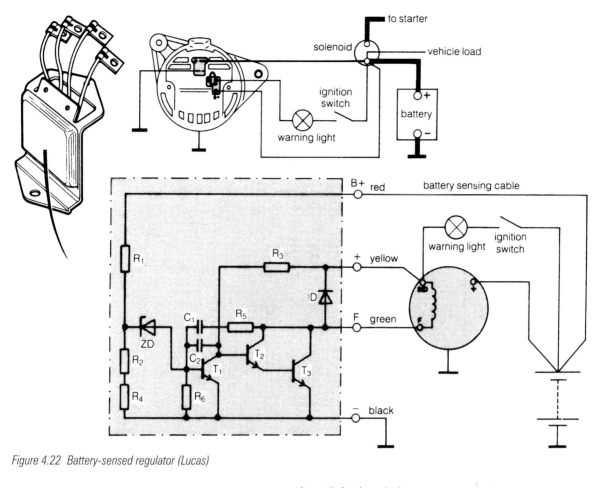

Figure 4.22 Battery-sensed regulator (Lucas)

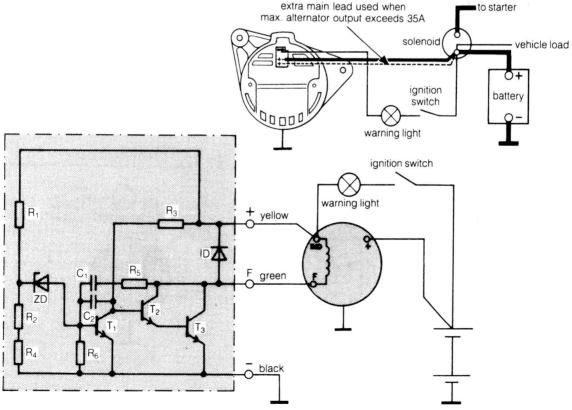

Figure 4.23 Machine-sensed regulator (Lucas)

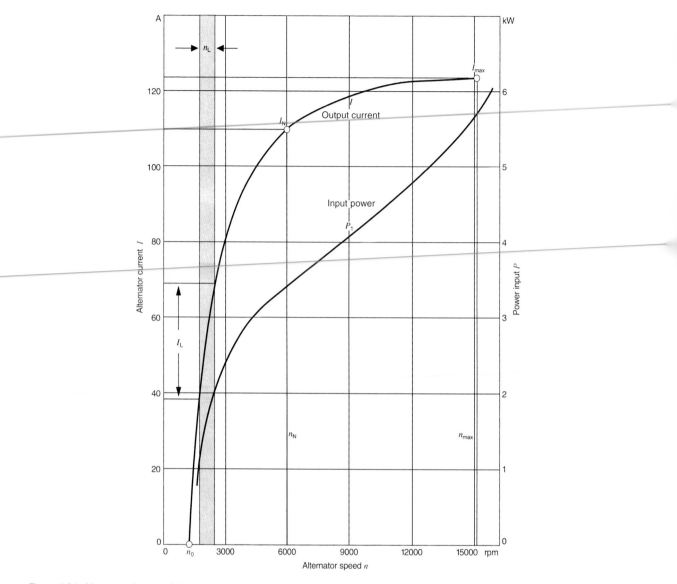

Figure 4.24 Alternator characteristic curve

4.4.1 Special features in current designs

Over-voltage/surge protection

Over-voltages can occur in the vehicle system and generally the alternator must be protected against these. They can occur as heavy loads are switched on or off or if a wiring fault occurs which causes sudden load disconnection and consequent voltage peaks. A number of methods are used to provide this protection:

- Zener diode rectifiers: used in place of the normal rectifier diodes, zener diodes limit high-energy voltage peaks and provide protection for the whole vehicle against over-voltage.

- Surge-proof regulators: extra protection built into the regulator electronics via high electrical strength of the internal components. This technique only protects the alternator itself.

- Surge protection diode: fitted in the field circuit, if over-voltage occurs this diode conducts and shorts the field circuit to stop the alternator charging.

Alternators are not generally fitted with reverse-polarity protection. Accidental reverse connection of the battery (or jump leads to another vehicle) will cause a catastrophic current to flow through the rectifier and destroy the alternator and other equipment.

Neutral point third harmonic

Alternators with star-connected windings can benefit from an additional increase in output by connection of the neutral point of the windings to a pair of output diodes. Thus the alternator would have four node points connected to diodes giving four positive diodes and four earth diodes (see Figure 4.25).

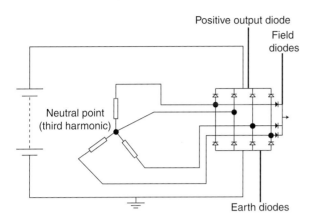

Figure 4.25 *Additional diodes to utilise third harmonic II-diode alternator*

In theory the voltage at the star point is zero, but in reality a potential is generated at a frequency that is three times the frequency of any of the individual phases. By connecting this point to output diodes, the energy that is normally lost can be superimposed on the alternator output phases to give a power increase of approximately 10%.

Improved stator construction
Improvements in the winding technology and material has allowed optimised stator winding to be created that improves the efficiency of the alternator. An example of this is used in DENSO alternators. They have introduced the world's first SC (segment conductor) stator windings with a rectangular conductor for their stator coil. By raising the winding density (space factor) from 45% to 70%, DENSO made the SC-type alternator 20% lighter and increased the output so that it is 50% higher than a conventional type.

General view   Cross section

Figure 4.26 *DENSO alternators – SC-type winding*

Multi-function regulators
Multi-function regulators are employed in many current designs of alternators. These allow the alternator to include built-in intelligence and self-monitoring, and they do not need field excitation diodes. The circuit for this type of regulator is shown in Figure 4.18. The main features are:

- 'Engine running' signal can be taken from the L terminal which also switches the warning lamp.
- Terminal W provides and engine speed signal.
- Alternator field excitation is implemented via a ramp. This prevents torsional vibration due to torque jumps and contributes to the smoothness of the engine.
- The voltage regulator field circuit pulse-width signal is provided as an output so that other vehicle systems can monitor alternator loading.

4.5   FUTURE DEVELOPMENTS IN CHARGING SYSTEMS

As intelligence in the vehicle and its sub-systems grows, the main developments will be in the efficient control and management of electrical power and distribution in the vehicle. We have already discussed energy management controllers fitted in vehicles that can manage the effective use of power in critical situations. In addition to this, alternators fitted with communication interfaces allowing bi-directional communication between the alternator and other sub-systems will contribute to 'smart' power management systems, some of which are already available in certain current vehicle types.

As we move towards hybrid vehicles for emission reduction, integrated starter-generators will become commonplace and these must be fully integrated into the vehicle system rather than just being a charging system. These systems will provide energy recovery in addition to contributing to vehicle performance (via energy boosting). This technology needs different battery technology than that currently utilised. In addition, system voltages must be much higher in order to transmit the required power. For these reasons, charging systems will evolve at an accelerated pace in the future. Integrated starter-generator (ISG) technology is discussed in more detail in *FMVT: Book 2 Powertrain Electronics*.

Chapter 5

STARTING-MOTOR SYSTEMS

what is covered in this chapter ...

- ■ Starting a combustion engine
- ■ Types and characteristics of starter motors
- ■ Electrical circuits
- ■ Future developments in starting systems

5.1   STARTING A COMBUSTION ENGINE

5.1.1 Introduction

A starter motor converts electrical energy stored in the battery into a mechanical force (torque) to start the internal combustion engine. The system must be capable of supplying sufficient power to rotate the engine at the minimum speed required to successfully initiate the combustion process in the engine cylinders. In modern vehicles this is approximately 100 rpm.

The internal combustion engine is not self-starting and this minimum speed is required to allow the engine to form a reasonably well-atomised fuel mixture in the cylinder and compress it sufficiently for combustion to take place. In addition the starting motor must be able to operate with the very high cyclic torque demand required when rotating an internal combustion engine at cranking speed. The speed must be adequate to allow the momentum of the moving parts to carry the engine over from one firing stroke to another.

Basic requirements

The power requirement to achieve a suitable speed depends upon the size and type of an engine and the ambient conditions. To start a warm engine of 1.5 litre displacement under normal conditions, approximately 1.2 kW is required. The same engine under low-temperature conditions would require approximately 4 kW.

The power at the shaft of the starter motor is the product of torque and speed, that is:

$$P = T\omega$$

where:

P = Power (watts)
T = Torque (Nm)
ω = Angular velocity (rad/s).

By definition, torque is a turning moment and is the force exerted at a given radius, as shown in the Figure 5.1.

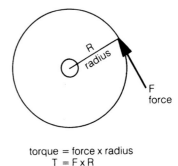

torque = force x radius
T = F x R

Figure 5.1 Torque is the product of force and radius

A starter-motor pinion driving an engine flywheel must exert sufficient torque to provide breakaway from the static condition, i.e. it must rotate the engine from standstill and accelerate up to cranking speed. Interestingly the main consideration that affects the torque required to start the engine (apart from its type – spark or compression ignition) is not the total displacement of the engine but the displacement of the individual cylinders. This dictates the peak torque which must be overcome to generate the compression pressures in the cylinders, i.e. larger cylinders require larger starter motors, not necessarily larger engines.

To provide the high power, the motor electrical circuit must have very low resistance such that a high current, of hundreds of amps, can flow freely. The cables and switches must withstand the large load and the motor must be capable of converting the energy in an efficient manner. Naturally a starting system will not function properly unless the battery can provide the high current demanded. In addition, under these conditions, the battery voltage cannot fall excessively as this affects the motor speed.

The starting process

All vehicle electric starter motors operate in a similar sequence as follows:

- Drive engagement: when the driver requests an engine start. The starting motor has to first establish a mechanical link between itself and the engine.

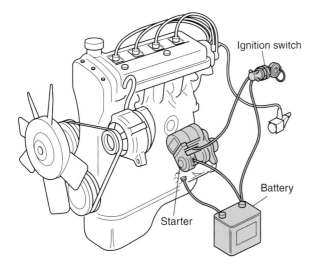

Figure 5.2 Typical starter motor system components and layout

The starter motor is mounted somewhere on the engine block, normally via a flange-type mounting, and drives a gear wheel mounted on the engine flywheel at the back of the engine. The general system arrangement is shown in Figure 5.2.

On requesting a start, the starter motor drive pinion must move into position and engage with the flywheel teeth. If tooth-to-tooth blocking occurs, then the engagement system must compensate for this and turn the pinion so that the teeth misalign and then engage correctly, thus being positioned properly for torque transmission. This status is a prerequisite before the motor can be supplied with full battery current to start the engine.

- Torque transmission: once the drive pinion is fully engaged into the flywheel ring gear teeth, transmission of torque to rotate the engine can begin. At this point, the motor can be switched on with full power. This is normally effected via a solenoid switch which is appropriately rated to handle the large current with minimal electrical resistance. The motor begins to rotate and, due to the transmission ratio between the starter and engine, a large amount of torque is applied to the crankshaft to overcome the static friction and rotate the engine. The compression and expansion in the engine cylinders means that the torque required varies considerably during the process. In addition, this affects the engine speed; the cyclic accelerations and decelerations of the crank shaft can be quite high. This is shown in Figure 5.3.
- Engine start-up: a warm, modern, fuel-injected engine will normally start within two revolutions. When cold, the engine needs longer. Generally though, as soon as fuel is injected/ignited the engine will generate its own torque and therefore increase

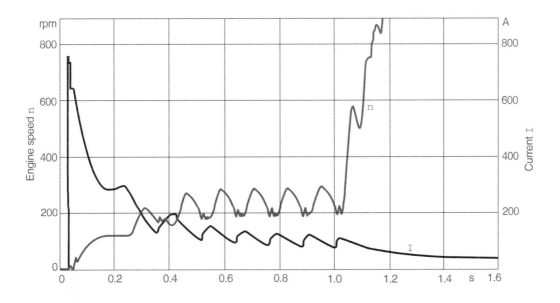

Figure 5.3 Starter motor speed and current during a start process

the rotation speed of the engine. After a short time the engine out accelerates the starter and at this point, even if the motor is still powered, the torque must not be transmitted back from the engine as this will over-speed the starter motor and cause permanent damage. Mechanisms are built into the starter to prevent this.

- End of start process/release: as soon as the driver realises the engine has started and releases the starter motor, the solenoid circuit disconnects the electrical power to the motor and the drive pinion then disengages from the flywheel ring gear and returns to the rest position. The motor is then fully disengaged and unpowered and can freewheel to a standstill.

Key Points

An internal combustion engine is not self-starting. It needs an external device to rotate the engine to initiate combustion. In light vehicles this is an electric motor – the starter motor

The starter motor drives the engine via a toothed ring gear fitted to the flywheel. A pinion on the starter motor engages this when starting and disengages once the engine fires

Starter motors operate at low voltage (~10 to 12 volt) and hence require very large currents in order to generate sufficient power

5.2   TYPES AND CHARACTERISTICS OF STARTER MOTORS

5.2.1 DC motors

The DC motor is universally adopted in vehicle starting-motor system. The basic principle of operation is discussed in Chapter 1 of this book, but we will look at the specific technology in the application in more detail here. In the past, motors with electromagnetic fields have been predominant, but the availability of improved permanent magnet materials has enabled the construction of lightweight, compact starting motors that utilise this technology.

General construction features
Constant rotation and a steady torque are required for the starting motor so a number of armature conductor coils are needed. These coils are set in slots around a laminated soft-iron core. The end of each coil is soldered to a soft copper commutator segment that is insulated from the adjacent segments with mica (see Figure 5.4):

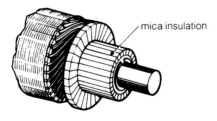

Figure 5.4 Commutator

Armature conductors are made in the form of thick copper strips for minimum electrical resistance. The electrical contact to the armature is made via carbon

brushes, often composed of carbon and copper, and these are held in contact with the commutator via springs (see Figure 5.5).

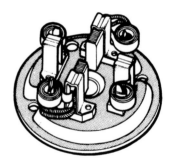

Figure 5.5 Brush springs

The standard armature and commutator arrangement allows the brushes to supply the armature conductor that is positioned where the flux has greatest density. When the torque generated rotates the armature and this conductor is pushed away, another conductor takes its place. By using a number of conductors, near-uniform rotation is obtained. A typical armature has approximately 30 slots for the conductors; the greater the number the smoother the rotation.

A typical field coil arrangement is shown in Figure 5.6.

The field coils are made of copper or aluminium alloy and are wound in a direction which produces N and S poles. Each coil is bound with tape to provide insulation. In the case of two-pole field coils (as shown in Figure 5.6) one end of the coil is connected to a brush and the other end is attached to the starter terminal. By using more poles a more powerful starter motor is obtained. Figure 5.7 shows a two-brush, four-pole motor in which the total magnet strength of the field is doubled as the current is made to form other field paths. The polarity of the poles is N–S–N–S and the diagram shows how the yoke (or barrel) forms part of the magnetic circuit.

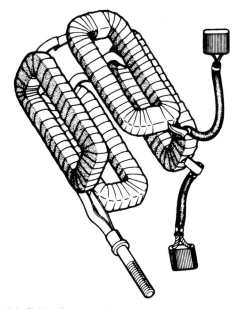

Figure 5.6 Field coil construction

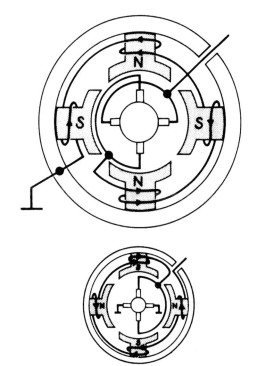

Figure 5.8 A four-pole, four-brush motor

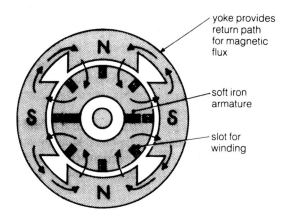

Figure 5.7 Magnetic circuit, four-pole, two-brush motor

A four-pole, four-brush motor is shown in Figure 5.8.

In this design the current from the field is fed to the two insulated brushes, so the reduced brush resistance allows more current to flow. Current is the same throughout the circuit so two other insulated brushes must be fitted.

A starter motor is generally in use for only brief periods of time and thus plain sintered bronze bushes are employed for the armature bearings (non-reduction gear starters).

Series wound motors

This motor has the thick field coils arranged in series with the armature, and all the current that passes to the armature also goes through the field. This gives the strongest possible flux strength. Figure 5.9 shows a simple series-wound motor.

When current is supplied to the motor, the combined effect of the current in the armature and the field windings distorts the magnetic flux and thus generates a torque that pushes the armature away from the field pole.

The series-wound motor has the characteristic of high-peak torque at zero speed and a high no-load speed as shown in Figure 5.10.

The torque output of a motor is directly proportional to the product of magnetic flux and current. In a series motor these are at a maximum at zero speed so the torque will also be at a maximum. As armature speed increases a back-emf is generated in the armature and this opposes and decreases the armature current. The back-emf is due to the tendency of the motor to act as a generator; as the armature moves through the magnetic flux, an emf is induced into the conductors. As the polarity of this induced emf is opposite to the applied voltage across the armature, the emf acts against the supply, hence the term 'back-emf'.

This increase in back-emf with speed and decrease in current causes the torque output of the motor to fall gradually. This makes the series motor very suitable for engine starting as the high torque at standstill is ideal for providing the breakaway torque needed to start the engine which then reduces to a much lower value once the engine is turning over.

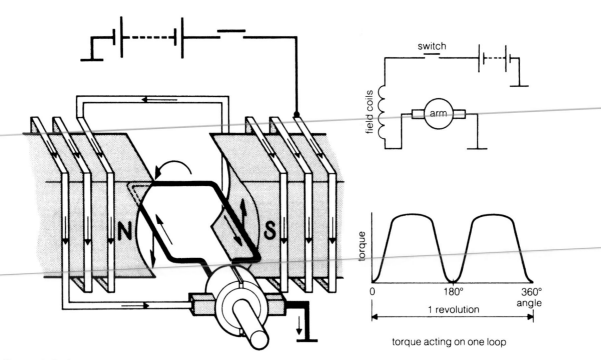

Figure 5.9 Series wound motor

The speed of the motor varies inversely with the field strength. Under load the field is saturated and no variation in speed occurs. When under light or no load, the rise in back-emf reduces the armature and field current. This causes the field to diminish and hence the motor speed rises. In theory the motor speed will rise to infinity but practically, motor damage due to over-speed will occur when run in this condition for any length of time.

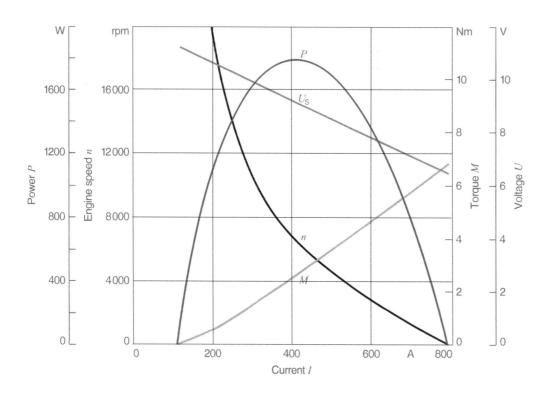

Figure 5.10 Characteristics of a series wound motor

Series-parallel motors

Figure 5.11 shows a series-parallel motor.

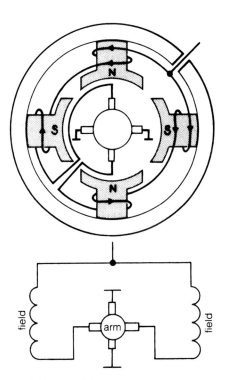

Figure 5.11 Series-parallel motor

This arrangement has the field coils in series with the armature but connects two pairs of coils in parallel. Current flowing in the armature divides as it enters the motor, half of the current passes through each of the field coils. The advantage of this arrangement is that a lower field resistance can be achieved and hence the motor can handle more current and thus produce more torque.

Permanent magnet

A more common arrangement in current designs is to replace the electromagnetic field with permanent magnets and this gives a significant benefit with respect to the power:weight ratio of the motor. When used in conjunction with a planetary gear set, a very compact starting motor system can be produced.

The torque/speed characteristic of the permanent magnet motor is similar to a shunt-type motor (not described here) but can be manipulated with the inclusion of flux concentrators adjacent to the pole magnets as shown in Figure 5.12.

The leading edge of the magnet is replaced by a piece of soft iron and this short-circuits part of the magnetic flux. The primary flux is reduced under no-load conditions and the no-load speed then increases. This means the speed characteristic becomes similar to the series motor.

In the vicinity of the short circuit, the soft-iron pole edge offers the flux resulting from the stator flux and the

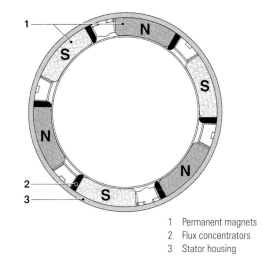

1   Permanent magnets
2   Flux concentrators
3   Stator housing

Figure 5.12 Permanent magnet motor – flux concentrators

armature flux a path of low magnetic resistance (known as reluctance). The result of this is that the overall flux is greater than a motor without flux concentrators and thus produces higher torque. Thus the torque characteristic becomes closer to a series motor.

The characteristics of the permanent magnet motor with flux concentrators are shown in the graph in Figure 5.13 and it can be seen that they are very similar to the series motor.

5.2.2 Pinion engaging mechanism

The drive pinion of the starter motor has to be engaged with the flywheel ring gear teeth before any torque can be transmitted to rotate the engine. There are two main methods for this on light vehicle starting systems.

Inertia

This method was employed extensively in the past for small to medium-size petrol engines. It is not generally used now as developments in technology have reduced the cost of pre-engaged starters. Nevertheless, an understanding of this technology is useful as it is prerequisite to understanding the pre-engaged-type starter.

Inertia is the property of an object to resist changes in velocity unless acted upon by an outside force. For the inertia starter drive, this property is used to drive the pinion along its shaft (axially) and slide into mesh with the flywheel ring gear. When the pinion becomes fully engaged, the rotation then drives the flywheel.

A typical arrangement is shown in Figure 5.14.

When the motor is operated, the sudden acceleration of the armature and the inertia of the pinion causes the pinion to move along the helix towards the motor. In this process the pinion engages with the flywheel aided by a chamfer on the teeth. The sudden shock as torque is transmitted is absorbed by a compression spring. When the engine starts, the flywheel speed out-accelerates the pinion and this throws it back along the helix and

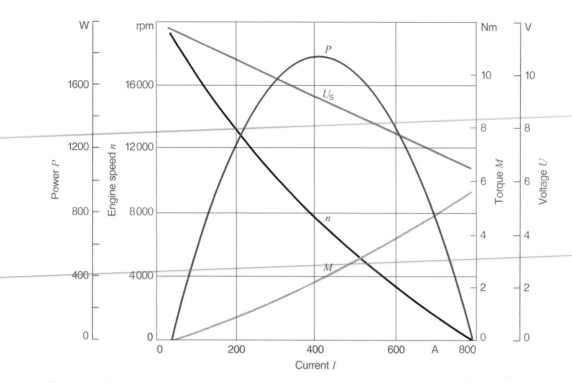

Figure 5.13 Characteristics of a permanent magnet motor

disengages the drive. The ejection is quite rapid and a spring is also employed to cushion the pinion against this shock force. The pinion can be arranged 'outboard' (it moves away from the motor) or 'inboard' (it moves towards the motor). The latter is most common as this reduces the bending stresses on the shaft.

An important point to note is that inertia engagement is not suitable for diesel engines. The cyclic acceleration and deceleration during cranking is much higher (due to high compression pressures) and this can cause premature disengagement of the drive. Also note that the inertia mechanism has special requirements for lubrication to prevent the build-up of clutch dust.

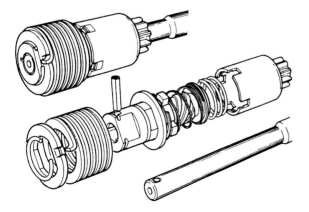

Figure 5.14 Inertia-type starter drive engagement

Pre-engaged

This is the most common design for light-vehicle starting systems. The pinion engagement is performed by an electrical solenoid which is integrated into the starting motor. In addition to its mechanical engagement role, the solenoid acts as a relay switch to delay the passage of full motor current until the pinion is fully engaged with the flywheel. When the engine fires, the pinion does not fully disengage until the driver releases the switch. This feature overcomes the problem of premature ejection of the pinion during an isolated firing stroke.

Figure 5.15 shows the main constructional details of a typical pre-engaged type starter motor. A solenoid plunger is connected to an operating lever. This is pivoted to the casing at its centre and forked at its lower end to engage with a guide ring. This ring acts against the clutch/pinion assembly. Helical splines formed on the armature shaft engage with the driving part of this assembly. These splines cause the pinion to rotate slightly as it moves axially along the shaft to engage with the flywheel. A strong return spring in the solenoid holds the lever and pinion assembly in the disengaged position.

The operation of the system is as follows:

- When the starter switch is operated, the solenoid winding is energised and the solenoid plunger is drawn inwards against the force of the return spring. The plunger is connected to the pinion engaging lever which consequently pushes the pinion/clutch assembly forward (due to lever action) for engagement with the flywheel teeth. The helix arrangement between the pinion/clutch assembly

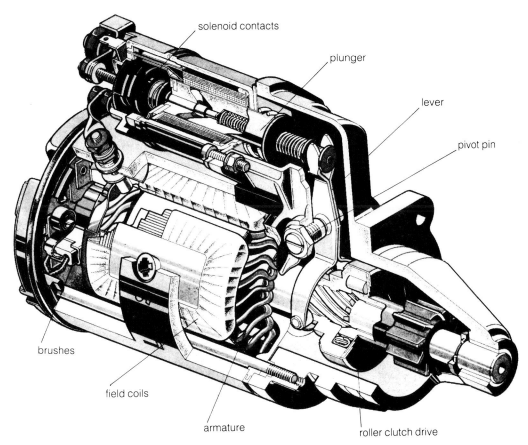

Figure 5.15 Pre-engaged starting motor (Lucas M50)

and the armature shaft allows slight rotation of the pinion during the engagement process and helps to prevent tooth-to-tooth blocking. This promotes full meshing of the pinion and flywheel ring taking place before the motor is powered for cranking the engine. At this point the motor is not energised.

- Assuming the pinion and flywheel teeth are misaligned (i.e. not blocking) the pinion can fully engage with the flywheel ready to transmit torque. Once the plunger reaches its limit stop, the solenoid contacts are closed and this connects battery power to the motor. If the teeth are blocked, a spring in the plunger/solenoid mechanism compresses allowing the solenoid contacts to close. This energises the motor, thus turning the armature, which then allows the teeth to misalign. Once this occurs the pinion drops into the fully engaged position for full torque transmission. The armature torque, in combination with the helix forcing the pinion against its stop on the shaft, ensures the maximum tooth-to-tooth contact area whilst cranking. This also prevents torque transmission until full engagement of pinion and flywheel occurs (see Figure 5.16).
- Releasing of the starter switch de-energises the solenoid and allows the return spring to open the solenoid contacts and withdraw the pinion from the engaged position. The solenoid plunger and lever assembly are connected with a certain amount

of deliberate 'play' that ensures the motor can be disconnected electrically before retraction of the pinion assembly takes place. This is necessary when the engine fails to start and the starting sequence has to be aborted. At this point the pinion is engaged under full cranking torque. When the power supply to the solenoid is switched off, there must be sufficient plunger travel to ensure that the solenoid contacts open. If this were not the case, the pinion engaging lever could hold the plunger in place with the solenoid contacts closed and it would not be possible to stop the motor.

5.2.3 Torque transmission

One-way clutch

All types of pre-engaged starter motors transmit torque to the engine flywheel via an overrunning or one-way clutch. The main function of this mechanism is to ensure that torque is transmitted in one direction only, i.e. from the starter motor to the engine. This prevents the engine from driving the starter when it fires (when engine speed will be greater than starter-motor speed). If the drive connection between the starter and engine were not disconnected under these conditions, the starter motor armature would be driven to excessively high speed and this would cause fatal damage to the motor.

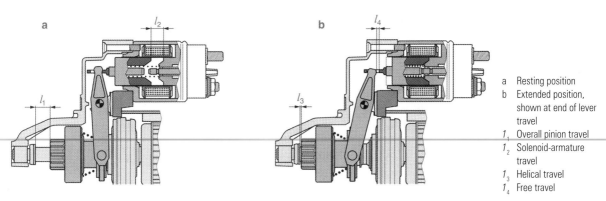

a   Resting position
b   Extended position,
     shown at end of lever
     travel
l_1 Overall pinion travel
l_2 Solenoid-armature
     travel
l_3 Helical travel
l_4 Free travel

Figure 5.16 Pre-engaged starter – drive engagement

In certain designs of starter motor (commercial vehicle types) this clutch performs an additional function of torque limitation to prevent overloading of the starter motor itself. There are two main types of overrunning clutch in use:

- Roller-type clutch: this is the most common type encountered on light-vehicle starting systems. The central component is the clutch shell with a ramp-type roller race. The clutch shell forms the driving member and is connected to the armature shaft via a helix spline. The frictional link between the pinion shaft (i.e. driven member) and the clutch shell is formed by cylindrical rollers that are able to move within the roller race. When the mechanism is at rest the springs force the rollers into constricted space between the roller race in the clutch shell and the pinion shaft. The rollers lock in place (due to the ramp constriction), and via friction they transmit force from the clutch shell to the pinion shaft when torque is applied from the armature (see Figure 5.17).

When the torque transmission is reversed, i.e. the engine tries to drive the motor, the friction between the pinion shaft and the rollers pushes the rollers into the wider part of the roller-race ramp. This disconnects

to frictional force at the roller surfaces between clutch shell and pinion shaft and allows the coupling to slip, thus preventing drive from engine to starter motor.

- Multiplate clutch: most common in larger starter motors found on commercial vehicles. This clutch type contains a multiplate clutch pack which is preloaded via a disc spring. In order to transmit torque the clutch pack is compressed under load via a helix arrangement through which torque from the armature to the engine is transmitted. This tends to compress the clutch pack and driving torque is thus transmitted via the friction faces of the clutch plates. This arrangement has an inbuilt limit stop to prevent compression of the clutch pack beyond a design limit. Therefore, at a designed maximum torque limit, the clutch will slip thus limiting torque transmission and preventing damage to the motor itself. Under reverse torque/overrun, the clutch pack disengages due to 'unwinding' of the helix. This releases the friction forces between the clutch plates and hence disconnects the drive completely (see Figure 5.18).

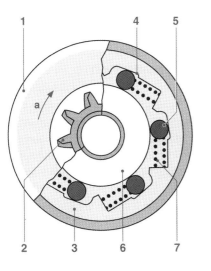

1   Cap
2   Pinion
3   Driver and
     clutch shell
4   Roller race
5   Cylindrical
     roller
6   Pinion shaft
7   Springs
a   Direction of
     rotation

Figure 5.17 Roller-type clutch

1   Driver flange
2   Disc spring
3   Laminated core
4   Clutch race
5   Stop ring
6   Stop collar on output shaft
7   Helical spline on output shaft

Figure 5.18 Multi-plate clutch-type pinion drive – section view

Reduction gear

In a conventional starter-motor arrangement, the pinion rotates at the same speed as the motor armature. Normally the pinion/clutch assembly is mounted directly on the armature shaft and in order to generate sufficient torque, the motor must be relatively large, and therefore heavy. If reduction gearing is utilised, a motor of the same power rating but with higher speed/lower torque characteristics can be employed, and due to this the motor can be 30–40% lighter. In addition a smaller, lighter starter motor allows designers a higher degree of freedom when designing the engine compartment and placing other equipment in it.

The reduction gear starter also has a higher apparent inertia (note that the base inertia of the armature is multiplied by the gear ratio squared) and this provides a considerable 'flywheel effect' which damps out instantaneous speed variations during cranking and helps to carry the engine through the cylinder top dead-centre position smoothly. As a result, the engine speed is consistent during cranking when the fuel is injected and this has a positive effect on the fuel injection pattern, which aids the starting process. For engines with fewer cylinders, this 'flywheel effect' ensures that the high peak torques of each cylinder can be overcome with a relatively low amount of starting power.

Reduction gear starters commonly use planetary gears or a spur type gearbox:

- Planetary-type gears: planetary gear systems are favoured in starter motors manufactured by European manufacturers. Planetary gears are compact and can offer low gear ratios (see Figure 5.20). The gear geometry offers high torque generation with minimal noise. The planetary gearing has a fixed internally toothed ring gear (the 'annulus'). The drive input is via the 'sun' gear which is attached to the armature shaft. The 'planet' gears (normally three of them) are in engagement with the sun and annulus. As the planet gears 'orbit' around the sun gear, their bearing shaft journals drive the output shaft which carries the helix/pinion/clutch assembly. The arrangement is shown in Figure 5.19.

The transmission ratio can be calculated as follows:

$$\text{Transmission ratio} = 1 + \frac{\text{Number of teeth on annulus}}{\text{Number of teeth on sun}}$$

In standard designs, the sun and planet wheels are steel and the annulus is a composite plastic. In more demanding applications, the annulus is also made of steel. Generally the transmission ratio is in the region from 3:1 to 6:1 and this allows optimisations of the starter motor to match the engine characteristics. Higher transmission ratios allow increased speed for better warm-starting performance whereas lower ratios allow more torque for improved cold-start capability.

- Spur-gear type: an alternative to the planetary gear arrangement is the spur-gear type. This

design of starter motor is preferred by far-eastern manufacturers and involves a different general construction and arrangement of the components (although the components are the same). The general design is shown in Figure 5.21.

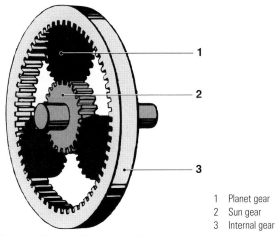

1 Planet gear
2 Sun gear
3 Internal gear

Figure 5.19 Epicyclic gear set schematic

Figure 5.20 Starter motor reduction gear set

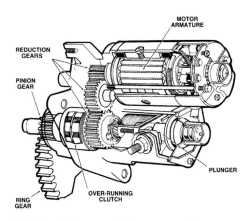

Figure 5.21 Reduction gear starter – spur-gear type

Note that the motor and solenoid are effectively reversed with respect to their relative positions when compared with the standard design. The motor armature is effectively in the piggy-back position and drives the pinion/clutch via reduction gears which give an overall transmission ration of approximately 3:1. The solenoid sits directly behind the pinion/clutch and acts directly upon it to move it in/out of mesh with the flywheel. The motor used is a standard four-pole machine but runs at high speed to generate the necessary power and this is converted to torque at lower speed via the gears. The armature and reduction gears are mounted in ball or roller bearings due to the high rotating speed of these parts. These units are well proven and are commonly used in the application range of 1–1.5 kW for light-vehicle starting systems.

Key Points

The starter motor has a series or series-parallel field winding which gives it the ideal characteristic to generate maximum torque at zero speed. Modern starter motors use powerful permanent magnet fields and as such are lighter and smaller

Most starter motors are pre-engaged. They use a solenoid to fully engage the starter motor pinion with the flywheel teeth before the motor is energised and torque transmitted to the engine

Many modern starter motors use small high-speed motors and reduction gear sets. This allows the construction of smaller, lighter starter motors

The starter motor pinion is fitted with a one-way clutch to prevent the engine from driving the motor as, if this happened, the motor would be destroyed due to over-speeding of the armature

The starter motor drives the engine via the flywheel ring gear with a 10:1 gear ratio

5.3   ELECTRICAL CIRCUITS

5.3.1 Starter-motor control

Solenoid switches

The current supply to the starting motor is always a significant amount (hundreds of amps) and this must be controlled via a special switching arrangement commonly known as a starter solenoid. The main purpose of the solenoid is to switch the large current to the starter motor by using a smaller 'control' current and this means the starter motor cabling can be kept as short as possible between the starter motor and the battery. This helps to reduce unnecessary electrical resistance in the supply circuit and ensures that maximum power can be delivered to the starter with minimal losses due to resistance and cable heating.

A simple solenoid arrangement is shown in Figure 5.22.

This is a single coil/single stage solenoid typical of the type used with inertia-type starter motors. In this application the only function is to switch the electrical supply to the motor. Effectively the solenoid is a heavy-duty relay controlled via a signal wire from the ignition switch.

For pre-engaged type starters the solenoid is built into the starter motor and performs two functions:

• it moves the drive pinion/clutch assembly outwards to engage with the engine flywheel ring gear
• it switches the current flowing into the motor armature.

A typical design of a pre-engaged solenoid is shown in Figure 5.23.

The solenoid core protrudes into the solenoid coil from one side, while the plunger protrudes from the

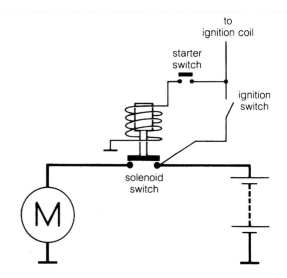

Figure 5.22 Starter-motor solenoid

other side. The distance between the core and the plunger represents the total travel of the plunger. The solenoid windings, core and plunger form the magnetic circuit. The electrical wiring arrangement is shown in Figure 5.24.

When the solenoid is energised, the magnetic field draws the plunger into the coil. This movement is utilised to first move the pinion into engagement (via a lever) and then to close the solenoid contacts (switch). Two windings are generally employed and these are known as 'pull-in' and 'holding' windings. The pull-in winding has its earth return path via the motor armature (see

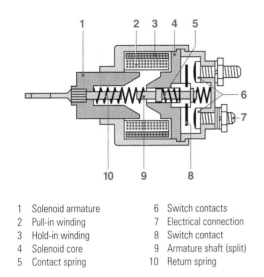

1	Solenoid armature	6	Switch contacts
2	Pull-in winding	7	Electrical connection
3	Hold-in winding	8	Switch contact
4	Solenoid core	9	Armature shaft (split)
5	Contact spring	10	Return spring

Figure 5.23 Pre-engaged solenoid

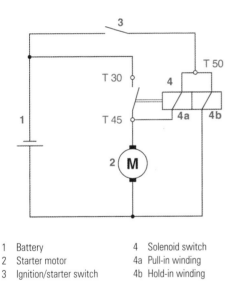

1	Battery	4	Solenoid switch
2	Starter motor	4a	Pull-in winding
3	Ignition/starter switch	4b	Hold-in winding

Figure 5.24 Electrical wiring arrangement

Figure 5.24) whereas the holding winding has a direct earth connection via the body. When the solenoid is initially energised current flows through both windings and this generates the strong magnetic field needed to overcome the forces required to engage the pinion fully, and to provide sufficient field strength to overcome the large air gap between the plunger and the coil.

As the plunger travels into the magnetic field the air gap reduces and thus the field strength increases. Once the plunger reaches its final position, closing the solenoid contacts, the field strength required to maintain this position is much less. Therefore, due to the fact that the earth path for the pull-in winding is via the motor armature, once the solenoid contacts close, the pull-in winding is effectively short-circuited (thus switched off). The field strength of the holding winding alone is sufficient to hold the plunger in position until

starter operation is complete. This arrangement reduces thermal stresses in the solenoid yet allows sufficient magnetic forces to be generated for the required functionality. It also reduces the overall drain on the battery as the pull-in winding is low resistance and can draw up to 50 A in some cases.

Power supply and cables

The power supply to the starting motor has a significant effect on its performance. The cable arrangement must be as short as possible and dimensioned appropriately to minimise volt drop to avoid cable heating and power loss. Generally the starter motor duty cycle is very short, but in exceptional circumstances the current flowing may be high for longer periods and hence the supply cable and switching components must be rated to deal with this operation mode without suffering damage.

Another factor to be considered is temperature as elevated temperatures will increase resistance in the cables. To determine the permissible temperature rise a transient current density of 30 A/mm^2 is taken together with the short-circuit current for the starter motor and these factors dictate the required cross-section of the power cable.

$$q_w = \frac{I_k}{J}$$

where:

q_w = Cable cross section (mm^2)
I_k = Short-circuit current of the starter motor (A)
J = Current density (taken as 30 A/mm^2).

The electric circuit of the starter motor is shown schematically in Figure 5.25.

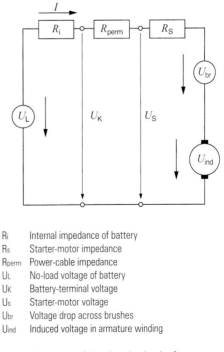

R$_i$	Internal impedance of battery
R$_s$	Starter-motor impedance
R$_{perm}$	Power-cable impedance
U$_L$	No-load voltage of battery
U$_K$	Battery-terminal voltage
U$_s$	Starter-motor voltage
U$_{br}$	Voltage drop across brushes
U$_{ind}$	Induced voltage in armature winding

Figure 5.25 Schematic of the electric circuit of a starter motor

The voltage at the battery terminals is the open circuit voltage minus the voltage drop due to the battery's internal resistance. The voltage available to the starter motor is further reduced by the voltage drop in the cabling. The actual voltage at the commutator is further reduced by voltage drop at the brush contact face, which is approximately 1.2 V per brush pair (irrespective of current) totalling 2.4 V for positive and negative brushes. In addition, the armature itself has resistance, and also a back-emf is generated when the armature rotates in the magnetic field.

The main technical parameters that affect the performance of the starting system which can be checked and improved are:

- battery – well charged, good condition, low internal resistance
- cabling – appropriately sized and minimum length to reduce voltage drop
- starter motor itself – good condition of solenoid contacts and brushes to minimise volt drop.

The starter-motor solenoid has two functions. It acts as a relay to switch the high current from the battery to the motor when required. In addition, for a pre-engaged type starter, it provides the force to move the pinion into mesh with the flywheel

The cabling between the battery and starter motor must very thick and as short as possible to minimise power losses due to voltage drop.

The solenoid employs separate pull-in and holding windings. This reduces current draw and prevents excessive heating yet still provides the necessary magnetic force

5.4   FUTURE DEVELOPMENTS IN STARTING SYSTEMS

Starter-motor technology has improved with the introduction of smaller, lighter motors with greater power density, and these improvements in technology have made possible the installation of starter motors which can perform reliably over the life of the engine even under the most extreme conditions. The biggest problem is that once the engine is running, the starter motor is dead weight. By combining the starter motor with the generator as a single electrical machine considerable weight savings can be made. This technology is under development and is known as ISG or integrated starter-generator. There are additional benefits to be gained with such a system, for example energy recovery (during braking or overrun conditions) and energy boosting (where a short-term power boost for the engine is needed).

A typical starter-generator arrangement is shown in Figure 5.26.

This includes the flywheel/cutch assembly. The motor itself is an AC multi-phase machine with an inverter drive system that can operate in motor or absorb mode to generate torque for starting, or absorb torque for regeneration.

ISG systems are discussed in more detail in *FMVT: Book 2 Powertrain Electronics*.

Figure 5.26 Typical starter-generator arrangement

Chapter 6

POWER DISTRIBUTION

what is covered in this chapter ...

- ■ Electrical circuits in the vehicle
- ■ Vehicle wiring systems
- ■ Circuit diagrams
- ■ Vehicle networks and communication buses
- ■ Future developments in vehicle power distribution and network systems

6.1　ELECTRICAL CIRCUITS IN THE VEHICLE

Vehicle wiring systems used to be relatively straightforward. With the adoption and integration of electronic control systems in vehicles, in combination with more sophisticated equipment demanded by the user, the complexity of vehicle electrical systems has accelerated. A modern vehicle has an extremely complicated electrical power distribution, communication and control system. Although the systems are complex, they can be more easily understood by breaking them down into functional groups and then studying the interaction between these. Figure 6.1 shows some of the systematic groups in a modern vehicle.

- Power supply: this is provided by the generator when the engine is running. The battery acts as a storage buffer and stores energy for starting as well as providing power for consumers like parking lights etc. when the engine is not running.
- Engine and powertrain management: in the past, ignition, fuelling and transmission control

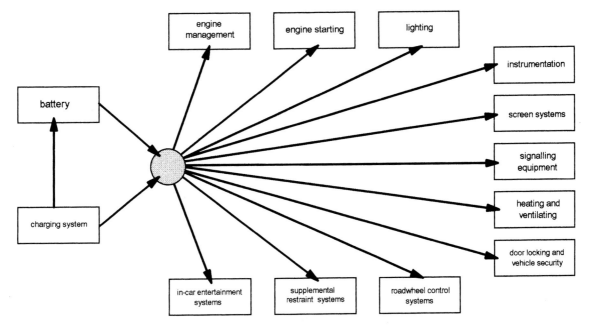

Figure 6.1　Vehicle electrical systems

were handled separately. The current trend is to integrate these control systems to harmonise their operation and to ensure that their functionality is complementary. This is particularly important in meeting current and future emissions regulations.

- Starting system: the starter motor and associated sub-systems allow the driver to start the engine, from any ambient condition, without needing any manual interaction or adjustments. In a modern vehicle the starting process requires appropriate actions from the engine control systems in addition to the starter motor cranking the engine. This is necessary to reduce engine emissions as well as to optimise the efficiency of the start procedure.

- Lighting system: appropriate lighting systems are specified by law so that the presence of the vehicle is clear to other road users in the dark or in conditions of reduced visibility. In addition to allowing the driver to see, front/forward lighting has to have a provision to prevent dazzling other road users.

- Instrumentation system: all road vehicles must be fitted with an instrument to indicate road speed. In addition, other indicators/instruments must be visible to the driver to highlight fault conditions in critical vehicle systems and also to indicate fluid levels or temperatures.

- Vision systems: these systems are fitted to ensure or promote good visibility for the driver and include windscreen wipers, heaters and washers.

- Signalling systems: these systems include direction indicators and audible warning systems (horn, reversing alarm etc.).

- Heating, ventilation and air conditioning (HVAC): this is provided to heat or cool the environment in the vehicle and to ensure a good through-flow of fresh, clean air for passenger comfort and driver alertness.

- Security systems: these include door locking, window closure and security devices (e.g. alarm and immobiliser systems).

- Dynamic stability and control: this includes systems to help control the vehicle in safety critical situations, for example anti-lock brakes, traction control, stability control, brake force distribution.

- Driver safety systems: these are passenger safety systems to protect vehicle occupants, and include airbags and seatbelt tensioners.

- In-car entertainment: this mainly covers equipment for driver and passenger entertainment, for example radio equipment, CD and mp3 players. This technology also includes driver information systems (for example GPS systems) and driver communication systems (in-car cell phone equipment).

The functional groups above are handled in separate chapters in this book, where they are studied in more detail.

The interconnecting hardware which allows the interaction and communication of the vehicle sub-systems is the main subject of this chapter. The physical interconnection of the system components exists as the vehicle wiring harness. This consists of cables and connectors to form the interfaces between components and to allow junctions in the system to direct power to the consumers that need it. The individual circuits need appropriate protection against fault conditions and this is provided via fuses or circuit breakers.

In addition, the wiring harness provides a communication network. This is becoming much more significant in modern vehicles with integrated sub-systems. Hybrid interfaces (analogue and digital signals via individual wires) to communicate between devices and components are inefficient in complex systems. They require extensive cabling which increases weight and cost. In addition, the greater the number of wires and connectors in the system, the greater the potential for faults, and this reduces the reliability of the system as a whole. The answer is provided by vehicle bus systems that allow digital communication between intelligent devices, control units, sensors and actuators. These are now commonplace in modern vehicles and allow additional functionality as well as weight/cost reduction.

Key Points

The wiring system of the vehicle has two main tasks: to transmit electrical power to the consumer components when they need it and to communicate and share information, data and signals around the vehicle components

Vehicle wiring systems have become much more complicated over the years. This increases the weight and complexity of the system

6.2 │ VEHICLE WIRING SYSTEMS

6.2.1 Wiring harness and cables

Introduction

Each main electrical component in the vehicle needs a source of energy and a circuit around which the electricity can flow. The supply cable (from the battery) is commonly known as the *feed* or *supply* wire. The circuit path is completed via the *return* or *earth* wire. This naming convention is due to the fact that, in most cases, the return path back to the battery is made via the vehicle frame or earth.

The various consumers must be connected to the supply via a cable network with low electrical resistance as this will minimise power losses. In addition, strength and durability are important for the reliability of the system. Generally, copper stranded cables are used as this gives a good combination of flexibility, low resistance and moderate cost.

Where several cables run together they are formed into a harness or loom. Depending on their application and operating environment, harnesses are finished in a number of different ways:

- In-vehicle (behind trim): spaced or spiral taping. This allows flexibility and heat dissipation but has limited resistance to mechanical forces.
- In-vehicle (behind dashboard): fabric or foam tap. This reduces noise (squeaks and rattles) due to movement; it has good resistance to abrasion.
- Engine compartment: fully bound with tape or sleeved with PVC sleeving or tubing. This provides a high degree of protection against the elements, high abrasion resistance but reduced heat dissipation.

To provide the maximum protection, individual cables to consumers will normally only leave the main harness at the point where that component is situated. The design of the wiring harness is critical to the reliability of the electrical system and the following factors must be taken into account during the design phase:

- cable runs must be as short as possible to reduce volt drop and cabling cost
- the number of connections and junctions must be minimised
- adequate and appropriate circuit protection must be available
- there must be appropriate protection against the surrounding environment
- ease of installation and test during production
- ease of access for replacement/testing during service life.

These factors, in addition to the complexity of the vehicle components, dictate the wiring system of the vehicle, its layout and the components used. Modern techniques of design use computer simulation to test various electrical systems models in combination with power management strategies to assess their combined effectiveness. This helps to reduce the development time of the wiring systems that are required in modern vehicles.

Automotive cable construction

The cable used in automotive wiring systems is generally multi-stranded and insulated. The size and number of individual copper wires dictates the overall cross-sectional area of the cable and this is the main factor that dictates its current-carrying capacity. These cable strands are packaged/surrounded by an insulating material that provides mechanical strength and resistance against damage. In the past, cotton and rubber were used as insulation material for the copper core of the insulated cable. Generally these have been superseded by PVC (polyvinyl chloride) plastic. Specific automotive-grade PVC polymers allow improved high-temperature performance at up to 105°C in extreme conditions. PVC is very durable, has high dielectric strength and a high resistance to moisture, fuels, lubricants and solvents found in the automotive environment. It is also relatively cheap to produce and is easy to process. Normally the insulation thickness is scaled to the conductor cross-section, but many modern vehicles employ cabling with reduced insulation thickness in strategically located circuits. This reduces weight and cost but also improves heat dissipation. A general rule is that cables with an area of less than $2.5\,\text{mm}^2$ can use the thinner insulation. Figure 6.2 shows the difference in these cable types.

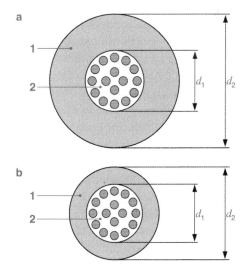

a) Type FLY with standard insulation thickness
b) Type FLRY with reduced insulation thickness
1   Insulation
2   Conductor made up of individual standards
d_1 Conductor diameter
d_2 Overall wire diameter

Figure 6.2 Different cable types – cross-section

An important safety point to note is that PVC cables give off dangerous fumes when heated – when incinerated, PVC releases hydrogen chloride. In addition, heat-damaged PVC cabling must be handled with care to prevent personal contamination as unacceptably high levels of dioxins can be transferred via direct contact. The industry is now looking at alternatives to PVC in vehicle wiring systems for future applications.

Cable colours/identification

In order to aid identification of the vehicle circuits in a wiring harness, the cables are normally colour coded. Unfortunately, the colour code is country and even manufacturer specific. This complicates matters when trying to diagnose faults in vehicle circuits. The wiring harness data for that particular vehicle model must be consulted and this is available from the manufacturer or other companies that specialise in providing wiring information (e.g. www.autodata.ltd.uk).

As an example, vehicles that were made in the UK conformed to a British Standard known as AU7. That standard defined seven basic colours for the vehicle main circuits. These were appended with a tracer colour to further identify the specific circuit. Most wiring diagrams are black and white, so letter codes are used to identify the cable colours on the diagram. The seven basic colours are shown in Table 6.1.

For example, a green wire is a fused ignition feed. A green wire with a red trace is left-hand indicator supply whereas a green wire with a white trace is right-hand indicator feed. As electrical equipment in cars became more sophisticated this standard was revised. In the

1980s it became BS AU7a and included additional colours for extra equipment being found as standard or optional in cars of that generation. Table 6.2 shows typical applications and colour codes.

European vehicles generally conform to DIN standards which dictate cable colours (DIN 47 002) and terminal designations (DIN 72 552). Cable colours can be manufacturer specific, but they follow similar general trends. Note that there is no correlation between the BS and DIN standards. This highlights an important point: the correct manufacturer data must be available when any detailed or involved work is to be carried out on a vehicle wiring system.

The DIN terminal designation system is commonly used and it defines the function of the terminals of a device. The terminal codes are not wire designations as different components connected to the ends of a single wire will have different terminal codes at each end. Typical designations are shown in Table 6.3.

Ford has developed a method called FSC (function-system-connection) for identifying cables, and has used this since the mid-1990s across all Ford models in all global markets. The advantage is a standardised system that allows unambiguous numbering of circuits and standard colour coding of cables (based on DIN specifications). The FSC current circuit numbers are grouped into areas of application as follows:

- Function: a number between 1 and 99 is assigned according to the circuit function. Basic functions are:
  31 – ground circuit
  30 – battery voltage
  29 – battery voltage, fused or protected.
  The numbers are generally harmonised with the DIN terminal codes. An 'S' after the function code means a switched function.
- System: two letters identify the system. The first is the system group, the second is the sub-system concerned within that group. For example:
  L = Lighting system (system group)
  G = Indicator (sub-system).
- Connection: this is a number between 1 and 99. Within a system, the connections of a component

Table 6.1 BS AU7 basic colours and functions

Black	Earth
Brown	Battery feed
Purple	Fused battery feed
White	Ignition feed
Green	Fused ignition feed
Red	Sidelight circuits
Blue	Headlight circuits

Table 6.2 Wire colour-code examples

Circuit wiring	BSI colour	Letter code (British)	Letter code (DIN)
Earth wire from component to earth tag	black	B	SW
Ignition switched fused supply, e.g. instrument, indicators, brake and reverse lights	green	G	GN
Battery supply from fusible link box	brown	N	BR
Fused permanent supply, e.g. side lamps, interior illumination	red	R	RT
Fused supply, e.g. central door locking	slate (grey)	S	GR
Fused supply, e.g. headlamps	blue	U	BL
Ignition switched supply to passenger compartment fusebox	white	W	WS

Terminal definition

1	ignition coil, distributor low-tension circuit

Ignition distribution with two insulated circuits
1a	to ignition point set I
1b	to ignition point set II

Ignition coil, distributor
4	high-tension circuit

Ignition distributor with two insulated circuits
4a	terminal 4, from coil I
4b	terminal 4, from coil II
15	switch-controlled positive downstream from battery (from ignition switch)
15a	in-line resistor terminal leading to coil and starter

Glow-plug switch
17	start
19	preglow
30	line from battery positive terminal (direct)
31	return line from battery negative terminal or ground (direct)
31b	return line to battery negative terminal or ground via switch or relay (switch-controlled ground)

Electric motors
32	return line*
33	main connection*
33a	self-parking switch-off
33b	shunt field
33f	for reduced-RPM operations, speed 2
33g	for reduced-RPM operations, speed 3
33h	for reduced-RPM operations, speed 4
33l	rotation to left (counterclockwise)
33r	rotation to right (clockwise)

*Polarity reversal of 32/32 possible

Starter
45	separate starter relay, output: starter; input: primary current

Terminal definition

Flasher relay (pulse generator)
51	input
49a	output
49b	output to second flasher relay
49c	output to third flasher relay

Battery swticing relay
50a	output for starter control

Start-locking relay
50e	input
50f	output

Start-repeating relay
50g	input
50h	output

AC generator (alternator)
51	DC voltage at rectifier
51e	DC voltage at rectifier with choke coil for daylight operation

Starter
52	starter control (direct)
53	wiper motor, input (+)
53a	wiper (+), end position
53b	wiper (shunt winding)
53c	electric windshield washer pump
53e	wiper (brake winding)
53i	wiper motor with permanent magent and third brush (for higher speed)
55	front fog lamp
56	headlights
56a	high beam with indicator lamp
56b	low beam
56d	headlight flasher contact
57	parking lamps (in some export markets)
57a	parking lamps
57L	parking lamps, left
57R	parking lamps, right

Figure 6.3 Wiring terminal designations

are given connection numbers, but only one number is used to define all the connections to a component. A suffix to the connection code (a letter between A and Z) denotes branches from wires which have the same potential and lead to the same component. For example, a code of 31S-LC3A means:

31	**S**	**LC**	**3**	**A**
Function	*Additional info*	*System*	*Connection*	*Additional info*
Ground	Switched	Courtesy lamps	Switch connection	Branch

Cable rating

Rating of the cable is critical in order to efficiently transfer the power to the electrical consumer with minimal losses. It is also important not to overrate the cable as this increases weight (and hence fuel consumption) of the vehicle as well as increasing manufacturing costs. The cross-sectional area dictates the maximum current permissible, but in addition the cable length contributes to the resistance of the cable. This factor is important when considering voltage drop as long cable runs need to be overrated with respect to cross-section. This is to compensate for volt drop losses due to the length.

For automotive circuits multistrand cable is used and historically this was specified by the number of strands (more strands equal greater cross-sectional area). Generally, each strand has a diameter of 0.3 mm. Table 6.3 shows typical sizes and applications.

Generally, cables are specified in cross-sectional area (mm²). Note that a 14-strand cable is approximately 1 mm². The conversion calculation is shown below:

$$\frac{14 \cdot \pi \cdot 0.3^2}{4} = 0.989 \sim 1\,mm^2$$

In order to specify the correct cable size the current draw of the consumer must be calculated as follows:

$$I = \frac{P}{V_n} \quad \text{or} \quad \frac{V_n}{R}$$

where:

I = Current
P = Power of consumer
V_n = Nominal supply voltage
R = Resistance of consumer.

From this, the ideal cross-sectional area of cable can be derived:

$$A = I \cdot q \cdot \frac{l}{V_{vl}}$$

where:

A = Minimum cross-sectional area of cable required
I = Current drawn by consumer
q = Resistivity of copper ($0.0185\,\Omega\,mm^2/m$)
l = Cable length
V_{vl} = Permissible voltage drop (normally 10% of supply voltage).

Once the ideal cross-section is known, reference must be made to standard cable sizes and the next-highest cable cross-section chosen.

Once the cable size has been chosen, it is advisable to check the actual voltage drop.

$$V_{vl} = I \cdot q \cdot \frac{l}{A}$$

where:

V_{vl} = Actual voltage drop
I = Current drawn
q = Resistivity of copper ($0.0185\,\Omega\,mm^2/m$)
l = Cable length
A = Cross-sectional area of chosen cable.

Also, the current density of the circuit should be checked.

$$S = \frac{I}{A}$$

where:

S = Current density (for short-duty cycles, S must be $<30\,A/mm^2$, in general about $8.5\,A/mm^2$)
I = Current drawn
A = Cross-sectional area of chosen cable.

Printed circuits

A printed circuit board (PCB) is commonly used in applications where there is high component density in a limited space (e.g. electronic control units, fuse boxes, instrument panels). In these applications a more reliable and compact arrangement can be formed with this technique. The material used for a circuit board has an insulated base onto which is bonded a thin layer of copper. After printing the circuit image on the copper, the board is immersed in acid. This removes the unwanted copper and leaves a number of conductors in the shape of the circuit image (see Figure 6.4).

Table 6.3 Cable ratings and applications

Conductor size No. of strands/diam. (mm)	Maximum current rating (ampere)	Application
9/0.30	5.75	Lightly loaded circuits
14/0.30	8.75	Ignition circuits, side and tail lamps, general body wiring
28/0.30	17.5	Headlamps, horns, heated rear windows
65/0.30	35	Ammeter circuit
120/0.30	60	Alternator charging circuit (heavy duty)

Table 6.4 Cable cross-sectional ratings

Nominal wire cross-sectional area mm^2	Approximate number of individual strands	Maximum resistance per metre at $+20^{\circ}$C mΩ/m	Maximum wire diameter mm	Nominal insulation thickness mm	Maximum wire external diameter mm
0.5	16	37.1	1.1	0.6	2.3
0.75	24	24.7	1.3	0.6	2.5
1	32	18.5	1.5	0.6	2.7
1.5	30	12.7	1.8	0.6	3.0
2.5	50	7.60	2.2	0.7	3.6
4	56	4.71	2.8	0.8	4.4
6	84	3.14	3.4	0.8	5.03
10	80	1.82	4.5	1.0	6.5
16	126	1.16	6.3	1.0	8.3
25	196	0.743	7.8	1.3	10.4
35	276	0.527	9.0	1.3	11.6
50	396	0.368	10.5	1.5	13.5
70	360	0.259	12.5	1.5	15.5
95	475	0.196	14.8	1.6	18.0
120	608	0.153	16.5	1.6	19.7

These conductors provide soldered connections for the component parts. In the case of many PCBs, such as instrument panels, the connection interface is via a multi-pole plug and socket. PCBs employed in instrument panels use wafer-thin copper foil which can be easily damaged by excessive current. This should be noted during diagnostic testing – always ensure that appropriate test equipment is used which will not damage the circuit. PCBs used in fuse boxes are a much thicker 'bus bar' type construction (see Figure 6.5) which can handle amps or tens of amps. Connectors, fuse and relay interfaces are soldered directly to the PCB. In this application, the fuse box normally forms the main junction point of the whole vehicle electrical system.

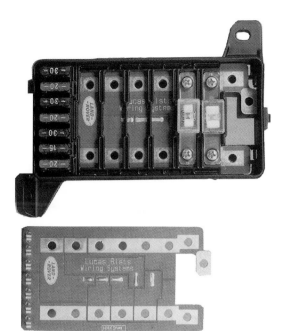

Figure 6.5 PCB fusebox fitted with seven Autofuses and two Pacific fuses (Lucas Rists)

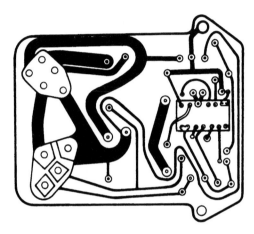

Figure 6.4 Printed circuit board for a wiper control showing copper conductors

- low contact resistance
- high insulation resistance between adjacent conductors
- high resistance to contamination
- easy to assemble
- protection against incorrect connection
- locking capability to prevent accidental disconnection or backing out of terminals.

Correct use of appropriate connectors is essential for the overall reliability of the wiring system. This is particularly important when repair work is carried out. If possible, the same type of connector or terminal used by the manufacturer should be chosen. These are not always easy to source, so if an alternative is used it must be of at least the same quality and have the same performance capability. In addition, it should harmonise with the existing wiring system.

Terminals

Terminals are used as interfaces between components and the wiring system. In the past, fork and eyelet-type terminals have been widely used (see Figure 6.6).

These have been superseded by more sophisticated designs.

Terminals like the one shown in Figure 6.7 are used on engine components (injectors, sensors etc.) and suffer the most arduous conditions. They are completely sealed to prevent dampness entering the contact zone. In addition, they are self-latching and must be unlocked by applying pressure at the correct point. These features provide the highest level of reliability which is essential in the under-bonnet environment.

6.2.2 Wiring system interfaces

Introduction

Terminals and connectors are used as interfaces between different parts of the wiring harness to form junctions or breakout points. In addition, they are used at components to allow disassembly and re-assembly of individual parts. Typically, wiring interfaces have to endure:

- vibration
- temperature extremes
- dampness/humidity
- aggressive liquids and gases
- corrosion.

These effects can cause an increase in contact resistance which in turn causes overheating of the connection and further damage. In worst cases a complete open circuit fault can occur, or short-circuits between neighbouring conductors. A connector system must possess the following attributes:

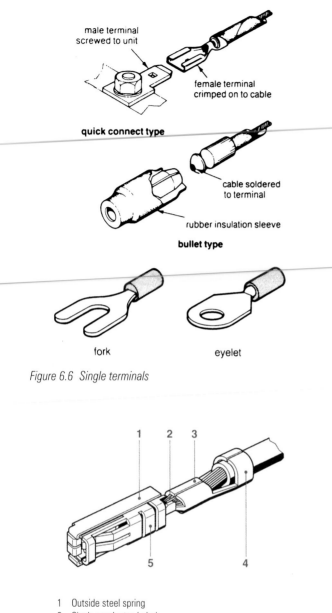

Figure 6.6 Single terminals

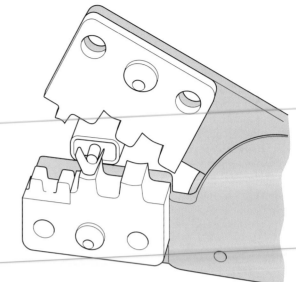

Figure 6.8 Crimping tool

1 Outside steel spring
2 Single conductor (wire)
3 Conductor crimp
4 Insulation crimp
5 Wave-shaped interior design

Figure 6.7 Terminal used in a connector assembly – blade type

During repair work a suitable crimping tool of the correct type must be used to fit terminals to wire ends. The conductors and insulators must be properly clamped and the terminal should be insulated against moisture ingress to prevent corrosion (see Figure 6.8).

Connectors

Connector systems are used to join cable ends together, normally in groups of cables to form junctions. In the past, simple bullet or lucar blade connectors were used (as shown above), but as vehicle electrical systems have become more complex these have been replaced by more sophisticated and reliable connector systems

which employ locking, non-reversible, high-density connector blocks. These normally feature special round pin or flat blade-type terminals (see Figure 6.9).

Many circuits on modern vehicles operate with very low currents (milliamps) and these are susceptible to leakage paths (via damp ingress) and electrolytic and fretting corrosion. Connectors for these circuits must combat these problems and are generally sealed using diaphragm or annular sealing elements. Often terminals used in these applications are gold plated to reduce contact resistance to a minimum. Many vehicle circuits are now safety critical and have to perform consistently over long periods of time, yet they may only be passing very small currents used for diagnostic and plausibility checks (for example airbag systems). This is particularly demanding as failure of a connector could be fatal.

Many of these modern connector systems, although more reliable, will not tolerate incorrect handling

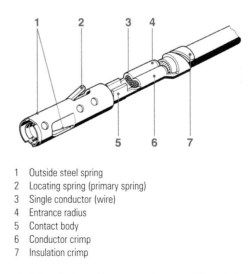

1 Outside steel spring
2 Locating spring (primary spring)
3 Single conductor (wire)
4 Entrance radius
5 Contact body
6 Conductor crimp
7 Insulation crimp

Figure 6.9 Terminal used in a connector assembly – pin type

as well as traditional connector types. They can be damaged easily when 'probing' during fault finding, and the sealing systems employed can be completely ruined by inappropriate treatment. This can create very obscure faults as the resulting water ingress causes the tracking (i.e. unintentional conductivity) across the various low-current circuits which are effectively shorted together. Handling of these connectors during repair or diagnostic work should be undertaken carefully and with appropriate consideration for maintaining the quality of the electrical connection.

Modern connector systems have a variety of features in their design such as positive-mate and anti back-out measures to ensure that the connections are fully and reliably made. They also feature clips to enable their retention to the body and trim as this prevents rattles and reduces strain on the cables and sealing systems. A selection of typical connector types is shown in Figure 6.10.

6.2.3 Circuit protection

Vehicle circuit protection is necessary to prevent damage to the wiring system if a fault should occur that causes excessive current to flow in the circuit (i.e. a short circuit). It essentially forms a 'weak link' which gives way when the circuit current exceeds a design limit, and this prevents overheating of the wiring. Car electrical systems have the potential to generate hundreds of amps from their power sources (alternators and batteries) and it is important that the system is protected from excessive fault currents which could cause a fire. Generally this protection is in the form of fuses, fusible links or circuit breakers:

Fuses

Automotive fuses are available in many different forms and have evolved over the years. In the past, the glass cartridge fuse was commonly used on British-manufactured vehicles (similar in form to mains plug-type fuses (see Figure 6.11)). This basically consists of a short length of tinned wire connected at both ends to metal caps and enclosed in a glass tube. A strip of paper, colour coded and marked with the fuse rating, is placed in the tube adjacent to the wire. When the current through the fuse exceeds the rated limit, the fuse blows (i.e. the wire melts) and the circuit is broken.

The ceramic-type fuse, used in the past on European vehicles, is similar in operation to the glass fuse (see Figure 6.11). The body of the fuse is ceramic and the current conductor is a copper strip formed around the body. Cheaper versions of this fuse are available with plastic bodies, but these should be avoided as they can cause problems in service. If the fuse connection is not tight, heating will occur; this melts the plastic body which deforms and causes an open circuit.

By far the most common type of fuse in use on vehicles today is the blade-type fuse (see Figure 6.12) (also known as the ATO type). These are available in a number of current ratings and can be identified by the colour of their bodies, as shown in Table 6.5.

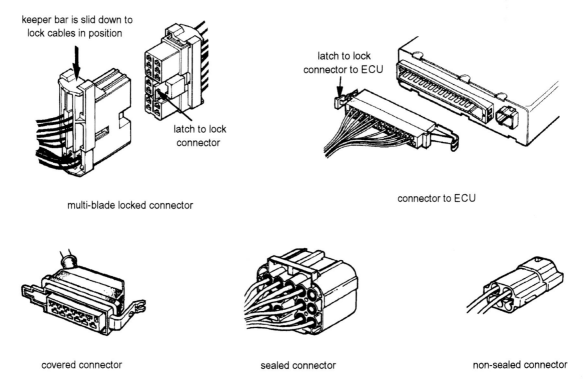

Figure 6.10 Cable connectors – various types in use

Table 6.5 ATO fuse colour code

Colour	Current rating (A)
violet	3
tan	5
brown	7.5
red	10
blue	15
yellow	20
clear	25
green	30

In addition mini and maxi versions of this fuse are available to match more closely specific requirements (see Figure 6.13). These fuses have a favourable performance in service for vehicle wiring systems. Their blowing performance is very consistent and therefore it is not necessary to oversize the cabling. Blade-type fuses can be easily accommodated in a compact fuse or relay box and mounted in the vehicle or under the bonnet with minimum space requirements.

Fuse selection
Generally when a fuse blows there is a circuit fault and this should be investigated. A fuse should always be replaced with one of the same value. The fuse protects the wiring and not the consumers! Therefore, the size of the fuse is appropriate to the wire size. Installing a fuse of higher rating will cause the wiring to overheat if a fault occurs and this could lead to a fire in the vehicle.

Fuses are specified according to their stated rating. This could be the continuous current-carrying capacity or the fusing value. The ratio of these two parameters

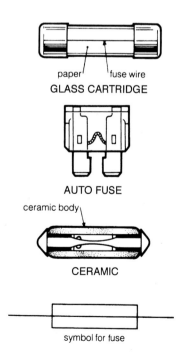

Figure 6.11 Types of fuses

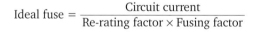

Figure 6.12 Blade-type fuse

is known as the fusing factor. Note that glass cartridge fuses are specified according to their fusing value whereas ceramic fuses have their current-carrying capacity stated. For both of these types of fuse, the fusing factor is approximately 2. For example, an 8 A ceramic fuse will blow at 16 A and a 20 A glass fuse will carry a continuous circuit current of 10 A maximum (without nuisance failure).

Blade-type fuses have superior performance in that their fusing factor is much lower (approximately 1.35 at 25°C) and hence they respond more quickly to an over-current situation. This means that the fuse value can be matched more closely to the circuit current rating and the circuit wire size can be optimised rather than being over-specified. They are rated with maximum circuit current capacity (shown in Table 6.3, page 122).

Another factor to consider is temperature. Fusing action is temperature dependent and the fuse rating must be compensated if high (or low) temperatures occur where the fuse is located. Figure 6.14 shows the temperature re-rating factor to be applied.

For example, a fuse located in an under bonnet fuse box operates at around 60°C. The circuit current is 10 A. The ideal fuse rating can be calculated as follows:

$$\text{Ideal fuse} = \frac{\text{Circuit current}}{\text{Re-rating factor} \times \text{Fusing factor}}$$

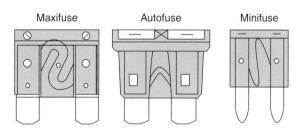

Figure 6.13 Maxifuse, autofuse, minifuse – blade-type fuses

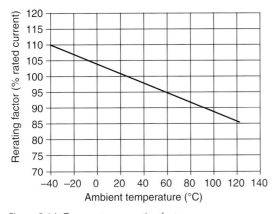

Figure 6.14 Temperature re-rating factor

$$= \frac{10\,\text{A}}{95\% \times 0.75} = 14\,\text{A}$$

In most cases temperature effects can be excluded as fuses are only available in a certain range of sizes, but if temperature extremes are encountered and the ideal fuse rating calculated is available in a standard fuse size then this fuse should be selected.

Fusible links

A common way of protecting main battery circuits is to use a fusible link. These can be in the form of special fusing wires soldered onto cable ends at the battery connection or as cartridge-type elements mounted in specific fuse boxes located near the battery. They form heavy-duty fuses that will rupture in the event of a catastrophic short circuit and this reduces the risk of a fire if an accident causes the main battery cable to short to earth. Figure 6.15 shows the common types.

Cartridge-type elements are most common and have replaced wired fusible links. These are also known as Pacific-type fuses. They are available in sizes up to 120 A. The internal construction is shown in Figure 6.16.

Circuit breakers

Circuit breakers employ a bi-metallic strip to control contacts that carry current in the protected circuit. When a current overload occurs, the strip heats up and bends; this opens the contacts and interrupts the circuit. There are two types of circuit breaker available depending upon the application – the manual reset type and the auto-reset type. The construction of a typical manual re-set type is shown in Figure 6.18.

Figure 6.15 Fusible links

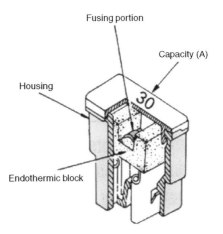

Figure 6.16 Cartridge-type elements

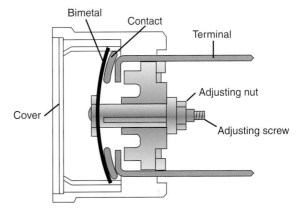

Figure 6.17 Circuit breaker – auto reset type

If a manual circuit breaker trips, it remains an open circuit and it can be re-set by removing it and inserting a small metal rod to snap the bi-metal strip back into the contact closed position. Circuit breakers are commonly placed in the fuse-box inside the vehicle. They are used to protect high-current circuits which have large in-rush currents, for example motor drive circuits (e.g. power windows, power sunroofs, central locking) and heated screens.

Auto-reset or cycling thermal breakers are used commonly in lighting circuits as in this application a short circuit will cause the light to go on and off repeatedly rather than fail completely. Therefore, the driver should be able to bring the vehicle to rest safely. The basic construction is shown in Figure 6.17.

The current overload heats the bi-metal strip which expands and breaks the circuit connection. With no current flowing, the strip cools and contracts back to its original shape which then closes the contacts and reinstates current flow in the circuit, thus re-setting the breaker automatically. This operation repeats at low frequency whilst excess current is flowing in the circuit.

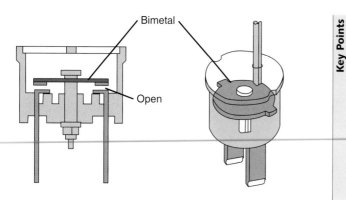

Figure 6.18 Manual-reset circuit breaker

Cables for automotive applications are generally of the PVC insulated multi-strand type. The thickness and number of strands dictates the current-carrying capacity of the cable. It is important that the cable has the required capacity to prevent overheating and excessive volt drop

The individual cables are bundled together to form a harness. Normally the colour of the cable is used to identify its purpose or status. A number of standards are used to define the colours used

Connectors are used as interfaces or junctions, and terminals are used to connect the cables to components. It is important to use the right connector and that it is fitted to the cable properly either by soldering or crimping

In order to protect the wiring from excessive currents due to short-circuit faults, some form of fuse can be fitted. There are a number of different types of circuit protection and it is important that, if replaced, the same current rating is used. Never replace a fuse with one of higher value!

Alternative circuit protection types are circuit breakers or fusible links. Fusible links are generally used to protect high-current circuits if an accident occurs that causes major damage to the wiring harness. Circuit breakers are re-settable and are used on circuits with high in-rush currents (e.g. motor circuits)

6.3 CIRCUIT DIAGRAMS

6.3.1 Introduction

Wiring or circuit diagrams are essential tools when undertaking detailed repairs or fault-finding on vehicle electrical systems. They act as a map for the system so that the route taken by flowing currents to and from components can be seen clearly. This helps considerably in understanding how the system or a component works. In addition they provide information regarding component locations and wiring junctions. The main problem is that, unlike general industrial engineering practice, there is very little standardisation, and hence most manufacturers have their own methodology for creating and presenting wiring diagrams. Therefore, specific manufacturer information must always be sought.

Certain aspects of wiring system technical information follow conventions, for example symbolic representation. Knowledge of these conventions will help when dealing with diagrams which do not conform to standards, as much of the information will be the same. It should also be noted that it will be assumed in any diagram that current flows from left to right and/or from top to bottom.

6.3.2 Wiring diagrams

Symbols

Many of the symbols used in vehicle wiring diagrams conform closely to those laid down by the IEC (International Electrotechnical Committee). They form the smallest element of any wiring diagram and are the simplest way to represent a device or component. They can illustrate clearly how a device operates or how technical sequences are executed. They do not necessarily replicate the design or form of the device they represent. Typical examples of symbols used in automotive wiring diagrams are shown in Tables 6.6 and 6.7.

Block diagrams

These are commonly used to give an uncomplicated overview of a system or sub-system and its function. Usually they do not give details of internal component circuitry and just show the most significant elements. Wiring is usually represented in single pole form. The block diagram can be used as an initial reference point for understanding more detailed wiring diagrams. An example of a Motronic system in block diagram form is shown in Figure 6.19.

Schematic diagrams

Schematic diagrams show the circuit and its components in detail. In addition, they show the current paths and detail of how the circuit operates, often including detail of internal circuitry in component parts. Schematics can be shown in assembled representation, and in this way the mechanical interconnection of parts (switches, relays etc.) is shown by broken or dotted lines. Alternatively, detached representation shows the current paths with

Table 6.6

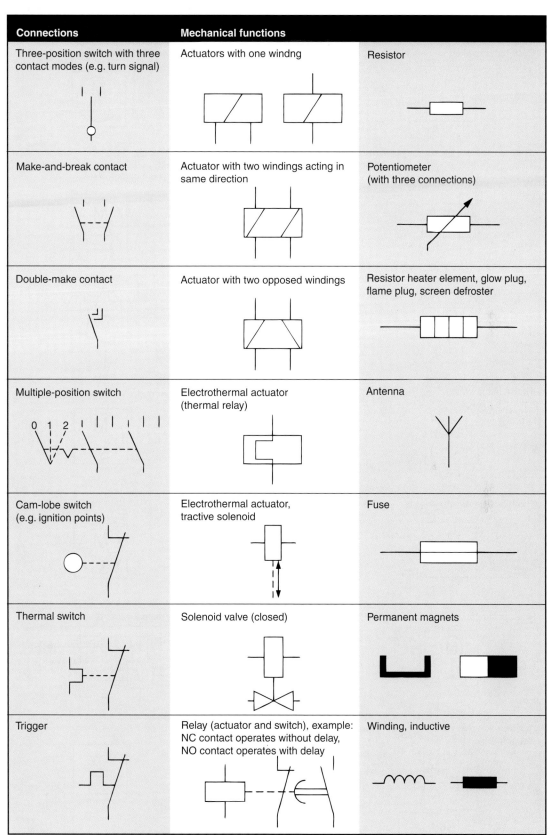

Connections	Mechanical functions	
Three-position switch with three contact modes (e.g. turn signal)	Actuators with one windng	Resistor
Make-and-break contact	Actuator with two windings acting in same direction	Potentiometer (with three connections)
Double-make contact	Actuator with two opposed windings	Resistor heater element, glow plug, flame plug, screen defroster
Multiple-position switch	Electrothermal actuator (thermal relay)	Antenna
Cam-lobe switch (e.g. ignition points)	Electrothermal actuator, tractive solenoid	Fuse
Thermal switch	Solenoid valve (closed)	Permanent magnets
Trigger	Relay (actuator and switch), example: NC contact operates without delay, NO contact operates with delay	Winding, inductive

Table 6.7

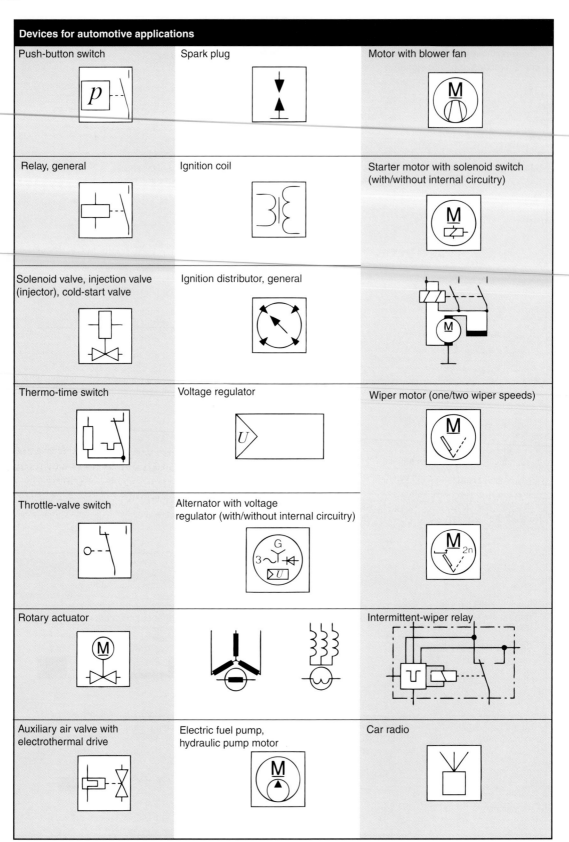

Devices for automotive applications

Push-button switch	Spark plug	Motor with blower fan
Relay, general	Ignition coil	Starter motor with solenoid switch (with/without internal circuitry)
Solenoid valve, injection valve (injector), cold-start valve	Ignition distributor, general	
Thermo-time switch	Voltage regulator	Wiper motor (one/two wiper speeds)
Throttle-valve switch	Alternator with voltage regulator (with/without internal circuitry)	
Rotary actuator		Intermittent-wiper relay
Auxiliary air valve with electrothermal drive	Electric fuel pump, hydraulic pump motor	Car radio

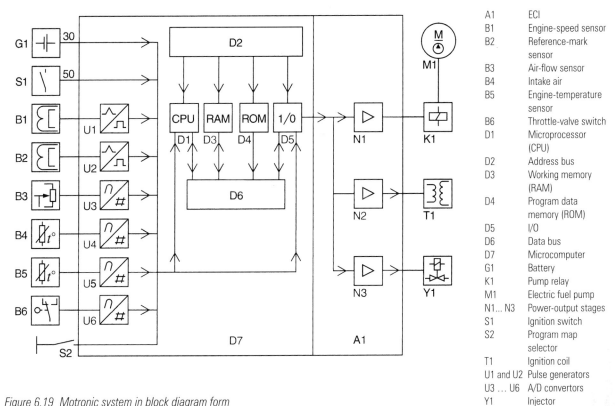

A1	ECI
B1	Engine-speed sensor
B2	Reference-mark sensor
B3	Air-flow sensor
B4	Intake air
B5	Engine-temperature sensor
B6	Throttle-valve switch
D1	Microprocessor (CPU)
D2	Address bus
D3	Working memory (RAM)
D4	Program data memory (ROM)
D5	I/O
D6	Data bus
D7	Microcomputer
G1	Battery
K1	Pump relay
M1	Electric fuel pump
N1... N3	Power-output stages
S1	Ignition switch
S2	Program map selector
T1	Ignition coil
U1 and U2	Pulse generators
U3 ... U6	A/D convertors
Y1	Injector

Figure 6.19 Motronic system in block diagram form

priority given to clarity, and hence the component parts are not shown with their relative orientation or interconnection. The main purpose is to show clearly the function and operation of a circuit or component. An example of detached and assembled representation is shown in Figure 6.20.

Terminal diagrams

Terminal diagrams focus on the terminal designations of components and illustrate this at the connection points. Normally devices are represented by simple shapes with symbolic or pictorial representation of components. At each component the connections are marked with terminal codes which designate the function of the connection (not the wire designation!). This system has been designed to facilitate correct connection of devices and their wiring with an emphasis on repair and installation work. Typical terminal designations are shown in Figure 6.3 on page 121 and conform to a DIN specification (DIN 72 552). Figure 6.21 shows a typical diagram.

Current flow diagrams

Current flow diagrams are widely used by manufacturers and provide a clear overview of the most complex automotive electrical systems, including their numerous interfaces, in a concise, easy-to-understand way. Generally they show supply lines across the top of the page (battery and ignition) and an earth line across the bottom. The

'current flow' for the system or sub-system is depicted using tracks between the supply and earth lines, through the component internal and external circuitry, which is clearly shown on the diagram. Often the position of the track is numbered (similar to line numbers in a page of text) and this allows cross-reference to be made to other positions on the diagram, allowing connections between sub-systems to be highlighted. A typical example for an ABS system is shown in Figure 6.22.

Key Points

Wiring diagrams are extremely helpful in understanding faults. However, it is important that the correct information is available and used. Also, that the type of diagram methodology must be fully understood by the user, as this can vary considerably between manufacturers

Current-flow diagrams are very popular and easy to understand. Block diagrams give a simplistic overview which promotes understanding of a complex system

Schematics show the system, including internal detail of components, in a concise way so that function and operation can be seen clearly. Terminal diagrams focus on the function of the circuit using codes as identifiers

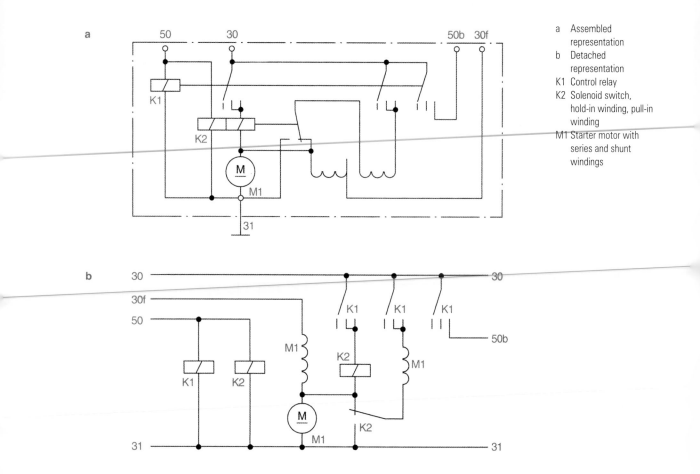

a Assembled
    representation
b Detached
    representation
K1 Control relay
K2 Solenoid switch,
    hold-in winding, pull-in
    winding
M1 Starter motor with
    series and shunt
    windings

Figure 6.20 Schematic of a starter motor (assembled and detached representation)

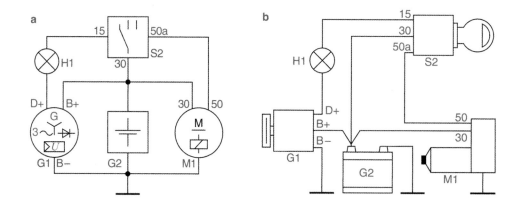

Figure 6.21 Terminal diagrams

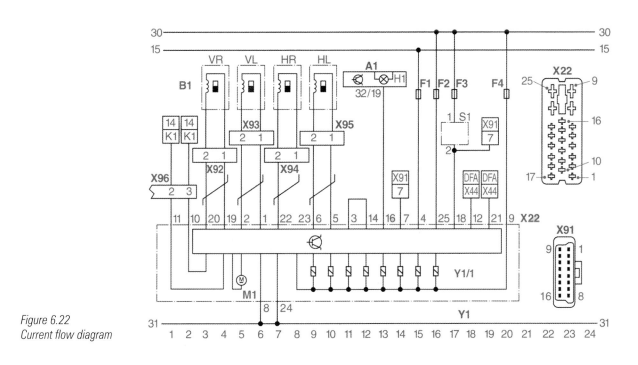

Figure 6.22
Current flow diagram

6.4   VEHICLE NETWORKS AND COMMUNICATION BUSES

6.4.1 Introduction

Vehicle networks have become commonplace in modern automotive electrical and electronic systems for a number of reasons:

- increased requirement for interaction of electronic control systems, to allow sharing of information between intelligent controllers
- to implement the above functionality with cable interfaces and point-to-point connections would mean extra cable and hence extra weight
- increasing requirement for cross-diagnostic and plausibility checking for complex, interacting systems or safety-critical systems (e.g. ABS, ESP)
- system expansion is easier to implement.

As the cost of electronic systems has reduced, this technology has become the most cost effective method for handling the large amount of data required and shared by modern vehicle control systems. The introduction of automotive-compatible serial data networks has expanded the capabilities for intelligent data transfer and sharing and is a logical development for modern vehicles.

Figure 6.23 shows the advantages of implementing a bus communication system in-vehicle. The reduced number of connections is clear.

Bus systems for different applications require different data transmission rate capability (also known as bandwidth). It is very common to see several networks on the same vehicle running at different speeds appropriate for the application. A number of typical groups are implemented with different performance requirements:

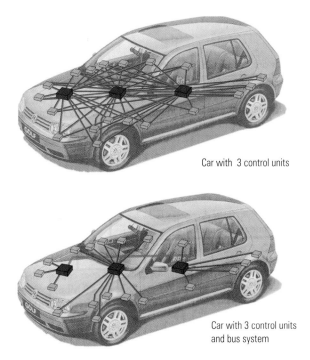

Car with 3 control units

Car with 3 control units
and bus system

Figure 6.23 Comparison showing increased complexity with point-to-point connection compared to a bus-based system for sharing data

- Entertainment/multimedia: mobile communications, radio, navigation.
- Body and convenience: lighting, HVAC, door locks, mirrors, etc.

- Powertrain: powertrain control, vehicle dynamic control, driver safety systems.

Figure 6.24 shows the typical speeds available at the time of publishing.

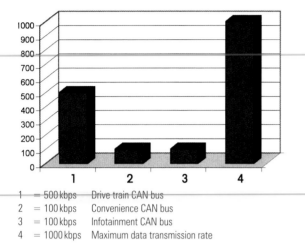

```
1 = 500 kbps    Drive train CAN bus
2 = 100 kbps    Convenience CAN bus
3 = 100 kbps    Infotainment CAN bus
4 = 1000 kbps   Maximum data transmission rate
```

Figure 6.24 Data transmission rates on the CAN bus system

6.4.2 Current technology

The most widely adopted vehicle network technology was developed by Bosch and is known as CAN (controller area network). This technology has established itself as the standard for vehicle manufacturers. However, it should be noted that there are a number of other network technologies available and under development.

CAN

The basic principle of the CAN bus is that individual modules (electronic control units or ECUs) are connected in parallel to the bus system. Each point of connection to the bus is known as a node and all of the connected nodes have equal priority. This means that all messages on the bus are available to all of the ECUs (i.e. nodes) at the same time. This is known as a multi-master system. The advantage of this method is that failure of one node does not impair bus-system access for the other connected nodes and this increases the overall reliability of the system. In addition, the system is designed with a high degree of inbuilt safety with respect to error checking and handling of transmitted data.

Figure 6.25 shows a typical system incorporating multiple networks. A basic system overview and operation are discussed below.

The basic principle is shown in Figure 6.26. Each control unit is connected to the bus, in parallel, by transceiver modules. The transceiver is a transmitter and receiver amplifier. It converts serial data into electrical signals on the bus (and vice versa). For clarity, a single CAN line is shown, but generally the signal is transmitted over a differential line as this provides superior electrical interference rejection.

The information is transmitted as electronic messages and each control unit can send and receive them via

the transceiver. A typical message would be a physical value, for example engine speed. This is converted into a binary number and then transmitted electrically as a serial bit stream on the CAN data bus as 1s and 0s (see Figure 6.27). All the other control units on the bus receive this data and can convert the bit stream back into a message ready for processing by the ECU.

Between the transceiver and ECU, the CAN module controls the data transfer process for the CAN messages to and from the ECU. It is divided into two sections – send and receive. The CAN module transmits data to the ECU via mailboxes (i.e. memory locations) which have read/write access to and from the ECU processor.

The CAN data bus can be in one of two states representing 1 or 0. The transceiver is connected to the bus line via an open collector as shown in Figure 6.28.

This results in two possible states on the bus line:

- transistor 'open circuit': high state via resistor, bus level high (logic 1)
- transistor 'closed circuit': low state, resistor shorted, bus level low (logic 0).

These are known as recessive and dominant states.

Consider three transceivers connected on a bus line (see Figure 6.29). It is clear that if any switch is closed, the bus line becomes status 0/status 1; if all switches are open, the bus line becomes status 1. Also, if the bus is in state 1 any node can overwrite this state to 0. This shows how the multi-master or broadcast system works, but there are some things to consider with this method:

- What if two control units send at the same time?
- What about fault handling?

In order to understand it more clearly, we will consider the send and receive process in more detail.

Data transmission

The following example looks at the transmission of engine ECU data to the dash panel insert (see Figure 6.31):

- First the engine ECU gets the required data value. This value is stored in the ECU microprocessor memory ready for transmission.
- This data is then passed to the transmit mailbox of the CAN module. An electronic 'flag' is then raised to indicate that data is ready for transmission.
- The data is converted into a message in the correct format for transmission according to the CAN protocol (see Figure 6.30). The main components of this protocol included in the message are:
  - identifier: states what the message data is
  - message content: actual data value
  - checksum: method or error protection
  - acknowledge: message acknowledgement.
  In addition:
  - other: start and end of frame messages, control message (size of data field).
- CAN module checks that the bus is active and if necessary waits until it is free. When the bus is free, the data is transmitted by the transceiver.

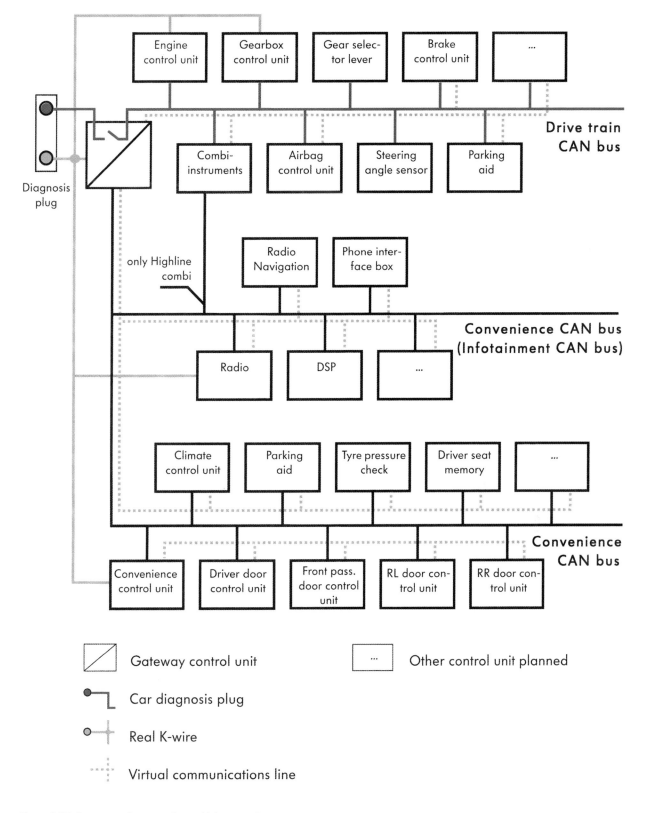

Figure 6.25 Bus system incorporating multiple networks

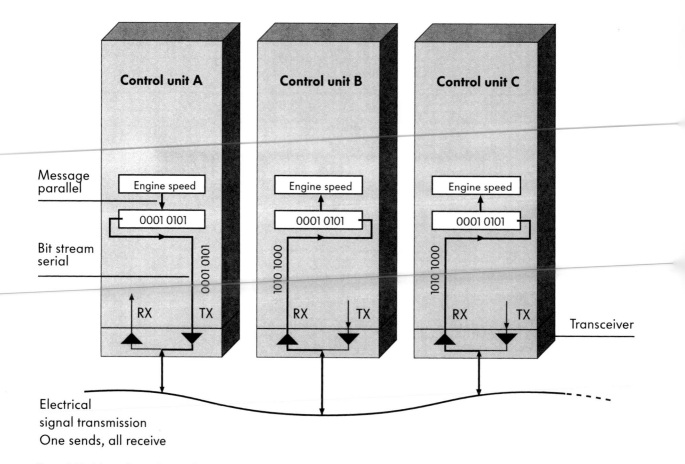

Figure 6.26 Information exchange of a message on the CAN bus

Figure 6.27 Electrical signal transmission in chronological sequence

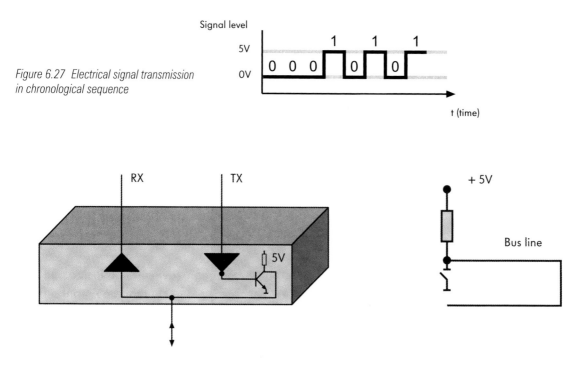

Figure 6.28 Transceiver unit – open collector

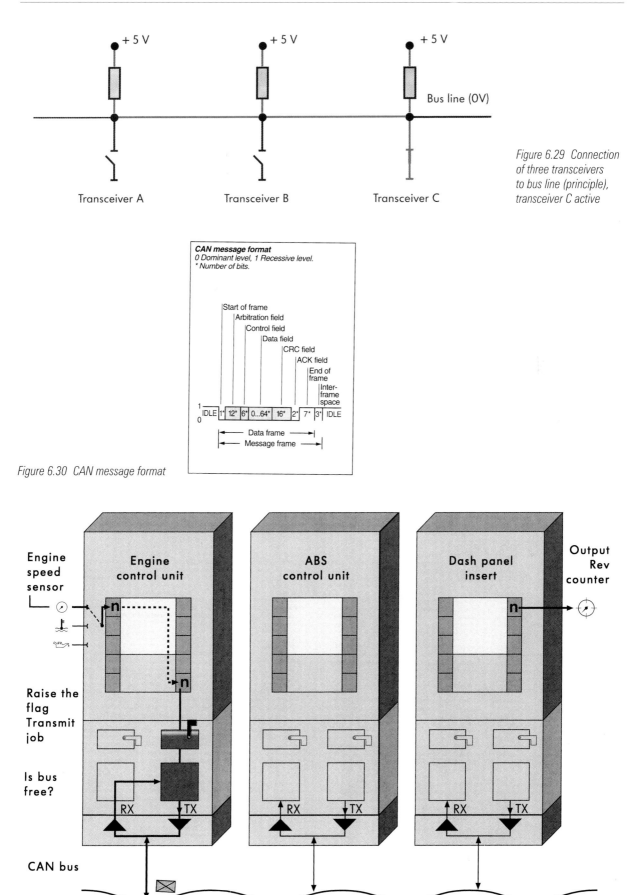

Figure 6.29 Connection
of three transceivers
to bus line (principle),
transceiver C active

CAN message format
0 Dominant level, 1 Recessive level.
* Number of bits.

Figure 6.30 CAN message format

Figure 6.31 CAN bus – data transmission

Data receive

All nodes on the CAN bus receive the transmitted data at their transceivers (see Figure 6.32). First the data is checked for errors and usability. This helps to detect local faults but still allows high data throughput on the bus. Using the checksum part of the protocol (CRC (cyclic redundancy check)) transmission faults can be detected. If no errors are found, an acknowledgement is sent to the transmitter confirming reception of the data intact. The message is then processed in the CAN module and a decision is made as to whether that message is relevant to that control unit (or node). If it is relevant, the message is placed in the receive mailbox, otherwise it is discarded. When the receive flag is raised, the ECU microprocessor knows new information has arrived. This data is then copied into the input memory of the microprocessor ready for use. Data exchange is repeated cyclically according to the cycle time setting.

Error handling

If several control units transmit data at once, there could be collision on the bus. This is avoided by using bus arbitration with the following strategy. Every node starts its transmission by sending an identifier and all the nodes monitor the bus traffic. The identifier sets the priority of the message and the message with the highest priority is assigned first access to the bus without delay. Transceivers respond to failure to gain bus access by automatically switching into receive mode; they then repeat the transmission attempt as soon as the bus is free.

The CAN protocol has an extensive error management system capable of detecting transmission errors with a high degree of certainty. Any node detecting an error can inform the other nodes via transmission of an error frame and the message can then be rejected by all nodes. Following this, an automatic retransmission is executed and these are monitored. If these become frequent, a control unit can be automatically switched off to prevent bus traffic being impaired.

LIN

This is an acronym for local interconnect network, which is a technology that has been proposed and developed by a consortium of manufacturers including Audi, Daimler-Chrysler, Volkswagen and Volvo. It is a low-cost alternative to CAN where high bandwidth is not required (for example comfort and convenience functions like window lift, central locking etc.). The main difference between LIN and CAN is that bus access in a LIN network is controlled by a master node so that no arbitration or data collision management in the slave nodes is required. Note that LIN is implemented as a sub-bus and as such fully integrates with a vehicle CAN network (see Figure 6.33). LIN is a complementary bus system and is not designed as a replacement for CAN. Its main application is where the throughput capability and versatility of CAN is not required.

LIN bus is generally implemented as a single-wire serial communications protocol using simple UART (universal asynchronous receiver transmitter) hardware (which is available on most microcontrollers as standard).

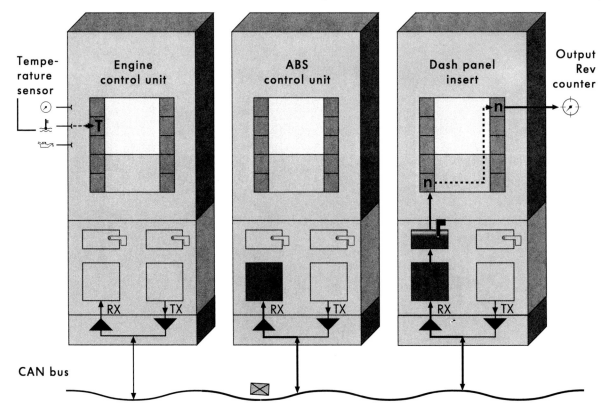

Figure 6.32 CAN bus – data receive

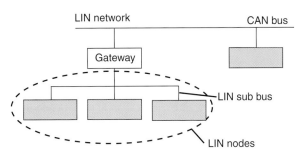

Figure 6.33 LIN

A particular feature is the self-synchronisation in the slave nodes without crystal or ceramic oscillators. These two factors together significantly reduce the cost of the electronic hardware needed for interfacing to the bus.

The specification of the line driver and receiver follows the ISO 9141 single-wire standard (with some enhancements). The maximum transmission speed is limited to 20 Kbps due to the requirements for electromagnetic compatibility (EMC) and clock synchronisation. A node in a LIN network does not make use of any information about the system configuration, except for identification of the master node. Nodes can be added to the LIN network without requiring hardware or software changes in other slave nodes. The size of a LIN network is typically less than 12 nodes (though not restricted to this), resulting from the fact that only 64 identifiers are available and also the relatively low transmission speed.

The typical applications for LIN are shown in Figure 6.34.

6.4.3 New developments

Due to the rapid developments in automotive technology, faster, near real-time performance capability for data transmission networks will be essential (for example drive or brake-by-wire systems). New bus systems are being developed and proposed for these applications. The leading technology is FlexRay which has already

been implemented in production (to an extent on the suspension control of the BMW X5). This technology has been developed by a consortium including Volkswagen, BMW, Daimler-Chrysler, General Motors and Bosch.

FlexRay

FlexRay has been designed to support the high-bandwidth needs of current and future in-car control applications. At the core of the system is the communications protocol. The protocol provides flexibility and performance and has the following features:

- time- and event-triggered communication schemes allowing deterministic, real-time performance of the data bus
- high error detection and error diagnosis capability
- sophisticated power down and wake-up mechanisms
- flexible extendibility and full scalability to enable upgrades
- collision-free bus access
- guaranteed message latency
- message oriented addressing via identifiers
- scalable system fault-tolerance via the support of either single or dual channels.

A hardware layer incorporating an independent bus monitoring feature provides further support for error management. The FlexRay system is targeted to support data rates of up to 10 Mbps with a gross of up to 20 Mbps possible. The system consists of a bus network and processors (ECU, electronic control units) similar to the CAN bus system. Each ECU has an independent clock and these are resynchronised frequently in order to guarantee high performance. The FlexRay network provides scalable fault tolerance by allowing single or dual-channel communication. For security-critical applications, the devices connected to the bus may use both channels for transferring data. However, it is also possible to connect only one channel when redundancy is not needed, or to increase the bandwidth by using both channels for transferring non-redundant data. Within the hardware layer, the FlexRay protocol provides fast error detection and signalling as well as

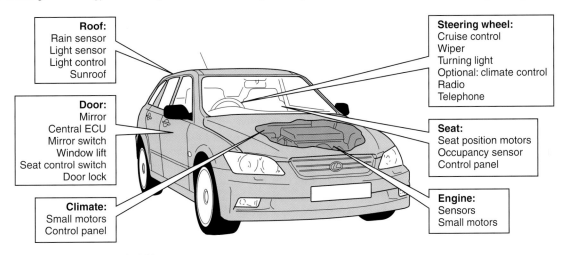

Figure 6.34 Typical applications for LIN

error management via an independent bus guardian which monitors traffic on the data bus for errors.

Why FlexRay and not CAN?

The main benefits of FlexRay are:

- it provides up to 10 Mbps data rate on two channels, or a gross data rate of up to 20 Mbps
- it significantly increases frame length (compared to CAN – 8 bytes per frame)
- synchronous and asynchronous data transfer is possible
- guaranteed data throughput performance during synchronous transfer (deterministic, real-time performance)
- it provides prioritisation of messages during asynchronous transfer
- it provides fault-tolerant clock synchronisation via a global time base
- it has error detection and signalling capability
- it enables error containment on the physical layer through the use of an independent bus guardian mechanism
- it provides scalable fault-tolerance through single or dual channel communication.

FlexRay has been specifically developed to support future requirements in the industry and it will become

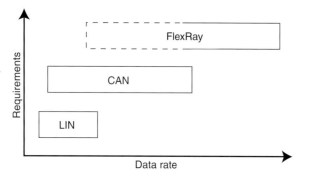

Figure 6.35 Relative performance comparison of bus systems

commonplace in the high-performance control systems mentioned above. In addition, FlexRay has the performance to support active and passive safety systems, collision avoidance and driver assistance systems.

Key Points

Vehicle networking allows sharing of data and the consequent reduction in cabling and complexity. This technology is essential in order to reduce the amount of cables in a modern vehicle to a manageable level with respect to cost and weight. It has now been adopted by most manufacturers in most models currently on the market

The most commonly used in-vehicle network technology is CAN. This was invented by Bosch

In order to cope with the amount of data, modern vehicles normally have more than one bus network. Each one runs at a different data transfer speed according to the requirements of the components connected to that bus. This reduces the load and hence increases the response time for critical components such as powertrain or dynamic safety systems

The buses are connected together at one point called a gateway. This allows a single access point for diagnostics

Other network technology seen in current vehicles is LIN. This is a lower-performance bus system suitable for body components such as door control systems (windows, mirrors etc.) It is cheaper to implement than CAN but is fully compatible with it

New technology that will be implemented in the future is FlexRay. This is a high-performance bus for safety-critical systems that need a high degree of performance and reliability. It has been specifically developed for X-by-wire systems (where X = brake, steering, drive, etc.)

6.5 **FUTURE DEVELOPMENTS IN VEHICLE POWER DISTRIBUTION AND NETWORK SYSTEMS**

The adoption of hybrid drive systems will have the biggest impact on future developments. We have mentioned these before with respect to the effect they will have on the design of traditional engine starting, power generation and battery systems. The adoption of this technology in mainstream production vehicles will be inevitable (if not essential) to achieve targets set by future emissions legislation. It will not only change the shape of all the above-mentioned sub-components, it will also alter the way that they interact with each other.

For the wiring and communication system, a major deviation from the current norm will be the adoption of higher-voltage power networks. This will be absolutely necessary in order to be able to store and provide the large amounts of power needed for vehicle traction in hybrid-drive powertrains. In addition, the power requirements of current and future vehicles will increase as an ever-growing number of comfort and control-related consumers are fitted. This is a trend which has been clearly demonstrated in the industry over the years. Higher power at 12 volts means more current and this leads to heavier, more expensive cables as well as lower efficiency in transferring this power.

Over the last few years, 42 volt systems have been discussed, and it is likely that this standard will be adopted in the future but initially in a complementary form. It is not likely that the 12 volt system will be replaced immediately, but it is likely that vehicle systems will use two power supply networks (see Figure 6.36), both of which will be controlled by a single energy management system. This system will coordinate the operation and function of the system components (ISG, batteries, converters and inverters), to optimise operation and control of the power supply system in such a way as to improve efficiency and cope effectively with peak demands. It is thought that the 42 volt system will become the standard once manufacturers of components in the industry adapt to it.

The latest generation of vehicle communication networks have been discussed above, and these have been and will be an important part of the development of future systems. However, these systems have high demands with respect to safety-critical operation, and in this respect the automotive industry is cautious and will only adopt this technology when it is well proven. The change and developments in these systems becomes less frequent over time, but the adoption of the technology in current vehicles and the advantages that this can bring is now well accepted by all manufacturers. The interaction of vehicle control systems via data buses is essential to achieve the overall performance required to fulfil customer/driver expectations. The harmonised operation of sub-systems and components becomes more critical with a sophisticated hybrid-drive powertrain (see Figure 6.37) and this presents the main challenge for vehicle communication networks in the future.

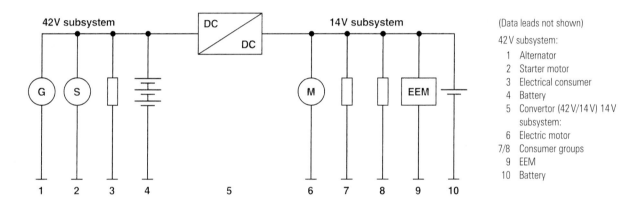

(Data leads not shown)

42 V subsystem:
1 Alternator
2 Starter motor
3 Electrical consumer
4 Battery
5 Convertor (42 V/14 V) 14 V subsystem:
6 Electric motor
7/8 Consumer groups
9 EEM
10 Battery

Figure 6.36 System architecture with 14 and 42 volt systems

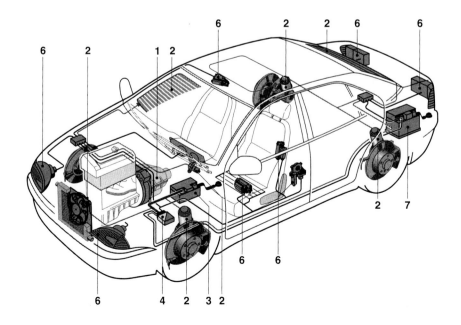

(Data leads not shown)

42 V subsystem:
1 Starter alternator
2 Consumer groups (42 V)
3 Battery
4 EEM with integral convertor (42/14 V)

14 V subsystem:
5 Electric motor
6 Consumer groups (4 V)
7 Battery

Figure 6.37 Hybrid drive with ISG and 14/42 volt power network

Chapter 7

COMFORT AND CONTROL SYSTEMS

what is covered in this chapter . . .

- ■ Heating, ventilation and air conditioning (HVAC)
- ■ Engine cooling
- ■ Vehicle closure and security
- ■ Driver comfort and assistance

7.1   HEATING, VENTILATION AND AIR CONDITIONING (HVAC)

These systems are integrated into the vehicle electronic control environment to automate minor adjustment processes, thus relieving the driver of these repetitive tasks. This reduces the possibility of driver fatigue and ensures that the driver can concentrate on the task of driving the vehicle. Some systems are designed to maintain the driver's environment at an optimum state; others help them and make their task of controlling the vehicle easier and more pleasurable. The main aim of these systems is to provide the driver with an environment of minimal stress.

7.1.1 Introduction

Several interior environment control systems, with different levels of sophistication, are employed in modern vehicles and these control air flow and temperature in the passenger compartment. This is necessary for a number of specific reasons:

- To maintain a comfortable temperature inside the vehicle according to the driver's requirements or preferences irrespective of the outside temperature. This helps to prevent driver fatigue and maintains alertness.
- To help maintain good visibility through all of the windows by way of an appropriate rate of air throughput inside the vehicle. This prevents the build-up of damp, humid air which could cause condensation on the inner surface of the windows.
- To clean incoming cabin air and remove dust, pollen and odours for maximum passenger comfort.

The optimum temperature for the driver is 20–22°C. Strong sunlight can increase the temperature inside the vehicle by up to 15°C above ambient, particularly at face level. This is the area where the effect of excessive heat is most dangerous and studies have shown that elevated temperatures from 25°C to 35°C can reduce sensory perception and reasoning by up to 20 per cent.

A comfortable interior temperature depends on the ambient temperature and the air flow inside the vehicle (which is in turn affected by vehicle speed). Table 7.1 outlines some typical temperature and flow scenarios that are encountered by the heating and ventilation system in the vehicle:

Table 7.1 Typical temperature and flow scenarios

	Low ambient temp. –10 °C	Moderate ambient temp. 10 °C	High ambient temp. 35 °C
Air flow rate (kg/min)	8	4	10
Required interior temp.	28 °C	22 °C	22 °C

Effective performance of the vehicle heating, ventilation and air conditioning (HVAC) system is essential for the comfort of the occupants of the vehicle. In addition, the performance and efficiency of this system can have a considerable impact on safety. If the system is not designed effectively or does not work efficiently there will be a detrimental impact on the levels of concentration that the driver can maintain.

7.1.2 Basic heating and ventilation system

A basic heater/ventilation system uses a centrifugal-type fan driven by a simple DC motor to boost the air flow through the vehicle interior. A heater unit connected to the engine coolant circuit is used to provide a heating source. A typical fan arrangement is shown in Figure 7.1.

Variable motor speeds are required and this is achieved by changing the applied voltage at the motor. This is commonly done using a simple resistor network (often the resistors are fitted into the air stream to cool them) or, alternatively, an electronic voltage controller. A typical control circuit is shown in Figure 7.2. This provides three fan speeds. Moving the switch through the three positions shorts out a resistor at each stage and steps up the applied voltage.

The temperature of the air coming into the vehicle is controlled either by mixing hot and cold air or by controlling the flow of coolant through the heat

exchanger in the heater unit. Note that this basic system is discussed in more detail in *FMVT: Book 1*. Figure 7.3 shows such a system.

This type of system was fitted for many years but has a number of disadvantages:

- temperature control has to be performed manually by the driver; this is a distraction for the driver and therefore reduces concentration and safety
- it is impossible to manually maintain the ideal temperature in the vehicle whilst driving due to the number of continuously changing variables that affect it
- air flow through the vehicle is a function of vehicle speed and fixed-speed fans, even if manipulated manually, cannot maintain the ideal throughput rate.

For the above reasons, the basic heating system designs are less common and they are normally only fitted to low-budget vehicles. Most vehicles from mid-range up are fitted with more sophisticated interior environment control systems.

7.1.3 Electronic controlled heating systems

As mentioned, the interior temperature of the vehicle is affected by ambient temperature and vehicle speed. Without automatic control, manual readjustment of the heater controls is needed. Alternatively, an electronic control system can adjust the operation of the heating system components to achieve the ideal temperature inside the vehicle. This can be done by measuring certain values like ambient temperature, interior temperature, vehicle speed etc. and using these values

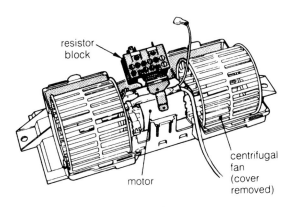

Figure 7.1 Heating and ventilation fan

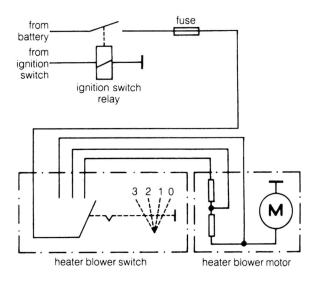

Figure 7.2 Control circuit for three-speed operation of a heating and ventilation fan

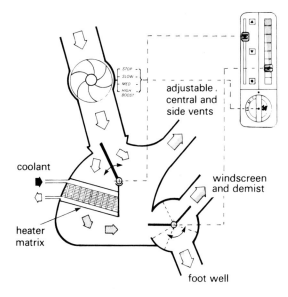

Figure 7.3 Heating and ventilation system

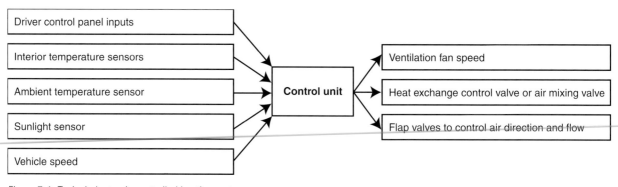

Figure 7.4 Typical electronic controlled heating system components and interactions

to adjust the operation of the system components in a closed-loop control system (see Chapter 2 for an explanation of control systems). An overview of the typical system components and interactions is shown in Figure 7.4.

Sensors in the vehicle monitor the temperature of the cabin via a small sampling system which takes measurements from the cabin air at strategic points. In addition there are sensors which detect sunlight shining into the vehicle. The driver has an input panel to select the desired air temperature and flow. In addition the system accounts for vehicle speed as this has an effect on air flow through the vehicle. By measuring the actual air temperature in the cabin, this can be compared with the driver input. Any deviation is used as an error signal which is applied to the control system which then makes the necessary adjustments on the actuators used in the system.

Typically for temperature control a PWM (pulse width modulated) solenoid valve is used to control the flow of hot coolant into the heat exchanger used for heating the interior air. The adjustments in the open/close ratio in the cycle periods regulate the flow from zero to maximum. For the air flow control, an electric servomotor gear unit is employed for adjusting cool/warm air distribution flaps. It is also possible to have independent left- and right-hand side control.

The limitation of this system is that it is not possible to cool the air. Therefore the application of such a system is limited in overall functionality. It is generally confined to the low–medium market sector cars or low-price vehicles. In many cases, particularly mid-range cars upwards, air conditioning is now fitted as standard.

7.1.4 Air conditioning/climate control

Introduction

As mentioned, even with sophisticated control the heater system is not capable of maintaining a comfortable cabin temperature unless it also has the capability to cool the incoming air. In many countries the ambient

temperature can be much higher than 20°C for most of the year and under these conditions the air must be cooled to maintain the required ideal environmental conditions in the vehicle. Cooling the air also reduces its humidity and cleans it and these factors are just as important as the reduction in temperature.

The basic principle of the refrigerator part of the air conditioning system is covered in detail in *FMVT: Book 1*. It involves the application of the basic laws of thermodynamics. Note the following points with respect to an air conditioning system:

- heat is a form of energy whereas temperature is the perception of the relative 'hotness' or 'coldness' of a body
- in order for heat to be transferred a temperature difference must exist
- the boiling point of a fluid (i.e. the point at which it changes from liquid to a gas state) depends upon the pressure.

In order to reduce the air temperature in the vehicle, the heat must be absorbed at low temperature (inside the vehicle) and at high temperature rejected (outside the vehicle). This can be achieved by using the change of state of a fluid at different pressures in a system, to absorb or reject heat at higher or lower temperatures. The basic air conditioning system uses two heat exchangers, one inside the car to absorb heat (the evaporator) and one outside to reject heat (the condenser). The working fluid circulates between these driven via a pump/compressor. This raises the pressure of the fluid and hence its boiling point for heat rejection. Once the heat has been rejected in the condenser, the fluid is allowed to expand at low pressure after passing through an expansion valve and into the evaporator. Here the fluid absorbs heat from the air, thus cooling it. The fluid then returns to the compressor to restart the cycle. In order for the system to operate, energy must be input and this is mechanical energy from the engine used to drive the compressor. This can be a considerable additional load. A simplified system overview is shown in Figure 7.5.

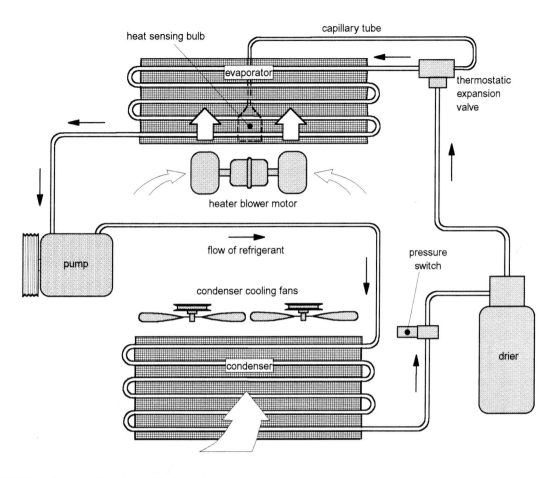

Figure 7.5 Schematic layout of an air conditioning system

Control system – climate control

The basic air conditioning system forms a switchable chiller/refrigerator unit to cool incoming air. The only additional control elements are air temperature sensors to detect/prevent ice formation on the evaporator. In addition there are pressure sensors to ensure that the refrigerant fluid pressure is correct for proper operation. If not, the compressor is disabled and the system becomes inoperative. Engagement of the compressor is done via an electric clutch. All of the sensors are connected to an ECU which controls the function and operation of the air conditioning system.

A further step forward from this is climate control. This system is a complete HVAC system for the vehicle. All environment control functions are completely integrated in its operation in order to provide the ideal driving environment at all times with minimal driver intervention. This is clearly an important safety feature in addition to additional comfort provided for the driver.

Such a system needs a large number of inputs and outputs (sensors and actuators) in order to be able to control the environment in the vehicle to the required tolerance taking into account the external factors of:

- vehicle speed
- ambient temperature and humidity
- sunlight.

An overview of a typical electronically controlled HVAC system is shown in Figure 7.6.

The system is controlled via an ECU which controls outputs to actuators, monitors the status and gives feedback via various sensors. It is a closed-loop system in order to maintain accurate control of the vehicle interior conditions.

The sensors in the system are as follows.

Sunlight sensor

Using a photo-optical element this sensor detects the intensity of the sunlight. The ECU then adjusts the air flow accordingly to compensate.

Temperature sensors

Usually these are thermistors, mounted in:

- the dash
- the blower air stream
- outside (ambient) air
- the air intake duct
- the foot wells
- the engine coolant
- the radiator fan switch.

System overview of an electronically controlled air conditioner
(the temperature is regulated evenly at the left- and right-hand sides of the passenger cabin as shown)

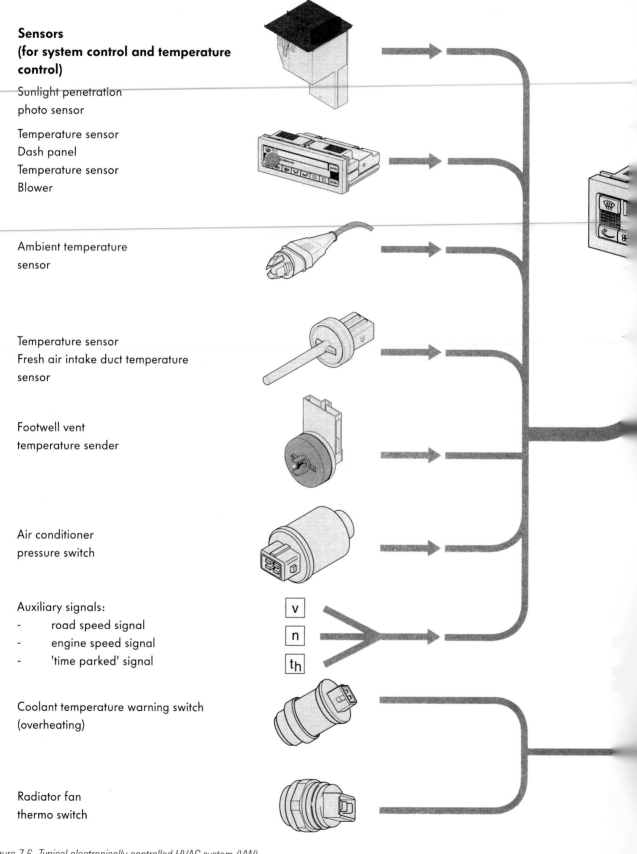

**Sensors
(for system control and temperature control)**

Sunlight penetration
photo sensor

Temperature sensor
Dash panel
Temperature sensor
Blower

Ambient temperature
sensor

Temperature sensor
Fresh air intake duct temperature
sensor

Footwell vent
temperature sender

Air conditioner
pressure switch

Auxiliary signals:
- road speed signal
- engine speed signal
- 'time parked' signal

Coolant temperature warning switch
(overheating)

Radiator fan
fan thermo switch

Figure 7.6 Typical electronically controlled HVAC system (VW)

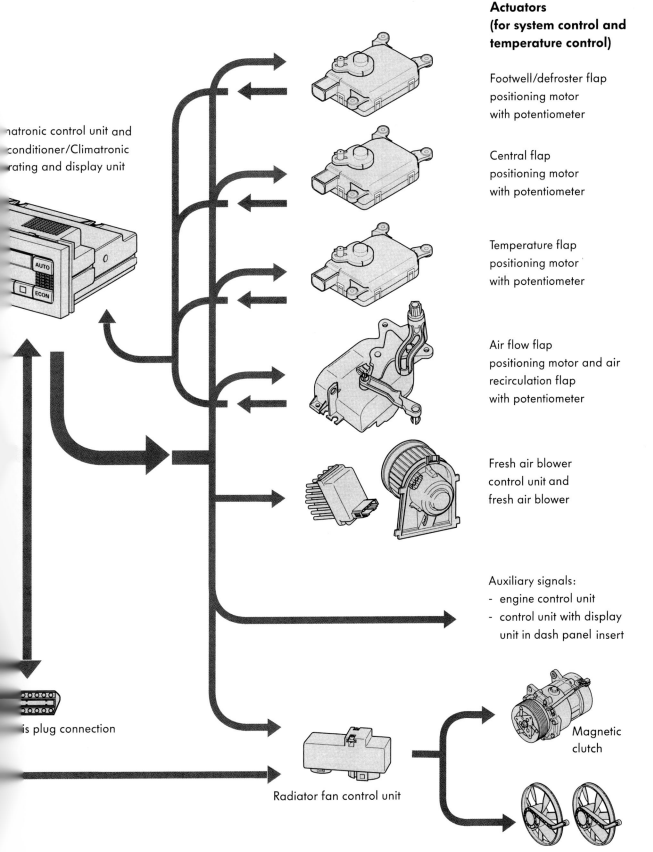

**Actuators
(for system control and
temperature control)**

Footwell/defroster flap
positioning motor
with potentiometer

Central flap
positioning motor
with potentiometer

Temperature flap
positioning motor
with potentiometer

Air flow flap
positioning motor and air
recirculation flap
with potentiometer

Fresh air blower
control unit and
fresh air blower

Auxiliary signals:
- engine control unit
- control unit with display
  unit in dash panel insert

natronic control unit and
conditioner/Climatronic
rating and display unit

AUTO

ECON

is plug connection

Radiator fan control unit

Magnetic
clutch

Radiator fan, right and
auxiliary fan

Pressure switches

Mounted in the refrigerant circuit, these monitor the system pressure to ensure that, during under- or over-pressure situations, the compressor is disabled. In addition, they are used to indicate the additional load imposed on the engine by the air conditioning compressor when the air conditioning is active. This information is used to adjust the operation of the engine cooling fans accordingly. Certain systems use dual-pressure switches known as high-/low-pressure switches so that the compressor operation is cut if the pressure is too high. It is also cut if pressure is too low such as in the case of a refrigerant leak.

Additional signals

The following are also monitored by the AC control system:

- vehicle speed
- engine speed
- vehicle stationary (parked) timer
- air quality
- driver input panel.

The actuators in the system consist of:

- various servomotors for positioning flaps to direct air flow in the system
- a heater blower motor with variable speed controller
- a compressor clutch
- radiator and condenser fans.

Operation

The main interface for the driver to set the required conditions in the vehicle interior is via the dash-mounted control panel. A typical example is shown in Figure 7.7.

Once the driver has set the required temperature, the climate control ECU regulates the mix of hot and cold air to maintain the target temperature irrespective of the external conditions. A considerable advantage is that the ECU has far more signal inputs than a simple heater control system and hence more parameters can be monitored by the control system. Thus, it can calculate in advance the thermal result of any manual inputs from the driver. The ECU controls heating and cooling via water-control valves and AC compressor operation. It also monitors the system status to ensure that the correct prerequisite pressures and temperatures of the system are in place before activating

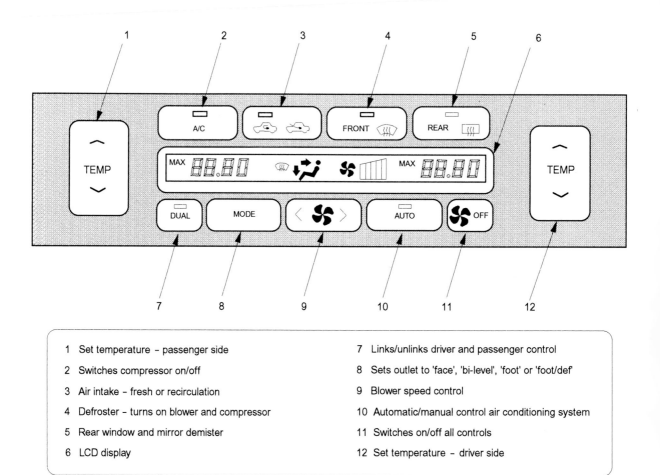

1 Set temperature – passenger side	7 Links/unlinks driver and passenger control
2 Switches compressor on/off	8 Sets outlet to 'face', 'bi-level', 'foot' or 'foot/def'
3 Air intake – fresh or recirculation	9 Blower speed control
4 Defroster – turns on blower and compressor	10 Automatic/manual control air conditioning system
5 Rear window and mirror demister	11 Switches on/off all controls
6 LCD display	12 Set temperature – driver side

Figure 7.7 Control panel for climate control

the system and during operation. An overview of the system is shown in Figure 7.8.

Many climate control systems are linked to other control units via the CAN bus. This allows the extra information such as road speed and engine speed to be monitored easily. This bi-directional communication is also used to optimise and integrate the operation of the system harmoniously within the vehicle. For example, under full load, the AC compressor can be switched off to prevent parasitic losses during acceleration and thus optimise performance and drivability. (When engine power is used to drive the compressor (or other auxiliary consumer or load) when it is not really needed, this is called a parasitic loss.)

Key Points

The correct environmental conditions inside the vehicle are essential to ensure driver alertness. A basic heater system needs constant readjustment by the driver in order to maintain the optimum temperature and air flow through the vehicle

Key Points

Electronic control of the heating system ensures that the conditions in the vehicle can be stabilised according to the passenger settings irrespective of the external conditions of the vehicle

Air conditioning uses energy input from the engine, via the compressor, to initiate a process whereby heat is absorbed from the vehicle interior at low temperature (by the evaporator) and rejected outside the vehicle at higher temperature (by the condenser)

A combined system with electronically controlled heating and air-conditioning is known as climate control. This system has many sensor inputs for all the external and internal conditions so that it can provide the optimum environment inside the vehicle according to driver preferences

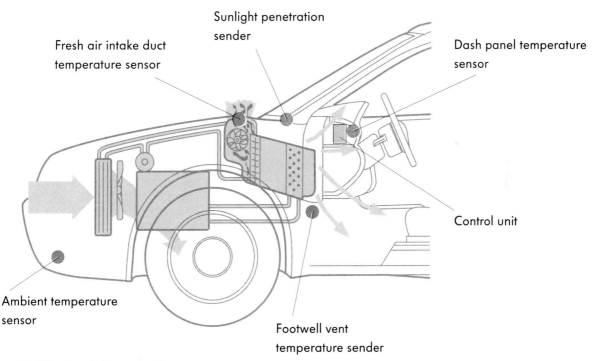

Figure 7.8 *Clilmate control sensor positions*

7.2   ENGINE COOLING

7.2.1 Radiator cooling fans

Cooling fans supplement the air flow through the radiator when the flow is insufficient to transfer all of the heat energy. This typically happens when the vehicle is stationary. Under normal driving conditions, air flow due to vehicle movement is more than sufficient to carry the heat energy away from the engine, in the coolant, via the radiator. When the vehicle is stationary, with the engine running, the lack of air flow causes heat build up. An electric fan mounted directly on the radiator is normally thermostatically controlled so that when the temperature rises above a certain value, the fan switches on automatically and removes the excess heat energy via the air flow. The advantage of an electric fan for this purpose is:

- there are no parasitic losses – the fan is only used when required
- it is easy to accommodate, particularly for transverse engine installations
- it is possible to closely control engine temperature in conjunction with the engine thermostat.

Figure 7.9 shows a typical installation.

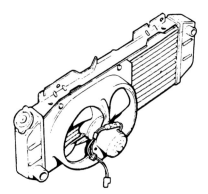

Figure 7.9 Electric cooling fan

A plastic fan is fitted to the armature shaft of a DC motor. This is mounted on a frame directly adjacent to the radiator to provide the appropriate air movement. A typical control circuit is shown in Figure 7.10.

The simple circuit in Figure 7.10 uses a bi-metal thermal switch located at the radiator side of the thermostat housing. The switch operates the cooling fan at about 90°C and switches off at approximately 85°C. In the circuit shown, the power to the fan is via a relay which is ignition controlled. A relay is often used, particularly if two fans are fitted. It is not uncommon for the cooling fan to be permanently fed so that it can run on after the engine has been stopped.

More sophisticated cooling fan operation can be achieved with a small microprocessor-based control unit. This is typical where air conditioning is fitted as in addition to the engine cooling fan. A compressor cooling fan will be fitted, which is very similar in construction to the engine cooling fan. A typical fan control system for engine/condenser cooling is shown in Figure 7.11.

In this system there are three fans, one engine cooling fan and two condenser fans. The inputs to the control unit are engine temperature and refrigerant pressure. The unit performs the following functions:

- it switches the radiator and condenser fans at appropriate speeds
- it signals interchange with the powertrain control system
- it monitors coolant temperature
- it times the operation of the coolant run-on pump.

The fans are switched on in various combinations of speeds in order to achieve the desired cooling effect for the air conditioning operation and engine temperature control. On some vehicles, the fan motors are run in series for lower speed and in parallel for full-speed operation.

7.2.2 Controlled engine cooling systems

Introduction
All engines employ thermostatic control of the coolant temperature to ensure that the engine operates at the optimum for maximum efficiency. In addition, the thermostat control allows a faster warm-up time by allowing the coolant flow to bypass the radiator during

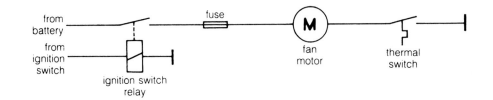

Figure 7.10 Control circuit for engine cooling fan

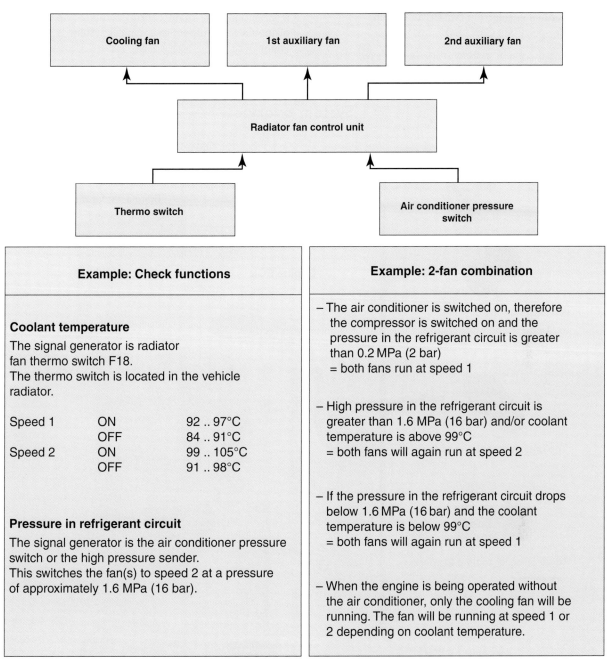

Figure 7.11 A typical fan control system for engine/condenser cooling (VW)

the warm-up phase. The operation of engine cooling systems is discussed is *FMVT: Book 1*.

Motor manufacturers are under increasing pressure to reduce exhaust emissions and increase engine efficiency. The traditional cooling system has come under scrutiny to observe where improvements can be made to optimise engine operation. In the past, running the engine at a fixed temperature has been acceptable, but with load-dependent engine temperature adjustment made possible, improvements can be made in fuel economy, particularly at part load. In addition, CO (carbon monoxide) and HC (hydrocarbon) can be reduced with this technique.

Operation

The main target of a electronically controlled cooling system is to allow the engine operating temperature to be set to a specific value depending on the engine load. The temperature set-point information is stored electronically in the engine ECU. The actual value is stored in a look-up table and this depends on the following sensor inputs:

- engine speed (from crank position sensor)
- engine load (from mass air flow meter)
- coolant temperature (sensors located in head and radiator outlet)

- interior heater selection (via driver switch)
- vehicle speed (via CAN bus).

The required system temperature is achieved using a coolant control unit connected to the ECU and this is essentially the main control actuator. An overview of inputs and outputs of a typical system is shown in Figure 7.12.

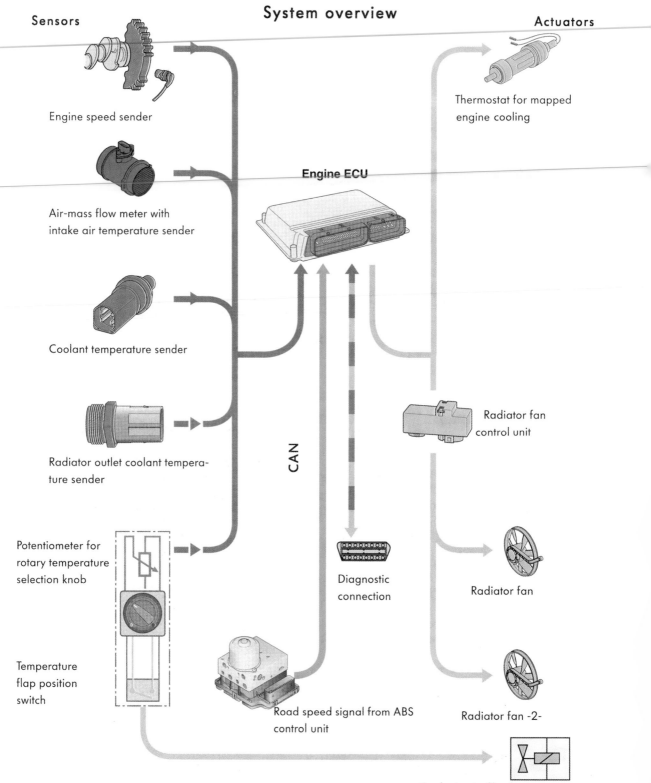

System overview

Sensors

Engine speed sender

Air-mass flow meter with intake air temperature sender

Coolant temperature sender

Radiator outlet coolant temperature sender

Potentiometer for rotary temperature selection knob

Temperature flap position switch

CAN

Engine ECU

Diagnostic connection

Road speed signal from ABS control unit

Actuators

Thermostat for mapped engine cooling

Radiator fan control unit

Radiator fan

Radiator fan -2-

Coolant cut-off valve two-way valve

Figure 7.12 Electronic coolant control system – inputs/outputs

The coolant control unit replaces the thermostat and is essentially a thermostatic control valve. The detail of one design is shown in Figure 7.13.

This is basically a traditional wax thermostat but with the addition of a resistive heating element supplied with current from the ECU via a PWM (pulse width modulated) signal. When energised, the heating resistor heats the wax thermocouple. This expands the wax inside and extends the lifting pin which causes the thermostat to open. Thus, thermostat opening and closing is not just a function of the coolant temperature at the thermostat housing, but also as specified by the ECU in accordance with the engine operating conditions.

Figure 7.14 shows the temperature variation of a typical electronically controlled cooling system as a function speed and load. The lines on the graph are isobars (lines of constant temperature) at the temperatures shown.

Note that temperatures are higher in the part throttle range. This improves performance and reduces fuel consumption/emissions. As speed and/or load increase, the engine temperature is reduced. This increases power output as the heating of the induced air by the engine is reduced.

In addition, the ECU controls switching of the cooling fans. The fans' switching thresholds are stored in a map as a function of engine temperature, load and vehicle speed. Hence fan switching is adapted and implemented closely to the actual engine requirements.

This reduces unnecessary noise and contributes to improved emissions and fuel consumption. Switching of the fan motors is executed via relays to control the high-inrush current.

Engine thermal management

As more demands are made to increase the efficiency of the combustion engine, designers have to look at all sources of wasted energy around it. Basic thermodynamic laws dictate the energy conversion during combustion and a large amount of this energy is lost in the process as heat to the cooling system. In order to dissipate this energy and prevent overheating, it is necessary to lose power via some additional components (for example a water pump to circulate coolant, a radiator fan to create air movement) and these losses can be minimised in conjunction with thermal management of the engine. As mentioned above, the electronically controlled cooling system can be combined in a system with an electric water pump and a variable-speed radiator cooling fan to provide a full engine thermal management system with electronic control. An overview of the main components in a typical system is shown in Figure 7.15.

The benefit of this system is that all of the related thermal control components are managed by an electronic control system that can monitor the engine and vehicle operating conditions and adapt the engine thermal control accordingly. The operation of the components is fully harmonised and this improves the efficiency of the system as a whole. It also allows a

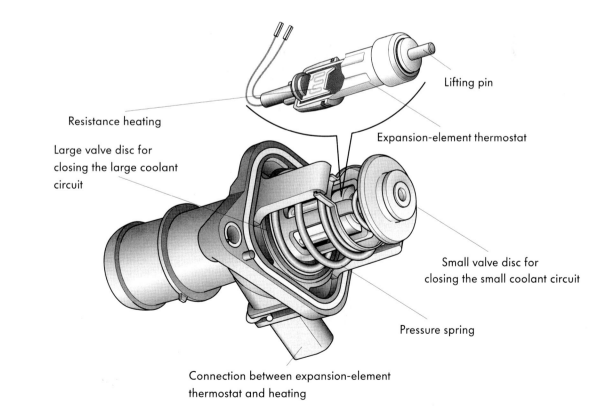

Resistance heating

Large valve disc for closing the large coolant circuit

Lifting pin

Expansion-element thermostat

Small valve disc for closing the small coolant circuit

Pressure spring

Connection between expansion-element thermostat and heating

Figure 7.13 Coolant control unit (thermostat for mapped engine cooling)

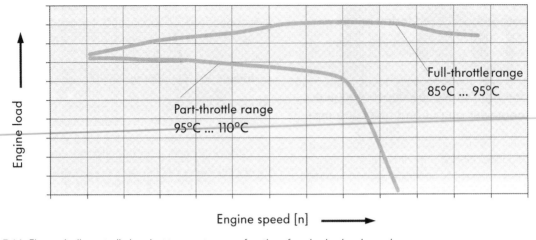

Figure 7.14 Electronically controlled coolant temperature as a function of engine load and speed

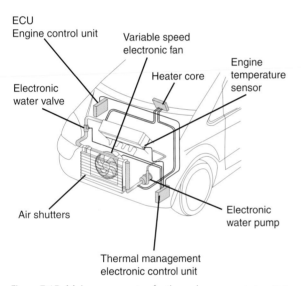

Figure 7.15 Main components of a thermal management system (valeo)

degree of redundancy, that is, if one component fails, the others can compensate intelligently. The main advantages of this system are:

- Accurate matching of engine temperature to speed and load conditions via electronic coolant valve (increased efficiency – reduced exhaust emissions).
- Engine temperature rise characteristic at start-up is improved. This reduces engine emissions during this operation phase (which is critical for compliance with emission regulations).
- Operation of energy consumers (i.e. fan, coolant pump) is optimised thus reducing parasitic loads on the engine. Fan and pump speeds are matched to actual requirements.

- Coolant circulation can be maintained after engine shut-off. This prevents hot spots/localised overheating in the engine. In addition, passenger compartment temperature can be maintained for a considerable period.

Thermal management of the engine is an important step in the development of more efficient internal combustion power units. This technology will be implemented more frequently in order to achieve future emission legislation and it will be essential with respect to combustion engines in hybrid powertrains where energy management and conservation is of paramount importance.

Key Points

Electric radiator cooling fans are efficient due to the fact that they are only switched on and use power when they are needed; this is achieved via thermostatic control

More sophisticated engine cooling fan controls have variable speeds and multiple fans to ensure the correct cooling flow is provided under all conditions

Electronically controlled or mapped cooling systems allow adjustment of the engine operating temperature according to speed and load conditions. This can increase engine efficiency, reducing fuel consumption and emissions. In addition, it promotes a higher maximum power to be achieved

Further refinement and optimisation of the cooling system components have made possible a complete, electronically controlled engine thermal management system. This provides the optimum engine thermal conditions under all operating conditions. In addition, the system has built-in redundancy due to the fact that one component can compensate for another component failure (to an extent)

7.3   VEHICLE CLOSURE AND SECURITY

7.3.1 Doors, windows and sunroof

Window lifters

Electrically operated windows are now common in most vehicles. Nearly all systems use a small DC motor to provide the motive force to raise and lower the window glass in the frame. Motor operation and direction control is provided via a three-position rocker switch located in the door or within easy reach of the seated occupant. If the vehicle is equipped with electric windows all round, it is common for the driver to have a master panel which allows for the operation of all of the windows. In addition, the driver can normally disable all of the passenger windows via a button on this panel.

Force is transmitted from the motor to the window glass via a gearbox and lever mechanism. Alternatively a flexible rack or cable assembly can be used. Both arrangements are shown in Figure 7.16.

The motor drive is usually via a self-locking worm reduction gear. This ensures that the window cannot move unintentionally or be forced open when the motor is not energised. In order to protect the motor and the wiring, thermal protection is fitted in the circuit. This can be built into the motor body (thermal trip) or done externally via thermal circuit breakers. This prevents damage to the system if the switch is held in an operating position for too long or if the window stalls due to ice etc.

A typical electric window wiring circuit is shown in Figure 7.17. This shows a rear-passenger window circuit. The rest of the system has been omitted for clarity. The driver and rear-passenger switches are effectively in parallel. Either switch can operate/reverse the motor via movement of the appropriate ganged switch to supply the motor with a current of suitable direction. In addition, the isolation switch can be seen which disconnects the earth (return) path for the rear-passenger switch when activated by the driver.

Generally, more sophisticated systems are now fitted to vehicles rather than the simple reversing motor and switch arrangement. The motor itself can be fitted with a microprocessor controller which features a speed and position sensor so that the electronic controller knows the actual motor speed, direction of rotation and window position. It is also fitted with current sensors that monitor current and torque at the motor. The window lift control unit is generally mounted in the door with the motor and forms decentralised (or localised) intelligence in the vehicle system. It is capable of interfacing with other vehicle systems via the CAN or LIN bus to provide additional features and intelligent functionality in the system. Typically these are:

- integrated total closure of windows, sunroof, door locking and security system
- automatic one-touch closure including user protection via an anti-jam back-up feature
- full motor protection, thermal overload sensing and over-current protection.

Sunroof closure

Electric operation of the sunroof is very commonplace in modern vehicles where this accessory is fitted as standard equipment by the manufacturer. Electrical operation provides a safety benefit in that the driver only has to operate a switch rather than turning a handle while driving.

Power-window drives

a System with link mechanism, **b** System with Bowden cable.
1 Drive motor, **2** Guide rail, **3** Driver, **4** Link mechanism, **5** Bowden cable.

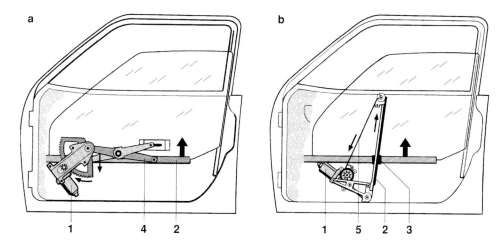

Figure 7.16 Electric window drive mechanisms (cable and link)

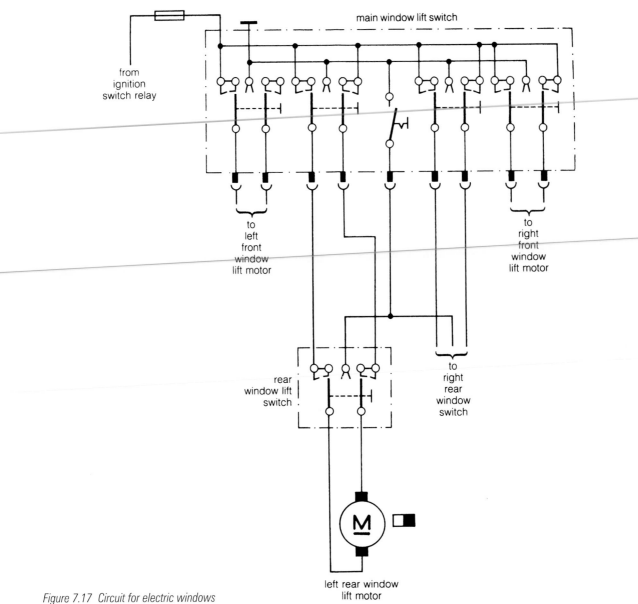

Figure 7.17 Circuit for electric windows

The manufacturer equipment sunroof is normally a tilt-and-slide type and, when electrically operated, a switching arrangement must be used to stop the motor in the roof closed position but allow tilt or slide operation from this position via the switch. This is done via a limit switch and latching relay, but in modern systems a microprocessor handles motor direction and roof position according to driver selection. Sensors (Hall or microswitches) are used to detect the limit positions and the closed position. The motor is normally a DC permanent magnet type which drives the roof panel via a push-pull cable. In addition, a modern microprocessor-based control unit can add extra functionality which improves the convenience of the sunroof and its operation. These are:

- one-touch open and closure
- opening to pre-set positions via a control knob
- integration with vehicle 'total closure' command

- variable-speed motor control to decelerate the motor smoothly when reaching limit positions
- electronic motor protection
- automatic closure via a rain sensor.

Central locking

Central locking of the vehicle door locks has become a standard feature on nearly all vehicles. Often the door-locking action is remote controlled and can be combined with activation of an alarm and immobiliser. The system consists of actuators mounted in all of the doors, the boot/tailgate and the fuel filler cap. When the driver locks the driver's door either with the key or via a remote, the actuators are activated by a control circuit and this secures the vehicle. Various actuators are available, but they fall into two categories:

- electric
- pneumatic.

Early electrical systems used solenoid actuators, but these have a restricted operating stroke and can draw large currents. A simplified solenoid actuator circuit is shown in Figure 7.18.

The electric servomotor type is more commonly used now (Figure 7.19). This incorporates a small DC motor with a reduction gear rack drive which gives a large linear operating force, in both directions, over a long stroke. The interface to the lock mechanism is via a rod or lever to actually implement the change of status of the mechanical door lock to the locked or unlocked position. The actuator force direction is controlled by reversing the supply to the motor and this executed via the central-locking controller which can be a stand alone unit or a function integrated into a body electronics module.

Pneumatic systems are also employed by manufacturers and are well proven. An advantage is that operation of the system is nearly silent. The actuators incorporate diaphragm elements which convert pressure to displacement/force and are connected to the lock mechanisms via a rod/lever as above. Pressure above atmospheric moves the actuator in one direction and below in the opposite direction (atmospheric pressure is approximately 1 bar; below this is a vacuum condition). The pressure is generated by a pumping unit mounted in the boot. An electric motor inside the pumping unit drives the pump assembly and this generates the required positive or negative pressure, according to the motor direction, to execute locking or unlocking. This action is controlled via the central-locking control unit which can be integrated into the pumping unit. A typical system is shown in the wiring diagram (Figure 7.20).

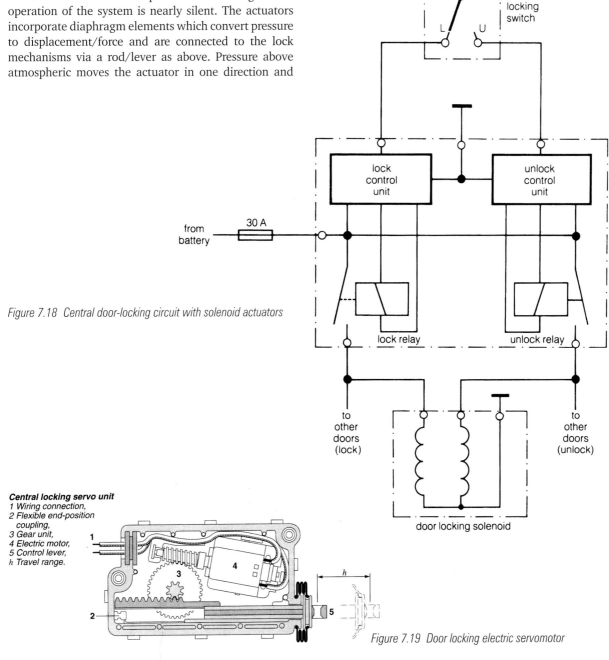

Figure 7.18 Central door-locking circuit with solenoid actuators

Central locking servo unit
1 Wiring connection,
2 Flexible end-position
*   coupling,*
3 Gear unit,
4 Electric motor,
5 Control lever,
h Travel range.

Figure 7.19 Door locking electric servomotor

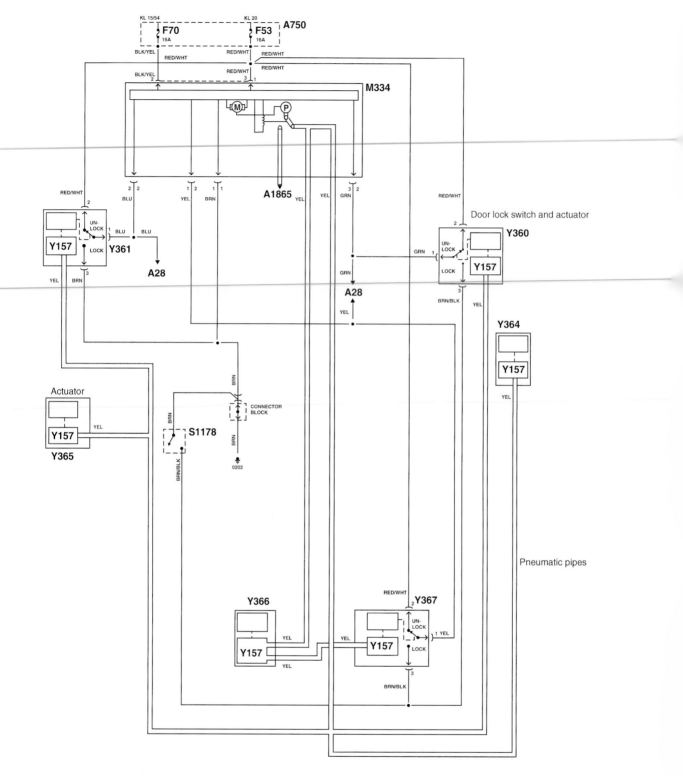

Figure 7.20 Schematic diagram for a pneumatic door-locking system

With either of the above systems, switches are fitted in one or both of the front doors so that when the driver inserts the key and turns the lock manually, this signals to the central locking controller to take the required action and implement locking or unlocking of the vehicle.

Many systems incorporate a dead-locking facility. This means that when the vehicle is locked from the outside, the door locks are jammed so that they cannot be opened from the inside (i.e. by smashing a window). This can be implemented by additional actuators which block the normal lock in the locked position. This feature can be implemented irrespective of the type of lock actuators and some vehicles have combined pneumatic/electrical locking systems. Additional enhancements that can be included in a modern electronically controlled locking system are:

- integration with total closure command including deadlocking
- activation of door locks when the vehicle moves (passenger protection against car jacking)
- automatic unlocking during a crash (via acceleration sensor)
- automatic interior light illumination on unlock/entry.

Current developments in locking systems include passive entry systems. These allow the driver to lock and unlock the vehicle's doors without touching a key. In addition, starting and stopping the engine is done by pushing a button. The driver uses a passive key device which detects a low-power signal emitted from the vehicle when the driver approaches. The passive key automatically responds to the vehicle by emitting an encrypted code. The vehicle receiver processes the code and sends it to an entry/locking ECU. This confirms the key code, and when the driver touches the door handle the entry ECU unlocks the doors. To start the engine the driver simply pushes an ignition button. The engine ECU allows the engine to start only when the key code is read and confirmed again.

In future, all of the mechanical parts of the door-lock mechanism are likely to be replaced by a completely electrical/electronic solution. Modern electronic systems are now at least as reliable as a mechanical system and can be accommodated more easily in the door structure. With this system the exterior door handle and lock arrangement can be dispensed with and this gives a cleaner exterior vehicle line. The lock assemblies will communicate to the controller via the vehicle communication bus and this allows sophisticated fault diagnosis and handling strategies to be implemented. The main benefits of this system are:

- reduced size and weight of the lock
- easy manufacturing; locks can be programmed individually after installation during production or service/repair
- no door handles
- integrated, intelligent functions with other vehicle systems are easy to implement.

7.3.2 Vehicle security

Immobiliser

Many vehicles are fitted with electronic immobiliser systems to prevent unauthorised use of the vehicle. The immobiliser prevents starting or running of the engine (or both) via interruption of the relevant circuits. This can be executed as a software function of the vehicle system (factory-fit systems known as electronic immobilisers) or via hard-wiring (retro-fit systems known as electrical immobilisers). Both systems carry out the same function as defined above. When the driver leaves the car, or at the latest when it is locked, the system arms. No specific action is required by the driver, hence the vehicle cannot be left unprotected.

Figure 7.21 shows a typical overview of an electrical immobiliser. This uses relays to interrupt the essential vehicle operation circuits.

Typically the circuits to be deactivated in the immobiliser will be the starter solenoid switch feed, the fuel pump circuit and the ignition circuit. For diesel engines an electric shut-off valve is normally fitted and this circuit can be interrupted. Alternatively a fuel solenoid valve could be installed.

Electronic immobilisers, fitted as standard by most manufacturers, are more sophisticated. The operation is integrated with the engine electronics and prevents operation via a sub-routine in the engine management system operating program. This is far more complex than the electrical immobiliser and nearly impossible to bypass. Also, it can be implemented easily on diesel or petrol engine management systems. The system overview is shown in Figure 7.22.

Immobilisers are activated passively by the following methods:

- Remote transmitter: either radio or infrared, this is used to lock the vehicle central-locking system and in doing so activates the immobiliser.
- Key transponder: integrated in the key is a coded transponder which is read via an aerial located at the ignition switch. Data is exchanged when the ignition key is inserted and no action is required by the driver.
- Coded keypad: a few vehicles have used this system. The system arms automatically after engine shut off. The key code must be entered on a dash-mounted key pad in order to start the vehicle. This method is slightly less convenient.

In addition, the immobiliser system normally incorporates a prominent, flashing LED to indicate to potential thieves that the vehicle is protected.

Alarm systems

Vehicle alarm systems are often incorporated into a complete vehicle security package including an immobiliser and central deadlocking. In addition, they can be retro-fitted to increase the security of older or high-risk vehicles. The main function of the alarm system is to emit a warning signal when an unauthorised

Immobiliser with interrupt circuits

1 Transmitter (remote control), **2** Immobiliser ECU, **3** Receiver (remote control), **4** Microcomputer (**4a**), with battery connection (**4b**), **5** Relay, **6** Central door-locking system, **7** Status display, **8** Starting system, **9** Engine-management ECU, **10** Electric fuel pump (gasoline engine) or fuel supply (diesel engine).

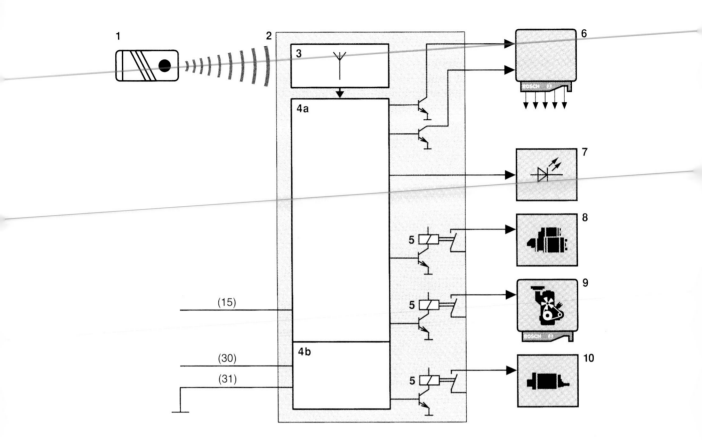

Figure 7.21 Overview of an electrical immobiliser

attempt is made to enter the vehicle or tamper with it. Typically the warning signal consists of a siren and flashing hazard lights.

A number of technologies are utilised to protect the vehicle and interior:

- Contact switches at the door, boot and bonnet.
- Ultrasonic interior sensor: using interior-mounted transceivers, the inside of the passenger compartment is flooded with an ultrasonic field. Any disturbance (due to breakage of glass, illegal entry) changes the amplitude and phase of the ultrasonic signal and this triggers the alarm.
- Microwave interior sensor: similar to the above but a higher-frequency signal that is less susceptible to false alarms. This is often used in soft-top/cabriolet vehicles.
- Shock sensor: a piezo-electric accelerometer senses impacts and vibration on the vehicle structure.
- Tilt detection: changes in vehicle position, including rate of change, are monitored. If these exceed a threshold (due to illegal movement of the vehicle) then the alarm is triggered.

- Voltage drop: the rate of change of the battery voltage is monitored, and if significant current is drawn (e.g. for the interior light or ignition) the alarm is triggered.

Almost all alarm systems are activated remotely and their function is integrated with an immobiliser system. Figure 7.23 shows the protection offered by a typical system.

The heart of the system is an electronic control and evaluation unit that can be incorporated in the siren. A typical system overview is shown in Figure 7.24.

The system can be activated via infrared or radio signals. The transmitter unit is either a key-fob device or it can be built into the body of the ignition key itself. An infrared unit transmits the digitally encoded signal to a receiver in the car, similar to a television remote. Therefore it must be pointed at the receiver unit in order to work. Radio signal units are more commonly used and are much more secure. They emit a weak radio signal that is received by the vehicle system. They are not directionally sensitive and can incorporate additional security techniques like rolling codes (i.e. the digital code changes each time the key is operated). This prevents the use of code-scanning devices to enter the vehicle, but it also means that sometimes it is necessary to resynchronise the key with the vehicle. Figure 7.25 shows a typical radio transmitter system.

Immobiliser with coded intervention

1 Transmitter (remote control), **2** Immobiliser ECU, **3** Receiver (remote control), **4a** Microcomputer,
4b Microcomputer with battery connection, **5** Coding unit, **6** Central door-locking system, **7** Status display,
8 Engine-management ECU.

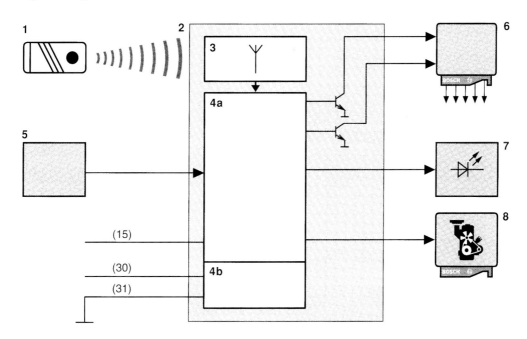

Figure 7.22 System overview – electronic immobiliser

Alarm system (example)

Protected areas: Basic system
① Doors, boot, filler cap, engine bonnet, glove
   compartment (central locking system, contact switch),
② Starting system (ignition and starting switch),
③ Car radio.

Protected areas: Auxiliary systems
④ Passenger compartment (ultrasonic field),
⑤ Wheels, overall vehicle (vehicle-tilt sensors).

Alarm components:
❻ Remote control (transmitter),
❼ ECU (receiver),
❽ Direction-indicator lamps
   or low beam (flashing signal),
❾ Horn (audible signal).

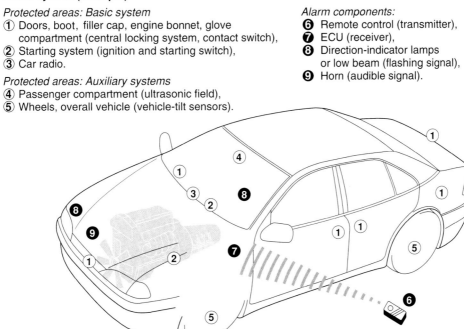

Figure 7.23 Protection offered by an alarm system

Alarm system with electronic protection against wheel theft and tow-away

1 Transmitter (remote control), **2** Alarm-system ECU, **3** Receiver (remote control), **4** Microcomputer (**4a**), with battery connection (**4b**), and input stage for wheel-theft and tow-away protection device (**4c**), **5** Car radio, **6** Ultrasonic receiver, **7** Door-contact switch, **8** Contact switch for bonnet, boot, and glove compartment, **9** Position sensor with evaluation unit, **10** Relays, **11** Starting system, **12** Horn, **13** Ultrasonic transmitter, **14** Direction-indicator lamps or low beam, **15** Status display.

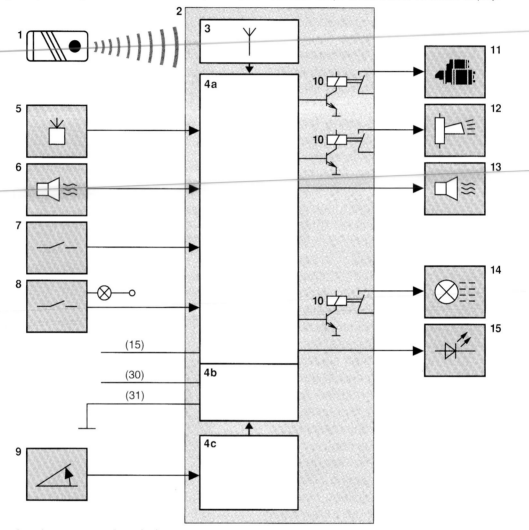

Figure 7.24 Complete alarm system – schematic view

Key Points

Window-lift systems and sunroof closure systems use permanent magnet DC motors, gearboxes and cable or lever drive mechanisms to convert the rotary motion into a linear force to open/close as required. The motor is simply reversed by reversing the supply polarity in order to change the direction of force

Most window/sunroof closure systems benefit from electronic control (via an ECU) which provides additional features in operation, for example integration with an alarm system for automatic closure or one-touch operation with built-in safety features

Central-locking systems allow the driver to completely close and lock the vehicle in one single action. Often this is initiated by remote control. Passive entry systems mean that the driver does not even have to do this – they just approach the car, it recognises them and unlocks!

Immobiliser systems can be electrical (where they physically 'cut' engine running or starting circuits with relays) or electronic (where the immobilisation is done within the ECU software). Most immobilisers are passive and require no action by the driver to activate them. Often they are integrated with central-locking or alarm systems

Alarm systems are used to protect the vehicle and contents by emitting an audible and visual signal when the vehicle is under attack. They detect intrusion into the car via interior sensors. Often the siren has a battery back-up to prevent deactivation of the system by disconnection of the battery. High-quality alarms systems conform to the Thatcham Category standards (see www.thatcham.org/security)

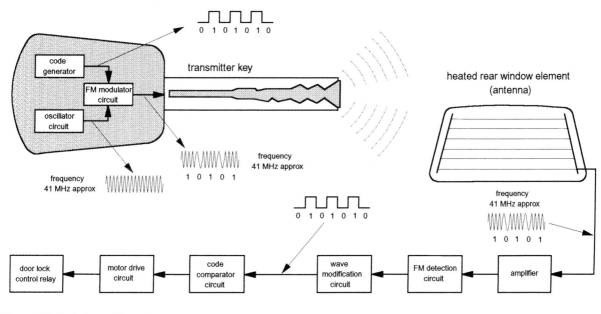

Figure 7.25 Radio transmitter system

7.4 DRIVER COMFORT AND ASSISTANCE

7.4.1 Cruise control

Cruise control relieves the driver from the task of maintaining a constant speed over an extended period of time, for example when driving on a motorway. The system can maintain a particular speed irrespective of gradient, headwinds etc. thus reducing the possibility of driver fatigue.

It is becoming a common accessory in modern vehicles. This is because most vehicles have electronic controls already capable of performing this feature. No additional parts are required, unlike in the past where additional actuators were needed to be fitted to the throttle assembly and additional cruise control units had to be installed in the vehicle. Modern cruise control systems perform the function with existing components and the cruise controller is merely a software extension in the engine management system.

The system works as a closed-loop controller for vehicle speed (see Chapter 2). The desired speed is set by the driver and the actual speed is monitored by the system via vehicle speed sensing. Any deviation is fed back to the controller as an error. The controller then adjusts the throttle position to compensate and try to maintain the desired speed. A diagram of the process is shown in Figure 7.26.

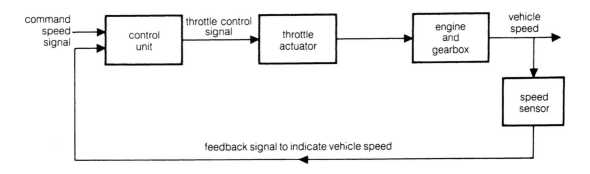

Figure 7.26 Control loop – cruise control system

The main system components are:

- Controls: mounted near or on the steering wheel, this selects on/off and operation mode. Typically:
  - activate/set: this sets the current speed as the desired target speed. It can also sometimes have up/down to increase/decrease the desired target speed;
  - off: this switches off cruise control but retains the last set speed in memory;
  - reactivate: the vehicle returns to the last-set speed.
- Vehicle speed sensor: most vehicles have an electronic speedometer with a sensor that can be utilised. Alternatively, ABS wheel-speed sensor signals could be used.
- Cruise control unit: commonly an engine/powertrain ECU function in modern vehicles.
- Throttle actuator: this is not necessary for drive-by-wire (electronic throttle or EGAS (electronic gas pedal)) systems; older systems used pneumatic or electrical actuators.
- Brake and clutch switches: if either pedals are operated, the cruise control operation is suspended until the driver operates the reactivate command via the control lever.

Figure 7.27 shows how the components integrate within the cruise control system.

The speed signal is processed and compared with the desired value. This gives the error signal for the control loop. The acceleration and speed controller process this signal to generate the throttle position demand which is applied to the throttle actuation control system.

The system is deactivated by the switch-off logic circuit if the driver lever 'off' switch, clutch or brake are activated. Also, this happens automatically under the following conditions:

- minimum speed threshold is crossed (approximately 20 mph)
- the speed difference threshold becomes too great between actual and desired speed.

In addition, operation of other vehicle dynamic control systems will deactivate cruise control operation, e.g. stability control activation. When the reactivate control is given, the vehicle accelerates to the last speed-set point and then the speed controller takes over to maintain constant vehicle speed. If the driver accelerates beyond the set speed and then releases the throttle, the vehicle will gently decelerate to the set speed at which point the cruise control resumes speed control. The system is not deactivated under these conditions.

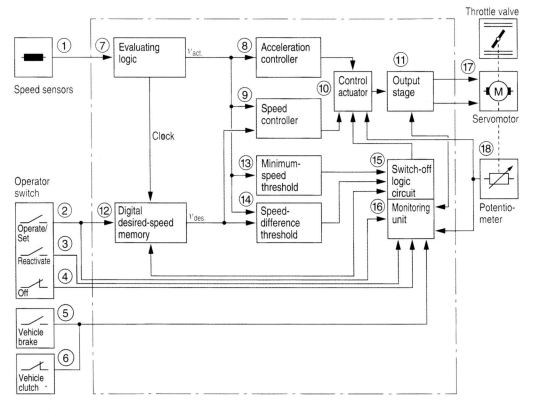

Figure 7.27 Block diagram – cruise control system ECU and components

New developments – adaptive cruise control

This technology allows an addition to the basic cruise control system by introducing the ability to automatically adjust the vehicle speed to maintain a set distance to the vehicle in front according to that speed. That is, the vehicle is capable of safely following a vehicle in front that is travelling at a slower speed than the set speed of the cruise control system.

If the vehicle in front is travelling at a constant speed, a car with ACC (adaptive cruise control) can follow at the same speed and constant distance because the distance is proportional to speed. The constant time gap is equal to the time required for the front of the car with ACC to reach the position of the rear of the vehicle in front and can be expressed by:

$$\text{Time gap} = \frac{\text{Clearance}}{\text{ACC vehicle speed}}$$

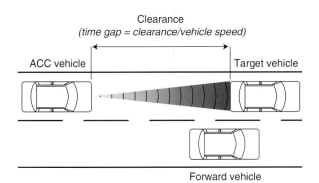

Figure 7.28 *Adaptive cruise control – time gap*

Switching between normal cruise control condition and ACC modes is done automatically by the system which can adapt immediately to changing traffic conditions, e.g. a car pulling into the gap in front and reducing the distance between vehicles.

The ACC system uses a microwave radar transceiver to measure the distance to the vehicle in front. This sensor is mounted at the front of the vehicle (behind the bumper) and includes all of the necessary control electronics and processing power. It is therefore known as the ACC sensor and control unit. Apart from this sensor, the other inputs and outputs in addition to the normal cruise control system are:

- engine management system with electronic throttle/ fuel injection control
- electronic brake control system with pressure-increase capability (ESP).

A system overview is shown in Figure 7.29.

The ACC sensor detects the distance to the vehicle in front using radar. The fundamental principle is that the time between transmission and reception of the radar beam is measured, and from this the distance can be calculated (known as 'echo timing'). If the target object is moving, the echo signal undergoes a frequency shift relative to the transmitted signal and this gives rate of change of distance information (Doppler effect). The ACC sensor/controller uses this information to calculate distance to the vehicle in front. The sensor is shown in cut-away view in Figure 7.30.

The ACC system is integrated with the other sensors and actuators fitted to the vehicle via the CAN bus. It uses existing hardware and this reduces installation and implementation costs.

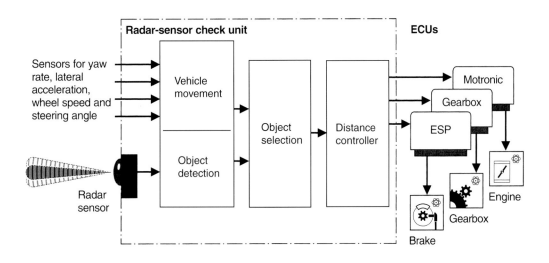

Figure 7.29 *ACC – structure and components of system (Bosch)*

Figure 7.30 ACC sensor (Bosch)

The system interfaces to the drive train control via the engine control/throttle (and can thus control engine/vehicle speed) and also with the brake control system (ABS, ESP) in order to be able to reduce the vehicle speed if necessary. In addition, yaw sensors, wheel-speed sensors and steering angle sensors give the ACC system information about the vehicle positional dynamics (see Figure 7.31).

The main operational features of the ACC system are:

- Cruise control: operation as a standard cruise control system.
- Constant gap: determination of gap and maintenance of this calculated by the ACC sensor. Intelligence built into the sensor selects the target vehicle. The required distance is calculated and then implemented by the system. The driver can also adjust the time gap according to the driving conditions and this is done via selection buttons in the steering wheel.

- Bend detection: the ACC can take into account bends in the road (to a limited degree). Adjustments are made to the speed and acceleration characteristics to compensate for this.

ACC is a clear step forward in the development of systems to improve the safety of the driver by taking over tasks that require high levels of concentration for extended periods of time. It is likely that as the technology improves, the system will evolve further and progress towards providing an autopilot mode for the driver that can react more quickly and drive more safely than a human being!

7.4.2 Parking assistance

Modern vehicle designs may have reduced visibility due to improved body aerodynamics and this can be a particular disadvantage to the driver when trying to park the vehicle. It can be very difficult for the driver to see all possible obstacles from the driving position and also to judge the distance to fixed objects. This often leads to an inefficient use of available parking space. In order to make the process of parking the vehicle easier for the driver, many vehicles are specified with parking aids as extra equipment and increasingly this feature is becoming standard on many mid- to upper-market sector vehicles.

The parking assistance systems warn the driver of his proximity to an obstacle either by visual or audible means. Certain systems incorporate a camera which provides the driver with a visual display of the vehicle rear end, but most systems use discrete ultrasonic proximity sensors flush fitted into the bumper. These sensors can be fitted at the rear only (see Figure 7.32) or at the front and rear to provide full, all-round sensing capability (see Figure 7.33).

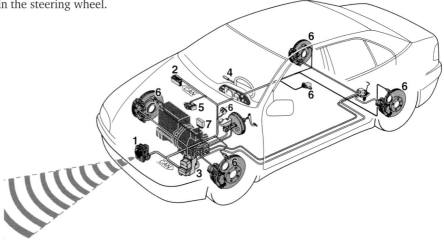

Figure 7.31 ACC system showing interfaces

Sensing range of the ultrasonic sensors as used for backup monitoring

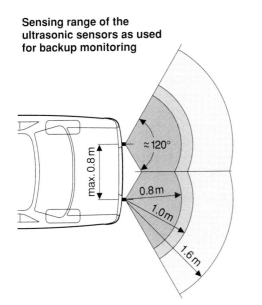

Figure 7.32 Rear sensors

Sensing range of the parking system with all-round monitoring facility

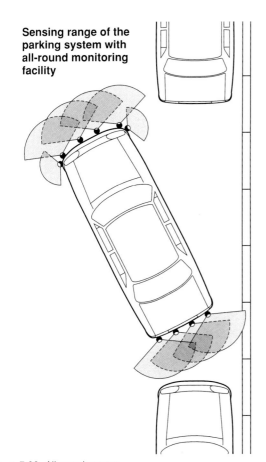

Figure 7.33 All-round sensors

The sensors are connected to an ECU which provides power to them as well as triggering them and evaluating the received signal. Once this information has been processed, it is sent to the driver display unit which consists of LCD or LED visual display elements. In addition, an audible warning tone for the driver can be implemented which increases in frequency as proximity to an object reduces.

The system uses the pulse-echo principle to detect proximity to objects. When the system is operated the ECU excites the sensor element for approximately 150 μs, and due to post-pulse oscillations the sensor produces an ultrasonic pulse of 1 ms duration. The sensors then switch to listen mode to receive the reflected sound wave. The ECU processes this signal and uses the information to calculate the distance to the object from the wave transit time. (Note: the parking sensor is discussed in more detail in Chapter 2.)

Systems with rear sensors only are normally activated only when reverse gear is selected. All-round monitoring systems activate front sensors at low vehicle speeds (<10 mph) and rear sensors with reverse gear engagement.

The ECU monitors the system and sensors. All errors are stored in non-volatile memory for access via the appropriate fault-code reading system. Note that the sensors have local intelligence and are connected to the ECU via a bus to transmit and receive signals and data (see Figure 7.34). This reduces the wiring and noise influences and thus improves the detection reliability.

7.4.3 Seats

Adjustment

Electric positioning of the seat is a common feature of luxury-class cars. The benefit of such a system is that when controlled by a microprocessor ECU, the position of the seat for a specific driver can be stored in memory so that when that driver uses the vehicle, they can recall the stored seat position immediately. This feature can also include:

- steering column position
- door mirrors.

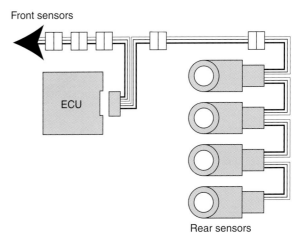

Figure 7.34 ECU and sensors connected via a bus (DENSO)

Figure 7.35 shows a seat design which includes the actuators to enable this feature. As many as seven electric servomotors can be incorporated to perform the following functions:

- seat height adjustment (front and rear of the seat)
- longitudinal positioning (fore and aft)
- cushion depth adjustment
- back-rest tilt adjustment
- lumbar support
- head-restraint position.

In addition, the seatbelt anchor points can be included on the seat frame and are therefore adjusted in the seat adjustment process. This provides the best possible fit for the occupant and so contributes to overall safety. When the anchor points are attached to the seat frame, the seat structure is reinforced so that it is capable of withstanding the forces encountered in an accident as applied by the seatbelt mountings.

Figure 7.36 shows the layout of a typical system with four adjustment motors. The servomotors drive the gearbox assemblies via shafts. The gearboxes are

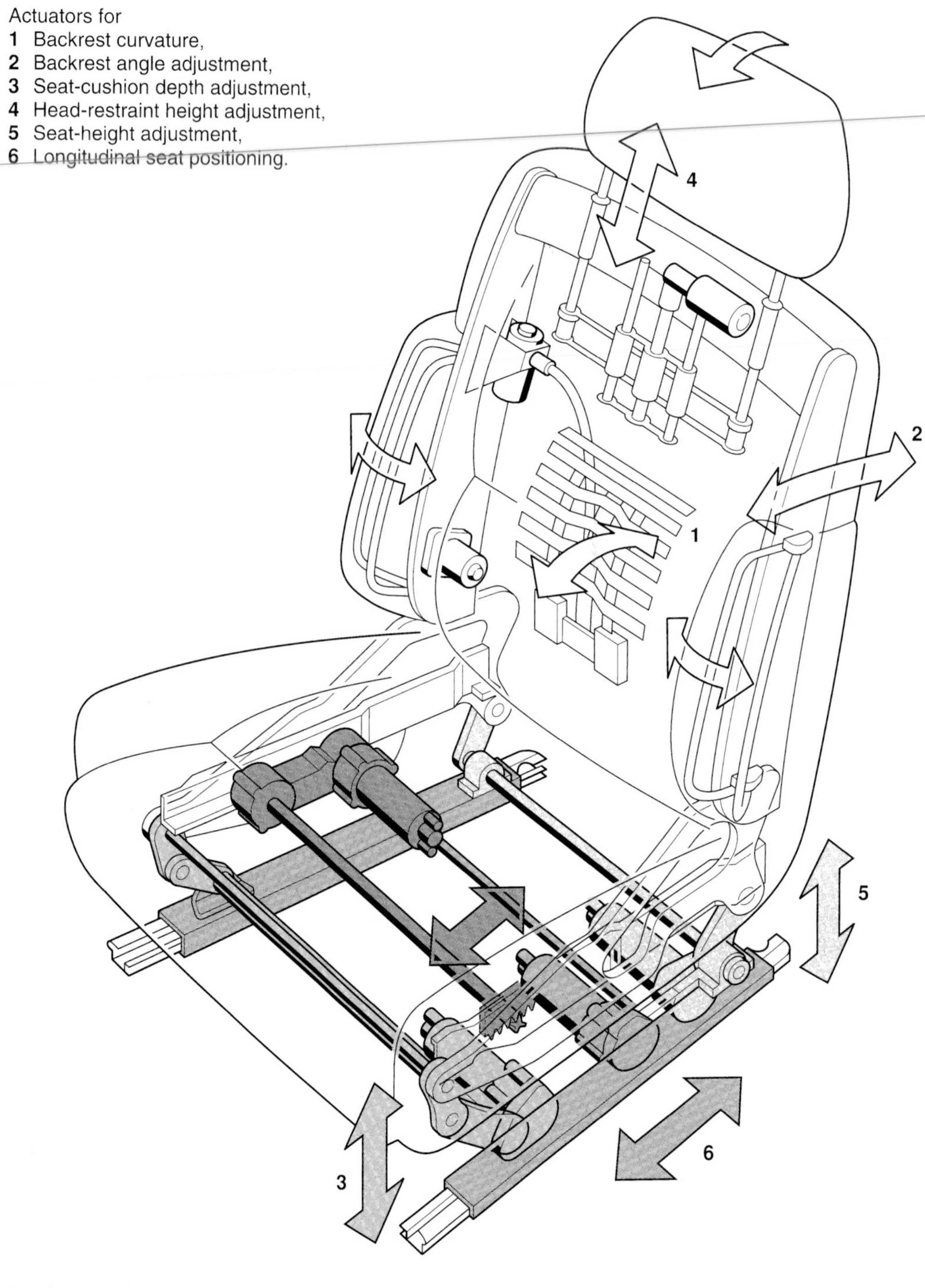

Actuators for
1 Backrest curvature,
2 Backrest angle adjustment,
3 Seat-cushion depth adjustment,
4 Head-restraint height adjustment,
5 Seat-height adjustment,
6 Longitudinal seat positioning.

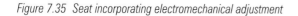

Figure 7.35 Seat incorporating electromechanical adjustment

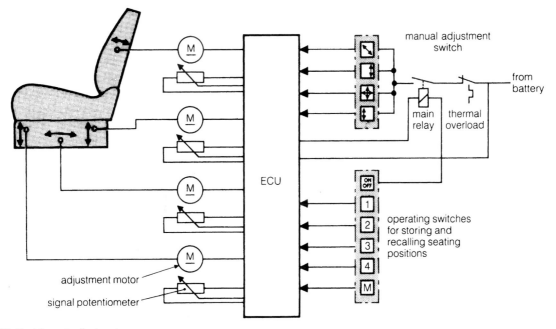

Figure 7.36 Electric seat adjustment

normally the worm and wheel type and this transfers the rotary motion to linear movement that acts directly on the seat frame. The system has feedback position sensors. Figure 7.37 shows a typical gearbox arrangement which incorporates a potentiometer for this purpose.

When required, seat position data is stored by the user in the ECU memory via the control interface. This can be recalled by the seat occupant and the ECU then activates the seat motors until the preselected seat position is achieved automatically.

Heating

Seat heating is a feature normally associated with Swedish manufacturers, but it is commonly available on most luxury-class vehicles. The seat pad and backrest of the front seats (only) are fitted with thermostatically controlled heating elements which can be switched on by the individual seat occupant when required. Most systems allow a low or high setting to be selected.

In addition to the obvious benefits in cold weather, seat heaters can contribute to a reduction in back pain or discomfort caused by long-distance driving.

Key Points

Cruise control implements a closed-loop control system to maintain a given speed set by the driver. This relieves the driver of the task of maintaining a fixed speed which can be tiring over an extended period of time

Adaptive cruise control not only maintains the speed of the vehicle, it also adjusts this taking into account the distance to the vehicle in front, ensuring that a safe gap is maintained. The system uses a radar sensor to detect the distance of the gap. The system can adjust vehicle speed via the throttle and also apply the brakes to slow the vehicle if necessary

Parking sensors use reflected ultrasonic waves to detect the proximity to obstructions. Sensors can be fitted at the rear only, or at the front and rear giving all-round protection. Normally four sensors are fitted at the rear and four or six are fitted at the front

Seat adjustment and heating are normally fitted to luxury-class cars, but both can contribute to safety by ensuring the correct position of the occupant in the seat every time and also by reducing fatigue via increased passenger comfort

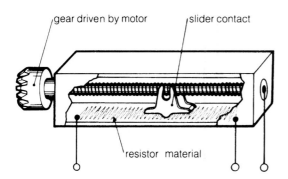

Figure 7.37 Potentiometer for sensing seat position

Chapter 8

SIGNALLING AND VISION

what is covered in this chapter . . .

- ■ **Lights**
- ■ **Screens**
- ■ **Mirrors**
- ■ **Signalling**

8.1 LIGHTS

8.1.1 Introduction

Exterior lighting is an essential part of the vehicle basic equipment to allow the vehicle to be identified easily at night or in conditions of poor visibility. In addition, the driver must be able to see in these conditions and the lighting system fulfils this purpose. There are many regulations which stipulate the type of lights which can be fitted for legal road use. Some of these lights are essential and are fitted as standard equipment and some of them are additional equipment fitted according to vehicle use or specification. The basic configuration of the vehicle lighting system consists of the following:

- side and rear lights (position or marker lights including the number plate at the rear)
- interior illumination (instruments and passenger compartment)
- main forward driving lamps (high and low beam)
- rear fog lamps (high-intensity rear light for use in conditions of fog or falling snow)
- reversing lamps (illuminated when reversing to warn of movement and to provide illumination)
- brake lights (illuminated when the brake is applied to warn other road users that the vehicle is slowing down)
- direction indicators and hazard lights.

In addition there are:

- spot lamps (long-distance lights switched on with main beam)
- front fog lamps (used in foggy conditions with side or dipped headlamps to illuminate the road immediately in front of the vehicle without producing glare)
- daytime running lamps (for certain markets a lighting system must be provided for use in the daytime; normally it is provided via head/side lamps).

A typical lighting circuit is shown in Figure 8.1. Most lighting systems use an earth return circuit with the lamps connected in parallel. In this circuit, switch 1 is for the side/marker lamps, switch 2 is for the headlamps (in addition to switch 1) and switch 3 selects main or dipped beam.

Usually each lighting circuit is fused individually. This reduces the possibility of failure of the whole lighting circuit if a fault occurs. It is also common to use relays to reduce the length of cables supplying current to the headlamps. This reduces voltage drop and losses. The lighting circuit shown in Figure 8.2 is typical of a more modern vehicle.

8.1.2 Light sources

Light intensity

The light intensity (also known as luminous intensity) is the power to radiate light and produce illumination at a distance. Luminous energy refers to the source of light and it is measured in candelas (cd), one candela being the approximate illumination emitted by one candle.

The amount of light which falls on a surface is called the illumination, and the intensity of this is measured

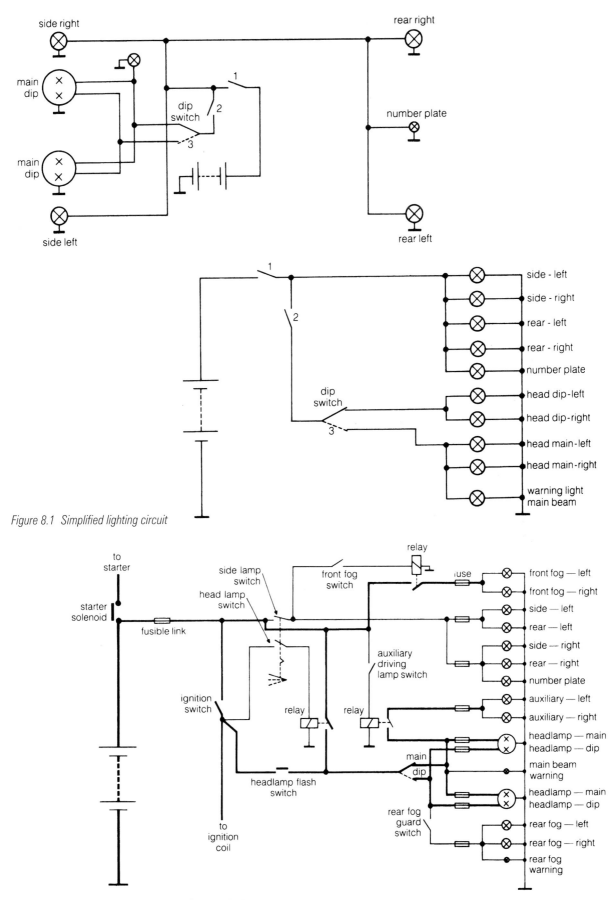

Figure 8.1 Simplified lighting circuit

Figure 8.2 Lighting circuit incorporating fuses and relays

in lux. The brightness of an illuminated surface varies according to:

- the reflective properties of the surface
- the luminous intensity of the light source
- the distance between the light source and the surface.

A surface illumination of one lux is obtained when a lamp of one candela is placed one metre from a vertical screen. When the distance is increased the intensity of the illumination decreases by the square of the distance, i.e. if the distance is doubled, the intensity will reduce to a quarter of the original value.

Luminous intensities of some typical vehicle bulbs are shown in Table 8.1.

Table 8.1 Luminous intensities of some typical vehicle bulbs

Bulb application	Intensity (cd)
Brake lamp bulbs	60 to 180
Tail lamp bulbs	4 to 12
Rear fog lamp bulb	150 to 300
Main beam	>200 000

Conventional incandescent bulbs

Conventional-type vehicle bulbs are thermal radiators which generate light from heat energy. This means that the light output is proportional to the heat generated at the filament. A typical low-wattage vehicle bulb is shown in Figure 8.3.

The tungsten filament is supported by wires connected to contacts in the brass cap. When the correct voltage is applied, the filament reaches a temperature of approximately 2300°C and white light is produced. Operating at higher or lower voltages than specified will reduce the performance and life of the bulb. Generally the air is evacuated from inside the bulb glass. This helps to reduce oxidation and vaporisation of the filament and extends the working life. In larger wattage bulbs of this type (e.g. for headlamp applications) the bulb glass is charged with an inert gas at low pressure and this can significantly increase the operating temperature of the filament (and hence light output) of the bulb.

Halogen bulbs

During the life of a conventional bulb, the tungsten filament vaporises and deposits on the inner surface of the bulb glass. This causes it to turn black which significantly reduces the light output from the bulb. This fact has led to the near extinction of this bulb in headlamp applications. The halogen-type bulb is a considerable improvement as it produces a much higher light output, has greater efficiency and a longer service life. Halogen refers to a group of chemicals (iodine and bromide) which are added to the gas charge inside the bulb to overcome the evaporation problem and thus extend the service life. In addition, due to this gas charge, it becomes possible to use filament temperatures approaching the melting point of tungsten and this produces high levels of luminous power when compared to a conventional bulb. A typical dual-filament headlamp bulb is shown in Figure 8.4.

The evaporation of the tungsten from the filament is part of a cyclic process which regenerates the bulb (see Figure 8.5). As the tungsten evaporates, it moves from the hot filament towards the glass envelope, it combines with the halogen and forms a new compound (tungsten halide). This compound moves via convection back to the hot gas region around the filament (instead of depositing on the glass). At this point, the tungsten halide splits and the tungsten is redeposited back onto the filament; the halogen particles that are released are returned to the gas.

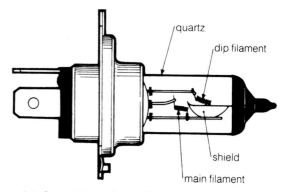

Figure 8.4 Quartz-halogen lamp bulb

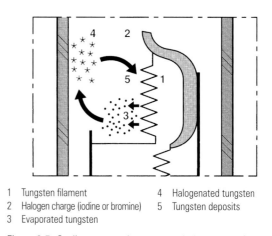

1	Tungsten filament	4	Halogenated tungsten
2	Halogen charge (iodine or bromine)	5	Tungsten deposits
3	Evaporated tungsten		

Figure 8.5 Cyclic regeneration – quartz-halogen bulb filament

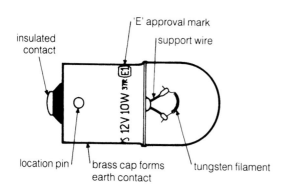

Figure 8.3 Filament light

To maintain this regeneration process the bulb must operate at a temperature of around 300°C. This is achieved by using a small bulb of quartz glass which can withstand the heat load and can also withstand the pressure of being charged with fill gas at several bar. This helps to reduce the tungsten's inherent tendency to evaporate.

An important point when handling these bulbs is not to touch the quartz glass. Even minute traces of oil or grease can lead to harmful deposits that can attack and destroy the glass during the operating cycle.

Gas discharge

Gas-discharge lamps are a recent development in lighting technology for automotive applications. The basic principle is well established and used extensively in industry, for example low-pressure sodium street lamps and fluorescent lighting. Gas discharge refers to the electrical discharge that occurs when an electric current flows through a gas and causes it to emit radiation.

As a light source, this technology is well suited for human vision. It provides longer-range lighting with better distribution of the light on the road surface. Durability of a gas-discharge lighting system is such that it lasts the entire life of the vehicle, it is not necessary to replace the bulbs as they do not wear out. In addition, the packaging of the lamp system allows a high degree of freedom to the vehicle designer as it is possible to create headlight units of a more compact design.

Operation

The general construction of the gas-discharge bulb is shown in Figure 8.6. It is filled with the noble gas xenon and a mixture of metal halides. The system is operated by an electronic ballast unit that controls the ignition and operating processes. To start the light emission process from the lamp, an ignition voltage of approximately 10–20 kV is applied across the electrodes. This ionises the gas between the electrodes and provides an electrically conductive path in the form of an arc. Once the conductive path has been initiated, a regulated supply of AC current at 400 Hz heats the lamp body so that the metallic charge is vaporised and light is radiated.

The lamp can take several seconds to ionise all of the particles and generate full illumination. In order to accelerate this process, a high start-up current is applied by the electronic ballast unit until the bulb reaches full luminous power. At this point the control system monitors and limits the lamp current and applies an operating voltage of about 85 volts which is sufficient to maintain the luminous arc. A typical system layout is shown in Figure 8.7.

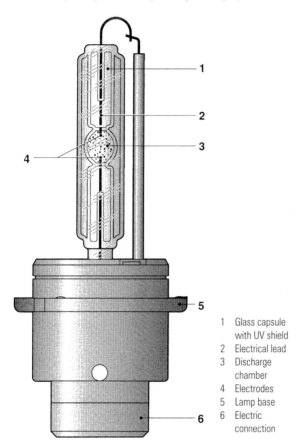

1	Glass capsule with UV shield
2	Electrical lead
3	Discharge chamber
4	Electrodes
5	Lamp base
6	Electric connection

Figure 8.6 Gas-discharge bulb

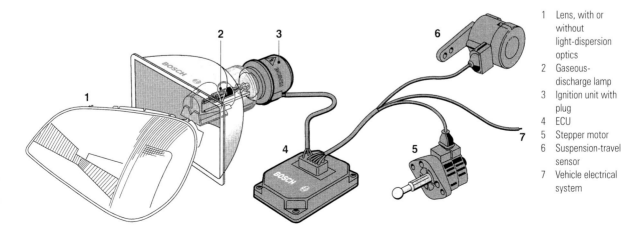

1	Lens, with or without light-dispersion optics
2	Gaseous-discharge lamp
3	Ignition unit with plug
4	ECU
5	Stepper motor
6	Suspension-travel sensor
7	Vehicle electrical system

Figure 8.7 Main components – gas-discharge headlamp

Note that gas-discharge lighting systems are generally always fitted with headlamp washers and automatic levelling systems in order to optimise the system under all operational conditions and prevent glare to other drivers due to the high luminous output of the system. Generally, the gas-discharge lamp is applied to dip-beam only. They are used in combination with conventional lighting technology to provide main beam, i.e. a four-headlamp system. The reason for this is that the start-up time for the light source of a gas-discharge lamp is still too long for the near-instantaneous requirements of switching between main and dipped beam.

The advantages of a gas-discharge lighting system can be summarised as follows:

- long service life, no mechanical wear, systems last the life of the vehicle
- extremely favourable light source with respect to intensity and distribution of the light
- highly efficient system, high light output for relatively low power consumption.

New technologies (LED)

A new technology employed increasingly in vehicle lighting systems is the LED (light-emitting diode). Until recently LEDs have not been available as a high-power light source and thus they have been employed mainly in instrumentation. With developments in technology, LEDs are much brighter and also come in a wider range of colours. They are being employed in a greater number of automotive applications and they are rapidly becoming the future of automotive lighting. LEDs allow automotive manufacturers to increase their styling flexibility due to their small size. At the same time, they can provide a light source that is more durable and longer lasting than any other light source currently available.

The main advantages of using LEDs are:

- rugged, low-voltage light source
- small optical source, improved light utilisation
- compact size allowing unique styling options
- no IR or UV emission
- environmentally friendly (e.g. no mercury)
- fundamentally long lasting (they last the life of the vehicle).

The main applications where LED lighting is currently used on the vehicle are as follows.

Exterior:
- turn signals and repeaters
- tail lamps and side marker lamps
- brake lights including high-mount brake lamps
- rear combination lamps
- back-up lamps
- rear fog lamps
- puddle lamps.

Interior:
- map lights
- reading lights

- interior dome lights
- door lights
- ambience lighting
- switch and instrument lighting.

LED technology provides an attractive light source that can be employed in the vehicle to improve the interior ambience and also to provide feature lighting of components (see Figure 8.8). For exterior applications they have a considerable advantage due to their efficiency. This means that for a given output they draw less current. Therefore, problems due to voltage drop, which can decrease the light output from an incandescent bulb considerably, are no longer a significant issue in lighting circuits employing LED technology. A typical high-power LED light source for automotive applications is shown in Figure 8.9.

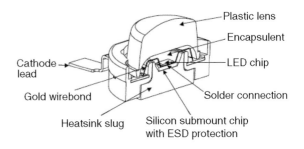

Figure 8.8 Interior LED lighting

Figure 8.9 Typical high-power LED light source for automotive applications

An important safety benefit of the LED is switching time. The light-up time of an LED is much less than an incandescent light source and this can provide a valuable benefit with respect to reaction time when used in brake-light applications, reducing braking response times by two-tenths of a second (an extra 5 metres of stopping distance at motorways speeds).

LED lighting offers better visibility in poor weather and the LED light source has a very long life (100 times longer than an incandescent bulb). This can reduce service time and costs as they can be fitted for life with no maintenance requirement.

LED technology is not employed in front lighting applications as it has not been approved under European legislation. This is likely to change soon and will promote the widespread adoption of the LED as the next-generation technology for forward lighting systems (at the time of writing, Audi and Lexus had already announced new vehicle models employing this technology). The main advantages of LED forward lighting are:

- increased styling possibilities due to the compact form of the LED lamp
- high-performance, efficient light source with low power requirements
- instant on, no warm-up time required
- life-of-vehicle operation
- safety advantage: long life and shock/vibration resistance
- maintained high performance through working life
- mercury-free light source
- dimming capability, efficient optical designs
- active front lighting system (AFS) compatible (static and dynamic)
- robust with high reliability, no moving parts.

When fitted to a vehicle for forward lighting, the LED lamp element has its own control unit which can vary the light output by altering the current supply. The temperature of the LED has a significant impact on its light output. Heat is generated at the semiconductor junction and, in addition, heat from the engine compartment can affect the light source. The control unit manages this and protects the LED element from damage due to over-temperature. It is possible to control the light output to provide main and dipped beam. Also, the unit can be used in conjunction with halogen or gas-discharge light sources (in a four-headlamp system).

The light intensity of LED headlamps is currently slightly inferior with respect to gas-discharge lamps, but the LED is superior with respect to the colour temperature. Table 8.2 shows the different available light sources compared.

The main target is to illuminate the road with light that is as close as possible to natural light and the LED is much closer to natural daylight than any other light source. This factor alone has a significant positive effect on reducing driver fatigue.

Table 8.2 Colour temperature – different available light sources compared

Light source	Colour temperature (K)
Natural daylight	6000
LED	5500
Xenon	4000
Halogen	3000

Implementation of LED front lamps allows the designer of the vehicle a high degree of freedom to integrate the lighting assemblies into the overall vehicle design form. This is due to the fact that the LEDs are much smaller and can be arranged in blocks to create a unique design signature or statement on the vehicle. In addition, due to the zero maintenance requirement, the LEDs can be installed so that the space behind them can be used more effectively in the overall vehicle design.

Figure 8.10 LED front lamps

8.1.3 Front lighting

Lamp assemblies

The main components in a vehicle lamp assembly for forward lighting consists of the following basic components:

- light source
- reflector
- lens.

The light source emits a beam which is then distributed via the reflector or lens according to the lamp type and the driver requirements (i.e. main/dip beam) (see Figure 8.11). In general, the headlamps' illumination range is proportional to the lens area, whilst the luminous efficiency is a function of the reflector depth.

An ideal reflector gives a beam of light which illuminates the road far ahead in addition to the area immediately in front of the vehicle. Normally, reflectors are shaped in a parabolic form and coated with aluminium to give the required reflective property. The reflector collects as much light as possible from the source in order to maximise the headlamp range. It is imperative that the light source is placed at the focal point of the reflector (see Figure 8.12).

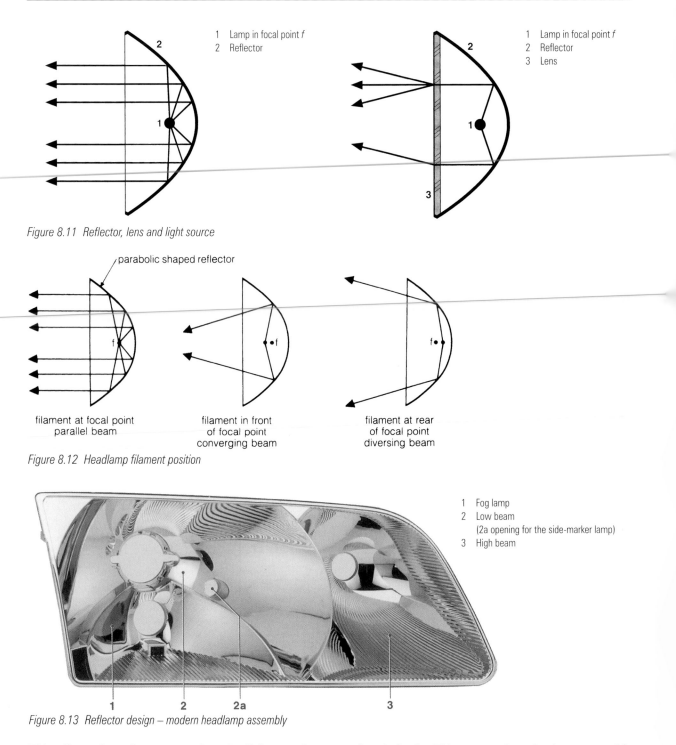

1 Lamp in focal point *f*
2 Reflector

1 Lamp in focal point *f*
2 Reflector
3 Lens

Figure 8.11 Reflector, lens and light source

parabolic shaped reflector

filament at focal point
parallel beam

filament in front
of focal point
converging beam

filament at rear
of focal point
diversing beam

Figure 8.12 Headlamp filament position

1 Fog lamp
2 Low beam
  (2a opening for the side-marker lamp)
3 High beam

Figure 8.13 Reflector design – modern headlamp assembly

This allows the reflector to project the light rays in the form of a parallel beam. Other positions can put the lamp out of focus and this can reduce illumination and dazzle oncoming vehicles. Note that modern lamp assemblies and bulbs are prefocused and no adjustment is necessary. Also note that correct installation of the bulb is important for the same reason.

Modern design techniques have enabled the optimisation of reflector designs to improve headlight function with respect to light distribution. In addition, these designs incorporate optimised reflectors for the specific lamp function (main, dip, fog etc.) with reduced depth. This means that the lamp assembly can be integrated as part of the vehicle design with a reduced physical space requirement. A typical example is shown in Figure 8.13.

The purpose of the lens is to provide the required illumination pattern on the road surface. It does this by refracting, dispersing and focusing the light emitted from the reflector. The lens is moulded to form a number of prismatic sections which provide the required patterns for main and dipped beam in addition to any other lamps included in the assembly. The main beam requirement is a long-range, penetrating light

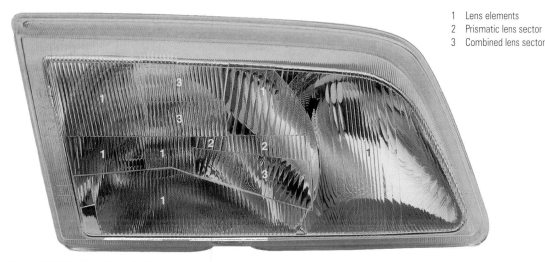

1 Lens elements
2 Prismatic lens sector
3 Combined lens sector

Figure 8.14 Traditional lens design

beam, whereas dipped beam provides a low-level beam which gives a well-illuminated pool of light in front of the vehicle but biased towards the near side. A typical traditional lens design is shown in Figure 8.14.

Note that many modern headlamp designs with sophisticated reflectors are fitted with a completely clear lens. This is due to the fact that CAE/CAD (computer aided engineering/computer aided design) techniques have produced sophisticated reflectors that perform the light-distribution process from the light source without the need for a refractive lens. This reduces the weight of the headlamp assembly as a clear plastic rather than a refractive glass lens can be employed.

An alternative design concept to traditional headlamps is the PES (poly-ellipsoidal system) design concept (see Figure 8.15). This concept uses imaging optics to improve the technical performance of traditional headlamp systems. A conventional headlamp uses a lens to provide the light diffusion whereas the PES lamp uses a combination of a reflector and lens to project the required light beam using a principle similar to an overhead projector. In the case of the lamp unit, the image being projected is the light-distribution pattern generated by the light source in combination with the reflector. A cut-off screen is integrated to provide the dip-beam pattern. The main advantage of the PES headlamp is that a much smaller lamp assembly can produce the same (or better) beam pattern than a traditional, large-surface lamp assembly. In addition, the beam shape and cut-off can be designed with high accuracy. Note that the PES concept normally combines the high beam, low beam, side and fog lamps in a single lighting strip which requires only a low clearance height. This allows high flexibility in the vehicle design with respect to incorporating the front lighting assembly.

The human eye has a finite response time when moving from a brightly lit area to a poorly lit area (and vice versa). Therefore, the forward lighting system must provide a facility to prevent dazzling the driver of an oncoming vehicle. In addition, the beam patterns

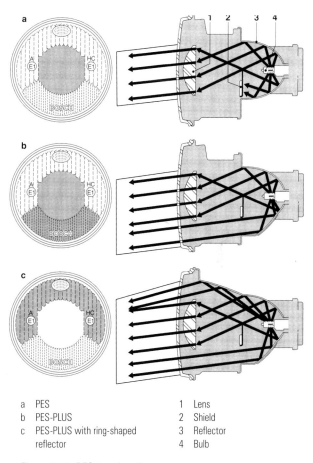

a PES
b PES-PLUS
c PES-PLUS with ring-shaped
   reflector

1 Lens
2 Shield
3 Reflector
4 Bulb

Figure 8.15 PES-type headlamps

must be graduated to prevent eye strain. A front headlamp system incorporates a main and dipped beam arrangement which is selectable by the driver to prevent glare to oncoming vehicles. A typical dip-beam pattern is shown in Figure 8.16.

The high beam is produced by a light source located directly in the reflectors' focal point causing the light to

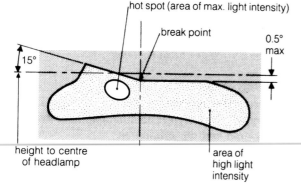

Figure 8.16 Light pattern for European-type headlamp, dipped beam, left dip

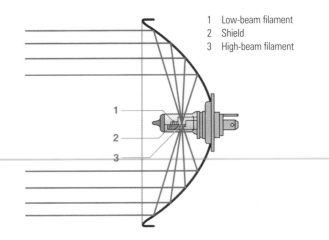

1 Low-beam filament
2 Shield
3 High-beam filament

Figure 8.18 Main beam

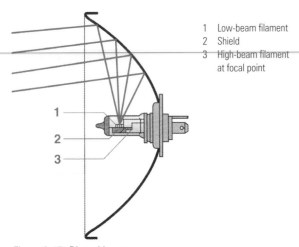

1 Low-beam filament
2 Shield
3 High-beam filament at focal point

Figure 8.17 Dipped beam

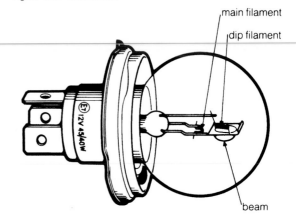

main filament
dip filament
beam

Figure 8.19 Twin-filament bulb

be reflected along a plane parallel with the reflectors' axis (see Figure 8.18). The maximum light output of the high beam is a function of the reflectors' mirrored surface area. Dipped beam is the primary light source most commonly employed whilst driving at night due to traffic density. Dipped beam is provided by redirecting the light rays downwards as shown in Figure 8.17.

When a twin-filament bulb design is employed, dipped beam is implemented via a beam deflector or shield placed adjacent to the dip filament in the bulb. Modern headlamp designs using single-filament bulbs use complex lens/reflector combinations to achieve the same result. A traditional, twin-filament incandescent bulb is shown in Figure 8.19 where the filament shield for dipped beam can be seen clearly. Halogen twin-filament bulbs are very similar in this respect.

To provide a single lens/reflector design which produces optimised dipped and main beam functionality is a challenge and often a compromise of beam pattern. In the past, four-headlamp systems reduced this compromise by providing dedicated lamps units for main and dipped beam separately. In this way, the lamp unit reflector and lens could be designed specifically for the purpose of providing the appropriate light-beam distribution. The outer lamps provided the dipped beam pattern, and when main beam was switched on

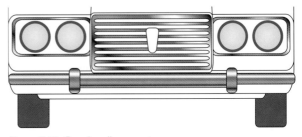

Figure 8.20 Four-headlamp system

the inner lamps were illuminated in addition to provide the long-range light source (see Figure 8.20).

This technique is commonplace with modern vehicle lighting systems, as mentioned previously. Sophisticated lens designs for each application require an individual light source appropriately positioned to achieve the maximum efficiency for the design. Hence, twin-filament bulbs are less commonly fitted. In addition, where mixed light source technology is used (e.g. gas-discharge-dip, halogen-main) then individual source/reflector/lens arrangements for each lamp type (main, dip, fog) become essential to achieve the optimum lighting efficiency and performance.

Levelling

In order to adapt for changes in vehicle load which can have an effect on the aim of the headlamps, in Europe a

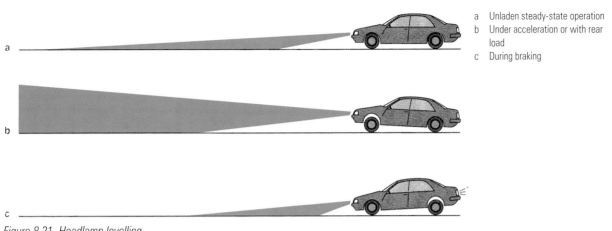

a Unladen steady-state operation
b Under acceleration or with rear load
c During braking

Figure 8.21 Headlamp levelling

headlamp levelling system is now mandatory in all road vehicles. This allows the driver to adjust the headlamp aim to maintain good range of the lamps and to prevent dazzling drivers of oncoming vehicles. Figure 8.21 illustrates the effect.

The system adjusts the lamp aim by slightly altering the inclination angle of the headlamp assemblies. Simple systems can employ a mechanical, Bowden cable system connected to a control knob located close to the driver. Most commonly employed is the electric system which uses servomotors to adjust the position of each lamp unit. The main system components are:

- sensors on the vehicle axles to measure vehicle inclination due to load
- a control unit which calculates inclination angle of the vehicle and responds by activating the headlamp servomotors appropriately
- servomotor actuators to adjust the tilt angle of the headlamps.

The most basic systems have manual control. This is activated by the driver and allows the headlamp beam to be lowered by a number of pre-set positions according to the load in the vehicle. The next level of sophistication is the automatic headlamp level systems and these fall into two main categories.

Static systems

Static systems simply compensate for the variations in vehicle load due to passengers and luggage. In addition to the suspension sensor, the system monitors

vehicle speed to decide if the vehicle is in steady-state operation. From this information, the control system adjusts the headlamps to offset vehicle inclinations that are registered over a period of time. The control system makes adjustment to the headlamp aim when first moving off, then again once the vehicle speed has stabilised. The system is deliberately slow reacting to ensure that the headlamp aim is not overcorrected.

Dynamic systems

The dynamic system can distinguish clearly between the operating modes of the vehicle and, similar to the static system, it uses suspension sensors and vehicle speed sensing, but it is capable of establishing and responding to deceleration and acceleration of the vehicle. The system operates in the same manner as the static system whilst the vehicle is in steady-state operation. As soon as the vehicle brakes or accelerates the control system switches to dynamic mode. This enables faster processing of the incoming sensor information and high-speed operation of the headlamp adjustment servomotors. In this mode, the beam readjustment can be made in fractions of a second. Thus the driver has optimum vision at all times. When the vehicle returns to steady-state operation, the beam adjustment mode switches back to the static, slow-response mode. A schematic diagram of a typical dynamic system is shown in Figure 8.22.

Cleaning

Headlamp cleaning systems are commonly fitted to upmarket versions of vehicles but can also be found as optional equipment. They are essential and

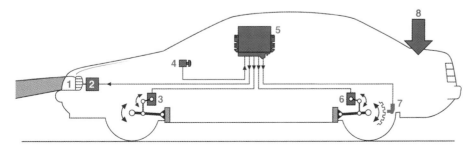

1 Headlamp
2 Actuator
3 Front-suspension travel sensor
4 Light switch (on/off)
5 ECU
6 Rear-suspension travel sensor
7 Wheel-speed sensor
8 Load

Figure 8.22 Dynamic headlamp levellling system components

mandatory if the vehicle is fitted with gas-discharge headlamps. The main function is to remove dirt from the headlamp lens which can reduce the illumination power of the headlamps considerably. This makes a significant contribution to safety as it ensures the optimum illumination of the road surface. Note that a new development in this area is the application of a dirt sensor (see Chapter 2) to activate the system automatically when required. The main functional requirements of the system are:

- cleaning efficiency of >70% on a lamp with intensity reduced to 20% due to dirt
- sufficient water reserve for at least 25 cleaning cycles
- functional at all ambient conditions.

Two main designs of headlamp cleaning systems are in common use as follows.

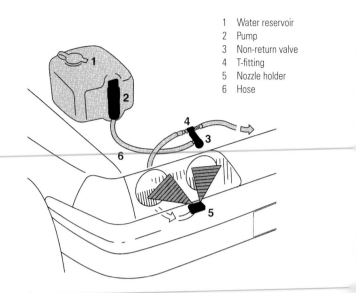

1 Water reservoir
2 Pump
3 Non-return valve
4 T-fitting
5 Nozzle holder
6 Hose

Figure 8.24 High-pressure wash system

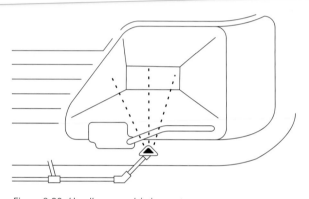

Figure 8.23 Headlamp wash/wipe system

Wash and wipe system

This is similar to windscreen wipers. The wiper arms are driven by small electric motors which incorporate parking switches so the blades always park off the main lens area. Washers are similar to screen washers and use the same water reservoir as water consumption is not excessive.

However, this system can only be used on a glass lens with a simple flat surface. Due to this restriction it is not employed very often now as the shapes of modern vehicle headlamps are too complex to be cleaned effectively by this method.

High-pressure wash system

This system is much more common in modern vehicles as it can be used with glass or plastic lens headlamps of complex shape. The system cleans the lens via the application of a high-pressure jet of cleaning fluid (water/screen-wash mix). This effectively washes the lamp surface, but the success of the system operation depends upon:

- the distance between the nozzle jet outlet and the lens
- the size, speed and impact angle of the washer jet
- the composition of the cleaning fluid.

Many systems are fitted with extending nozzle jets. These retract completely into the bumper when not in use and so do not detract from the vehicle styling lines. When the system is activated, the jet nozzle extends from the bumper and moves into the optimum spray position in front of the lens; this considerably improves the effectiveness of the system. Note that the nozzles extend due to the water pressure generated by the system pump. The system is simple and effective. The main challenge is to optimise the jet so that it can clean the lens effectively at different vehicle speeds. The components of a typical system are shown in Figure 8.24.

Auxiliary lighting

Auxiliary lamps are fitted at the front of the vehicle to supplement the operation of the obligatory lighting systems. They are designed to give a beam shape and light output specific to the application:

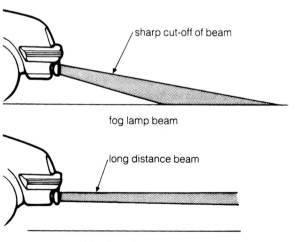

sharp cut-off of beam

fog lamp beam

long distance beam

driving lamp beam

Figure 8.25 Auxiliary lamp beams

The most common auxiliary lights are as follows.

Front fog lamps

Designed for use in fog or falling snow, these project a wide flat-topped beam with sharp cut-off to illuminate the road immediately in front of the vehicle without causing glare. They can be fitted above or below the bumper and:

- they must both be at the same height as each other
- they must be equidistant from the centreline of the vehicle
- the illuminated area must be no more than 400 mm from the widest point of the vehicle
- they must be switched separately from the headlamps.

Driving (spot) lamps

These are appended to the main beam headlamps to give enhanced long-range visibility. They provide a concentrated, far-reaching beam of light. They must be:

- not higher than 1200 mm above the ground
- not lower than 500 mm from the ground
- not more than 400 mm from the widest part of the vehicle
- switched with main beam (i.e. in conjunction with the dipping facility).

If these lamps systems are fitted as aftermarket extras it is important that they are wired correctly and use relays to prevent overloading any of the vehicle's switchgear.

Parking lights

Most vehicles are fitted with side lamps at the front in addition to the headlamp units, or integrated within them. These have a wattage of less than 7 watts and are visible from a reasonable distance. In the past, these lights could be used when driving in low lighting conditions although it is now illegal in the UK to drive during the hours of darkness with sidelights alone. In this case, sidelights are now parking lights and are generally used to show the position of the vehicle when parked on the road in the dark.

Adaptive lighting

This is a new technology being implemented by a number of manufacturers. An adaptive front-lighting system (AFS) redirects the headlamps individually in a horizontal plane taking into account the steering angle and vehicle speed. The benefit of this is that the system can improve visibility during night-time cornering thus ensuring safer driving in these conditions.

The system is controlled by an ECU which calculates the required swivel angle of the headlamp unit using steering angle and vehicle speed information. The entire headlamp light distribution is swivelled by up to ±15° as a vehicle negotiates the bend thus illuminating the road ahead at a wider angle. This dynamic movement of the light distribution provides a significant gain in safety due to the increased range of illumination along the road. On winding roads visibility can therefore be increased by up to 50% depending on the curve radius.

Typically the control unit receives the data which is available from the CAN bus, and from this the current driving situation can be established. This data is processed by the control unit and converted into control signals which are transmitted via a LIN bus (for example) to the servomotors installed in both headlamps. These motors swivel the lighting module in accordance with the road course. The AFS ECU can also be used to control the headlamp-levelling actuators in the headlamps. A typical arrangement is shown in Figure 8.27.

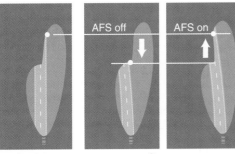

Straight   Curve

Figure 8.26 AFS – adaptive front lighting system

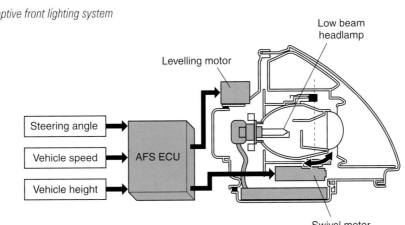

Figure 8.27 AFS system components for headlamp swivelling and levelling

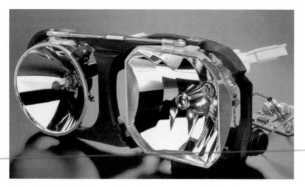

Figure 8.28 AFS lamp unit with common swivel strategy

A further refinement of such a system is the option to implement different swivel angles for the reflectors that are at the inner or outer radius of a curve. An example of a common swivel strategy is the swivelling of the 'inner' headlamp with a given swivel angle and the 'outer' headlamp with half that swivel angle. In addition, there is the option to swivel main and dipped beams separately according to road conditions.

8.1.4 Rear lighting

Tail lamps
Tail lamps mark the presence of the vehicle (from behind) to other road users. The vehicle must be fitted with two European-approved lamp units of not less than 5 watts. They must be:

- between 1500 mm and 350 mm from the ground
- spaced more than 500 mm apart
- positioned so that the distance between the edges of the vehicle and the illuminated area is not less than 400 mm.

The rear number plate of the vehicle must be illuminated at night by a lamp unit connected to the tail-lamp circuit. This is designed to make the number plate visible to other road users; note though that the bulb itself must not be visible from behind the vehicle.

Stop lamps
These are fitted to alert following drivers to the fact that the vehicle is braking. Two stop lamps illuminating a red diffused light must be fitted which switch on when the footbrake is applied. They must be 'E' marked (European standard approved) lenses visible through a given angle. Generally they are 21 watts and are often combined with a tail lamp in a single bulb or lamp unit. In this case the ratio of intensity between the two functions must be at least 5:1. The lamps must be positioned:

- between 150 mm and 350 mm from the ground
- symmetrically, at least 400 mm apart.

In addition, for modern vehicles in the European and US markets a supplementary high-level stop lamp must be

fitted positioned at the vehicle centre line. These high-mount units are often integrated into the body design or rear window and incorporate LED technology due to space limitations. Note though that the response time of an LED is ideally suited to the stop-lamp function.

Fog lamps
Rear fog lamps are used to indicate the position of the vehicle from behind when visibility is extremely poor. They are generally used in fog or falling snow. One or two rear lamps can be fitted and must only operate in conjunction with headlamps or front fog lamps. They must also be switched separately from the front fog lamps, and:

- they must be positioned between 250 mm and 1000 mm from the ground
- they must be positioned more than 100 mm from any stop lamp
- if two lamps are fitted they must be symmetrical
- if one lamp is fitted it must be on the vehicle offside or centreline.

Fog lamps are normally fitted with a 21 watt bulb and a lens with a large surface area. Both must be 'E' marked.

Reversing lamps
These are designed to illuminate the area behind the vehicle when reversing. No more than two lamps can be fitted and they must not exceed 24 watts. The light should be switched on automatically when reverse gear is engaged and the ignition is switched on.

8.1.5 Interior lighting

Numerous complementary lighting systems are fitted inside the vehicle. There is no specific legislation for these and hence manufacturers are free to equip vehicles in any way they choose. Good interior light includes switchgear and appropriate illumination of the driver controls and is important to provide a safe, relaxing environment for the driver.

Interior lamps
Also known as dome lamps, these illuminate on entry to the vehicle, either via door switches or via integration with the vehicle security system. Often the interior lamps are fitted with a time delay unit to allow the occupants to find and fasten seat belts etc. on entry. In addition, these lamps can be activated automatically on ignition key 'off', so that the occupants have light to exit the vehicle safely. These functions are often implemented via a central body electronic module which controls the operation of interior lights, in addition to other accessories, implementing logical features as described. Map lights are also fitted to illuminate specifically the area in front of the occupants for reading purposes. These lamps are designed to provide a light source which does not distract the driver. Additional interior lighting is fitted to many vehicles to illuminate storage areas such as glove compartments or the boot loading area.

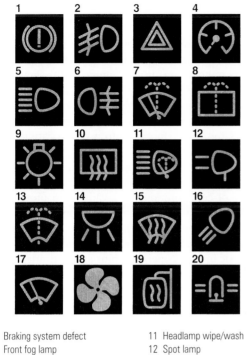

Figure 8.29 European standard symbols for warning lamps

1 Braking system defect	11 Headlamp wipe/wash
2 Front fog lamp	12 Spot lamp
3 Hazard-warning flashers	13 Windshield washer system
4 Instrument-panel illumination	14 Interior lighting
5 High beam	15 Windshield defroster
6 Fog warning lamps	16 Floodlamp
7 Windshield wiper and washer	17 Windshield wipers
8 Rear-window washer	18 Ventilation/heater fan
9 Main headlamp switch	19 Heated mirror
10 Rear-window defroster	20 Rotating beacon

Instrumentation

Controls for the vehicle accessories and equipment must be clearly visible at night in order to maximise ease of use for the driver. In addition, it is common that the display-instrument lighting intensity can be adjusted manually or automatically (via a rheostat or electronic voltage controller). Indicator lamps are used to monitor various operating conditions and some of the colours for these are specified in a uniform European code. Examples are shown in Figure 8.29.

Comfort and convenience controls must be gently backlit so that they can be seen by the occupants but without causing glare or distraction for the driver. Switch illumination is necessary to allow the driver to identify specific functions and to assist orientation.

Key Points

Light output is measured in **candela** which is a unit derived from candle power. The power of light falling on/reflected by a surface is measured in **lux**. When the distance is increased between the light source and the reflective surface, the intensity of the illumination decreases significantly (i.e. by the square of the distance)

For headlamp applications, traditional incandescent bulbs have been replaced by halogen types due to their superior light output. Note that these are now being replaced by new technology such as gas-discharge light sources, and LED technology will be used in the future

Gas-discharge lamps use a high-voltage arc through gas to generate the high-intensity light source. The arc is controlled by an electronic ballast unit to control the light source. Note that this lamp technology is always used in conjunction with automatic levelling and cleaning technology to prevent glare to other drivers

Modern vehicle lamp assemblies are designed using computer-aided design and simulation techniques. Complex reflector shapes can generate the required beam pattern without the need for a sophisticated lens. Often, headlamps of this type are fitted with a completely clear plastic lens

Headlamp levelling provides active compensation to headlamp beam deviation caused by vehicle loading. More sophisticated systems can compensate for acceleration and braking effects. Active front lighting is a development of this technology. In addition to levelling compensation this system can direct the headlamp beam in the direction of intended travel. This improves road illumination and safety

Developments in rear lighting technology are mainly due to the ability to use different light sources other than incandescent bulbs. LED technology is to the forefront here and allows compact lamp units to be created with advanced features like substitution of lamp types (i.e. a stop lamp fails so a tail lamp can be used in its place as a temporary measure). Also, one lamp can execute more than one function due to multicolour LED light sources. In addition, LEDs have a very fast response compared to an incandescent bulb lighting up time and this provides a valuable safety benefit, particularly with respect to brake lights

8.2 SCREENS

8.2.1 Cleaning

Front wiper

A front wiper system is essential on all vehicles to ensure good visibility for the driver under all weather conditions. This fact makes an efficient screen cleaning system an absolute essential contribution to road safety. The fundamental requirements are as follows:

- the system must clear the windscreen of snow, ice, dirt and rain
- the wipe area must be a specific size in accordance with regulations
- it must be a practically noiseless operation
- it must operate over a wide temperature range
- it must be capable of handling overload (e.g. blades frozen on the screen)
- it must be corrosion proof.

The force required to drive the wiper system can be considerable in modern vehicles due to the complex curvature of the windscreens which require long wiper blades. The drive motor must generate the required power. In the past, shunt-type motors were used, but for modern vehicle applications powerful permanent magnet motors are used. Figure 8.30 shows the typical layout of a wiper system. The motor power is transformed to low speed/high torque via a worm gear reduction drive. This drives a crank mechanism which converts the rotary motion into a reciprocating linear motion.

The design of the wiper system is subject to legislation that defines the required wiped area. A number of configurations are available to provide the required patterns and these are shown in Figure 8.31.

The wiper system is generally controlled via a driver lever or stalk near the steering column. Most systems have basic bi-speed operation plus an intermittent wipe function. There are also a number of enhancements available to improve the convenience of the system.

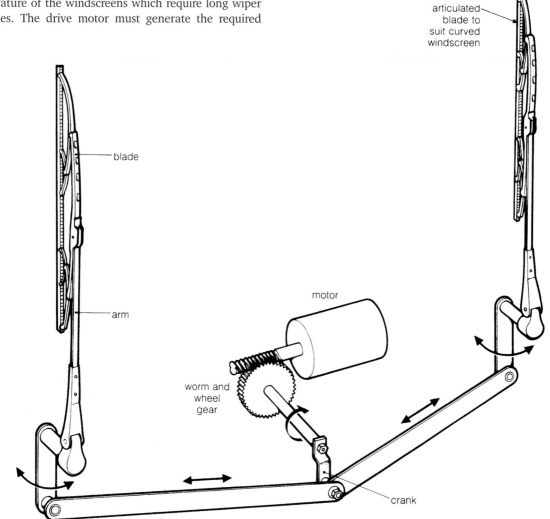

Figure 8.30 Layout of a typical wiper system (simplified link-type drive)

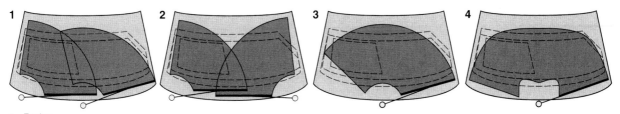

1 Tandem
2 Opposed-pattern system
3 Single-lever system, not controlled
4 Single-lever system with lift control
… Legally prescribed visibility area (USA)

Figure 8.31 Wiper system – wiped area patterns

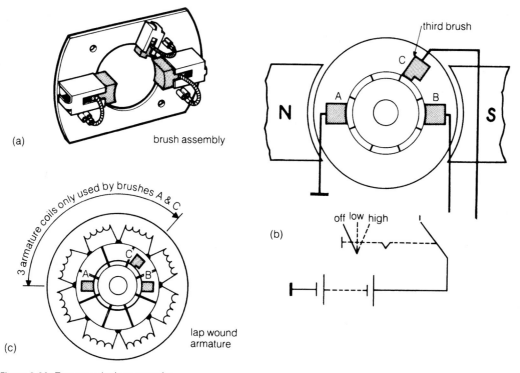

Figure 8.32 Two-speed wiper operation

Two-speed operation

All front wipers have a least two-speed operation. Low or normal speed gives approximately 50 wiping cycles per minute (a wiping cycle is one full back-and-forth motion of the blades). High speed gives approximately 70 wiping cycles per minute. The actual value of these speeds is defined in country-specific legislation.

The method of achieving the two speeds with a simple permanent magnet motor involves the inclusion of a second brush on one side of the commutator giving three in all. This is shown in Figure 8.32.

When the switch supplies current to brush 'B', low-speed operation is obtained. If high-speed wipe is selected then current is supplied via brush 'C'. This moves the armature magnetic field out of the magnetic circuit of the yoke, thus having a field weakening effect. Weakening the field increases the motor speed but reduces the torque and this setting should not be used under high load conditions, e.g. snow build up on the screen.

Self-switching and self-parking

When the wipers are switched off it is essential that they rest in a position that does not impair the vision of the driver. This is difficult to achieve manually so all wiper systems are fitted with either a self-switching or self-parking function. When the driver switches the wipers off, the wiper motor continues to run until the wiper blades are at the end of the stroke, off the screen (known as self-switching). In some cases, the wiper blades move to a position beyond the normal wiping arc so that they are completely off the screen. This is known as self-parking. The switching assembly that allows this function is normally mounted at the motor gearbox. A simple arrangement which demonstrates the principle is shown in Figure 8.33.

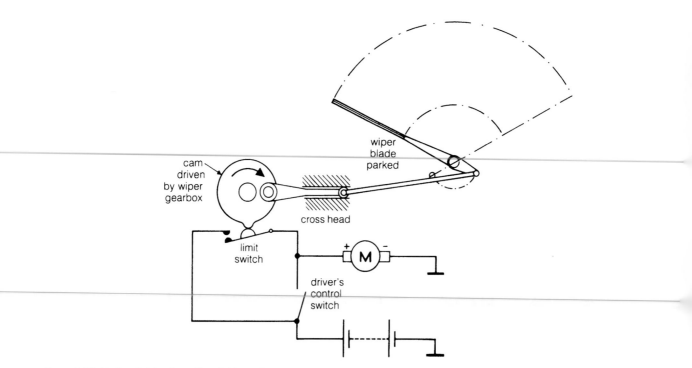

Figure 8.33 Limit switch to give self-switching action

The limit switch is in parallel with the driver switch so that both switches must be open before the motor stops, i.e. the driver switch must be off and the blades in the park position. However, this simple arrangement is not sufficient as, due to the motor inertia, it is possible for the motor to 'run on', passing through the limit switch open position, and thus the wiper will not park. The solution is to brake the armature in addition to cutting the supply and this is implemented electrically using the principle of regenerative braking. Figure 8.34 shows a typical switching arrangement.

The limit switch contacts are changeover instead of normally closed. When the limit position is reached, the supply to the motor is cut and the motor armature is short-circuited via an earth connection on each side. Any residual energy in the armature is then dissipated via current flowing through this circuit and the motor stops abruptly thus preventing any run on.

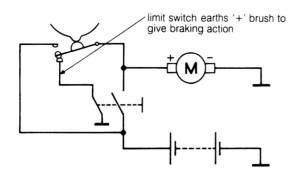

Figure 8.34 Regenerative breaking

Self-parking is an extension to self-switching and allows the wiper arms to be positioned off the screen when not in use. This improves the vehicle dynamics and wind noise and provides better visibility for the driver. In order to achieve this a complex, mechanical linkage system allows an extended wiping arc when the motor is reversed. Thus, when the self-parking mechanism is activated (via switch off of the driver switch) the wiper motor stops and reverses in sequence to achieve the extended stroke. In modern vehicles this action is controlled via a wiper ECU or alternatively a body electronic ECU (in conjunction with intermittent functions).

Intermittent wipe

Light rain or spray conditions need regular but infrequent use of the wiper system. This is achieved via an intermittent wiping function fitted to most vehicles. When selected this mode operates the wipers for a single sweep every few seconds. An extension to the basic function allows the driver to select the time delay between wipes according to the conditions. Due to the regenerative braking system used, the intermittent wipe function is provided by a timer relay that is integrated into the self-switching circuit. A typical circuit diagram is shown in Figure 8.35.

The circuit that activates the intermittent relay is a pulse generator which generates a pulse of sufficient time to allow the motor to move the limit switch beyond the 'park' position. The time difference between the pulses is controlled by an electronic circuit using an R–C network or timer microprocessor. Typically the time difference can be adjusted by a suitable driver control between 2 and 40 seconds.

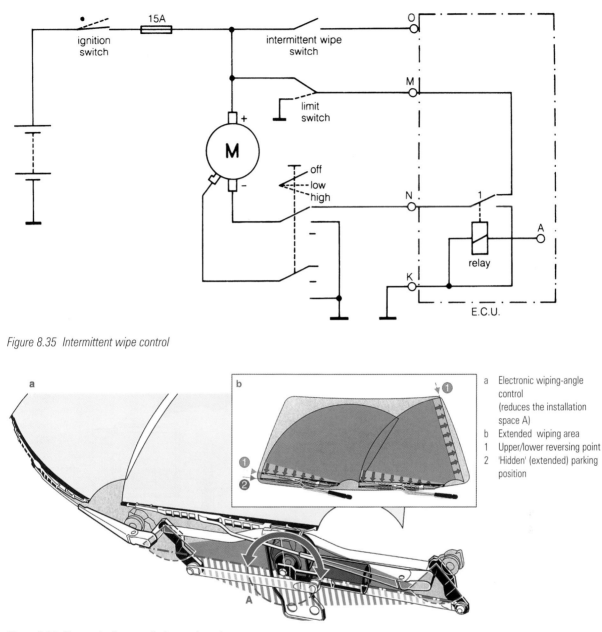

Figure 8.35 Intermittent wipe control

Figure 8.36 Electronically controlled reversing wiper motor system

a Electronic wiping-angle control (reduces the installation space A)
b Extended wiping area
1 Upper/lower reversing point
2 'Hidden' (extended) parking position

Electronic wiper motors

Many vehicles are being fitted with wiper motors that incorporate integrated control electronics. The advantage is that the motor can be continuously reversed by the electronic controller and hence produce the required reciprocating motion directly. This means that the installation space required for the wiper linkage is less and provides more flexibility to allow the maximum wiped area (see Figure 8.36).

Sensors detect wiper blade position and motor speed and torque, thus the electronic controller can ensure the correct operation of the wiper arm irrespective of friction or wind speed. In addition, when used in conjunction with a rain sensor, the motor speed can be matched exactly to the conditions. An interesting point is that it is possible to fit a separate motor for each blade with no mechanical linkage. An electronic controller synchronises the operation of the blades; communication between the motor controllers is via CAN or LIN bus. The advantage of such a system is that it requires less installation space and is lighter.

Additional features

Many wiper systems feature additional logical features to enhance the basic operation of the system. This is achievable due to the high level of integration of the electronic control systems of modern vehicles:

- Intermittent time as a function of road speed: the wiper control systems account for vehicle speed and reduce the delay time as road speed increases.

- Automatic operation of wipers: the wiper system is fitted with a rain sensor (see Chapter 2) that can adjust intermittent time and full operation of the wipers automatically according to the intensity of the rain on the windscreen as measured by the sensor.
- Automatic wash/wipe sequence: when the screen washers are activated, the wipers automatically operate for a number of sweeps to wash and clear the screen without the driver having to switch the wipers on/off.

Rear wiper

Rear wiper systems are fitted mainly to hatchback or estate cars. The technology is similar to front wiper systems in respect of:

- motor technology and self-switching arrangements
- intermittent and continuous wipe operation
- wash/wipe operation sequence.

Two-speed operation is not required. Also, generally, only one wiper arm is fitted, therefore complex linkages are not needed. A general trend is towards electronically reversing motors as the need for a mechanism to convert rotary to linear motion is not then required. This also allows a wider wiping arc of up to 180° if necessary, and the weight/complexity of the motor mechanics is reduced. Typically the service life of a rear wiper is much shorter as its operation is less critical to safety than the front wiper system. Typical wiper patterns for a rear wiper are shown in Figure 8.37.

Washers

Screen washers are fitted to complement the wiper operation (front, rear and headlamp). Normally they are electrically operated from a driver stalk and employ simple centrifugal pumps powered by small DC motors (see Figure 8.39). These generate fluid pressures of approximately 0.7 bar and this is sufficient to provide a jet of fluid on the windscreen via two or four jets mounted on the bonnet or integrated in the wiper blade itself. The cleaning fluid (water mixed with additive) is held in a separate container of approximately 2 litres (more if the same reservoir supplies headlamp washers >5 litres). The screen-wash additive helps the cleaning action but also lowers the freezing point of the fluid. Often the washer jets are heated to improve performance in freezing conditions. A typical pump design is shown in Figure 8.38.

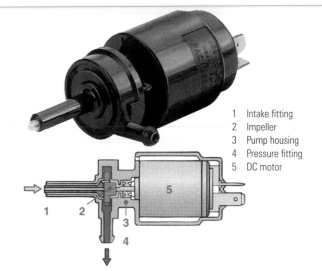

1 Intake fitting
2 Impeller
3 Pump housing
4 Pressure fitting
5 DC motor

Figure 8.38 Washer pump design

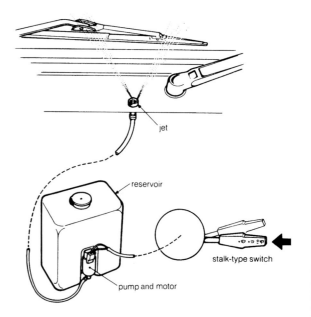

jet

reservoir

stalk-type switch

pump and motor

Figure 8.39 Windscreen washer system

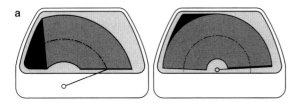

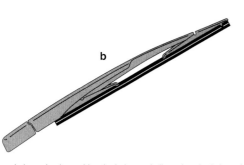

a Rear-window wiped area (the shaded areas indicate impaired view of passing vehicles)
b Rear-window wiper arm (plastic)

Figure 8.37 Typical wiper patterns for a rear wiper

Note that often a single pump supplies front and rear screen wash (if both are fitted). This is achieved via bi-direction operation of the pump which has two outlets (to the front and rear screens). The pump is switched to rotate in the appropriate direction according to whether rear or front screen wash is required. Of course it is also possible for an individual pump to be fitted, one for the front and one for the rear. Often screen-wash operation activates the wipers to execute a number of sweeps automatically to clean the screen (as mentioned above).

8.2.2 Heating

Rear screen

Most vehicles are fitted with an electrically heated rear screen. This helps to clear and prevent condensation which can impair the driver's rear view. The heating element consists of a strip or wire element bonded to the glass surface. When supplied with current the element has a heating effect just sufficient to evaporate the condensation. Note that the element consumes a considerable amount of power as it has to heat a large area. Therefore the current supply to the heated rear window is nearly always via a relay to minimise power loss due to voltage drop in the cable. Operation of the heated rear window is normally only possible with the ignition on, and often only when the engine is running. In addition, timer units can be fitted so that it is not possible to leave the unit switched on for a long time as this could put excessive load on the charging system. A circuit diagram for a simple heated rear window system is shown in Figure 8.40.

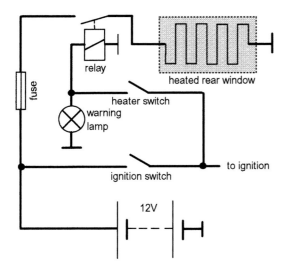

Figure 8.40 Heated rear window circuit

Front screen

Many vehicles are now fitted with heated front screens. These help with fast defrosting of the screen in harsh weather. The screen heating elements must be much more discreet in order that they do not impede the driver's vision. This is achieved by bonding micro-thin elements within the glass which generate sufficient heat to melt snow and ice. Due to that large surface area the current draw is considerable, and for this reason heated front screens are equipped with timer controller to prevent excessively long periods of use. In addition, they normally only operate when the engine is running.

Often the operation of heated screens is monitored when a central electronic control unit is fitted to manage the body electronics. If the battery condition or charging system operation is compromised by these significant consumers they can be switched off by the control unit in order to conserve power in a critical situation.

Key Points

Most front wiper systems have two continuous speeds – low and high. The high speed is achieved with a second brush supplying current to the armature with a reduced field flux. This increases the speed but reduces the motor torque

In addition, most vehicles have an intermittent wipe function. This activates the wipers for a single sweep every few seconds. An intermittent wipe relay performs this task. It is activated by an electronic timer circuit and is connected into the wiper self-switching (parking) circuit

All wiper systems must be able to continue after switch-off until the blades reach a suitable position off the screen. This is known as self-switching. Some wiper systems actually move the blades off the screen when switched off. This is known as off-screen self-parking

Electronic wiper motors are being fitted to many vehicles. These do not need an external crank mechanism as the motor is reversed by the electronics. This saves installation space. If two motors are fitted they can be synchronised electronically so that there is no mechanical linkage between them at all

Rear-screen heaters are very common. Front-screen heaters are also being seen fitted to vehicles. Note that screen heaters draw significant power from the electrical system and their operation is often controlled by a timer and/or monitored electronically

8.3 MIRRORS

8.3.1 Exterior

Position adjustment

An electrical actuation system can make the process of adjusting the door mirrors safer for the driver. This makes the task easy for the driver who is therefore more likely to adjust the mirrors appropriately for good rear vision. It is particularly helpful for the driver when adjustment of the passenger side mirror is required. Electric adjustment of mirrors is quite commonplace in modern vehicles. A typical circuit arrangement to adjust the mirrors via a joystick-type switch is shown in Figure 8.41.

The mirror glass is fitted to a frame inside the mirror housing which has lateral and horizontal movement, thus allowing the mirror glass to pivot up/down and left/right. The movement is controlled by two small reversible permanent magnet motors to provide actuation in each plane. In the circuit shown in Figure 8.41 each mirror has its own switch, but it is also possible to use a single switch for both mirrors. When the switch is pressed to vertically tilt the mirror, the switch cage A is moved downwards and the two contacts B and C make a circuit with the − and + surfaces D and E. Conversely, when the switch stalk is moved upwards, B contacts the positive surface and C contacts the negative surface. In this switch position, the potential applied to the vertical tilt motor is opposite to that given when the switch was in the previous position. This causes the motor (and hence the mirror) to move in the opposite direction.

Heating

Where electric adjustment of the mirrors is fitted, it is common that electric heating of the mirror glass is also featured (hence electric mirrors!). Heating the surface of the mirror glass provides fast clearing of condensation or ice and this ensures good visibility for the driver in poor weather conditions. Heating is implemented via an embedded resistive heating element within the mirror glass structure. Often the mirror heaters are linked to the operation of the heated rear window and this overcomes the need to have a separate switch arrangement.

8.3.2 Interior

Auto-dipping interior mirror

Automatic dipping rear-view mirrors can identify excessively bright headlight beams behind the car and darken the mirror glass to prevent glare for the driver. An electronic control unit varies the darkening effect quickly and continuously according to actual ambient light conditions.

The automatic dip function makes use of a transparent, electrically conductive material that becomes increasingly impervious to light when an electric current is applied to it. A very thin layer of this material is inserted between the actual mirror reflector and the outer glass. The mirror also contains two photoelectric cells. One of these faces forward and determines the ambient light intensity. The second is in the rear-facing surface of the mirror and reacts when a bright light strikes it from behind the car. If this light is very much brighter than the ambient light intensity, the photoelectric cell generates the necessary electrical signal immediately. The electrically conductive layer darkens and the image in the mirror no longer dazzles the driver.

An extension to the basic function of the automatic dipping interior mirror is available with an additional light sensor that can switch the dipped-beam headlights on or off automatically according to the ambient light level.

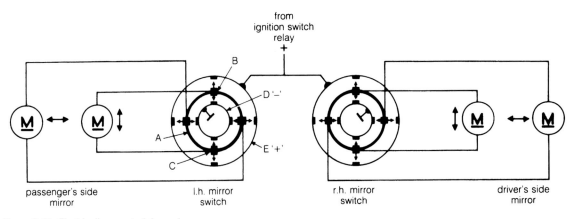

Figure 8.41 Electrically operated door mirrors

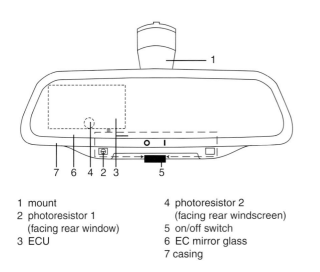

1 mount
2 photoresistor 1
   (facing rear window)
3 ECU

4 photoresistor 2
   (facing rear windscreen)
5 on/off switch
6 EC mirror glass
7 casing

Figure 8.42 Auto-dipping interior mirror

Key Points

Electric adjustment of mirrors allows the driver to alter the external mirrors easily via a switch inside the vehicle. The movement of the mirror glass is implemented by small electric motors, one for each movement plane

Often electric mirror adjustment is combined with mirror heating to assist driver vision during cold weather driving. Mirror heaters are often switched in conjunction with the heated rear window

Auto-dipping rear-view mirrors use photoelectric sensors to compare ambient light with light shining on the mirror surface from the headlamps of the vehicle behind. If the light on the mirror is greater than ambient by a predetermined threshold, the mirror glass is darkened by the electronics to prevent glare for the driver

8.4   SIGNALLING

8.4.1 Visual

Visual indication of change of direction or movement is provided by turn signal lamps also known as indicators. In addition these lamps can be used to warn of potentially hazardous situations. They are amber illuminated lamps fitted to both sides at the front and rear of the vehicle; repeater lamps are fitted on each side of the vehicle. When switched on they must flash on and off at a frequency of 60 to 120 flashes per minute. A visual and audible indication of operation is also provided for the driver. The front and rear lamp units are subject to European approval regulations and the bulb must be rated at 15 to 36 watts. Normally a

21 watt bulb is fitted at the front and rear. A simple direction indicator circuit is shown in Figure 8.43.

When the switch (normally a stalk-mounted switch near the steering wheel) is moved to the left or right, current is supplied appropriately to the lamps. Interruption of the current to give the lamp-flashing effect is effected by a flasher unit situated on the supply side of the switch. It is also possible to make left- and right-hand side lamps flash together to give a hazard warning. This is activated via a dash-mounted switch. A typical hazard warning and indicator switching arrangement employing a single flasher unit for both indicator and hazard functions is shown in Figure 8.44. The flasher unit provides the

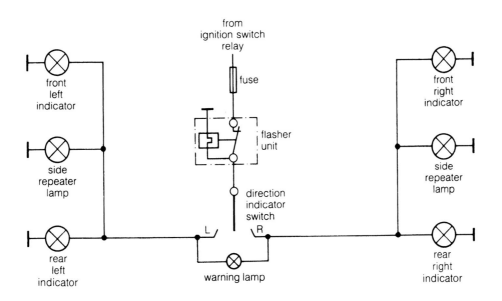

Figure 8.43 Directional indicator circuit

on/off switching of the indicator/hazard lamps. In the past these have been thermal-type units (i.e. the lamp current heats a bi-metal element to switch the lamps on/off cyclically).

These have been replaced by electronic flasher units as they are more efficient and reliable than thermal types (see Figure 8.45). They provide a clear, audible 'click' during operation, they are not susceptible to voltage fluctuation and they can be designed to give a clear indication of bulb failure via a distinctive increase in flash frequency.

Generally switching of the bulb current is executed via relay contacts which are triggered via an pulse-generator integrated circuit. A schematic of a typical electronic flasher unit is shown in Figure 8.46.

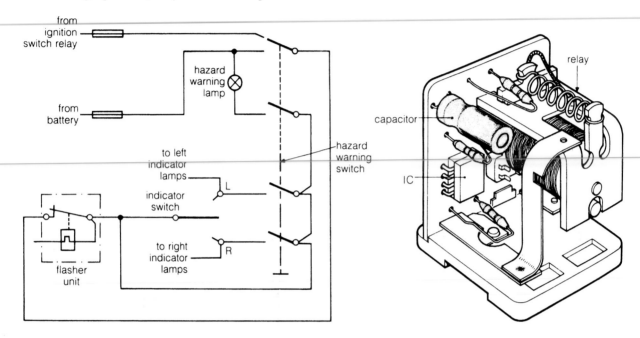

Figure 8.44 Hazard warning circuit

Figure 8.45 Electronic flasher unit (Lucas FL19)

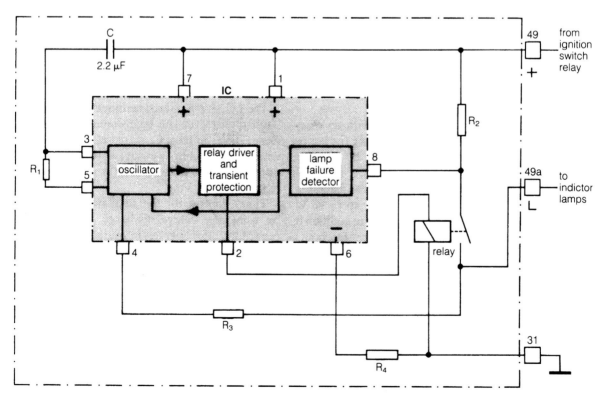

Figure 8.46 Electronic flasher unit circuit

The integrated circuit has three main sections:

- an oscillator
- a relay driver
- a lamp failure detector.

A voltage regulator inside the unit ensures that the flash frequency remains constant over the operating voltage range. Timer control for the oscillator circuit is achieved using an R–C network to give the required flash frequency of ~90 cycles per minute with a 50% duty cycle. Pulses from the oscillator are passed to the relay driver which is a Darlington amplifier. This provides the current pulses to energise the relay coil. The lamp failure detector senses the voltage drop across resistor R_2. This resistor senses the current to the signal lamps, and in the event of a bulb failure the lower current flow will give reduced voltage drop across the resistor. The lamp failure detector circuit senses this and the flash frequency is increased by a factor of two to warn the driver.

Note that common practice is to integrate all timer functions into a central body electrical module. In this case, the flasher unit does not exist as a standalone unit but its function is integrated with other timer/relay circuit applications in a single control unit.

8.4.2 Audible

Motor vehicles for road use must have audible signalling devices that produce an appropriate sound of the correct magnitude. These are commonly known as 'horns'. Most horns are electrically operated and the sound is generated by oscillating a diaphragm magnetically or pneumatically. The sound produced should be appropriately loud but also pleasingly musical. It is often the case that two horns are fitted, high and low frequency. The high-frequency sound overcomes traffic noise whilst the low-frequency tone will carry over a greater distance. The physical size of the horn defines its frequency and loudness. Note that horns should be mounted to the car body via an 'elastic' flexible coupling to prevent the transmission of oscillations to the vehicle body work as this would reduce the horn's loudness and sound quality. A number of different horn types are in use.

High-frequency horn

These are commonly used. An electromagnetic vibrator (trembler) circuit excites a steel diaphragm at about 300 Hz which causes a tone disc to oscillate at about 2 kHz. The combined oscillation provides a highly penetrating note. Figure 8.47 shows the detail of the magnetic vibrator circuit used.

When the horn button is pressed (sometimes mounted on a stalk but more generally as a button on the steering wheel) a current of about 4 amps flows in the field coil. This generates a flux which attracts the armature. After the armature has moved a given distance, the contacts open causing the magnetic field to

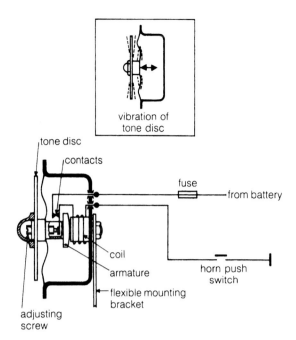

Figure 8.47 High-frequency horn and circuit

collapse. The natural spring property of the diaphragm returns the armature to its rest position and closes the contact. The process then restarts cyclically.

Wind-tone horns

These use a very similar circuit to the high-frequency horn to generate the required oscillations, but instead of exciting a tone disc this design resonates a column of air in a trumpet, similar to a wind instrument (see Figure 8.48).

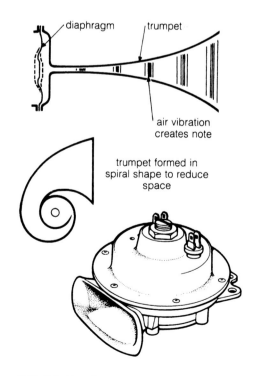

Figure 8.48 Wind-tone horn

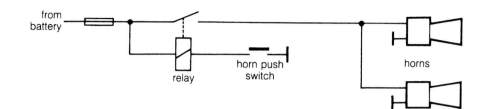

Figure 8.49 Horn circuit with relay

The frequency of the generated sound is a function of the trumpet length. Therefore, for packaging reasons, the trumpet is formed in a spiral shape. In most cases, these horns are fitted in pairs with complementary frequencies. If twin horns of any kind are fitted, a relay must be used in the circuit to prevent volt-drop due to excessive cable length. A simple, typical circuit diagram is shown in Figure 8.49.

Air horns

These consist of a trumpet through which air is forced via an electrically driven air pump. Vibration of the air column in the trumpet is initiated by the diaphragm at the end. When the horn is operated, the air compressor pump drives air through the trumpet which deflects the diaphragm allowing air to escape into the trumpet itself. This causes a pressure drop which then allows the diaphragm to close. The cycle then repeats continuously. The frequency of the diaphragm vibration combined with the trumpet length dictates the sound output. These units are fitted in pairs and are often used as sirens for emergency vehicles.

Key Points

Turn signal flashers use an electronic flasher unit as a pulse generator. This switches the lamps on and off during use at the required frequency. In addition, the flasher unit warns the driver of bulb failure by increasing the flash frequency

Turn indicators are used as hazard warning indicators by flashing both sides at once (i.e. all indicator lamps, left and right). In modern vehicles, the same flasher unit performs hazard and indicator functions

Horns provide an audible signal and must be fitted to all vehicles. Generally they use an electrical trembler circuit to provide the excitation frequency which oscillates a diaphragm to produce the required sound output. The actual sound-generation method depends on the type of horn

It is important that the horn is mounted on a flexible connection to prevent vibrations being passed to the car body itself which would reduce the horn's sound output. If twin horns are fitted then a relay must be used to prevent voltage drop and reduced performance

Chapter 9

SAFETY SYSTEMS

what is covered in this chapter . . .

■ Vehicle dynamic (active) safety
■ Driver and passenger (passive) safety

9.1 VEHICLE DYNAMIC (ACTIVE) SAFETY

A number of factors can affect the safety of a vehicle when driving on the road:

- the condition of the vehicle and its running gear
- ambient conditions (weather, visibility, road surface, traffic)
- driver capability (reaction time etc.).

Developments in technology have allowed the integration of active safety systems. These are systems that can override the driver input, if necessary, based on inputs from sensors. They use microcontroller-based calculation to decide on appropriate evasive action in a critical situation. They can stabilise the vehicle's handling response and maintain steerability. They can react much quicker than a human driver and thus actively contribute to the safety of the vehicle and its passengers. An example is the ABS (anti-lock brake system; the abbreviation is derived from the German name *Anti-Blockier System*). ABS can override the driver-applied brake pressure at the wheel in response to a wheel-speed sensor signal that indicates the speed and acceleration of the wheel. If the wheel decelerates too quickly and approaches an impending wheel lock (and loss of grip) the ABS reduces the brake pressure until the wheel begins to accelerate again. This is a cyclic process which takes place many times a second, controlled by a microprocessor with no driver intervention. It maintains the maximum possible braking force but prevents the loss of grip and driver control.

ABS is a good example of an active safety system as it was probably the first system of this kind to have an impact on the market. Technical developments have brought other systems, for example:

- TCS (traction control system)
- ESP (electronic stability program)
- ACC (active cruise control).

New developments will bring greater enhancements. Developments in software and hardware reliability will realise fully x-by-wire systems (where x = brake, steer, drive etc.) with high reliability and safety integration levels so that control of the vehicle in critical situations will be a function of the electronic system and not down to driver skill or reaction.

9.1.1 ABS (anti-lock brake system)

System overview

The basic function of the car braking system is to allow the driver to control the vehicle speed by absorbing inertia energy from the vehicle mass and converting it to heat. The braking system allows the driver to stop the vehicle completely and to prevent the vehicle from moving when parked. Successful operation of the vehicle brakes relies on a certain level of friction (or grip) being maintained between the road wheel and the road surface. If the level of friction between the tyre/road interface is insufficient during braking (perhaps due to the road surface, ice, etc.) then brake force cannot be transmitted and braking efficiency is reduced.

Most drivers cannot judge the point at which the wheels lock. An additional complication is that the friction coefficient at each wheel could be different and the driver cannot control brake force at each wheel individually. When the wheels skid, the driver has very little control on the directional stability of the vehicle and therefore the probability of an accident is high. The

ABS detects if any of the wheels are about to lock and regulates the brake pressure at that wheel to prevent this. As a result, maximum braking force can be transmitted and the driver can retain control of the vehicle.

An ABS function can be added to an existing automotive braking system that consists of a standard servo-assisted master cylinder with a twin-circuit hydraulic circuit brake system. (The details of standard vehicle braking systems are covered in *FMVT: Book 1*). The basic hydraulic brake system allows the driver to apply brake force at each wheel via a hydraulic circuit. In addition, as shown in Figure 9.1, the ABS components consist of:

- wheel-speed sensors
- ECU
- hydraulic modulator.

System components and operation
The basic principle of the system is that the wheel speed is monitored via sensors by the electronic control unit so that it can determine the point at which the wheel is about to skid and thus lose grip. When this point is reached, the control unit can reduce the brake pressure at that wheel via valves in the modulator assembly. This prevents wheel lock and the wheel begins to accelerate again due to the reduced brake pressure. At this point the modulator valve assembly reapplies hydraulic pressure at the brake mechanism until the wheel decelerates and approaches the critical point before skidding, when the brake pressure is reduced again. This apply-release-apply cycle continues many times a second, individually at each wheel, until the driver releases the brake

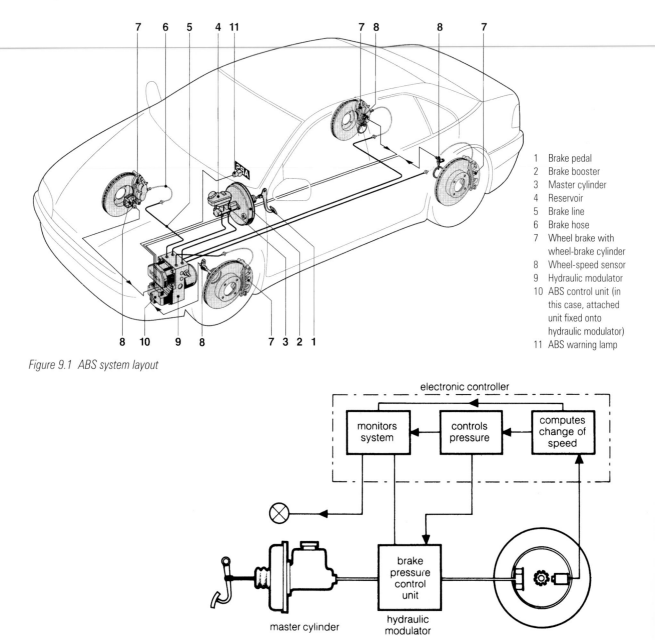

1   Brake pedal
2   Brake booster
3   Master cylinder
4   Reservoir
5   Brake line
6   Brake hose
7   Wheel brake with wheel-brake cylinder
8   Wheel-speed sensor
9   Hydraulic modulator
10 ABS control unit (in this case, attached unit fixed onto hydraulic modulator)
11 ABS warning lamp

Figure 9.1 ABS system layout

Figure 9.2 ABS control system (closed loop)

pedal or the vehicle speed is reduced to approximately walking pace whereby the ABS system then deactivates automatically. This allows the vehicle can come to a complete halt. This process of apply-release-apply based on sensor signals is a good example of a closed-loop control system (see Figure 9.2).

The hydraulic modulator assembly consists of a number of valves that can open or close the hydraulic circuits between the master cylinder, brake cylinders and a return pump (see Figure 9.3). In modern systems, 2/2 solenoid valves (i.e. two connections, two positions) control pressure application and pressure reduction to and from the brake cylinder. The return pump controls the pressure release and returns fluid to the master cylinder from the brake cylinder during the pressure reduction phase. Generally, a pair of valves are allocated for each wheel's hydraulic brake circuit. All of these components are often contained within the modulator assembly complete with the ECU electronics. Note that it is also possible to use a single 3/3 valve per wheel (i.e. three positions; apply pressure, hold pressure and release pressure), but these have generally been superseded by the 2/2 type used in pairs.

Wheel-speed sensors are the main ABS ECU input to monitor the wheel speed and acceleration status. Wheel-speed sensors can be passive or active. They are incremental rotation sensors that produce analogue or digital signals for processing via the ECU to determine instantaneous wheel speed. (Sensors of this type are discussed in more detail in Chapter 2.) A vehicle is normally fitted with one sensor per wheel (depending on the ABS version). Typical wheel-speed sensors are shown in Figure 9.4.

The ABS ECU evaluates the signals from the wheel-speed sensors. From these signals the acceleration/deceleration of the wheel, brake slip, wheel reference speed and vehicle speed can be derived. This information is processed by a microcontroller and the necessary reactions are calculated and sent to the hydraulic modulator via the output stage as control signals for the valves and pump. The main functional parts of the ECU are:

- Input stage: filters and timer/counters that receive and condition the wheel-speed sensor signals ready for further processing and calculation in the ECU.
- Processing unit: a microprocessor evaluates the signals from the wheel-speed sensors and compares them with reference values. Using sophisticated control algorithms, the ECU calculates the desired reaction needed and sends this data to the actuators.
- Power stage: output data from the microprocessor is converted into signals to operate the system actuators in order to achieve and implement the desired output and reactions.
- Monitoring unit: there is a monitoring circuit that continuously checks that the ABS system is functioning correctly. If a fault is detected, the ABS feature is switched off and the driver is warned via a dashboard indicator lamp. Normal braking function remains unimpaired.

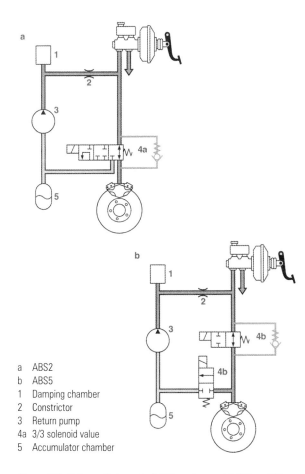

a ABS2
b ABS5
1 Damping chamber
2 Constrictor
3 Return pump
4a 3/3 solenoid value
5 Accumulator chamber

Figure 9.3 Schematic layout of ABS systems with 2/2 or 3/3 valves

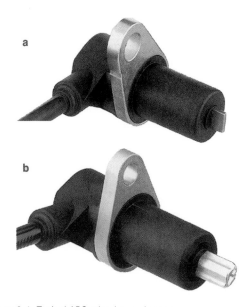

Figure 9.4 Typical ABS wheel-speed sensors

a Chisel-type pole pin (flat pole pin)
b Rhombus-type pole pin (lozenge-shaped pole pin)

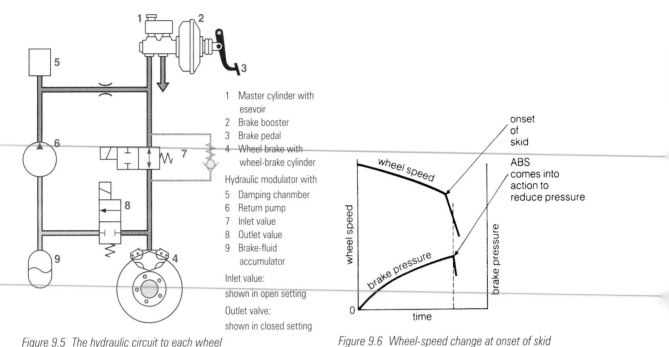

1 Master cylinder with
   esevoir
2 Brake booster
3 Brake pedal
4 Wheel brake with
   wheel-brake cylinder

Hydraulic modulator with

5 Damping chanmber
6 Return pump
7 Inlet value
8 Outlet value
9 Brake-fluid
   accumulator

Inlet value:
shown in open setting

Outlet valve:
shown in closed setting

Figure 9.5 The hydraulic circuit to each wheel

Figure 9.6 Wheel-speed change at onset of skid

The modulator forms the actuator part of the system. Its main duty is to regulate the brake fluid pressure to each wheel in accordance with the electrical signals sent by the ECU output stage. As mentioned above, the fluid passage to and from the master cylinder to each wheel brake cylinder is via the valve assembly in the modulator. The hydraulic circuit also includes an accumulator to store hydraulic pressure. The return pump pumps the hydraulic fluid from the brake cylinders back to the master cylinder. Figure 9.5 shows an overview of the hydraulic circuit to each wheel.

During normal braking operation, the solenoid valves are in the pressure application setting (as shown in Figure 9.5). The inlet valve is open and this allows fluid movement between master and brake cylinders so the braking can occur normally as required by the driver. If brake slip occurs due to a slippery surface, the solenoid valves are switched by the ECU into a *maintain pressure* setting. The connection between the master and brake cylinder is closed (via activation of the inlet valve) so that any increase in pressure applied by the driver does not increase the pressure at the brake cylinder. If this still does not reduce the possibility of slip, the pressure at the brake cylinder can be reduced by opening the pressure release solenoid. The inlet valve is still closed, hence the pressure at the brake cylinder is released and wheel lock-up does not occur. The fluid is returned to the master cylinder in this phase via the accumulator and pump. The cycle is repeated many times a second. In addition, each wheel is controlled separately and this allows maximum braking to be achieved at each wheel irrespective of the available grip. Figure 9.6 shows wheel speed and brake pressure plotted versus time during the onset of a skid.

Since its introduction, ABS has evolved considerably (see Figure 9.7) and benefited from the following advances in technology:

- improved valve design and response
- advances in electronic circuitry and components
- improved test methods and technology in the development of highly dynamic electronic control systems
- general developments in electrotechnical technology (sensors, relays etc.).

This has reduced the cost and physical size of the anti-lock brake system so that it is standard equipment on most vehicles. Note that if ABS fails to operate, then it does not affect the operation of the normal brakes, i.e. it is fail-safe. Latest generation ABS ECUs also employ dual processors which monitor each other for correct operation. Generally ABS has extensive self-diagnostic capabilities and can store faults to aid diagnostic procedures.

9.1.2 TCS (traction control system)

System overview

It is an important factor that critical, safety-related situations can occur not only when the wheels lock under braking but also when the wheels lose grip under acceleration forces (known as wheel spin). In both situations, the frictional grip at the tyre/road surface interface is lost and hence the driver loses control of the vehicle direction – the vehicle effectively becomes unstable.

During wheel spin it is very difficult even for an experienced driver to control the movement of a vehicle.

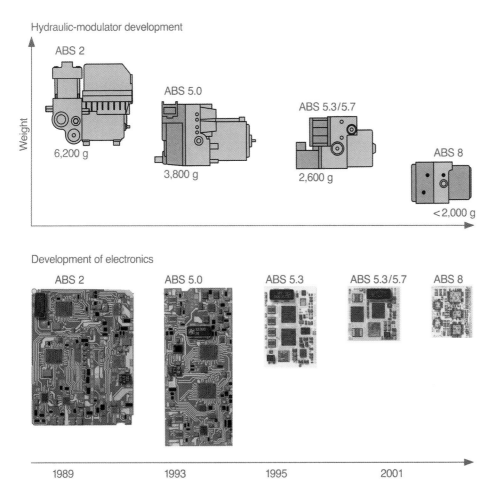

Figure 9.7 Evolution of ABS technology

Spinning of the wheels can be caused by over-zealous throttle usage, but with modern vehicles the torque produced at the wheels can easily exceed the tractive force transmission limit when the road conditions are less than ideal (rain, greasy road surface etc.). If this happens at speed it can catch the driver unaware and easily lead to a hazardous situation due to the loss of lateral stability. The problem is particularly noticeable when accelerating and turning at the same time, such as when joining a road at a T junction. This is because the differential applies most drive to the wheel that needs to rotate faster on the outside of the curve. In addition, for front-wheel drive (FWD), the weight tends to lift off the front wheels.

The introduction of traction control systems (TCSs) can overcome these problems and potential hazards by limiting the torque transmission at the wheels in a controlled and predictable manner. In addition, the system can help the driver to maintain control when the vehicle is driven on surfaces where tyre grip is low (snow, ice, etc.) and the possibility of the vehicle encountering surfaces with a different grip coefficient at each wheel (which leads to very unpredictable handling of the vehicle) is likely. The TCS provides increased vehicle stability and directional steerability when accelerating and this is particularly beneficial when accelerating hard. The TCS maintains the optimum level of slip at the wheels to allow the engine to transfer the maximum tractive force without compromising safety under given conditions.

System components and operation

TCS is a logical extension to ABS and shares the components. It is effectively a software extension to ABS with an additional interface to the engine control system. An overview of a TCS and its component layout is shown in Figure 9.8.

The traction control system regulates the slip at the driven wheels during driving. It responds as quickly as possible to maintain the optimum level of grip if a wheel begins to break away. In order to be able to do this, the system must establish a reference value to compare to the actual wheel speeds to establish the slip ratio. This can be done easily by monitoring the non-driven wheel speeds.

The system then calculates a reference or acceptable slip value which depends upon a number of factors based on the actual conditions at that time. These factors are:

- effective grip or coefficient of friction at the wheel
- tractive resistance at the wheels
- yaw velocity
- steering angle
- lateral acceleration.

The system regulates the slip at each wheel via control of the engine torque and brake torque at the wheels. Via this method, the slip at the driven wheels can be controlled to the limit of the conditions at the time. That is, it can be maintained at the reference slip level. The interventions which take place are as follows.

Drive torque

This can be regulated via the TCS interface to the engine control ECU. The TCS sends correcting values to the engine control system to reduce torque output in a controlled way. This depends on the speed of the torque reduction requirement (a function of the given conditions). In gasoline engines, drive torque can be reduced by the throttle valve position. This is suitable where slower, controlled intervention is needed by the TCS. If a fast reduction in torque is required to prevent a wheel breaking away, the system can demand this and it is implemented via interruption of fuel injection or via ignition angle retardation. These latter method provides an instantaneous response. The relative response time is shown in Figure 9.9.

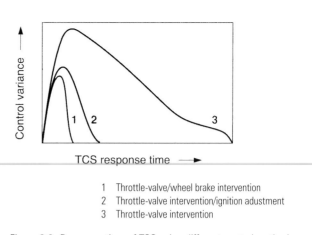

1 Throttle-valve/wheel brake intervention
2 Throttle-valve intervention/ignition adustment
3 Throttle-valve intervention

Figure 9.9 Response time of TCS using different control methods

For diesel engines, drive torque intervention is via the electronic diesel control system which can immediately adjust the amount of fuel injected to reduce engine torque. This can be executed in a slow or fast manner according to the demands sent via the TCS. Note that in common with current practice, the interface between the TCS and engine control ECU will generally be via the CAN bus.

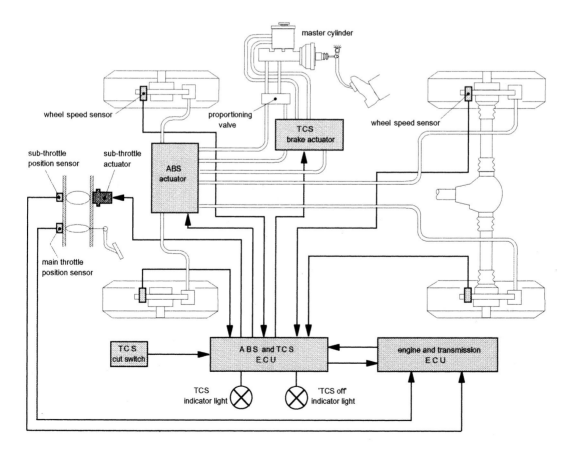

Figure 9.8 Traction control system

Brake torque

This is regulated at each wheel by the braking system hardware and control electronics (i.e. the ABS). The TCS requires an extension to the brake system as it must be able to actively generate brake system pressure on demand, i.e. without the driver applying pressure to the brake pedal. This can be achieved easily via the hydraulic modulator of a modern anti-lock brake system and is a function of most current ABSs.

The TCS has a number of structured controllers which maintain the stability of the vehicle based on inputs from the vehicle systems and sensors. Figure 9.10 shows the structure of these controllers.

The actuators are effectively the ABS and the engine ECU. The drive axle speed controller is used to regulate the speed of the drive axle via engine torque intervention. The transversal differential lock controller regulates the speed differential of the driven wheels via asymmetrical brake application. In this way, it replicates the action of a differential lock.

These two controllers together form the TCS. The drive axle speed controller regulates the engine torque and is used in situations where the available grip at both wheels is low. When the axle speed accelerates faster than the reference value, the loss of grip is sensed by the system and brake torque is applied symmetrically to the driven wheels. In addition, the engine torque is reduced. This allows the maximum acceleration under these conditions whilst the driver still maintains control of the vehicle.

The transversal differential lock controller regulates the torque distribution between the driven wheels. It is used where the available grip of the driven wheels differs considerably, i.e. the surface friction coefficient is different at each wheel. The wheel with the least grip (and hence torque transmission) sets the limit for available torque at each wheel due to the differential action. To counteract this, the controller applies the brake at the spinning wheel (i.e. the wheel with lowest torque transmission). This transfers torque and increases the torque at the gripping wheel and thus traction is increased. The asymmetric brake action is reduced once the differential speed reduces to zero and full traction is restored.

Note that the system continuously monitors the amount of brake usage and can determine the likely build up of heat at the wheels. This is taken into account and the system can reduce heat build up by control of engine torque (i.e. reduction over cumulative time period).

The TCS provides a considerable additional safety benefit for the vehicle occupants by helping the driver to maintain control of the vehicle under difficult conditions as well as day-to-day driving. The main advantages are:

- increased traction, the vehicle can be operated at optimum slip limit
- differential locking action without the hardware of a locking differential
- efficient implementation due to multi-use application of ABS components
- reduced tyre wear when compared to a mechanical differential lock
- reduced wear on drive-train components when encountering difficult grip surface conditions.

9.1.3 ESP (electronic stability program)

System overview

Human error accounts for a large proportion of road accidents. Unforeseen circumstances can cause the driver to over-compensate. The vehicle can reach a critical state where the lateral acceleration forces can be greater than any human driver can compensate for. The vehicle then becomes uncontrollable. The ESP system is a fast, closed-loop control system that uses the ABS and TCS component infrastructure and controllers to improve vehicle handling and response in critical situations. It does this through controlled intervention of the drive-train components (see Figure 9.11).

ESP uses the vehicle braking system to assist in steering the vehicle. It can apply the brakes on individual wheels in order to counteract under-steer or over-steer. ESP can also intervene at the engine to apply torque to the

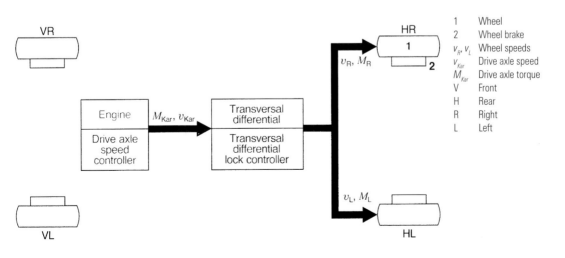

Figure 9.10 Structure of TCS controllers

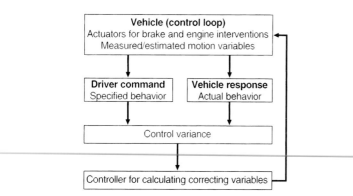

Figure 9.11 ESP control loop

wheels. Using a combination of braking and acceleration, individual wheels' ESP can help the driver to maintain control of the vehicle and reduce the risk of overturning the vehicle and/or an accident occurring.

ESP enhances vehicle safety in the following ways:

• it helps to maintain directional stability in critical or extreme situations

• it provides enhanced stability during everyday traffic situations like stopping the vehicle, accelerating, overrun, etc.

• the combined action of ABS, ETC and ESP improves braking distances, increases traction and gives better steering response in conjunction with improved stability.

Figure 9.12 shows an example of how ESP can contribute to vehicle stability by maintaining the vehicle's intended path even in extreme driving conditions.

System components

ESP prevents the vehicle dynamic motion from exceeding critical control limits. The system determines how the vehicle should respond in a critical situation when operating near these limits and monitors how the vehicle actually responds (via sensors). The difference between the two is an error signal that is applied to control actuators which attempt to minimise the difference by influencing the forces acting at the tyre/road surface interface. An overview of the system and its interfaces is shown in Figure 9.15.

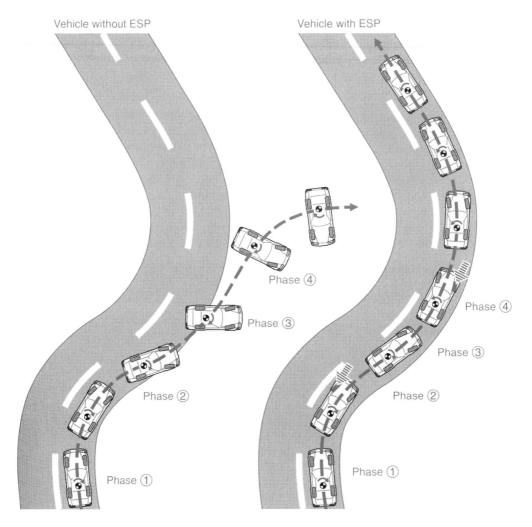

Figure 9.12 Comparison – with/without ESP in a critical situation

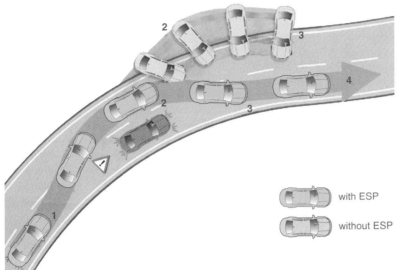

Increased braking force (Figure 9.14)

1 Driver steers, lateral force buildup
2 Incipient instability Right: ESP intervention at left front
3 Countersteer Left: Driver loses control of vehicle; Right: Vehicle remains under control
4 Left: Vehicle becomes uncontrollable, Right: ESP intervention at top front, complete stabilization.

Vehicle without ESP (Figure 9.13)

1 Vehicle approaches an obstacle
2 Vehicle breaks away and does not follow the driver's steering movements
3 Vehicle slides uncontrolled off the road

Vehicle with ESP (Figure 9.13)

1 Vehicle approaches an obstacle
2 Vehicle almost breaks away
   ESP intervention, vehicle follows driver's movements
3 Vehicle almost breaks away again when recentering the steering wheel
   ESP intervention
4 Vehicle is stabilised.

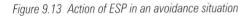 with ESP

without ESP

Figure 9.13 Action of ESP in an avoidance situation

Vehicle without ESP

Vehicle with ESP

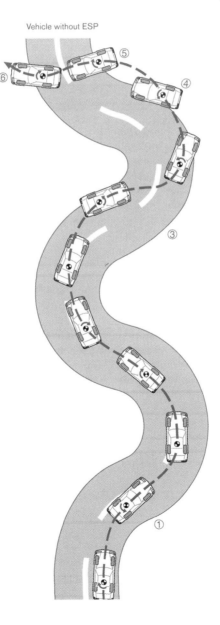

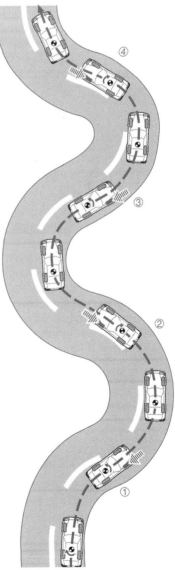

Figure 9.14 ESP operation during increased braking force

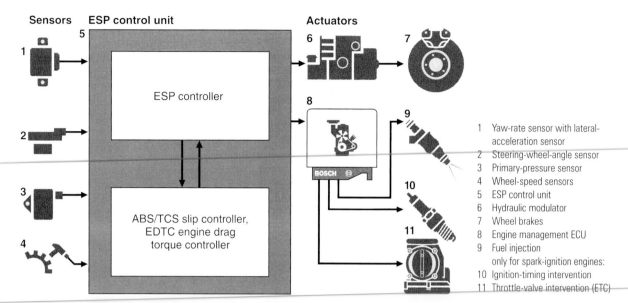

Figure 9.15 Overview of ESP system and components

The system consists of:

- Sensors that provide inputs of the vehicle dynamic state consisting of:
  - yaw rate sensor
  - steering angle sensor
  - brake pressure sensor
  - wheel speed sensors.
- Actuators to control the forces at the wheels.
- ABS hydraulic modulator.
- Interface to engine ECU.
- The ESP control unit with its sophisticated controller structure.

The system uses components of the anti-lock brake system and traction control system and can dynamically control brake forces at individual wheels. In addition, an interface to the engine control ECU allows control of wheel torque at driven wheels to adjust wheel-slip rates as required. To achieve this, the engine must be drive-by-wire, i.e. an electronic throttle actuator is part of the engine control system.

The main input signals are as follows:

- Input signals measured via sensors:
  - yaw velocity
  - steering-wheel angle
  - lateral acceleration
  - torque demand (via throttle position)
  - brake demand (via pressure sensor).
- Input signals inferred/calculated:
  - vehicle linear velocity
  - tyre forces and slip rates.

From these inputs, the following are derived:
- lateral forces at the wheel
- slip angle
- side-slip angle
- vehicle lateral speed.

System operation

The ESP controller sits hierarchically above the ABS and TCS controllers. It determines the vehicle dynamic state in real time based on information from the sensors. It uses this information to compare the actual vehicle response with the ideal vehicle response in a given situation. This provides the basis of an error signal. Figure 9.16 shows the structure of the controllers in the ESP system. It also shows the signal input and actuator output paths.

The required response of the vehicle is defined as the driver demand. The tyre grip factor (coefficient of friction between tyre/road interface) and the vehicle speed are also taken into account. These are estimated values derived from wheel speeds, lateral acceleration, yaw velocity and brake-system pressures. The required vehicle response is implemented by generating a corrective yaw moment (i.e. the yaw angle is the angle between a vehicle's actual heading and a desired or reference heading). In order to do this, the ESP controller intervenes and commands the ABS and TCS sub-controllers to generate appropriate slip forces at the wheels to influence the longitudinal and lateral forces. The ABS and TCS systems then execute the required slip commands via the actuator hardware.

The ESP control system monitors and controls two main status parameters:

- the yaw-velocity
- the side-slip angle.

From this information, the yaw moment (turning force at the vehicle axis) is calculated and this is required to achieve the ideal vehicle dynamic state. The limits of the vehicle dynamic capability are established from test-track data and this is stored in the ESP ECU as reference data. This data provides information about the relationship between the steering angle, vehicle speed and yaw velocity and this serves as a basis for the definition of desired vehicle motion.

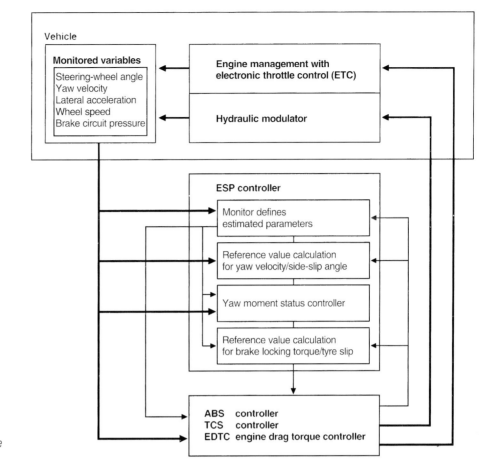

Figure 9.16 Controllers in the ESP system

The yaw velocity (turning speed at the vehicle axis) must be limited in line with the achievable grip of the vehicle tyres in contact with the road surface. This is essential in order to keep the vehicle on the calculated, desired path. For example, if the vehicle over-steers, the specified yaw velocity is exceeded (i.e. the vehicle rotates too quickly about its axis). The ESP responds by braking the front wheel on the outside of the curve radius which shifts the yaw moment to oppose the vehicle tendency to break away. If the vehicle under-steers, the yaw velocity is too low (i.e. vehicle rotates too slowly about its axis). ESP brakes the rear wheel on the inside of the curve radius to create a yaw moment (a turning force) to resist the vehicle's tendency to go in a tangential direction with respect to the curve.

In addition, the ESP system provides its data continuously to the ABS and TCS systems to allow maximum exploitation of these sub-systems under all conditions. During ABS operation the ESP provides the following data:

- lateral vehicle velocity
- yaw velocity
- steering wheel angle
- wheel speeds.

The subordinate ABS system becomes operative when the desired slip rate at any wheel is exceeded during braking. In order to measure this the system needs to establish vehicle speed accurately. This can be established by momentary under-braking of one of the wheels to determine the actual speed of the vehicle (also known as speed-over-ground) at its centre of gravity. This data can then be compared with actual wheels speeds so that slip and loss of grip can be established.

When TCS is in operation, ESP sends values to the TCS controller for:

- slip at the driven wheels
- slip tolerance between driven wheels
- engine torque reduction.

When wheel slip occurs, the TCS sub-controller becomes active to prevent the wheels breaking into uncontrolled wheel spin. The TCS limits engine torque under these conditions. In addition, braking torque can be applied to the spinning wheel (with certain limitations). The TCS receives values from the ESP system to adapt the specified slip and slip difference between driven wheels (in the form of an offset or adjustment value).

ESP therefore has two intervention strategies to stabilise the vehicle. It can use ABS or TCS to brake or accelerate individual wheels to keep the vehicle on the road and reduce the risk of an accident. When under control of the ESP, the basic function of the ABS and TCS systems becomes secondary. The ESP has priority over the two systems to command them in such a way as necessary to keep the vehicle stable and safe irrespective of the driving conditions. The system can support the driver in critical conditions but it cannot overcome the basic laws of physics. These will always govern the limiting factors with respect to how the vehicle will respond under a given set of conditions.

9.1.4 Electrohydraulic brakes

Introduction

Electrohydraulic brake technology is the next step in the integration of further electronic control for the braking system. It combines the function of the brake servo, ABS modulator and related functions like TCS and ESP in a single unit. When the driver operates the brake pedal, sensors are used to generate a demand value which is sent to the brake ECU. This information is processed according to a number of parameters and the required output is defined according to intelligent algorithms. These outputs are sent to the actuator, which in this case is the modulator assembly which generates the required brake force at each wheel.

In this form the system effectively becomes brake-by-wire. The system can control the hydraulic pressure at each wheel independently. In addition, it can respond independently of the driver input. All of the advanced electronic functions of the modern brake system like ESP, TCS and ABS are integrated. In addition, features like ACC (adaptive cruise control) which need automated brake response can be added easily.

Control of the brake force distribution can be executed electronically by the system. In addition, external braking factors such as engine inertia, engine parasitic loading and air drag can be taken into account when calculating the required retardation forces. Note also that the vacuum servo is no longer required as the modulator generates hydraulic pressure via a pump. The system has a high degree of redundancy and safety built in and it is possible to integrate it into existing vehicle designs. Therefore, brake-by-wire will probably become commonplace in the future.

System components and overview

A conventional brake system uses mechanical and hydraulic components to amplify the force applied at the brake pedal by the driver. It then distributes this force to the brake mechanism at each wheel in order to provide the retardation force necessary at the tyre surface interface. With an electrohydraulic (brake-by-wire) system, the brake actuation chain consists of:

- sensors
- brake system ECU
- pressure modulators (actuators)
- hydraulic pressure generator (hydraulic pump).

Under normal operation, there is no direct mechanical connection between the brake pedal and the brakes. The high-pressure generator can provide a rapid, dynamic pressure increase and thus, when under electronic control, the brake system can produce much shorter stopping distances with better handling and vehicle dynamics whilst braking. The main system components and their location on the vehicle are shown in Figure 9.17.

They are connected by a system of control wiring and hydraulic pipes. The actuator unit is shown in Figure 9.18 and consists of:

- actuator rod
- pedal travel sensor
- pedal travel simulator
- master cylinder
- fluid reservoir.

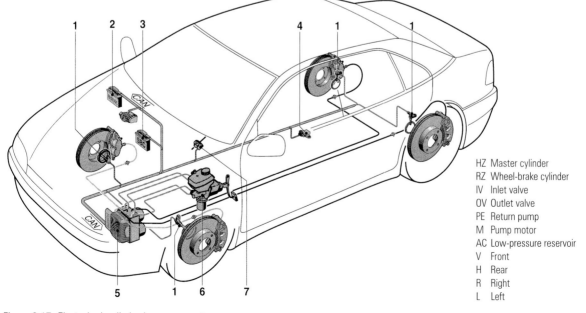

HZ	Master cylinder
RZ	Wheel-brake cylinder
IV	Inlet valve
OV	Outlet valve
PE	Return pump
M	Pump motor
AC	Low-pressure reservoir
V	Front
H	Rear
R	Right
L	Left

Figure 9.17 Electrohydraulic brake components

A number of sensor inputs are used to establish brake demand and the vehicle dynamic state. These are:

- pedal travel sensors (two for safety reasons)
- brake pressure sensors for accumulator pressure and brake-line pressures
- wheel-speed sensors at each wheel
- steering angle sensor
- yaw-rate sensor
- lateral acceleration sensor.

A schematic diagram of the system is shown in Figure 9.19.

Note the brake system isolating valves. Should the system fail or lose power, then these valves switch automatically to connect the master cylinder with the brake lines directly, thus allowing manual brake operation (with no assistance). This is a fail-safe feature. Two pedal travel sensors are fitted for the same reason, so that if one fails the other is immediately available. These features provide a high level of security and protection in the event of failure.

System operation

A brake demand operation by the driver, via the pedal, is detected by the system via the pedal travel sensors and a pressure sensor in the modulator which measures the actual pressure generated by the driver's foot. The information is processed in the ECU which calculates

1 Actuator rod
2 Pedal-travel sensor
3 Brake-fluid reservoir
4 Master cylinder
5 Pedal-travel simulator

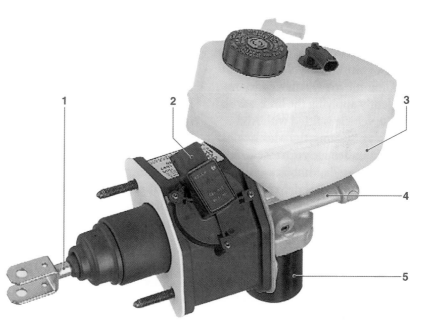

Figure 9.18 Actuator unit

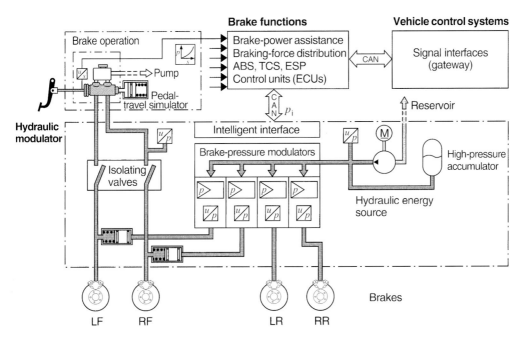

Figure 9.19 Overview of electrohydraulic brake system

the control signals to be sent to the modulator. Note that the brake ECU controls the following functions:

- brake boosting (servo assistance)
- ABS
- TCS
- ESP
- brake assistant,

taking into account the dynamic state of the vehicle and the driver demands. The ECU controls the brake pressure in the individual hydraulic lines to each wheel via pressure modulators. The brake pressure is generated by a hydraulic pump and accumulator assembly inside the modulator itself. Note that the master cylinder contains a brake pedal simulator which provides a reactive force at the brake pedal. This allows the driver to 'feel' the same pedal response as they would get from a conventional brake system. This feature is essential for user/driver acceptance of the system. The system can be programmed with an adaptive brake response such that the brakes provide more 'feel' with light operation but can give sharper, more dynamic response when the vehicle speed is higher or when the vehicle is operating in a more dynamic state.

The system can react quickly and additional features are built in to enhance safety and response time. For example, when the throttle is released, the system is primed with pressure in anticipation of a brake operation. This moves the brake pads into light contact with the disc so that the brakes can 'bite' and react very quickly. This has a significant benefit with respect to reducing stopping distances. In addition, during wet weather, the system can intermittently wipe the brake discs by moving the pads into gentle contact with the discs. This is done regularly and helps to increase brake performance during wet road conditions.

Vehicle active safety systems contribute to safety in a preventative way

The anti-lock brake system (ABS) allows the driver to maintain control of the vehicle during braking. The system measures the wheel speed at each wheel and can detect the onset of wheel lock. If this occurs, the brake pressure at that wheel is reduced by the system to prevent the wheel from locking. This is a cyclic process which is repeated many times a second to prevent wheel lock but maintain the maximum braking force at the wheel. The system operates without driver intervention

The system uses a hydraulic modulator which contains a valve assembly for each wheel and a hydraulic pump and accumulator to generate pressure for the system. The operation of the system is controlled via an ECU, and a wheel-speed sensor is fitted to each road wheel

The traction control system (TCS) uses the ABS component infrastructure to control wheel spin

and slip under driving or accelerating conditions. Effectively it works in the opposite way to ABS in that it allows the driver to maintain control of the vehicle whilst accelerating, whereas ABS maintains control under deceleration

The TCS prevents wheel spin and maintains wheel slip within limits by braking the spinning wheel in a controlled way, thus transferring torque to the opposite wheel on the driving axle. The system can also reduce engine torque via intervention with the engine ECU. The combination of these effects allows the driver to maintain control of the vehicle. The system operates automatically and no driver intervention is required

ESP is a software extension to ABS and TCS which integrates and harmonises these functions to enhance the dynamic safety of the vehicle. The system uses the ability to brake or apply torque at individual wheels in order to steer the vehicle in critical situations. It can do this as the ESP control software sits hierarchically above the ABS and TCS controllers which effectively become sub-systems of the ESP control structure

In addition to the components of the ABS/TCS system, the ESP system requires additional inputs in order to be able to establish the dynamic state of the vehicle. These include yaw and acceleration sensors. A steering angle sensor must also be fitted. This allows the ESP to establish the driver demand, the actual vehicle state and the reference state for the given set of conditions. From this information the system can calculate the error signal (difference between the actual and reference state) and the activate the actuators to correct or minimise the error (i.e. via braking or accelerating individual wheels). The reference state is derived from the driver demand and the physical limits to which the vehicle is restricted

Electrohydraulic brakes are also known as brake-by-wire systems. During normal operation there is no direct mechanical connection between the driver's foot and the brake system at the wheel. The system has a built-in pressure generator and modulator assembly which applies the hydraulic pressure at each individual wheel according to the conditions

The functions of servo assistance, ABS, TCS and ESP can easily be built in as the whole system is controlled by a brake ECU. The system uses pedal and brake pressure sensors to detect driver demand, and pressure sensors and wheel-speed sensors provide feedback signals to the ECU. The system has a fail-safe mode so that if the electrical system fails, valves allow hydraulic pressure direct from the master cylinder, generated by the driver's foot, to be applied at the brake cylinders

9.2 DRIVER AND PASSENGER (PASSIVE) SAFETY

Passive safety systems are designed to improve the level of protection of the driver and passengers in the event of an accident. The are designed to reduce the risk of injury and the severity of the consequences of an accident for the vehicle occupants. Many of the developments in vehicle safety have been due to advances in electronics and microprocessor technology. Figure 9.20 shows safety concepts for the vehicle and the influencing factors.

For many years passive safety systems consisted of seatbelt restraint systems. The developments in technology brought new technologies, for example:

- driver and passenger airbags
- side airbags
- seatbelt pre-tensioners
- roll-over protection.

Figure 9.21 highlights the main active and passive safety systems available to modern vehicle manufacturers and shows the components and their typical location on the vehicle.

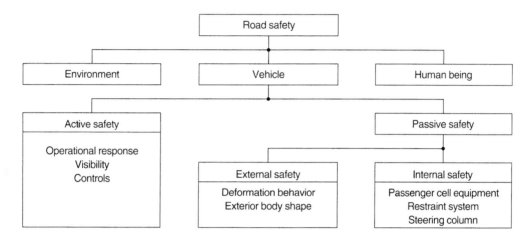

Figure 9.20 Safety concepts for the vehicle

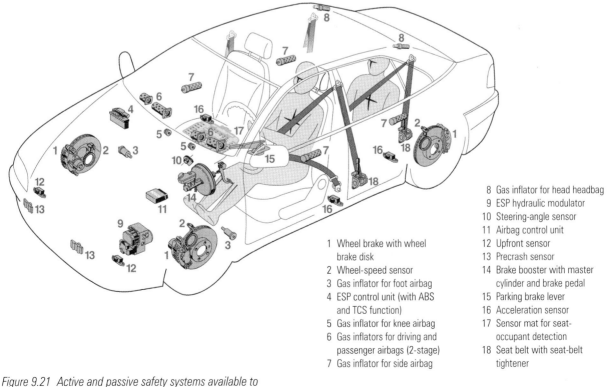

1 Wheel brake with wheel brake disk
2 Wheel-speed sensor
3 Gas inflator for foot airbag
4 ESP control unit (with ABS and TCS function)
5 Gas inflator for knee airbag
6 Gas inflators for driving and passenger airbags (2-stage)
7 Gas inflator for side airbag
8 Gas inflator for head headbag
9 ESP hydraulic modulator
10 Steering-angle sensor
11 Airbag control unit
12 Upfront sensor
13 Precrash sensor
14 Brake booster with master cylinder and brake pedal
15 Parking brake lever
16 Acceleration sensor
17 Sensor mat for seat-occupant detection
18 Seat belt with seat-belt tightener

Figure 9.21 Active and passive safety systems available to modern vehicle manufacturers

9.2.1 Airbags

Introduction

Front airbags are normally fitted to the driver and passenger side of modern vehicles. The main function is to protect the occupant from head and chest injuries that could be sustained in a collision with a solid object at up to 35 miles per hour and up to 60 miles per hour when in collision with another vehicle. A drawing of a typical inflated driver airbag is shown in Figure 9.22.

The system employs pyrotechnic gas inflators to inflate the airbag when a crash is detected by an electronic sensor system and ECU. Rapid inflation of the bag (approximately 40 ms) ensures that it is fully inflated before the passenger contacts it and this gives the highest level of protection. The airbag then deflates in a controlled way and thus absorbs the energy of the crash which has been imparted to the occupant. It does this with minimal surface pressures and forces and thus reduces or even prevents injury to the head and chest.

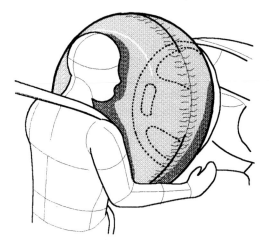

Figure 9.22 Driver's airbag

More recent developments in airbag technology have seen the inclusion of multiple airbag systems to provide maximum occupant protection. Side airbags provide protection for side collisions which account for about 20% of all accidents. Side airbags protect the head and upper body and are deployed from a roof cut-out in the form of inflatable tubes or curtains. Additional airbags can be deployed for the door or seat back-rest and are intended to catch occupants gently and protect them from injury if a side collision occurs. A typical side airbag installation is shown in Figure 9.23.

System components and overview

Figure 9.24 shows the main components of a typical airbag protection system, in this case a driver's airbag. The components are:

- an inflator and airbag assembly – mounted in the steering wheel
- front impact sensors – placed at the front of the vehicle
- airbag ECU – mounted centrally in the vehicle, consisting of all the evaluation electronics and triggering circuits
- driver warning lamp – mounted in the dash console.

Inflator and airbag assembly

This self-contained module houses the nylon fabric airbag, gas generator and igniter element. When a small electric current is applied to the igniter the heat produced causes the gas capsules in the gas generator to give off nitrogen gas to inflate the airbag. Figure 9.25 shows a cut-away view of a typical inflator assembly.

The electrical connection between the igniter element (also known as a squib) and the steering column is via a flattened cable wound in a similar manner to a clock spring. This maintains a reliable electrical connection at all steering-wheel positions.

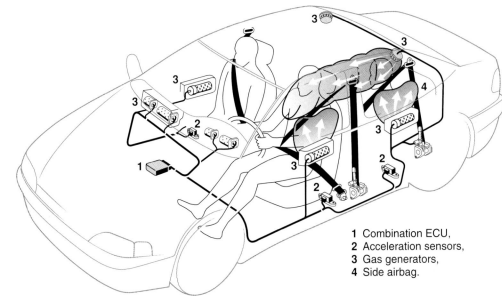

1 Combination ECU,
2 Acceleration sensors,
3 Gas generators,
4 Side airbag.

Figure 9.23 Side airbag installation

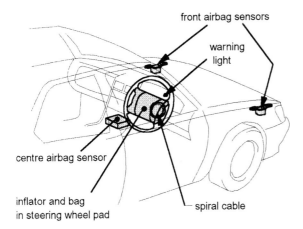

Figure 9.24 Airbag system layout

To prevent accidental triggering of the airbag due to a wiring fault (i.e. a inadvertent connection to the vehicle system voltage) the system uses an AC to fire the gas generator. The current is in the form of alternating current pulses at 80–100 kHz. A small capacitor effectively isolates the firing circuit from any DC. This is also essential after a crash to prevent accidental firing when occupants are being removed from the vehicle by emergency services.

Impact sensors

These are acceleration sensors which are mounted at strategic positions on the vehicle. They are also mounted within the airbag ECU itself (close to the centre of gravity of the vehicle). These sensors are of the surface micromechanical type and they form a complete spring-mass system on the surface of a silicon wafer. They have extremely low signal values (working capacitance of less than 1 pF) and hence the sensor assembly contains the sensing element complete with the evaluation electronics to ensure that the unit is not affected by interference or stray capacitance.

Airbag ECU

This is located at a central point in the vehicle and can have combined functionality by triggering the seatbelt tensioners and the side airbags as well. Figure 9.26 shows a simplified airbag ECU circuit.

The main functions of the airbag ECU are:

- housing of sensors
- back-up power supply
- airbag ignition driver circuit
- self-diagnosis circuit.

Impact detection is via acceleration sensors and an additional safety sensor (switch). This safety switch prevents accidental triggering of the airbag. It closes at

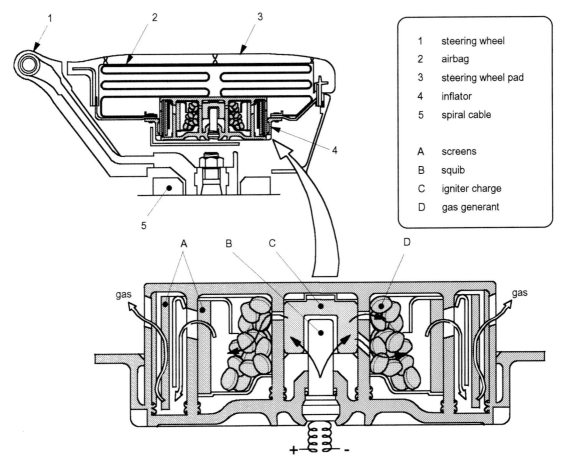

1	steering wheel
2	airbag
3	steering wheel pad
4	inflator
5	spiral cable
A	screens
B	squib
C	igniter charge
D	gas generant

Figure 9.25 Section through an inflator and airbag

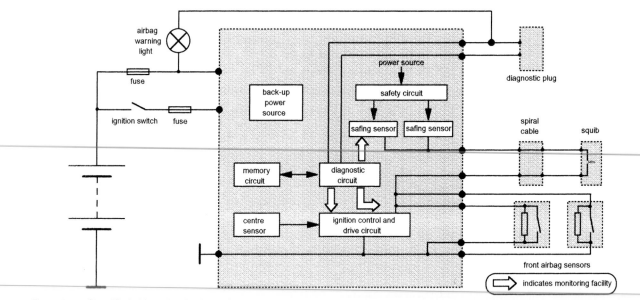

Figure 9.26 Simplified airbag circuit schematic

relatively slow deceleration rates and is connected in series with the power supply. Thus, the airbag will only trigger when the switch is closed. Figure 9.27 shows a simple mercury-type switch used for this application.

The back-up power supply function is essential to ensure that the system triggers even if power fails, and a voltage transformer and accumulator (capacitor) stores enough energy to supply the system for 150 ms which is sufficient for trigger activation. The ECU microprocessor receives all of the sensor signals and is programmed with algorithms that can reliably distinguish a real crash situation (based on data from crash testing). The system has a high level of inherent redundancy and plausibility checking. When a crash occurs, triggering of the airbag is effected by the igniter driver circuit which activates the gas generator. The system has a sophisticated self-check mode at start-up. Any problems are indicated via the driver warning lamp, and diagnostic data can be accessed via electronic tools (generally via CAN). After an accident occurs, the system retains crash recorder information and this is also accessible via the diagnostic interface.

System operation

When a vehicle collision is detected by the system sensors, the required response is calculated by the ECU processor according to pre-programmed information. The system works in conjunction with seatbelt tensioners (often using the same ECU) in order to coordinate and maximise the effect of both devices. In order to detect offset or oblique impacts, the ECU can take into account information from additional sensors like lateral acceleration sensors (where fitted). From the sensor data, the impact is analysed in sophisticated algorithms and the seatbelt tensioners and airbag are triggered with appropriate time thresholds according to the severity and type of impact.

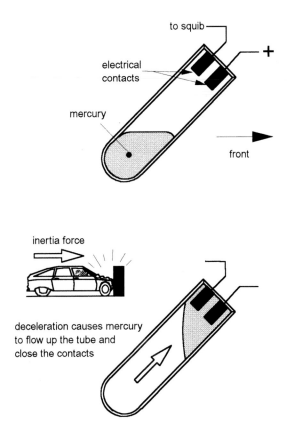

Figure 9.27 Mercury-type safety sensor

The electronic trigger circuit fires the gas generator and the airbag is inflated to full volume with nitrogen gas in approximately 30 ms. The airbag volume will be 30 litres for the driver and 60 litres for the passenger. Figure 9.28 shows the inflation process.

Driver airbags are generally inflated in 30 to 40 ms and passenger airbags in 80 to 100 ms. This is due to the

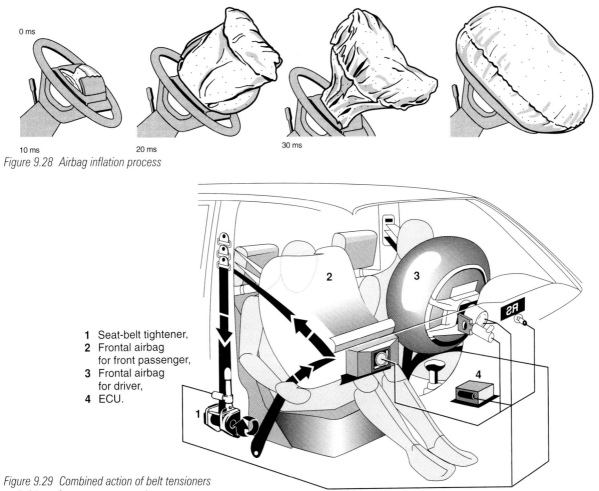

Figure 9.28 Airbag inflation process

0 ms
10 ms
20 ms
30 ms

1 Seat-belt tightener,
2 Frontal airbag
 for front passenger,
3 Frontal airbag
 for driver,
4 ECU.

Figure 9.29 Combined action of belt tensioners
and airbags for passenger restraint

fact that the passenger is further away from the glove compartment than the driver is from the steering wheel and the passenger airbag is bigger. The airbag response to the occupant hitting it is controlled deflation. This reduces the impact forces and absorbs the energy to reduce or prevent injuries. As soon as the airbag is fully inflated it begins to deflate. The whole process completes in less than 150 ms.

Developments in airbag systems have allowed the adoption of more intelligent systems which can react to a greater number of system inputs to tailor the response of the airbag according to a number of prerequisite conditions that can be taken into account:

- impact severity – via sensors in the vehicle crumple zones
- occupant presence, position and weight detection
- seat position detection
- networking via CAN of sensor information for more intelligent assessment of crash mode (e.g. vehicle speed, brake operation etc.).

This allows the system to respond in a more intelligent way, for example:

- controlled force of airbag in deployment via staged gas generators

- time-triggered deployment of airbag and belt tighteners according to crash severity assessment
- automatic transmission of emergency calls
- control and activation of other systems as appropriate (e.g. switch on hazards, open doors via central locking, switch off fuel pump, etc.).

9.2.2 Seatbelt tensioners

Introduction and function

Most vehicles are fitted with three-point inertia-reel seatbelts and these restrain the seat occupant when the vehicle is involved in a collision. An improvement to the basic function of the seatbelt can be gained via the inclusion of seatbelt tensioners. In the event of an impact, the belt tensioners pull the seatbelts tightly across the upper body and hold the occupant in a position as close as possible to the seat back-rest. This prevents excessive forward displacement of the occupant due to inertia effects of the body mass. Figure 9.29 shows the combination of belt tensioners and airbag systems for passenger restraint.

Mechanical inertia-reel seatbelts lock when a certain retardation (or deceleration) threshold is reached. The belt must absorb a considerable amount of energy even at modest speeds, but due to seatbelt slack, stretch and the inherent delay in the belt retractor, the seatbelt can only provided very limited protection at higher speeds and cannot guarantee that the occupant will not contact the steering wheel/dashboard.

Where seatbelt tensioners are fitted, they compensate for belt slack and stretch by retracting and tightening the belt strap automatically in the event of an accident. At an impact speed of approximately 30 mph, the system achieves its full effect within 20 ms of impact. This supports the operation of the airbag and retains the occupant for a suitable time until the airbag is fully inflated, at which time the occupant moves forward into the airbag and the energy imparted to the occupant by the crash is dissipated into the airbag as it deflates. To achieve maximum protection the occupants must decelerate with the vehicle with minimum movement away from their seats. This is achieved by triggering the belt tensioners immediately on impact to ensure restraint of the occupants as early as possible. The maximum forward displacement allowed should be less than 20 mm. Normally the tensioning process lasts between 5 and 10 ms. Figure 9.30 shows the retardation and displacement of a body at a given impact speed.

System components and operation

Seatbelt tensioners consist of a pyrotechnic gas generator similar to an airbag gas generator. When ignited, normally by the airbag/restraint system ECU, the rapid increase in pressure is applied to a plunger which, via a steel cable, rotates the belt-tightener reel and this then provides the force at the belt to restrain the occupant. Figure 9.31 shows a typical system.

In addition to systems that effectively rewind the belt, there are others which act at the seatbelt buckle. These units tension the lap as well as the diagonal part of the belt. They have an added advantage in that they

also prevent the tendency for the occupant to slide under the belt (known as submarining). For maximum protection both of the systems can be employed and triggered in a time-shifted manner. For example, the seatbelt tightener acts first, then, according to the severity of impact, the belt buckle tensioner is deployed a few milliseconds later.

9.2.3 Roll-over protection

Open-top vehicles lack a roof structure to protect the occupants in the event of the vehicle turning over in an accident. To improve safety, roll-over protection systems were developed which automatically provided the occupants with the necessary protection. Early systems used all-round sensing employing acceleration and tilt sensors to detect roll-over from any direction from horizontal. Current systems use latest technology sensing, for example micromechanical yaw rate and acceleration sensors. From the sensor information, the ECU calculates the probability and severity of a roll-over and then triggers the protective element (roll-over bar or head restraints) in a time frame of 30 to 3000 ms. The roll-over bar is activated by a solenoid which releases a pretensioned spring to bring it into the correct position. Alternatively, if head restraints are employed these are activated into the roll-over position by springs when triggered. Figure 9.32 shows how the extendable head restraints operate in a roll-over test.

This technology is now being considered for closed vehicles so that roll-over protection can be implemented via airbags and belt tighteners. This can prevent the

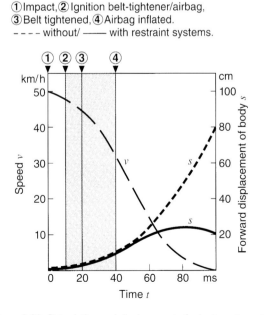

① Impact, ② Ignition belt-tightener/airbag, ③ Belt tightened, ④ Airbag inflated.
– – – – without/ —— with restraint systems.

Figure 9.30 Retardation and displacement of a body on impact

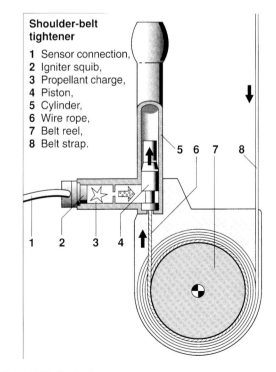

Shoulder-belt tightener

1 Sensor connection,
2 Igniter squib,
3 Propellant charge,
4 Piston,
5 Cylinder,
6 Wire rope,
7 Belt reel,
8 Belt strap.

Figure 9.31 Seatbelt tensioner system

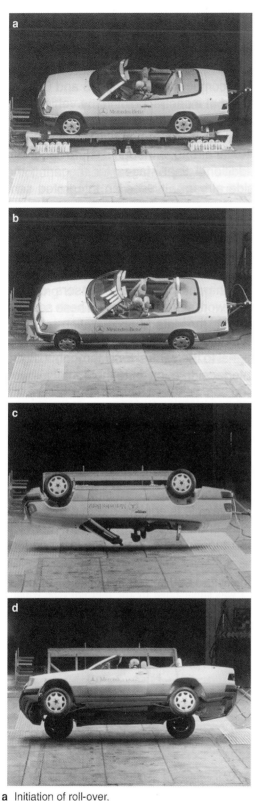

a Initiation of roll-over,
b Head restraints are triggered,
c Roll-over takes place,
d Vehicle lands on its wheels again.
(Source: Daimler-Chrysler)

Figure 9.32 Roll-over test showing action of extendable head restraints

occupants' limbs from being crushed by their own vehicle if they are thrown out of the window in an accident. It can also reduce injury to non-belted occupants.

Key Points

Vehicle passive safety systems are designed to protect occupants in the event of an accident. They are designed to reduce the severity of the consequences of an accident, i.e. the injury to the occupants

Airbags are used to absorb the energy which is imparted to the occupant during the sudden deceleration of an impact. They are fitted in front of the driver and passenger. They are also fitted at the side of the vehicle to protect the occupants from a side impact

Airbags employ pyrotechnic gas generators to inflate the bag fully in a few milliseconds. Once fully inflated, the occupant is cushioned and the energy of the impact is absorbed by the bag as it deflates. In addition, the occupant does not impact with a hard surface and hence the risk of injury is greatly reduced

The airbag system has sensors to provide information to an ECU. The ECU determines the impact occurrence and triggers the gas generators via a small AC. An AC is used as the input to trigger the igniter, as this can be decoupled with a capacitor. This prevents the possibility of a false trigger due to the application of a DC from the vehicle system (e.g. due to a wiring fault). The ECU has its own self-diagnosis and system check function

Seatbelt tensioners are complementary to the airbag system and keep the occupant in their seat for a short initial time during an impact. This allows time for the airbag to inflate fully before contact

The tensioners can act on the belt itself or at the belt buckle. They employ a pyrotechnic gas generators (similar to an airbag) to provide the rapid energy build-up required. They are normally triggered by the same ECU as the airbags as part of a complete occupant safety system. Normally the belt tensioner activates just before the airbag

Roll-over protection was developed originally for open-top vehicles but it can also be applied to closed vehicles to enhance occupant protection. For an open-top vehicle the protection is provided by spring-loaded head restraints or pop-up bars. For a closed vehicle, side airbags and belt tensioners are utilised. The system uses acceleration and yaw sensors to determine the roll-over mode and then triggers the protection accordingly

Chapter 10

INSTRUMENTATION SYSTEMS

what is covered in this chapter . . .

■ Driver information systems

■ Driver entertainment and communication

10.1 DRIVER INFORMATION SYSTEMS

10.1.1 Vehicle instrumentation and displays

Introduction

Years ago the vehicle instrument panel was relatively simple. It consisted of a number of simple instruments and warning lights which gave the driver basic information about the vehicle status. The most important basic visual displays are still fitted to all vehicles, but the instrument panel is now an important part of the vehicle system and communication infrastructure.

The technology employed in the instrument panel has also changed dramatically following developments in electronics. Even the simplest instruments are now fully electronic, though they may appear as an analogue gauge! The number of warning lights on the dashboard has grown with the advances in technology but the design of the panel is critically important. The driver cannot process too much information without being distracted from the task in hand (i.e. driving the vehicle). Therefore, it is necessary to design the instruments in such a way that the information is displayed clearly and concisely without being confusing. The basic functions of the dashboard panel are:

● speedometer and odometer
● engine speed
● remaining fuel contents indication
● engine temperature indication
● low oil-pressure warning
● generator malfunction warning
● warning lights for indicators, headlamp main beam.

Gauge and warning systems

In order to understand how the technology has evolved, it is useful to consider simple gauge and display systems. These are as follows.

Fuel contents gauge

Early gauge movements were moving-iron, cross-coil types, very similar in construction and operation to a simple ammeter. The tank sender unit was a variable resistor which was activated by a float mechanism. As the level in the tank altered, so did the current flowing in the gauge circuit, and hence this was measured and displayed by the gauge as fuel contents. This type of gauge was superseded by the thermal type which was cheaper and less sensitive to fuel movement (surge) in the tank. In this gauge mechanism, the current flowing in the gauge circuit heats a bi-metal element in the gauge to deflect the display needle. The more current flowing, the hotter the bi-metal and the further the needle deflects. This simple system has inherent damping and therefore does not react fast enough to display changes as the fuel moves whilst driving. However, one problem is that the current flow is of course dependent on voltage. To prevent voltage fluctuations of the vehicle system affecting the gauge readings, a voltage stabiliser is used which regulates the voltage supplied to the gauge assembly to a low level (normally 5 or 10 volts). A very simple stabiliser uses a bi-metal element to switch the supply voltage on and off which produces a mean voltage at the appropriate level according to the on/off ratio (known as the duty cycle). These have been completely replaced by electronic units which accurately regulate the supply voltage with minimal ripple. Commonly one stabiliser will supply the voltage to two or more gauges (i.e. fuel and temperature). A typical thermal-type fuel gauge circuit is shown in Figure 10.1.

The tank sender unit is a potentiometer connected to a float arm. As the fuel level changes, the position of the wiper also changes and this alters its resistive value. In this way the current flowing in the gauge circuit changes and the display reacts accordingly. In the past, simple wire-wound resistive elements were used, but for modern sender units printed circuits which employ thick film resistors are employed. These can be tuned accurately to take into account the complexity of the tank shape and this means that the fuel level indication can be more accurate.

Engine temperature gauge

For this application, the same gauge movement technology is employed as above. The gauge is also

supplied with a regulated voltage from a stabiliser, the only difference being the gauge sender unit. Normally this consists of an NTC (negative temperature coefficient) resistor element mounted in a brass screw-in body. This is mounted in the engine where it is exposed to coolant temperature at an appropriate point (e.g. thermostat housing). The NTC element is thermally sensitive and changes resistance as the temperature changes. As the engine temperature increases, the resistance of the NTC element decreases. This allows a greater current to flow in the gauge circuit and hence the display needle deflects further across the gauge display towards 'hot'. Note that the resistance of the thermistor is greater than the fuel tank sender so that although the two gauges work in the same way, the current flow in the temperature gauge is lower. The circuit is shown in Figure 10.2.

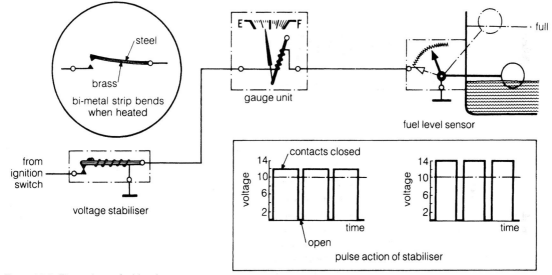

Figure 10.1 Thermal-type fuel-level gauge

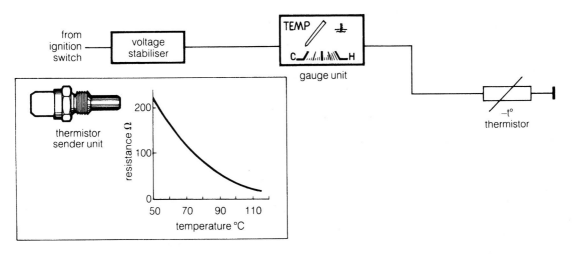

Figure 10.2 Thermal-type engine temperature gauge

Engine oil-pressure warning

Low oil-pressure warning is normally always signalled by a warning lamp. This may be supplemented by a gauge to indicate actual pressure. A warning lamp in the dash panel display is supplied with a voltage on one side and an earth path on the other via an oil-pressure switch. The switch is mounted in the oil gallery of the engine and is subjected to full oil pressure. The switch contacts are normally closed and then open when pressure is applied to a diaphragm. Thus, when the engine is not running (or has low oil pressure) the warning light illuminates. As soon as the minimum pressure is applied to the switch, the warning light extinguishes. The switch and circuit are shown in Figure 10.3.

Note that oil pressures in an engine vary considerably according to engine speed, load, temperature etc. In order to prevent indicating a false fault condition, the oil-pressure switch threshold is set quite low at 0.5 bar (7 psi). This prevents the warning lamp illuminating at idle speed with a hot engine, but note that oil pressure must be much greater than this when the engine is at higher speed or load. Therefore, this warning device is very rudimentary and gives a very imprecise indication of a fault condition. It is common for an oil-pressure gauge to be fitted as well in order to give a clearer indication of oil-pressure status, particularly in performance vehicles. Modern vehicles often employ more than one oil-pressure switch, with different pressure thresholds, mounted at different points in the engine. When used in conjunction with an evaluation circuit and a warning lamp or buzzer, this gives much more comprehensive protection against low oil pressure under all engine operating conditions.

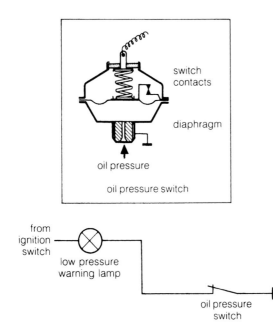

Figure 10.3 Spring-controlled diaphragm-type oil-pressure indicator

Battery warning lamp

This is also known as an ignition warning lamp as the lamp illuminates when the ignition is on but the engine is not running. On older vehicles with no electronic ignition, this condition could damage the ignition coil due to over-heating (if the 'points' were closed), hence the provision of a warning lamp on the dash panel. Operation of the lamp is via the generator circuit and hence this warning lamp is also known as the charge warning light. The dash-mounted lamp is supplied with an ignition supply on one side and earths via the generator rotor through the electronic regulator when the engine is not running. Once the engine starts and the generator begins to charge the battery, the circuit is switched off via the regulator. This shows that the generator is operating correctly, but note that it is only an indicator! There are several failure modes of an alternator which will not illuminate the lamp.

Tachometer/engine speed indicator

This is in the form of a dial to indicate actual engine speed. This prevents the driver from over-revving the engine and also helps them to maintain the engine speed at the optimum level via appropriate gear selection. In the past, the ignition circuit (low-tension) side was used to provide an appropriate signal for engine speed display. The frequency of the ignition pulses has a direct relationship to engine speed. This can easily be used by an electronic counter to calculate engine speed which can then be displayed via an analogue or digital display. Modern engine ECUs have a pulse train output which is used to drive the engine speed display.

Vehicle speed indicator

In the past, speedometers were purely mechanical instruments driven by a cable drive from the gearbox output shaft. Electronic speedometers have been in use for a number of years. These employ electronic odometers that are highly resistant to tampering and falsification of mileage readings. Some vehicles now have mileage counter information stored in the transmission control systems as well as on the dashboard so that the readings can be cross-checked for tampering. The speedometer display can be analogue or digital and the basis of speed measurement is an electronic pulse generator or sensor fitted to the differential or gearbox output shaft. This detects the movement of teeth on a pulse ring. The method is similar to that used for engine speed sensing (see Chapter 2). Analogue or digital technology can be employed in the sensor to produce a pulse train with a frequency proportional to speed. This can be easily evaluated by a microprocessor which counts the time difference between the teeth edges. From this information, and by knowing the appropriate calibration factor, the vehicle speed can be established and can then be conveyed to the display via an appropriate output driver circuit (or interface).

An international standard is in place for instrument symbols to avoid misinterpretation and allow simple multi-language support. The main symbols used are shown in Figure 10.4.

Vehicle condition monitoring

As vehicle service intervals have been extended by manufacturers, the need for appropriate condition monitoring of vehicle parameters, essential to safety, has become more commonplace. Vehicle service intervals are now more than 10 000 miles and can be up to 20 000 miles, and during these long intervals it is likely that components will wear and fluid levels need replenishment. So, to improve safety and reliability, condition monitoring becomes necessary. The degree of sophistication is manufacturer and model specific. All vehicles have basic condition monitoring as mentioned above which covers oil pressure, engine temperature etc. Generally, high-spec. vehicles have more sophisticated

monitoring systems which provide feedback to the driver in the areas of:

- bulb failure
- brake-pad wear
- engine oil level (and condition)
- essential fluid levels
- correct function of electronic safety systems (ABS, supplementary restraint system (SRS) etc.).

Developments in sensor technology can provide more sophisticated information than has been possible in the past (e.g. oil condition; see Chapter 2) and this level of technology is required to support current and future requirements for vehicle on-board diagnostics (OBD). It is a requirement for OBD applications that the vehicle can self-diagnose and that the condition of the engine between services is monitored in order to maintain exhaust emissions at acceptable limits. For this reason, condition monitoring becomes an essential, statutory function in modern vehicles.

Symbol	Information provided
	Brake warning light
	Turn signal/hazard indicator light (green)
	High beam indicator light (blue)
	Charge warning light
	Door open reminder light
	Hazard warning flasher indicator light
	Low washer fluid warning light
	Oil pressure warning light
	Glow plug indicator light
	Heated rear window indicator light
	Rear fog light indicator light
	Low fuel warning light
	Stop/tail warning light

Figure 10.4 Instrument panel symbols

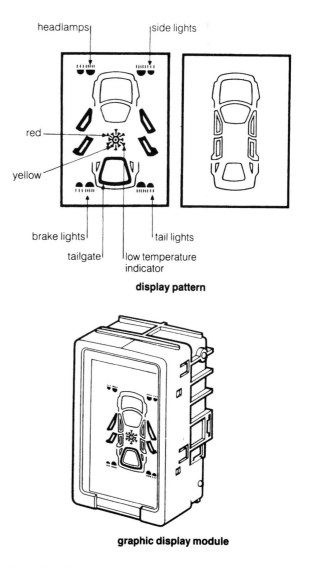

display pattern

graphic display module

Figure 10.5 Graphic display unit

Many systems incorporate warning lights, but with modern driver interfaces and electronic displays visual representation of the vehicle with a user-friendly graphical display is easily achieved. A typical graphical display unit is shown in Figure 10.5.

Modern vehicle condition monitoring systems employ microprocessor technology to monitor signals from various sensors placed at the critical components. Many sensors are just switches which indicate an 'OK' or 'Not OK' status of the component. An important factor is that the system self-checks and has inherent plausibility. That is, the system can detect if there is a wiring fault (e.g. open circuit) so that the driver is alerted if the system itself becomes faulty or unreliable. With microprocessor technology, this feature is easy to enable and more secure when compared to a simple warning-lamp circuit.

Basic condition monitoring can be provided by the following, relatively simple, sensor arrangements:

Bulb failure

Bulb failure can be detected via monitoring the current flowing to the respective circuit. If the current flow is reduced or stops, then a bulb has failed and this can be used as a signal to indicate the failure to the driver via a warning light or panel display. A common

technique in the past was to use a reed switch in the circuit to monitor the current. This consists of two or more contacts mounted in a glass vial to exclude contaminants. The vial is evacuated of air or filled with an inert gas to reduce arcing at the contacts. Closure of the switch contacts is achieved via magnetic flux which can be provided by a permanent or electromagnet. When electromagnetic operation is required, a coil is wound around the switch to create the magnetic field. A typical arrangement of the reed switch for bulb failure applications is shown in Figure 10.6.

In the arrangement shown in Figure 10.6, the reed switches are mounted in a bulb monitor unit which is located close to the lamp unit. There is a reed switch for each circuit (e.g. side, dip, main beam) and when the respective circuit is switched on, the bulb draws current and this closes the reed switch contact which illuminates the respective part of the display. If a bulb fails, the appropriate segment of the display does not illuminate and this indicates the failure to the driver.

Brake-lining wear

A sensing element consisting of a wire loop embedded in the friction material can be used to indicate that replacement of the brake pads is required. This is a useful safety feature, and where long service intervals exists it

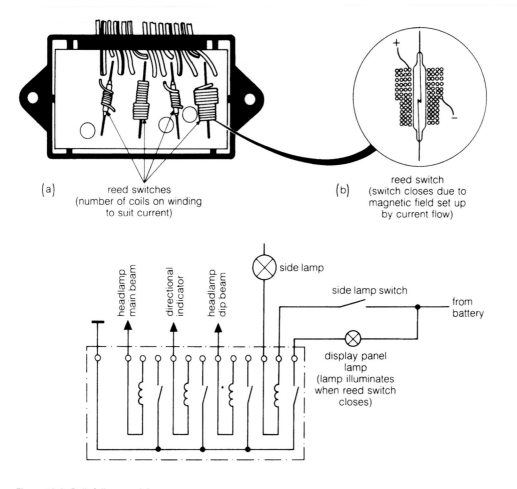

Figure 10.6 Bulb failure module

ensures that the driver is made aware of a safety-critical situation without periodic inspection. A very simple open-circuit system is shown in Figure 10.7(a).

The lamp will illuminate when the wire is exposed to the brake disc due to pad wear. The problem with this circuit is that it does not have a fail-safe mechanism. That is, if the circuit has a fault which causes an open circuit, the driver would not know his brakes were worn as the lamp would not illuminate. An improvement is to use a slightly more sophisticated circuit as shown in Figure 10.7(b) above. In this system, evaluation of the circuit integrity is performed by an ECU at switch on. If the circuit fails, or the pads are worn, then the driver is alerted via the panel warning lamp (switched on by the ECU).

Engine oil level

It is difficult to measure the engine oil level. Normally the engine has to be at a certain temperature and the vehicle must be level to establish the correct reading on a dipstick. A simple indication of correct minimal level can be established using a 'hot wire' measurement at the tip of a specially instrumented dipstick (see Figure 10.8).

A wire element in the dipstick, that is usually immersed in oil, is heated and the resistance is monitored. When the oil falls below a certain level, the resistance of the element changes when heated as there is no contact with the oil to dissipate the heat. This is monitored by an electronic circuit which then illuminates a warning lamp. This system relies on a good-quality connection

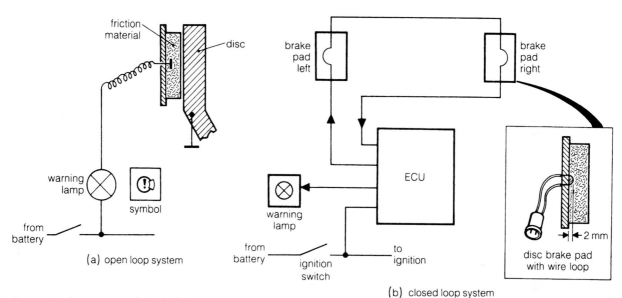

Figure 10.7 Sensor system for brake-lining wear

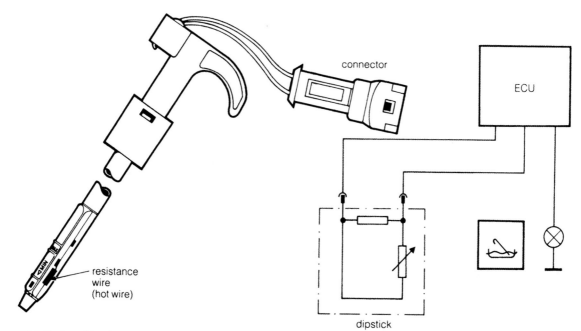

Figure 10.8 Engine oil-level sensor

in the circuit. In addition, the dipstick itself must be handled carefully to avoid damage to the sensor and wiring. Therefore the reliability is not good, so this technology has been replaced by more reliable sensors mounted permanently in the engine sump housing. These sensors can reliably detect the oil level and also its condition and form part of a sophisticated condition-monitoring system on modern vehicles which is used to determine service intervals dynamically according to the way the vehicle has been operated. These oil sensors are described in more detail in Chapter 2.

Essential fluid levels

These include brake fluid, washer fluid, coolant etc. A float-type switch can be incorporated to give a simple indication that the fluid level is above a minimum safe level. The float normally incorporates a magnet, and the switch element is normally a reed-type switch. The

warning is triggered when the magnet moves away from the reed switch sufficiently so that it opens and breaks the circuit. Examples of this arrangement are shown in Figure 10.9.

This circuit is normally fail-safe and some arrangement is made to test the circuit (for example when starting the engine) to verify the warning-light function and the circuit integrity.

Outside air temperature

A thermistor mounted on the vehicle exterior is now a common feature (see Figure 10.10). It is used to detect outside temperature to warn the driver of the possibility of black ice. The sensor is typically of the NTC thermistor type, similar to other temperature sensors used in automotive environments. An electronic evaluation circuit is incorporated in the dash panel which measures the resistance of the thermistor via a potential divider circuit. This a transferred to the display as a temperature reading in degrees Celsius, often with a warning symbol which illuminates at a critically low temperature to warn the driver that the temperature has dropped to freezing point.

Electronic driver displays

Until the late 1980s, conventional mechanical instruments and warning lights were commonly used to provide the driver with information and feedback. Advances in electronics and microcontrollers in vehicle systems have meant that the instrument panel of most modern vehicles is a microcontrolled sub-system which gives feedback to the driver via its interconnection into the vehicle network communication system, in addition to wired connections to sensors around the vehicle. The display elements in most vehicles are still analogue

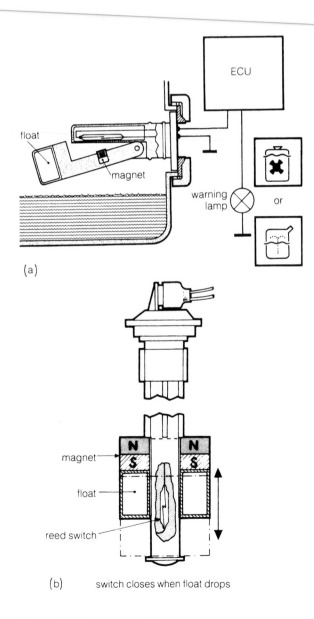

(a)

(b)   switch closes when float drops

Figure 10.9 Float system switch

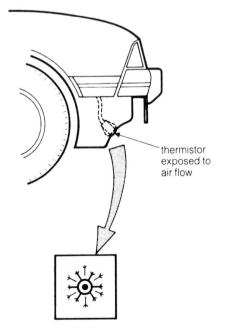

thermistor exposed to air flow

Figure 10.10 Air temperature sensor

displays, in most cases similar in appearance to the precision mechanical systems of the past. The main reason for this is driver familiarity, as the technology behind these simple gauge displays is sophisticated electronics of the latest generation. The advantage of electronic displays systems are as follows:

- the displays are more attractive and easier for the driver to read and process
- there are fewer moving parts
- combinations of display elements allow information to be prioritised before display
- they are more flexible and compact for integration into the modern vehicle dashboard.

A typical instrument cluster is shown in Figure 10.11.

In modern vehicles, the basic functions of the instrument panel are similar for all vehicles. The panel receives inputs via a data bus or direct signal inputs. All of the signal processing and calculation is executed via a microprocessor which then outputs the measured value to the indicator device driver. This could be a dot-matrix display, indicator lamps or a gauge display with a stepper motor-driven needle indicator for the driver interface. Figure 10.12 outlines this process.

Intelligent functions such as determination of service intervals, diagnostic functions etc. can be included as a function of the dash panel itself due to the integrated intelligence that it has on-board. In addition, in most modern vehicles, the dash panel forms a hub or gateway between the various bus systems used on the vehicle (for example CAN buses running at different data rates).

Various technologies are employed in the actual display elements, but these can be classified as *passive* (they reflect light falling on them) or *active* (they emit light themselves).

LED (light-emitting diode)

These are used extensively in modern displays due to their easy integration into electronic circuits and long life. They are an active light source and are now available in a wide range of colours (including white). They are employed for backlighting or warning lamp functions. A typical seven-segment LED display is shown in Figure 10.13.

LCD (liquid crystal display)

This is a passive display which normally requires backlighting. LCDs consume very little power and are suitable for small or large display modules. They use

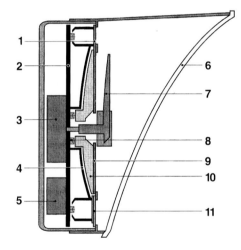

1 Tell-tale lamp
2 Printed-circuit board
3 Stepping motor
4 Reflector
5 Plug
6 View cover
7 Needle
8 LED
9 Dial face
10 Optical waveguide
11 LCD

Figure 10.11 Instrument cluster

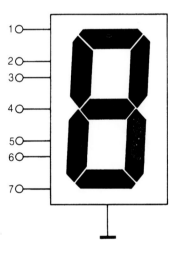

Figure 10.13 Figure-of-eight display with seven-segment LEDs

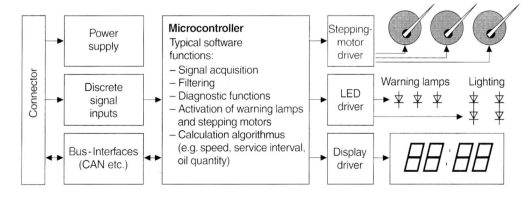

Figure 10.12 Signal processing in a microprocessor-based instrument cluster

the principle of light polarisation to create the display and can operate in positive or negative contrast (i.e. black figures on a light background, or light figures on a black background). The most common type is the twisted nematic LCD (TN-LCD). This terms stems from the twisted arrangement of the elongated liquid crystal modules between the glass plates with transparent conductors. This forms a 'light valve' layer which allows polarised light to pass through depending on whether a voltage is applied to the conductors. Figure 10.14 shows the construction of a display element.

The technology will support simple graphical display elements, but for more sophisticated requirements where display of infinitely variable information is needed more advanced LCD technology is required. STN (super-twisted nematic) LCD technology can provide moderate resolution in a monochrome display. DSTN (double-layer STN) LCD provides higher-resolution, simple colour displays. For complex image manipulation and display, small thin film transistor (TFT) displays are widely available and are used extensively in technology applications (for example in the mobile phone market). These can handle complex colour images at high resolution. In automotive applications they are used as GPS displays, reversing camera displays and multifunction displays for vehicle control and system setting (e.g. BMW iDrive – a concept from BMW to make the driver environment user friendly. Instead of switches, knobs and buttons, the cockpit is divided into two separate sections: the driving zone, containing all controls essential to driving, and the comfort zone, where a central consol controller regulates all of the vehicle's comfort functions).

VFD (vacuum fluorescent display)

This is active display technology with a wide available colour range. It is suitable for the display of numbers, words and bar graphs. Figure 10.15 shows a display element used for a digital seven-segment number display. Each segment of the display device consists of a filament that acts as a cathode to emit electrons, anodes (phosphor) and a grid which controls and evens out the flow of electrons. These are encased in a glass envelope under high-vacuum conditions. The cathode is made from fine tungsten wires which emit electrons when heated by an electric current. Normally these electrons are attracted to the positively charged grid, but when a segment of the anode is given a positive potential by applying a small voltage to it, some of the electrons pass through the grid, striking the anode and cause it to glow. The segments needed to form the display are arranged appropriately to perform the visual task.

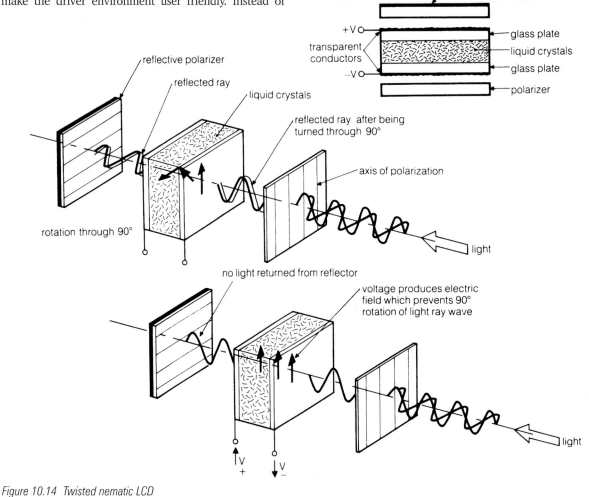

Figure 10.14 Twisted nematic LCD

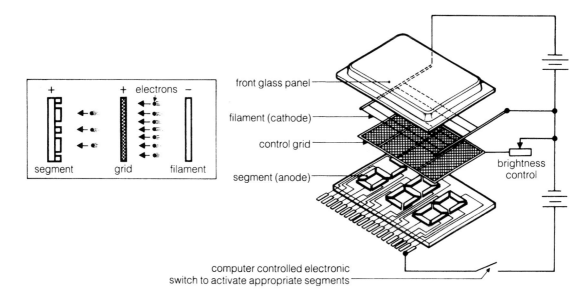

Figure 10.15 Vacuum fluorescent display

This technology is less common in modern vehicles as it has been superseded, but it was used extensively in first-generation electronic displays, particularly for digital speedometers either as seven-segment numeric displays or bar graph indicators.

CCFL (cold cathode fluorescence)
This is used for 'black screen' displays. Very bright display elements provide a high brilliance light source with good contrast. They are normally used in conjunction with a tinted screen/cover. This technology can also be employed to backlight displays.

DCEL (DC electroluminescence panel)
This is a solid-state device with a voltage applied across it which causes it to illuminate. It has very uniform light distribution and is an active light source. It is often employed to backlight LCD panels.

These display technologies can be used in combination to provide an attractive, user-friendly dash panel that displays the most relevant and important information to the driver in a succinct and efficient way. The efficiency with which the display panel communicates information to the driver is an important safety-related factor which must be optimised in a modern vehicle.

Head-up displays (HUD)
In a vehicle, conventional dashboard displays have a short viewing distance. When the driver is viewing the road and then has to switch to look at the instrument panel, a finite time is required for the driver to adjust his field of vision (typically 0.5 seconds). During this time the driver cannot focus on the road or the instruments and this is a safety-critical aspect. This situation can be improved with the adoption of a head-up display system which involves projecting important information onto the windscreen in the driver's viewing area. This generates a virtual image at an appropriate distance, which means the driver does not need to adjust his view or take his eyes off the road. Head-up displays were first pioneered in military fighter jets and helicopters to minimise information overload by centralising critical flight data within the pilot's field of vision. The basic principle is shown in Figure 10.16.

The HUD features an optical image generator which projects the image onto the inside of the windscreen as a reflection. The image generator can be active or passive illumination technology as described above. The virtual image created should not be too large or distracting. Therefore, it is positioned in an area of the windscreen with low road or traffic information content (for example in the corner of the screen). The HUD displays the most important information; it has to be concise to prevent driver distraction. Therefore, only safety-related information, warnings or route directions are displayed. The HUD is not a substitute for the standard dashboard display.

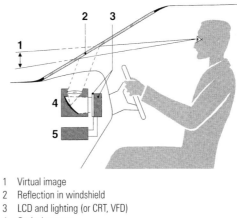

1   Virtual image
2   Reflection in windshield
3   LCD and lighting (or CRT, VFD)
4   Optical system
5   Electronics

Figure 10.16 Head-up display

10.1.2 Vehicle navigation systems

Introduction

Navigation in the vehicle is a process that the driver uses to get to their intended destination by means of directions or guidance. In the past, a driver would have to determine or plan a route using paper maps. Technology has made this job easier via dedicated programs or websites for route planning. The problem is that a planned route may be compromised due to traffic conditions. Also, if a given direction is accidentally missed, then the process of getting back to the original route can be difficult and time consuming for the driver.

A solution made possible via developments in technology is a vehicle navigation system. This system uses electronic maps and optimised route-calculation algorithms executed via a microprocessor for planning the best route according to the driver's requirements. This route can be offered to the driver online via a user interface providing audible and visual instructions as they travel (similar to a co-driver). It is essential that the actual position of the vehicle is known at all times so that this can be referenced to a map position. This can be achieved using satellite navigation technology which has become available for general use since the mid 1990s. This provides a dynamic route-calculation ability and thus the system can respond to actual traffic conditions by correcting the directions to avoid jams. This function can be implemented manually by the driver or automatically via traffic information signals.

Recently, handheld GPS (global positioning system) based navigation units have become very popular for in-vehicle use. They can be easily mounted in the driver's eye line and are completely removable for personal use. These systems are relatively cheap and very popular, but they rely entirely on receiving GPS signals from the transmitting satellites. In-built vehicle navigation systems are more sophisticated and use a combination of signals to determine the vehicle's position. In addition, their operation can be integrated and combined with other vehicle information systems and user interfaces, thus the operation of phone, entertainment and navigation systems can be fully harmonised and optimised. In this section we will concentrate on navigation system technology supplied by the manufacturer as original equipment.

Basic principle

The availability of signals for public use from GPS satellites has made navigation systems possible for general route and position finding. For general use, the GPS satellites transmit signals allowing positioning information to be established with accuracies of ±10 metres and this is more than sufficient for vehicle navigation use. GPS satellites were developed and provided for US military use and the signals generated produce highly accurate position information. Note though that these high-accuracy signals are encrypted and reserved for military use to prevent abuse of this useful information.

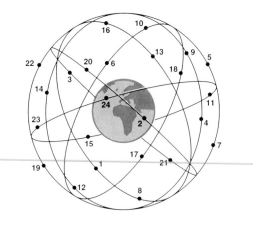

Figure 10.17 GPS satellites around the earth

There are 24 satellites which circumnavigate the earth every 12 hours in six different orbits (see Figure 10.17). Each one transmits a unique signal at approximately 50 Hz with their position information and a time signal. Due to the different transit times of this signal from each satellite, the signal received from each one has a time offset. The GPS receiver in the navigation system calculates the data transmission time by comparison with its own internal clock. Assuming that signals from at least three satellites can be received, two-dimensional position information can be derived from the time offset between the signals from each satellite (see Figure 10.18). With four satellite signals, three-dimensional positions can be established.

This position information can be established via GPS as long as good communication signals can be received from the satellites. If the connection between the GPS receiver and the satellites is compromised in any way, then real-time position information will be lost. The signals may be compromised due to:

- the surrounding landscape, valleys, hills etc.
- tunnels
- buildings.

The receiver must have line-of-site contact with the satellites (see Figure 10.19).

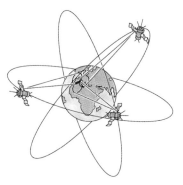

Figure 10.18 Connection to three satellites allows two-dimensional position information to be derived

Figure 10.19 Typical causes of loss of connection to satellite

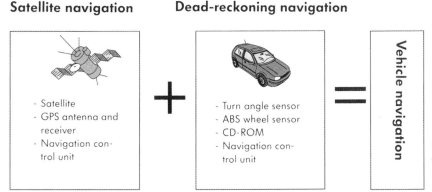

Figure 10.20 Principle of composite navigation

To counteract these problems, vehicle navigation systems use an additional method called *composite navigation* (also known as dead reckoning) to supplement the GPS information. This uses information from additional sensors in order the establish the distance moved and direction of movement of the vehicle. From this information the current position can be predicted (although with less accuracy than with GPS information). As soon as the satellite signals are available again, the system can update the driver with accurate position information. Using this technique, the GPS and composite methods work in a complementary way to overcome poor GPS reception and to ensure that the composite, calculated position information is accurate. In combination the systems provide an accurate basis for vehicle navigation (see Figure 10.20).

System components

An overview of the system components is shown in Figure 10.21.

The system employs the following components to perform the navigation function.

Navigation control unit

This is often integrated with the vehicle entertainment system to form a complete infotainment system. The advantage of this technique is that space which already exists in the dashboard in a convenient position for the driver is utilised for dual functionality. Also, the driver can operate the system (information and entertainment) from a single user interface. Systems of this type generally have a relatively large TFT touch-screen interface for route planning etc. In addition, the entertainment unit generally includes a CD-ROM drive which can be used as an appropriate media for handling map data. The advantage is that the maps can be updated easily and made readily available in this format. The user interface of a typical unit is shown in Figure 10.22.

Figure 10.21 In-car GPS-system overview (VW)

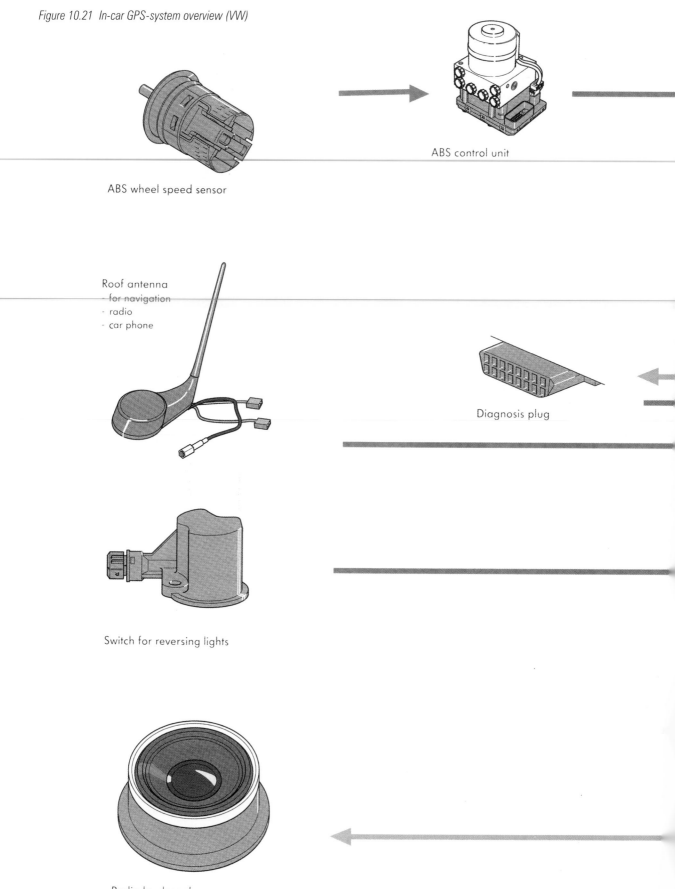

ABS wheel speed sensor

ABS control unit

Roof antenna
- for navigation
- radio
- car phone

Diagnosis plug

Switch for reversing lights

Radio loudspeakers

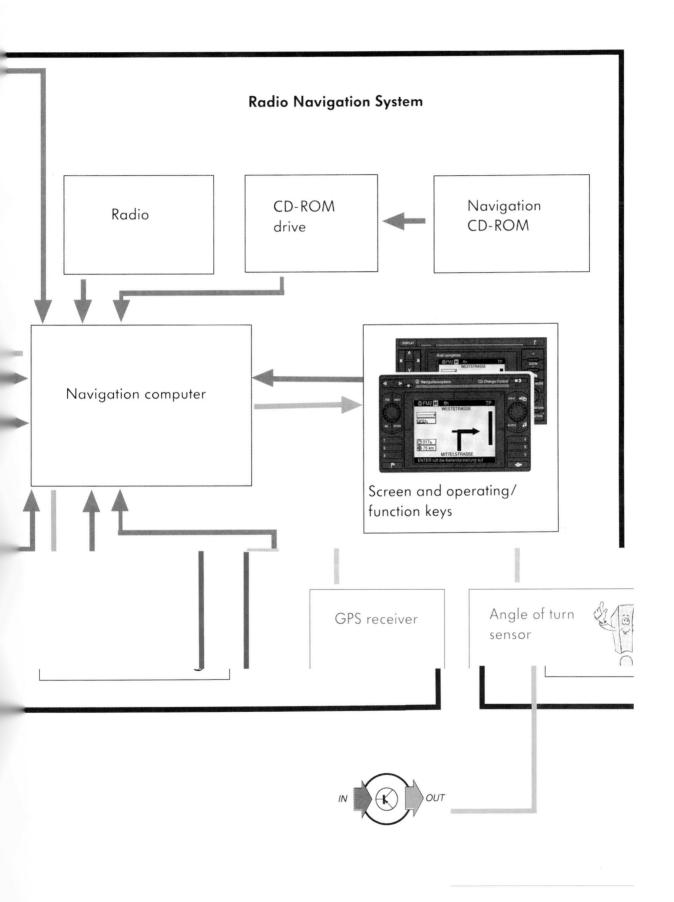

Radio Navigation System

| Radio | CD-ROM drive | Navigation CD-ROM |

Navigation computer

Screen and operating/ function keys

GPS receiver

Angle of turn sensor

IN   OUT

TIM button for retrieval of stored traffic announcements.

- New traffic announcements up to 4 minutes in length can be stored. When the system is switched on, each traffic announcement of the pre-set traffic radio station (TP Traffic Programme) is recorded. When you switch off the system, you can activate the Record mode for 24 hours by pressing the TIM button (press for longer than 2 sec.). In both cases, traffic announcement playback is started by pressing the TIM button. To start random track play, press the rocker button. To cancel playback, press the TIM button again.

Rocker button

- In **Radio mode**, pressing this rocker button to start automatic local station seek in the direction you are travelling.

Rotary push-button on left

- Press button to switch ON/OFF
  Turn switch to control volume

AS/ CD mix button

- In **Radio mode**, you can store the 6 stations with the strongest signals using this button. The stations are saved to the station keys on the set waveband - TP, FM or AM. The memory locations are allocated automatically and exclusively on memory levels FM2, AM2 and TP2.
- In **Audio CD mode**. you can play tracks at random by pressing this button.

If a CD changer is connected, you shuffle-play the CDs by pressing this button.

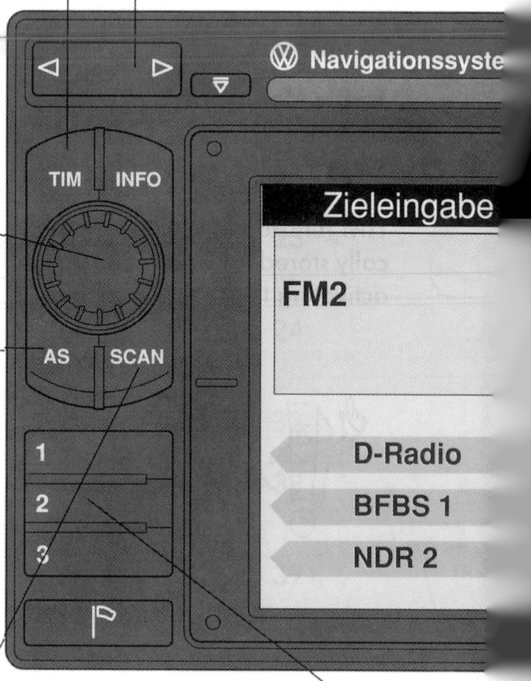

Scan button

- In **Radio mode**, all the station pre-sets can be played briefly by pressing this button. To pre-set a station, press this button again while the station is playing.
- In **Audio CD mode**, you can briefly play all the tracks on a CD by pressing this button. To select a track, press this button again while the track is playing.

Figure 10.22 User interface – in-vehicle GPS (VW)

Multifunction display

- Can be swivelled horizontally and vertically.

Button for changing over to night display mode

When you switch the low beam headlight on or off, the display automatically changes between daytime and night display modes.
You can switch over to the other display mode by pressing this button.
A photocell which is located below the button controls display brightness.

Flashing diode of anti-theft device

After entering the four-digit code number, the diode flashes if the ignition key has been removed from the ignition lock.

Button

- Select preceding menu or basic menu

Right-hand rotary push-button

- Turn: to select the menu fields and change the setting scales.
- Press: to confirm the menu fields.

SOUND button

For selecting the sound menu for the settings for bass and treble, the sound field (Balance and Fader) and the Volume Setup menu (basic settings for switch-on volume, traffic announcements (TIM), car phone, navigation and GALA).

AUDIO button

For selecting the basic audio menu.
Tone source selection: Audio CD (CD changer); Traffic radio TP1 and TP2; VHF FM1 and FM2; Medium Wave MW1 and MW2; Long Wave LW1 and LW2; other tone sources AUX; Radio mute

Station keys 1-6

- In **radio mode**, a single station can be assigned to each button from the six wavebands TP, FM, AM at memory levels 1 and 2.
  Storing a station: Select the station using the rocker button. To store a station, keep one of the station keys pressed until the programme switches to mute and a signal tone sounds. To select a station, press the corresponding button briefly.
- In **Audio CD mode**, select the CD in the tray by pressing this button. Buttons 1-6 correspond to the order of the CDs in the autochanger tray.

The unit integrates:

- the user control inputs via buttons and function keys
- multifunction colour display
- radio/CD entertainment system
- GPS receiver, connected via GPS external aerial
- map data via CD/DVD-ROM drive.

Turn angle sensor

This sensor is a vehicle yaw rate sensor (remember that the yaw angle is the angle between a vehicle's actual heading and a desired or reference heading) and it is used to establish the vehicle change of direction during composite navigation. If a yaw sensor is already fitted to the vehicle then that sensor can be used; the information is available via the CAN bus. If not, the yaw sensor can be fitted in the navigation unit itself. Yaw sensors are described in Chapter 2. Generally, if the sensor is fitted in the navigation control unit, then the tuning fork-type sensor is employed as this sensor needs no calibration and is:

- compact
- accurate
- highly immune to magnetic interference.

The sensor employs the principle of the Coriolis force to detect rotation of the vehicle about its axis. The sensor element is shown in Figure 10.23.

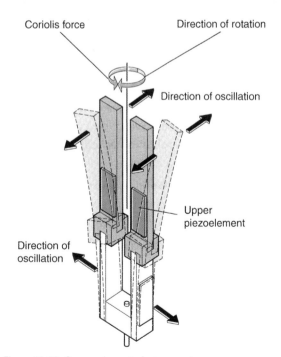

Figure 10.23 Sensor element of a turn angle sensor

Wheel-speed sensors

The signal from wheel-speed sensors (for ABS) are used to determine the distance travelled by the vehicle. In addition, in conjunction with the turn angle sensor, the curve radius can also be established. This information is essential during the composite navigation process.

Reversing signal

This is generally available from the reversing-light switch via the CAN bus. This allows the system to establish movement direction in order to accurately determine vehicle position.

GPS antenna

Good communication with the GPS satellites is essential for GPS navigation. Generally external GPS aerials are fitted and these can be combined with the entertainment system aerial or they can be mounted separately.

The entertainment system speakers are used to play back the audible direction from the navigation system. Note that manufacturer standard-fit navigation equipment generally includes a diagnostic interface via the vehicle's own diagnostic gateway. Using the appropriate equipment, error codes can be accessed and diagnostic procedures executed.

System operation

The processes involved during operation of the system are as follows.

Position finding

This involves the combination of composite and GPS techniques in order the establish the vehicle's current position and direction. A process known as 'map matching' allows the system to determine the vehicle's position with a high level of accuracy. The signals from the wheel-speed sensors and yaw sensor are compared to the stored map and the route profile. From this information, specific points (for example a right turn) are identified and the actual and estimated positions can be compared and the error compensated. This allows an accuracy of ±5 m to be established in urban areas.

Route calculation

The driver inputs their destination into the system at the beginning of the journey. Using the digital map information, the navigation system microprocessor calculates the best route. This route calculation can be adjusted by the driver to avoid specific points or to optimise the route with respect to distance or time. The route calculation timing is derived from the expected average driving time of each road section or element of the map.

Navigation

During the journey, an electronic voice gives verbal driver instructions in advance of turns or lane changes. In addition, the display screen gives simple visual signals (arrows etc.) which are directly in the line of sight to aid the driver in following the navigation system's recommended route. The route can be dynamically recalculated by the system if required by the driver (for example due to an obstruction) or if the driver misses an instruction.

The basic sequence of operation is as follows:

- Driver enters the destination via the user interface.
- Vehicle position is identified from the stored map data using satellite data to an accuracy of ±100 m.

- Once the vehicle is moving, the system uses map matching to increase the accuracy of the position data to approximately ±5 m.
- The system calculates the optimum route to the destination.
- The route information is given to the driver via audible and visual messaging during driving.
- During the trip, the distance and direction is continuously monitored via wheel-speed and yaw sensors.
- The system monitors whether the driver is following the prescribed route and alerts the driver if he deviates. If the driver stays on the deviated route the system dynamically recalculates a new route based on the current position.
- Once the vehicle reaches the intended destination, the driver is informed via an audible message.

In-vehicle navigation is currently a massive growth market, particularly for small, hand-held units. Note that these units can only navigate based on satellite information, they cannot use composite navigation as they are not integrated into the vehicle system and therefore cannot use the 'map matching' optimisation technique which improves accuracy. Nevertheless, as technology reduces in price, in-vehicle navigation will be standard and this is a useful addition to the vehicle instrumentation system for the driver.

Key Points

Instrument panels used in the past provided the driver with simplistic information about the vehicle status. Modern systems are much more complex and closely monitor the condition of the vehicle and engine for the purpose of dynamic service intervention planning and compliance with on-board diagnostic requirements

Basic instrumentation technology has been replaced by sophisticated electronic displays. These units form a connection node in the vehicle communication bus system whereby they can access information from sensors and actuators via the bus (normally CAN)

Key Points

Sophisticated electronic display elements have replaced conventional bulbs for warning lights and display illumination. It is interesting to note though that digital displays have not really been accepted in the market and the conventional dial-type indicator is still used to convey information even if it is operated by a sophisticated microprocessor-controlled stepper-motor drive

Head-up displays are the emerging technology for the automotive market, but this technology is well-established in the aerospace industry, particularly for military applications. With this system, the pilot (or driver) receives the most important information directly in his field of view

GPS navigation systems rely on signals which are sent from military satellites. These signals allow the current position to be derived from the time difference between transmitted signals. For two-dimensional positions, a connection to three satellites is needed. For three dimensions (i.e. position and altitude) a connection to at least four satellites is needed. There are 24 satellites orbiting the earth

In-vehicle navigation systems also use additional information from vehicle sensors to calculate distance and direction. This information, in conjunction with the GPS signals, allows accurate positioning to be determined even if the connection to the satellites is intermittent. In addition, the system compares the actual driven route with the digital map information. This is a technique known as map matching and allows the actual position to be determined to a very high degree of accuracy (<5 metres)

Digital map information is held on CD/DVD and can be updated easily. Often the navigation system is integrated into a complete infotainment system which incorporates entertainment, navigation and communication functions in a single, dash-mounted head unit

10.2 DRIVER ENTERTAINMENT AND COMMUNICATION

Driver entertainment systems started with the ability to fit a radio receiver in the vehicle. Today, nearly all vehicles have some form of basic entertainment or music playback system via a number of available media. As well as entertainment, these systems can provide essential information for the driver in respect of traffic and weather conditions.

Note that this section is designed to give an overview of technology involved and highlight the main terms used in this specialised field. In-car entertainment is a dedicated sub-section of the industry and as such there are specialist dealers who provides services and information to a level of detail beyond the scope of this book. They should always be consulted first when working with this area of vehicle technology.

10.2.1 Radio

Sound-wave transmission via radio waves

High frequency, electromagnetic radio waves propagate through the air at the speed of light. These waves can be made to vary in amplitude and frequency during transmission, and in this way an electromagnetic wave can be used as a carrier wave for signals at different frequencies. Sound waves are acoustic oscillations and the frequency range of the human ear is approximately 20 Hz to 20 kHz. Therefore it is possible to superimpose these sound frequencies onto a higher-frequency carrier wave in order to transmit them remotely. Of course, the sound-frequency oscillations must be converted into electrical oscillations first and this is done via a microphone. The high-frequency sounds wave can be picked up by a receiver which then reverses the process of combining the waves of different frequencies (known as demodulation) and the resulting, low-frequency oscillation can be converted back to sound via a loudspeaker. This is the basis of radio transmission of sound waves.

AM/FM

Sound oscillations can be superimposed on the carrier wave in one of two ways.

Amplitude modulation

The amplitude of the carrier wave is modulated at the frequency of the audio signals as shown in Figure 10.24.

This technique is applied in the short, medium and long waves.

Frequency modulation

The frequency of the high-frequency carrier wave is modulated at the low frequency of the audio signals as shown in Figure 10.25.

This technique is applied for VHF (FM) audio broadcasts and for the audio band of television.

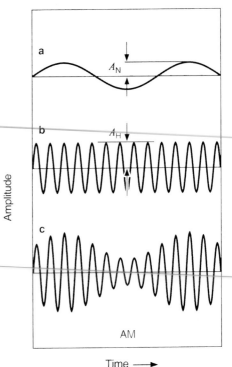

a   LF oscillation with amplitude A_N and frequency f_N
b   HF oscillation (non-modulated) with amplitude A_H and frequency f_H
c   HF oscillation, modulated

Figure 10.24 Amplitude modulation

The electromagnetic waves propagate by various means (as shown in Figure 10.26):

- long wave – as a ground wave along the earth surface
- medium and short wave – as above but also as a reflected wave
- VHF – practically in a straight line.

Long waves can be received over very long distances, irrespective of time of day. There are susceptible to local interference (electromagnetic radiation emitted by ignition interference, electric motors etc.). Medium- and short-wave reception improves at night due to atmospheric conditions but can suffer from fading. By far the best quality for analogue radio is achieved via FM/VHF transmission. The disadvantage is that these signals can only be received if a line-of-site connection to the transmitter is established. Any obstruction (buildings, hills, etc.) will affect the quality of the signal reception.

RDS (radio data system)

In addition to analogue sound waves, the carrier wave of an FM transmission can carry a limited amount of digital information. This is known as the radio data system or RDS. The amount of digital information which can be carried is limited as most of the available bandwidth is used for the audio signal. Nevertheless, the following information can be provided:

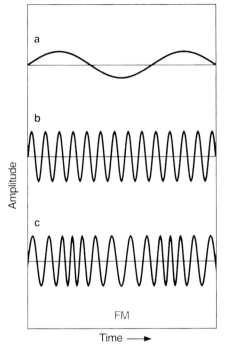

a   LF oscillation with amplitude A_N and frequency f_N
b   HF oscillation (non-modulated) with amplitude A_H and frequency f_H
c   HF oscillation, modulated

Figure 10.25   Frequency modulation

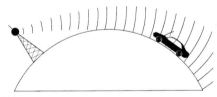

(a) Long wave
Propagation as ground waves. Long range (approx. 600 km)

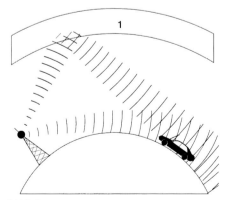

(b) Medium wave
Propagation partly as ground waves, partly as spatial waves which are reflected by the Heaviside layers

Figure 10.26   Electromagnetic wave propagation

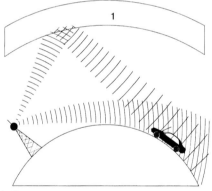

(c) Short wave
Propagation mainly as spatial waves. Very long ranges (depending upon the reflection capabilities of the Heaviside layer 1)

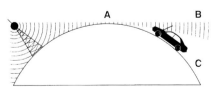

(d) VHF (FM)
Practically line-of-sight propagation. Short ranges (up to approx. 100 km).
A   Range: Only 'as far as the eye can see'
B   Range: As far as permitted by refraction
C   In 'shadow' (no reception)

- PS: programme service, allows the actual station name to be displayed in the radio display.
- Alternative frequency: information about available alternative frequencies. The RDS receiver checks the signal strength of all the alternatives and switches seamlessly if reception can be improved.
- PI: programme identity, the receiver makes a plausibility check with this code when it switches frequency to make sure that the same channel is received.
- TA/TP: Traffic announcement/programme. This indicates that a traffic announcement will be made. The driver can choose whether to interrupt a CD etc. automatically when a traffic announcement is made.
- PTY: programme type code. This indicates the genre of the broadcast (news, classical music etc.).
- PTY RT: radio text information. This allows a scrolling display of additional information, for example programme title, phone-in telephone numbers etc.
- EON: this signal allows the unit to transfer automatically to a traffic announcement being made on another station for the duration of the announcement.
- TMC: traffic message channel. Real-time digital traffic information which gives live status reports on traffic jams etc. This information can be used by navigation systems.

The RDS information is particularly useful and appropriate to vehicle radio systems due to the following enhancements that it brings:

- automatic retuning whilst travelling with no driver action required
- display of channel and programme information

- automatic playback of broadcast traffic information
- real-time digital traffic updates for navigation systems.

For these reasons, RDS is now standard on most in-vehicle equipment.

DAB

Digital audio broadcast (DAB) is the next-generation audio broadcast technology that ultimately will replace analogue broadcasting. Digital transmission of radio broadcasts is much more efficient than the equivalent analogue system with respect to data bandwidth and interference suppression on the transmitted signal. DAB broadcasts have the following attributes:

- reliable and interference-free reception
- very high-quality broadcasts
- additional features can be built into the receiver, for example pause of live broadcast or easy recording to disk/RAM
- additional display information is available
- many more channels are available due to multiplexing of broadcast channels.

The system transmits between five and seven broadcast programmes in a single transmission known as an *ensemble*. Data reduction techniques are used on each broadcast. The channels are then encoded with error correction and multiplexed together. Digital to analogue conversion is followed by mixing and filtering. Following this, transmission takes place at a frequency of 1.5 MHz.

The signal is received by the DAB tuner. It is decrypted, processed and then converted to left- and right-hand sound channels. In addition, data required for control and operation of the receiver is directed to the user interface. Figure 10.27 shows a DAB receiver.

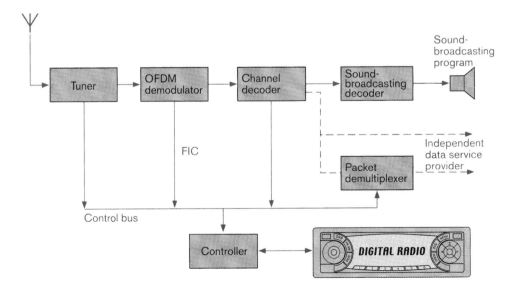

Figure 10.27 DAB receiver

Aerials

It is possible to fit an aerial in a preferred location on any vehicle, and this can be used with in-vehicle entertainment. Most vehicles have an aerial fitted as standard. The aerial converts the high-frequency carrier waves radiated by the transmitter into a signal that can be passed directly to the receiver for demodulation.

In the past, aerials have been mounted on the front wing, but this is less common now. Most aerials are roof mounted or alternatively they are integrated in the window glass or heated rear window element. The location of the aerial is critical to the performance of the receiver. Some typical locations are shown in Figure 10.28.

There are a number of different types of aerials according to the type of receiver and the mounting position. Typically, the 'rod'-type aerial, often retractable, is mounted on the vehicle in an area of high field strength such as edges or gaps (e.g. the roof, front and rear wings). They are particularly favourable as their length allows them to project beyond the vehicle's interference field. The angle of the aerial mounting position has an effect and is a compromise between the horizontal and vertical positions ideally required for AM and FM reception, respectively. It is clearly not possible to have one aerial in both horizontal and vertical positions. So the aerial is mounted at an angle. It is possible to mount more than one aerial where the receiver has a feature called antenna diversity. With multiple aerials, the probability of receiving a good-quality signal increases accordingly. A receiver with this feature can intelligently switch to the aerial with the best signal for the received transmission, and it can do this continuously during use (see Figure 10.29).

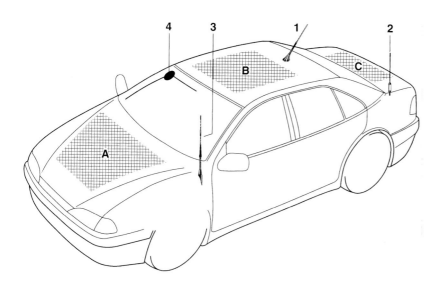

Suitable installation points:
1   Rear roof area
2   Rear wing
3   Front wing
4   Windscreen (exception with windscreen integrated antenna)

Unsuitable installation points:
A   Bonnet
B   Roof surface
C   Boot lid

Figure 10.28 Typical aerial locations on a vehicle

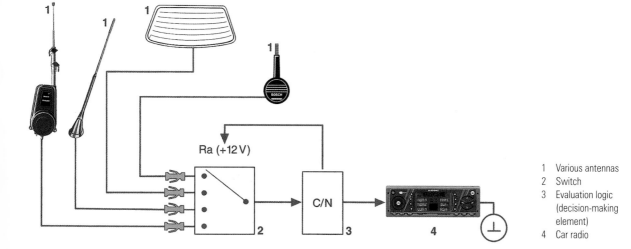

1   Various antennas
2   Switch
3   Evaluation logic (decision-making element)
4   Car radio

Figure 10.29 Antenna diversity system

Electric operation of retractable rod aerials is common and for this task a reversing, permanent magnet motor is employed which extends and retracts the aerial rod via a plastic cable drive. The receiver itself has a signal wire which is connected to a control relay that activates the aerial up or down when required. The drive arrangement of the cable is shown in Figure 10.30.

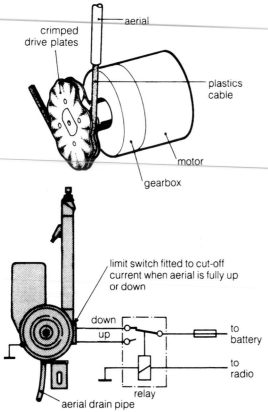

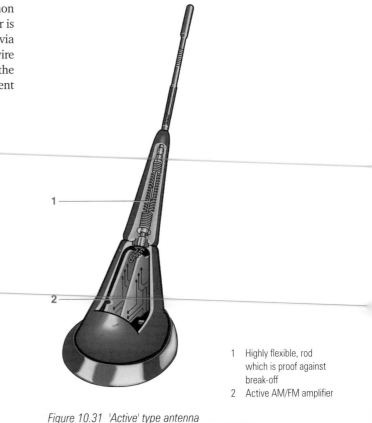

1 Highly flexible, rod which is proof against break-off
2 Active AM/FM amplifier

Figure 10.31 'Active' type antenna

Figure 10.30 Electric radio aerial

Active aerials are fitted with an integrated signal booster which means that losses in cables etc. can be compensated for. Therefore, the aerial can be fitted further away from the receiver, perhaps at the rear of the vehicle, away from the engine, which is itself a source of interference. A typical design is shown in Figure 10.31.

Aerials can be integrated into the window glass either as stand-alone aerial elements or using the heated rear window element. They are normally used in conjunction with an amplifier as they have low receiving power when compared to a rod aerial, but they are resilient to damage from external effects like damp or vandalism.

Due to the wide range of aerial equipment and mounting positions, an appropriate solution is always possible depending on the specific requirements. When an aerial is fitted to a vehicle a good earth connection between the aerial and the vehicle body ground is

essential for good reception and interference reduction. In addition, the connection to the receiver unit must be sound and properly terminated.

10.2.2 Music playback

Overview

As the media for storing music has evolved, so have the in-vehicle systems in order to play them. In-vehicle record players for playing vinyl discs never took off due to the sensitivity associated with this technology (i.e. a needle in a groove), but in the 1970s the eight-track stereo tape was ideal for in-vehicle music playback. However, this format never really established itself. The eight-track tape system was replaced by the music-cassette tape format and these were very successful until well into the 1980s, even though the sound reproduction quality was quite poor.

In the late 1980s the compact disc became the first cheaply available digital music format allowing high-quality reproduction and durable storage media. Compact discs have been by far the most popular music format in recent times until the MP3 became widely accepted due to the popularity of portable players for this media (e.g. the Apple iPod). MP3s allow efficient storage of music tracks due to the compressed format which retains a high proportion of the original sound quality. In addition, MP3 tracks can be played and stored on many kinds of modern electronic media like flash memory cards, hard disks and compact discs.

At the time of writing, MP3 is a widely accepted format that is increasingly being integrated into vehicle entertainment systems. It is likely that this trend will continue and it may be possible to store complete music collections in the vehicle on hard-disk based systems using computer-type interface technology (i.e. USB, fire wire etc.) to allow upload and download of tracks.

Current trends also indicate the growth of complete infotainment systems which integrate entertainment with information systems allowing a single user interface and combined, complementary technology to ensure that the driver has easy access to entertainment media as well as the latest traffic information warnings. A system of this type approaches the capability of a personal computer and it is likely that on-board PCs will become feasible which can easily perform information, entertainment and communication functions in an operating environment with which the user will be very familiar.

Compact disc

Invented originally by Phillips, the compact disc is a durable media which can store extremely high-quality, digitally encoded music tracks. The basic principle of operation is that the analogue sound-waves are digitised and stored as microscopic indentations (pits) on a spiral track etched or burned onto the surface of the disk. The areas between pits are known as 'lands'. Each pit is approximately 100 nm deep by 500 nm wide, and vary from 850 nm to 3.5 µm in length. The difference in height between pits and lands leads to a phase difference between the light reflected from a pit and that from its surrounding land. By measuring the intensity with a photodiode, it is possible to read the data from the disc. This produces a bit stream which can then be converted via digital-to-analogue electronics and then amplified to drive a speaker system.

The disc has no physical contact with the optical reader and therefore no wear occurs. Information on the disc has a very long life (but not indefinite) and recordable discs are fairly cheap so the user can create their own music discs (via a home computer).

Generally, the high-quality sound data must be reproduced on a high-quality sound system and amplifier to get the maximum benefit from the format. An in-vehicle CD player normally fits in the dashboard in the designed aperture for an entertainment unit. This allows playing of single CDs with manual changeover. Alternatively, a multi-disc unit or CD auto-changer can be fitted and the driver will not have to change the CD. This unit holds a number of CDs (generally six or 10) and it can be mounted in the boot (or dash if there is sufficient space). When the unit is loaded, all of the track information is read and the driver can select CDs and tracks from a play list displayed on the head unit. A typical auto-changer system is shown in Figure 10.32.

MP3

This music format has gained massive popularity recently (at the time of writing). The MP3 is digital audio encoding using an efficient compression format and algorithm designed to greatly reduce the amount of data required to represent the audio sound-waves yet still sound (to most listeners) like a faithful reproduction of the original uncompressed audio. The most important factors that have contributed to the success of this format are:

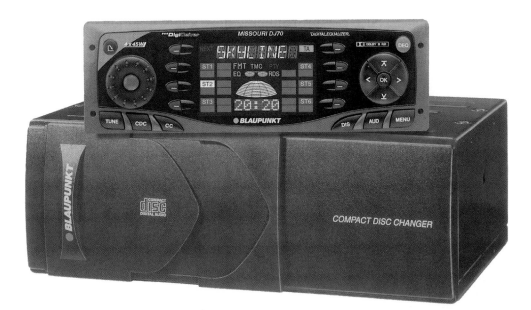

Figure 10.32 CD auto-changer

- highly compressed but small data files for the music tracks allow download and distribution via home computers and the internet
- the hardware for distributing or storing the files is flexible and efficient, they can be managed via flash memory, hard drives or data CDs or DVDs
- the popularity of the personal players used to listen to this music format.

In addition, the hardware needed to play and store music in this form is relatively small and hence ideal for in-vehicle applications. CDs and associated optical players/readers are large compared to flash memory readers or disc drives. In order to integrate MP3 playback in the vehicle system there must be an interface with the entertainment system. This could be via the following:

- A computer-type interface can be incorporated into the head unit to allow connection of external drives (i.e. USB etc.) with preloaded music tracks.
- A mini-jack connector to allow the direct connection of an MP3 player so that music can be output directly to the vehicle's system speakers.
- A memory card slot in the head unit allowing direct access to music tracks on a flash memory card. These cards are now available with 1 GB of memory in a physical package which is the size of a coin.
- An FM modulator which converts the sound signal from the MP3 player into an FM signal transmitted over a very small radius. This is then received via the head unit's FM receiver and played back via the entertainment system as a radio transmission.

A typical system is shown in Figure 10.33.

Speakers

The low-frequency AC signals generated by the output stage of the entertainment system must be converted into acoustic sound-waves at frequencies appropriate for the human ear (in the 20 Hz to 20 kHz range). This task is performed by the speaker system.

A simple speaker consists of a cone-shaped diaphragm which is suspended by a flexible rim. The cone moves back and forth to generate acoustic waves driven by the speaker's electromagnetic system. The diaphragms are cone-shaped for lower frequencies and dome-shaped for higher frequencies. High-quality speakers have cones manufactured from polypropylene, aluminium or ceramic. General-purpose speakers are made from paper. The general design and construction of a typical speaker is shown in Figure 10.34.

The current from the amplifier output stage causes the voice coil to oscillate so that the diaphragm vibrates and generates sound-waves. In order to prevent resonance, the speaker is often mounted in a box or enclosure filled with sound-deadening material. The diameter of the cone dictates the frequency range of the speaker. Large-cone speakers are optimal for low frequencies (known as woofers or sub-woofers). Small-diameter speakers are used for high-frequency sound-wave generation.

The speaker power is normally rated in watts and should exceed the amplifier output rating by 50%. Another property of the speaker is its impedance (resistance to AC current). This should be matched to the amplifier output to ensure the most efficient operation of the speaker.

Generally, it is not possible to produce the complete human frequency range with single speaker types. Often different speakers for different frequency ranges are employed in conjunction with additional hardware (crossovers) to ensure the sound signal is passed to the most appropriate speaker according to the frequency. Crossovers can be divided into active or passive types. The former divides the sound before amplification, the latter after. A typical crossover-based system layout is shown in Figure 10.35.

Modern in-vehicle entertainment systems with digital signal processing allow the generation of a well-balanced and optimised stereo effect, and a highly dynamic acoustic experience at any point in the vehicle interior.

10.2.3 Mobile telephones

Introduction

Car telephones were considered the ultimate luxury item at one time. With developments in technology, the mobile phone was miniaturised to the point where it became a hand-held device and this reduced the popularity of fixed car phones considerably. All mobile phones now use the GSM (global system for mobile communication) network for speech transmission. In addition, digital communication networks have brought additional possibilities for interaction, for example SMS (short messaging service (text)) messaging and MMS (multimedia messaging service (picture)) messaging. Furthermore, high-speed digital connections (via GPRS (general packet radio service) known as 3G) with sufficient bandwidth allow mobile internet and email access on hand-held devices. This has revolutionised portable communication which has left fixed car-phone technology behind.

The trend from these developments is the integration of mobile, hand-held devices into the vehicle environment. Wireless connections via standard interfaces like Bluetooth allow the integration of the mobile phone with the vehicle infotainment system. Features like hands-free operation and number selection via speech recognition become easily possible and a growing market exists for mobile-phone accessories for in-vehicle use.

Hands free

Section 26 of the Road Traffic Act 1988 now states that a driver

'who contravenes or fails to comply with a construction and use requirement as to ... not driving or supervising the driving of a motor vehicle while using a hand-held mobile telephone

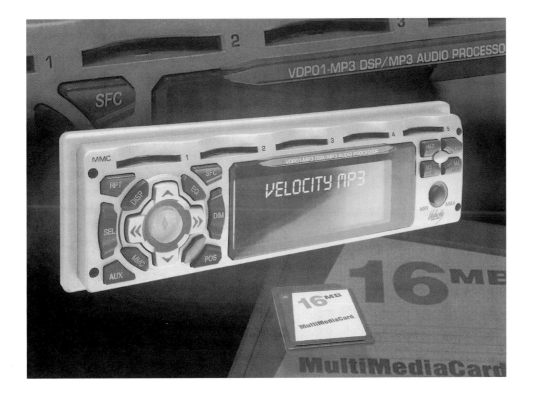

Figure 10.33 In-car MP3

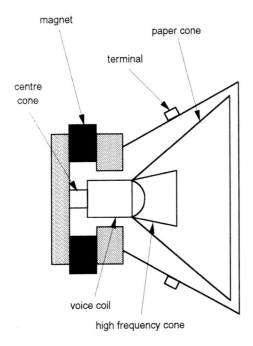

Figure 10.34 Construction of a twin-cone speaker

or other hand-held interactive communication device, or not causing or permitting the driving of a motor vehicle by another person using such a telephone or other device, is guilty of an offence'.

In laymen's terms, it is illegal to use a mobile phone without a hands-free device whilst driving and the offence is punishable by way of a fine and penalty points.

In response to this there is a growing market for hands-free devices to supplement operation of the phone and enable use of the phone whilst driving. In the simplest form, they can be headsets with a microphone that plug directly into the phone via a jack plug. Most are more sophisticated and use Bluetooth wireless technology. This system allows bi-directional data flow which supports transmission and reception of voice data. In addition, features like remote dialling, answering of calls etc. can be executed from the Bluetooth hands-free device without touching the phone itself.

Bluetooth is an industrial specification for wireless personal area networks (PANs). Bluetooth provides a way to connect and exchange information between devices such as mobile phones, laptops, PCs, printers, digital cameras and video game consoles over a secure, globally unlicensed short-range radio frequency.

Typical examples of an over-ear headset and speakerphone are shown in Figures 10.36 and 10.37.

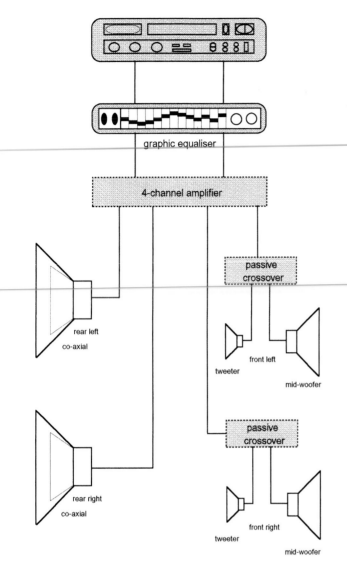

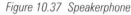

Figure 10.37 Speakerphone

Figure 10.35 Audio system with graphic equaliser and four-channel amplifier

An alternative is a car kit. These are fixed installations with a holder/cradle to charge the phone and connect to the additional speaker and microphone automatically when the phone is located in the cradle. These units can also integrate with the vehicle system by using the entertainment system speakers and via automatic mute of the radio or music playback during a call. These hard-wired systems are retro fitted via specialist installers who may also fit an external aerial for the phone system to improve reception.

The cradle is an essential part of the hands-free kit. It can be a simple unit to just hold the phone in an appropriate position, or it can be more sophisticated (as mentioned above) to form the interface to hands-free operation via a docking system. A typical installation is shown in Figure 10.38.

Figure 10.36 Over-ear headset

Figure 10.38 Hands-free phone cradle

Phone integration in the vehicle

Many vehicles are now offered with phone hands-free operation built in (via Bluetooth). The driver can easily answer and end mobile phone calls as they drive. It is not necessary to touch the handheld mobile phone once it is paired with the car. As a phone call is answered, the system conveniently mutes the car's audio system. Phone calls can also be initiated from the integrated system, either from the system's phonebook or dialled on the car's interface by the driver. On some Bluetooth communication systems using voice activation, a phone call can be initiated and the audio system muted without touching any buttons or user interface.

In addition, some aftermarket entertainment systems have a Bluetooth interface which means that this unit supports the hands-free operation and features of the phone once paired. A typical unit is shown in Figure 10.39.

Figure 10.39 In-car entertainment system with Bluetooth interface

The ultimate in phone integration is that the vehicle has a complete phone function built in. The driver places a SIM (subscriber identity module) card into a slot and the car effectively becomes a phone on wheels! (This is featured on the Porsche models and is known as PCM – Porsche Communication Management.)

Figure 10.40 Built-in phone function (Porsche)

Key Points

Driver entertainment systems consist of units which can play broadcast radio or preselected music tracks to the driver via an integrated hi-fi system built into the vehicle

Analogue radio signals are transmitted via a carrier wave. This wave contains the acoustic signal frequencies superimposed onto it. These are transmitted via frequency or amplitude modulation. When the signal is received, the sound frequencies are demodulated, amplified and sent to the speakers as electrical signals. The speakers convert electrical oscillations into acoustic vibrations which can then be heard by the human ear in the frequency range of 20 Hz to 20 kHz

Radio transmission technology is shifting to digital broadcasting (DAB) which offers high-quality sound with additional features like programme information etc. In addition, digital broadcasting allows more efficient use of the airwave frequencies so that more channels are available. A limited amount of digital information is already available from analogue networks in the form of RDS (radio data system). This provides basic channel and traffic information

In the past, in-vehicle music playback systems used magnetic tape to store analogue acoustic signals (eight-track and music cassettes). A dramatic improvement in sound quality occurred with the introduction digital storage media for music, the compact disc (CD). In recent years, the MP3 format has meant a huge improvement in convenience. This compressed data format allows many music tracks to be stored on physically small media systems (flash memory etc.). This allows the access and storage of large music libraries for in-vehicle use

In-car phones have been replaced by the hand-held mobile phone. The main growth area for vehicle use is the integration of these phones into the vehicle system. The driving force for this is legislation which prevents the holding of a phone whilst driving. Many aftermarket hands-free kits use Bluetooth bi-direction, shortwave radio, digital transmission technology to provide a seamless connection between the hands-free unit and the phone

Many cars now have a phone function integrated (via Bluetooth) allowing the driver to use their phone via an interface in the vehicle rather than via the phone keypad and screen. The system allows automatic connection of the phone to the hands-free system as soon as the driver enters the vehicle

Chapter 11

DIAGNOSTICS

what is covered in this chapter ...

- ■ Introduction
- ■ Diagnostic techniques
- ■ Application examples

11.1 INTRODUCTION

The diagnostic skill of a technician in the automotive industry is one of the key attributes which sets aside the top-performing, most valuable members of technical staff from the rest. Skilled diagnostic technicians are a valuable asset in the industry and most people who can demonstrate this ability are high-achieving master technicians who have the most interesting and challenging careers.

Diagnostics skills are a combination of applied knowledge and experience, logical thought process and an inquisitive nature. A technical mind instinctively wants to understand how something works.

Generally, a skilled diagnostic technician will have this profile, but it must be developed and optimised by experience and the correct guidance. This chapter is designed to give an overview of the application of tools and techniques. It is by no means exhaustive and is not offered as a substitute for manufacturers' detailed information. However, it will give the reader an insight into the area of automotive diagnostics. There are also some hints and tips on what to do when something that you do not understand or have never seen does not work!

11.2 DIAGNOSTIC TECHNIQUES

11.2.1 A logical approach

A logical approach to fault finding is essential in order to avoid wasting time and money. If a fault occurs on a vehicle and it is a known problem or you have come across it before, then by using your experience you can optimise the time spent rectifying the fault as you have some direction. Your diagnostic skills become apparent when you are looking at a problem that you have not seen before. In this situation, many technicians resort to changing component parts blindly. This is not acceptable for modern vehicles as these parts can be very expensive. A starting point is to use some method or philosophy to approach the problem. A simple but logical generic process (as shown in Figure 11.1) gives some structure to your actions.

Using a structure like that shown shifts the emphasis from *luck* to *skill* when identifying problems. This strategic approach will allow you to remain focused when dealing with a problem, ensuring that you use your time effectively and efficiently.

Always try to gather as much information as possible about the problem. Collect all of the documentation that you have. Talk to colleagues who may be able to support you with advice or their experience.

11.2.2 Successive approximation method

This method allows you to successively, physically check parts of a wiring circuit in a logical way so that

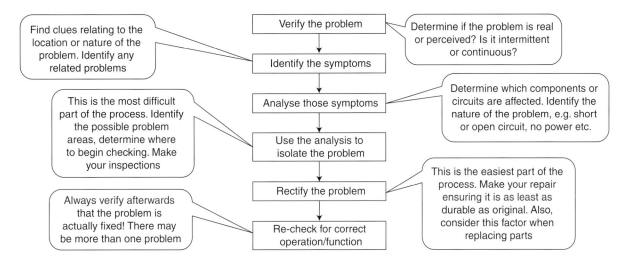

Figure 11.1 A logical approach

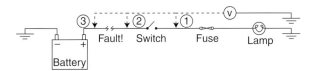

Figure 11.2 Fault-tracing via successive approximation method

with each check you will definitely get closer to the fault. This reduces the amount of time spent tracing electrical faults in the vehicle wiring system. If the circuit layout is not known or is complex, then a wiring diagram will help considerably. Figure 11.2 shows the basic principle.

The principle involves finding the middle of the offending circuit path. From this point you can use the appropriate test tool to check which side of the circuit has failed. Once you have identified this, you have immediately halved the problem! Next, you identify the halfway point of the bad part of the circuit, then make another check at this point. This technique rapidly reduces the size of the problem with each step. Finally, you will reach a point where the problem is easy to identify as you can locate a very specific area (for example a junction block) where the problem has to exist. This technique is very powerful and can be applied to any circuit.

11.2.3 Dealing with open circuits

Open circuits are normally identified by a loss of power. This can easily be checked with a voltmeter or test lamp via an open-circuit test. Generally the voltmeter has the advantage in that it does not damage any sensitive components, but it cannot identify a high resistance in an unloaded circuit. That is, the voltmeter tells you that a connection exists which can supply the voltage, but it does not tell you how good that connection is! An ohmmeter can also be used to check for open circuits,

but the circuit or component must be completely unpowered. Low resistances cannot be tested effectively with a ohmmeter.

11.2.4 Dealing with short circuits

Short circuits are where a direct path to ground exists. In an electrical circuit the current will always take the easiest path. If this happens, the circuit is overloaded and (hopefully) a fuse or other protection device will protect the circuit. Short-circuit detectors are available that switch the fault current on and off in the circuit (they are fitted in place of the blown fuse). It is then possible to identify the location of the fault using a compass or inductive ammeter. This means that it is possible to locate the fault without removing trim. The problem is that a high current still flows momentarily and thus, if the wire in the faulty circuit is small, it can still overheat. A better solution is to use a high-wattage bulb (>21 W). This will not overload the circuit but the intensity of the lamp allows you to distinguish a dead short from the normal circuit current as you systematically disconnect parts of the circuit. This method is particularly useful for tracing intermittent faults.

Examining the fuse can give information about the nature of the fault. If the fuse has 'blown' then a dead short exists. If it has overheated then an overload has occurred (this may indicate a component problem). If it has fractured, then the fuse itself could have fatigued and failed with no specific circuit fault.

11.2.5 Dealing with parasitic loads

Parasitic loads relate to current being drawn whilst the vehicle is standing inoperative. Most vehicles have a small, standing current draw due to electronic components (~50 mA), but more than this will flatten the battery over an extended period of, say, a few days. In order to isolate a load of this kind an ammeter must be connected in circuit with the battery. By removing the fuses, one by one, all the components which draw quiescent currents can be identified and eliminated. Once the offending circuit component fuse is disconnected, the drop in current draw will be seen at the ammeter. It is then possible to follow this current draw via the wiring system by disconnecting at appropriate wiring junctions. In this way the circuit component can be isolated.

11.2.6 Voltage-drop testing

Volt-drop testing is a dynamic test of the circuit under operating conditions and is a very reliable way of determining the integrity of the circuit and its components. With this technique, problem resistances in circuits which carry a significant current (>3 amps) can be clearly identified. For these circuits, even a resistance of 1 ohm can cause a problem (remember that $V = IR$, therefore a resistance of 1 ohm in a circuit carrying 3 amps will drop 3 volts across the resistance, i.e. 25% of the available voltage for a 12 volt system). Because the test is done whilst the circuit is operating, factors such as current flow and heating effect will be apparent. To test for volt drop, the voltmeter is placed in parallel with the circuit section to be tested. During operation of the circuit, any unwanted resistance will show as a voltage reading. In general, not more than 10% of the system voltage should be dropped between the source (the battery) and the consumer (the load). Voltage-drop measurements should be carried out on the return (earth) as well as the supply side of the circuit and generally voltage dropped on the earth side should be lower.

11.3   APPLICATION EXAMPLES

Some typical test applications and measurements are shown below.

some data for reference. This gives you a head start in the diagnostic process!

11.3.1 Sensors

Generally, most sensors produce a voltage that can be displayed on a voltmeter or oscilloscope. Many vehicle sensors measure dynamic properties and so the best way to test them is using an oscilloscope. This allows the user to see the high-frequency response of the sensor. Using a voltmeter, these elements of the signal would be lost. Some typical example wave-forms from chassis and body systems are shown in Table 11.1.

New sensor technologies can be explored with the oscilloscope. If a vehicle becomes available with a sensor that you have not seen before, as long as you know that the vehicle is working properly you can use it as a reference source. Take the time to do some research, find out which pins are supply, ground and signal. Then test the output and make a note of the signal and its response via voltage outputs at the respective pins. If the equipment allows, record the wave-forms for future reference, then you have a permanent record. Taking some time to do this could save you a lot of time later!

11.3.2 Actuators

Similar to sensor technology, the dynamic response of most actuators is a function of the input signals. These can be measured and recorded using an oscilloscope. Some typical examples are shown in Table 11.2.

Again, with actuator technology, take the time to do some research, explore vehicles with known functional equipment. Record the wave-forms electronically (or draw them) for reference. You will be glad you did when a problem occurs and you have already recorded

11.3.3 Power storage (batteries)

Battery testing and charging is discussed in detail in Chapter 3. You should refer to that chapter for more detail, but it is worthy to note the main points in the context of this chapter.

Maintenance
The amount of maintenance required for a battery is minimal and some batteries are described as 'maintenance free' (although this could be considered a relative term). It is important to note that all batteries need some periodic checks.

Due to advances in technology, battery fluid consumption is minimal or non-existent. Nevertheless, the physical condition of the battery and its electrical connections are essential for good performance. Bearing this is mind, it is important to regularly make a visual check of the battery, its mounting position and the integrity of the connections. If it is possible to access the cells, a check of fluid level and specific gravity should be made. Any large variation is an indicator of a problem.

Fault diagnosis
Most faults become more apparent when the conditions become more demanding (for example winter weather). Table 11.3 shows some typical faults and their possible causes.

A logical test procedure will identify the root cause of most battery-related problems:

- visual inspection
- specific-gravity check
- load test.

Table 11.1 Sensors

Sensor	Notes	Waveform
Hall effect	A square wave like this could be typical of a wheel-speed sensors or crank/cam sensor. Look for a symmetry and/or regularity of the wave form. These sensors should have a constant amplitude signal	
Thermistor	This is a typical temperature sensor signal over an extended time period. Look for a smooth signal as the temperature changes. Temperature is not a fast-changing quantity so high frequencies generally are noise!	
ABS inductive	An AC sensor wave form will vary in frequency and amplitude with speed. Look for symmetry and repeatability of the wave form	
Position sensor	Pedal position should show a smooth change of voltage as the pedal is moved, any noise or gaps in the signal will cause problems	
Pressure sensor	This is the voltage output from a fuel pressure sensor which allows the engine control system to dynamically adjust the fuel pressure. Look for a smooth, noise-free waveform	

Table 11.2 Actuators

Actuator	Notes	Waveform
Stepper motor	Simple square wave, look for constant amplitude and a cyclic, noise-free signal	
Idle speed actuator	This is an electromagnetic-type valve. The most important aspect is the regular shape of the wave-form and the fact that it is noise free	
Idle speed actuator	Rotary type, this is a simple square wave, varying frequency. Look for a clean signal, no noise!	
Idle speed actuator	Rotary type, slightly more complex wave-form, but nevertheless the same fundamental aspects apply. Look for a clean, regular signal	

Table 11.3 Typical battery faults and their causes

Fault	Cause
Undercharging	• Low alternator output, perhaps due to a slipping drive belt • Excessive drain on the battery, which may be due to a short circuit • Faulty alternator regulator • Terminal corrosion
Overcharging (excessive gassing)	• Defective cell in battery • Faulty alternator
Low battery capacity	• Internal or external short circuit • Sulphation • Loss of active material from plates • Low electrolyte level • Incorrect electrolyte strength • Terminal corrosion

It is important to check the surrounding sub-systems as well. Many problems which have the symptoms of a flat battery could be due to other problems like the charging or starter system.

11.3.4 Power generation (alternators)

Maintenance

Modern alternators are highly reliable machines that cover considerable vehicle mileage before needing any attention. In the past, replacement of components was feasible (e.g. brushes, bearings etc.), but with modern units failure normally indicates that the whole unit has reached the end of its service life and therefore replacement of the whole assembly is easily justified (reconditioned units are readily available).

The main requirements for maintenance are with respect to the external connections and drive belt. The electrical connections at the alternator carry a considerable current! Any loose or poor-quality connection will cause a resistance and this causes heating that damages the connection. This is a cyclic action and once it starts, failure will not be apparent until the vehicle has a flat battery. Therefore, it is advisable at service intervals to check the connection visually and, if in any doubt, via a dynamic volt-drop test to ensure the integrity of the connection.

The drive-belt tension and conditions should also be checked (see Figure 11.3). Insufficient tension is not always shown via the characteristic 'screeching' noise. If the alternator pulley can be turned via belt slippage then the tension needs increasing. Also, check the belt surface for cracks and a 'shiny' surface. In worn condition, vee-belts will not be able to transfer the torque to generate full power, irrespective of belt tension. Many manufacturers now recommend a set tension that should be checked with a suitable belt-tension gauge.

If the belt needs to be removed, take the opportunity to spin the alternator pulley by hand. Listen and feel for smooth bearing operation; any roughness or noise could indicate that failure is imminent.

Fault diagnosis

For alternator tests, it is important to check first that the battery is in good condition and charged and that the drive belt tension is correct. Assuming these are acceptable, a full charging check is the first step to diagnosing alternator faults. For this a suitable ammeter-voltmeter set is needed (see Figures 11.4–11.6).

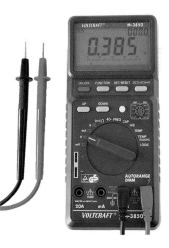

Figure 11.4 Multimeter

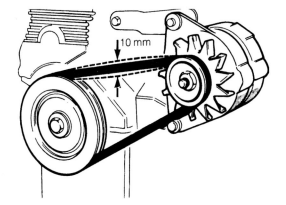

Figure 11.3 Belt-drive tension

Figure 11.5 Inductive ammeter

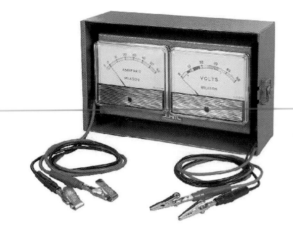

Figure 11.6 Volt-ammeter test set

indicates a rectifier failure; a glowing warning lamp could be a faulty regulator or wiring fault. Make sure that you are familiar with the type of alternator fitted as the warning light response to faults can vary.

- Check the voltage and continuity of cables between the alternator, battery and warning light (wiring details will help considerably). Check the electrical connections dynamically via the volt-drop method. This allows faulty connections to be clearly identified. Looks for signs of heating or corrosion at connectors and terminals.
- Additional tests can be carried out using an oscilloscope to look at the ripple currents. This waveform should be symmetrical and cyclic. Any variation indicates a problem with an alternator phase.

This allows monitoring of the charging current supplied to the battery in addition to the voltage. Modern equivalent meters have inductive current probes and these are easier to use as circuit disconnection of the battery is not needed. The important factor is to be able to monitor the battery charging current whilst the system electrical loads are activated. This test will also identify if the correct alternator is fitted to the vehicle. A working alternator will not charge the battery if it is insufficiently rated for the vehicle. The procedure is as follows:

- Run the engine at idle whilst monitoring battery current and voltage.
- Switch on steady consumers – headlights, fog lights, heated rear window and blower.
- Raise engine speed, watch the charging current. At idle speed current may flow from the battery as the alternator current is insufficient. Raising engine speed increases the output and so current should flow back into the battery from the alternator.
- Also monitor the battery voltage. If the charging current is positive (i.e. charging the battery) then battery voltage is less important but should be around 14 volts. Make sure it does not go over approximately 14.5 volts for a prolonged period as this could will cause overcharging of the battery. As with all figures stated in this chapter, it is essential that you always check the manufacturer's data. For example, in some cases alternator output can exceed 15 V on some 'smart charging' systems for a short time to boost the battery.

If the alternator can maintain battery charging under these conditions, then the system is working properly. If not:

- A visual check of the alternator warning light operation can give an indication of the nature of a fault. No warning light is a clear problem. Check the bulb and wiring. If these are functional, the alternator is at fault. Inverse operation of the lamp

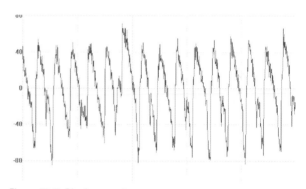

Figure 11.7 Ripple currents

11.3.5 Engine starting systems (starter motors)

Maintenance
The starter motor itself requires no regular maintenance. The most important factor for routine maintenance is the integrity of the energy supply chain, i.e. the battery and the cables. Battery maintenance is discussed above. The quality of the power supply cable connection is essential, particularly when you bear in mind the fact that the voltage during operation could be as low as 10 volts. You cannot afford to lose any voltage due to volt drop under these conditions. Terminals and connectors should be checked visually on a regular basis. They should always be clean and secure. Remember to check the earth connections at the battery and the engine – these are particularly important as they are easy to overlook.

Fault diagnosis
The parts of the starting system which cause the main problems are:

- battery
- terminals and connectors
- cabling

- solenoid
- starter motor.

Typical faults are shown in Table 11.4.

In addition, dynamic circuit checks should be carried out using the volt-drop method to identify resistances in the power cables. A voltage-drop test on the supply side should show now more than 0.5 volts and on the earth side no more than 0.25 volts. Also, place the voltmeter across the solenoid contacts and note the reading whilst the contacts are closed (see Figure 11.8). Any voltage indicates a resistance across the solenoid contacts suggesting that replacement is necessary.

If the starter system does not operate at all when the key is turned, note the response of the dash warning lights (or turn on the headlights). The problem could be an open circuit between the starter switch and starter, or it could be a faulty starter. To determine which, turn the key to the start position. If the lamps dim (due to current draw of the solenoid) then the circuit is intact. If not, then there is an open circuit or faulty connection between the switch and the starter solenoid terminal (DIN designation 50). It is then possible to trace the circuit path using a voltmeter or test lamps to locate the fault and this avoids unnecessary removal of the starter motor.

11.3.6 Power distribution systems (wiring and communication systems)

Maintenance

There are no specific maintenance requirements for the body electrical distribution and communications system. Preventative maintenance is not really possible. There are no consumable parts to be replaced and no regular maintenance can be carried out other than visual checks. The most important factor that is likely to cause problems is when modifications have been carried out. In these circumstances, always ensure that you carry out work to a standard which is at least as good as the manufacturer's original. Failure to do this will cause problems at some point in the future!

Fault diagnosis

If a section of a circuit has been identified as a region where a fault has developed, a detailed examination of the fuses, cables and connectors should be carried out. If a wiring diagram or other information is available this should be used in order to optimise the use of your time. Familiarise yourself with how the circuit works. After a visual inspection, tests using an appropriate test instrument should be carried out in a logical sequence. Make sure that you check the obvious and easiest aspects first and use your experience for a heuristic analysis. Intermittent faults are the most challenging and often

Table 11.4 Fault diagnosis

Symptom	Result of initial check	Possible cause
Low cranking speed	Lights dim when starter switch is operated	1. Discharged or defective battery 2. Poor connections between battery and solenoid 3. Tight engine
Starter does not operate	No lights or lights go out when starter is operated	1. Discharged or defective battery 2. Poor connections between battery and solenoid or between battery and earth 3. Severe short circuit to earth in starting motor
	Solenoid 'clicks' when starter switch is operated; lights unaffected	1. Poor connection between solenoid and motor 2. Broken or insecure earthstrap 3. Defective solenoid 4. Defective motor – most probably commutator or brushes
	No 'click' from solenoid; lights unaffected	1. Defective solenoid 2. Defective starter switch 3. Poor connections between starter switch and solenoid 4. Defective inhibitor switch (auto. transmission)
	Repeating 'clicking' from solenoid; lights unaffected	1. Broken holding coil in solenoid
	Repeated 'clicking' from solenoid; lights dim	1. Discharged or defective battery
	Lights dim when starter is operated and engine has seized	1. Pinion teeth jammed in flywheel 2. Engine has seized due to engine problem
Starter 'whines' but pinion does not engage		1. Dirt on helix (inertia drive) 2. Defective pinion engagement system (pre-engaged)

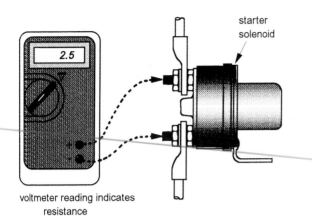

Figure 11.8 Volt-drop test to locate resistance

occur at faulty connectors. If possible try to identify the fault without disturbing the suspect connector as this can cause a temporary 'fix' where the fault cannot be located absolutely but will surely reoccur. Typical faults at connectors include:

- connector assemblies not locked
- terminals 'backed out'
- corrosion
- moisture
- terminal worn – connector surface contact force is insufficient.

Once the problem has been located it can be rectified. Make sure that any repairs are to the original equipment standards. Use replacement connectors of the same type as the original ones if possible. These can be difficult to source, so if a substitution must be made ensure it is fit for purpose, as convenient as the original equipment and, if visible, looks similar to the existing equipment.

Terminals and connectors can be cleaned and repaired to a certain extent. Remove connectors from the terminal block with care and if possible use the correct terminal tools (these are commercially available). Always dismantle the connector assembly according to the manufacturer's instruction. Terminal and connector assemblies are carefully designed and engineered to ensure good connections and reliability. Therefore, careful handling is important to ensure this quality remains. Special cleaning fluids and grease are available for connector assemblies and these should be used.

11.3.7 Comfort and control systems

Maintenance
Most of the systems in this category require no regular maintenance apart from perhaps lubrication (e.g. electric window lift, sunroof mechanism). The exception is the air-conditioning system. The system relies on a working fluid which contains a lubricant and it is important during regular vehicle service and inspection that the system pressure and fluid level is checked. It is

also important that any problems are rectified quickly as damage can occur to components (e.g. seals) if the system is out of action for an extended time period.

Fault diagnosis
Fault diagnosis for these system follows the same general principles as for any part of the system. All of the components in this category are fused and this should be the first point of call. Remember the following:

- use a heuristic approach to any problem
- familiarise yourself with the operation of the component or circuit
- check the components with the easiest accessibility first
- do not overlook the obvious.

Air conditioning/climate control systems generally need specialised equipment in order to test the system and diagnose faults. There are many specialised air-conditioning companies and in most cases it is better to delegate the task to a specialist! However, note that electronically controlled systems will have self-diagnostic functions, often accessible via OBD. Check if this is the case and use a scan tool to point you in the right direction by accessing the fault codes.

11.3.8 Signalling and vision systems

Maintenance
Generally, maintenance of vision systems (lights, screen, wipers) involves regular cleaning and checking of the equipment. Failure of bulbs on modern vehicles is often indicated on the driver display. If it is not, the driver should regularly check the lighting system to ensure that all of the equipment is working (a legal requirement) and that the lenses are clean. Windscreen wiper blades should be replaced regularly to ensure that the screen is effectively cleared. They are consumable items and should be replaced annually. Wiper arms also need inspection to ensure that sufficient force is generated to clean the screen properly. If this is not the case they should also be replaced. Headlamps may need readjustment and alignment to ensure optimum beam pattern and to prevent dazzle. Specialist equipment is needed for this task and should always be used.

Fault diagnosis
Lighting system faults are often caused by bulb or fuse failure. These systems have significant thermal shock and high-inrush current and this can cause a bulb or fuse to blow at switch-on. If a bulb blows it should be examined carefully as this can give an indication of where the problem could lie (for example a mirror effect on the bulb glass indicates a poor earth). Wiring checks follow the general rules mentioned above. Headlamp circuits draw a significant current and therefore volt-drop testing is appropriate to identify unwanted resistance. Earth problems at lamp units can cause very unusual responses during operation. Earth connections

should always be checked first when unusual lighting faults occur. Also, always check that the correct bulb is installed! There is a bewildering array of different bulb types which are very similar in form and this can be confusing for those who are not familiar with them. Make sure the right type is installed. Ask if a bulb has been replaced recently! Figure 11.9 highlights a process for fault diagnosis of lighting systems.

Wiper systems are generally reliable. Excessive wear in the linkage will be apparent by noise. In this case the mechanism must be replaced. Motor faults must be identified clearly before attempting to remove the motor assembly as this can be a significant task. If possible, try to get wiring information on the wiper system.

Self-parking mechanisms can be complex and vary from manufacturer to manufacturer. Parking switches are built into the motor and electronic controllers operate the system functions. A clear understanding of how the system works will help you in identifying the fault. If the motor is at fault, generally this will not be user serviceable and will require complete replacement.

Heated screens draw considerable current, normally controlled via a timer relay. Determine first if the screen is getting the required power. If not, inspect the circuit and components. If it is, check that the elements are intact. These can be broken easily but they are repairable with conductive paint. Use a voltmeter to identify the position of the break. Table 11.5 outlines a test sequence.

Electric window systems are generally reliable. In older systems, switch failure was common. These switches could be repaired if disassembled correctly and the contacts cleaned. Modern systems use electronic controllers and relays. Always check the fuses first, try to establish if the motor is drawing current or not. This identifies either a wiring fault or a motor fault. Check if the regulator mechanism is free or jammed/stiff. This will require removal of the door panel trim. As a guide, a test sequence table is shown in Table 11.6.

For signalling systems, inoperative horns are often caused due to failure of the unit or a poor connection. The reason for this is the exposed location of the horn. It is mounted at the front of the vehicle and is often exposed to extreme damp and weather. Generally, if the horn fails and the power supply integrity is good, then the complete unit must be replaced. Horns are often operated by relays. Check the circuit in a logical order (i.e. fuse first), bear in mind that the horn could be switched on the earth or the feed side.

Indicator systems usually fail due to bulb or wiring faults. These can be traced using known techniques mentioned above. Generally, electronic flasher units rarely fail, but even so it is worth checking by bridging the unit out. Normally, the whole system is wired to and from the hazard switch, so always check the operation of the hazards as this can give clues about the nature of the fault.

11.3.9 Safety systems

Maintenance

Safety-related systems have a high level of built-in operational security and redundancy and therefore have sophisticated self-monitoring functions. Dynamic safety systems use the vehicle brake infrastructure and therefore routine maintenance of the brake mechanical and hydraulic system becomes even more important. Passive safety systems do not generally have any maintenance requirements.

Fault diagnosis

These systems have sophisticated self-diagnosis functions and therefore alert the user to any problems which could render them inoperative. Part of this function is continuous self-checking. In order to diagnose faults, access to this information is imperative. Therefore an appropriate scan tool is a prerequisite. Many of the individual components are engineered to give a high degree of reliability and as such they can only be replaced and not repaired. Common faults for active safety systems relate to failure of wheel-speed sensors. These sensors operate in extreme environments at the wheel hub and failure can occur. However, in this case the electronic system recognises the fault and alerts the driver immediately. The technician can identify the problem using a scan tool and can check the signal from the sensor with an oscilloscope to confirm the diagnosis.

11.3.10 Instrumentation systems

Maintenance

There is no specific maintenance requirement for instrumentation or driver information systems. Once installed, the systems generally operate reliably throughout the life of the vehicle.

Fault diagnosis

Instrumentation faults can be diagnosed by breaking the system down into its components:

- the sensor or sender unit
- the instrument panel
- the wiring in between.

When considered in this way, the system is immediately simplified. If a problem occurs, try to understand how the system works. If possible, get information about the sender/sensor unit (resistance values, voltages etc.) and carry out the appropriate tests at the unit itself. It is likely, in most cases, that this will be the easiest part of the system to access. If you can confirm that the sensor/sender is working correctly then you can trace the wiring. Check connectors and junctions, the most easily accessible first. Remember to be careful tracing along the wiring system as any disturbance could temporarily 'fix' the problem and then it will be even more difficult to trace. Instrument panel signals normally interface

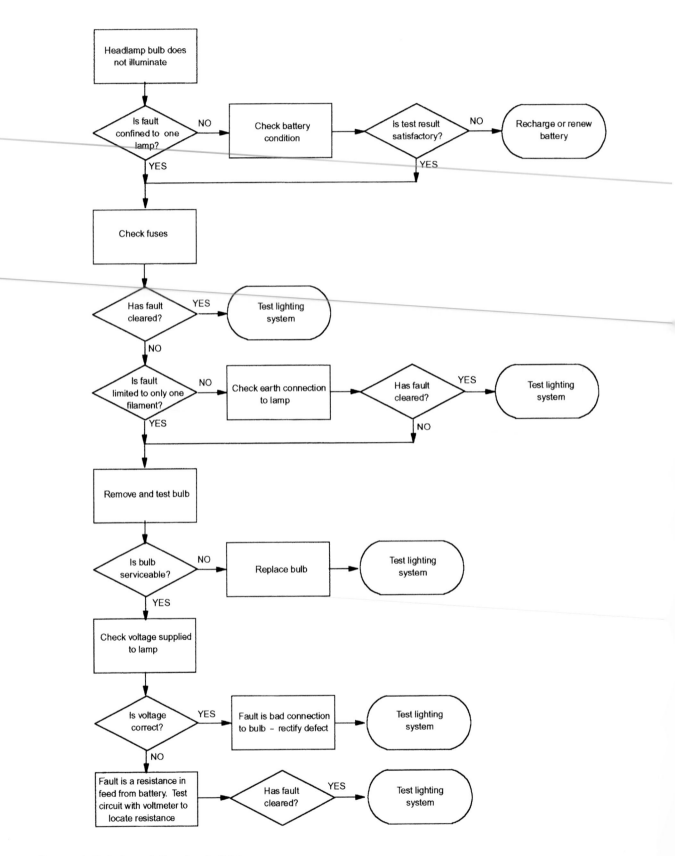

Figure 11.9 Fault diagnosis flow chart for lighting systems

Table 11.5 Test sequence when heated rear window fails to operate

Test	Result – Yes	Result – No
Is the fuse serviceable?	Proceed with test	Replace fuse
Is correct voltage applied to grid?	Check grid for open-circuit	Check circuit continuity and operation of relay

Table 11.6 Test sequence when left-hand side rear window fails to close

Test	Result – Yes	Result – No
Do front windows operate?	Check that driver's isolation switch is on	Proceed with test
Is fuse serviceable?	Proceed with test	Replace
Does right-side rear window operate?	Proceed with test	Check continuity from isolation earth switch to rear window switch and check feed to rear window switch
Expose left-hand-side switch: is supply voltage 12V?	Proceed with test	Check continuity between left- and right-hand switches
Measure output voltage from left-hand switch in up and down mode: is voltage 12V?	Fault is in limit switch or motor	Fault is in switch

via high-density pin connectors. These carry very small amplitude signals which can be easily affected by damp or moisture. Consider this and examine connectors and their operating environments carefully.

If it becomes necessary to remove the instrument panel (this should be the last port of call), do this carefully and considerately – no one likes a squeaky dashboard. All modern instrument panels are packed full of sophisticated electronics. If specific test equipment is available for checking the panel function then this should be used in preference to anything else. Disassembly of the instrument panel should be undertaken carefully, with manufacturer's instructions available, and in a static-protected environment. If it is not possible to fulfil any of these requirements do not attempt the job. Modern dashboard display systems form a node for the CAN bus and also act as a gateway between bus systems. In this case, diagnostic information is available via the diagnostic connector and this should be accessed first to get some indication where the problem might be before dismantling components.

11.3.11 On-board diagnostics

On-board diagnostics (OBD) are discussed in *FMVT: Book 2 Powertrain Electronics*. Remember that many chassis and body system components now use the same communication methods and techniques to share information as powertrain systems (e.g. CAN, LIN) and operate on the same network. Body and chassis diagnostic trouble codes (DTCs) are defined in the OBD

protocol standard and hence much useful information can be gained by exploiting the OBD functionality when troubleshooting. Generally, powertrain codes start with a P and body and chassis codes start with a B and C respectively. For more sophisticated control systems, accessing the DTCs should be the first step in a diagnostic procedure. In many systems, this will be the only way to start fault finding as the system and its components are so complex.

Some generic chassis codes are shown below.

C0000 – Vehicle speed information circuit malfunction
C0035 – Left front wheel-speed circuit malfunction
C0040 – Right front wheel-speed circuit malfunction
C0041 – Right front wheel-speed sensor circuit range/performance (EBCM)
C0045 – Left rear wheel-speed circuit malfunction
C0046 – Left rear wheel-speed sensor circuit range/performance (EBCM)
C0050 – Right rear wheel-speed circuit malfunction
C0051 – LF wheel-speed sensor circuit range/performance (EBCM)
C0060 – Left front ABS SOLENOID #1 circuit malfunction
C0065 – Left front ABS solenoid #2 circuit malfunction
C0070 – Right front ABS solenoid #1 circuit malfunction
C0075 – Right front ABS solenoid #2 circuit malfunction
C0080 – Left rear ABS solenoid #1 circuit malfunction
C0085 – Left rear ABS solenoid #2 circuit malfunction

C0090 – Right rear ABS solenoid #1 circuit
　　　　malfunction

C0095 – Right rear ABS solenoid #2 circuit
　　　　malfunction

C0110 – Pump motor circuit malfunction

C0121 – Valve relay circuit malfunction

C0128 – Low brake fluid circuit low

C0141 – Left TCS solenoid #1 circuit malfunction

C0146 – Left TCS solenoid #2 circuit malfunction

C0151 – Right TCS solenoid #1 circuit malfunction

C0156 – Right TCS solenoid #2 circuit malfunction

C0161 – ABS/TCS brake switch circuit malfunction

C0221 – Right front wheel-speed sensor circuit open

C0222 – Right front wheel-speed signal missing

C0223 – Right front wheel-speed signal erratic

C0225 – Left front wheel-speed sensor circuit open

C0226 – Left front wheel-speed signal missing

C0227 – Left front wheel-speed signal erratic

Some generic body codes are shown below:

B1200 – Climate control push-button circuit failure

B1201 – Fuel sender circuit failure

B1202 – Fuel sender circuit open

B1203 – Fuel sender circuit short to battery

B1204 – Fuel sender circuit short to ground

B1213 – Anti-theft number of programmed keys is
　　　　below minimum

B1216 – Emergency and roadside assistance switch
　　　　circuit short to ground

B1217 – Horn relay coil circuit failure

B1218 – Horn relay coil circuit short to Vbatt

B1219 – Fuel tank pressure sensor circuit failure

B1220 – Fuel tank pressure sensor circuit open

B1222 – Fuel temperature sensor #1 circuit failure

B1223 – Fuel temperature sensor #1 circuit open

B1224 – Fuel temperature sensor #1 circuit short to
　　　　battery

B1225 – Fuel temperature sensor #1 circuit short to
　　　　ground

B1226 – Fuel temperature sensor #2 circuit failure

B1227 – Fuel temperature sensor #2 circuit open

B1228 – Fuel temperature sensor #2 circuit short to
　　　　battery

B1229 – Fuel temperature sensor #2 circuit short to
　　　　ground

B1231 – Longitudinal acceleration threshold exceeded

Key Points

Try to employ a logical approach to your fault finding. This avoids wasting time and unnecessary replacement of components

Try to familiarise yourself with the system and attempt to understand how it works (assuming the information is available). This allows you to use your time more efficiently and effectively

Use a **heuristic** approach, i.e. use your experience with similar problems or scenarios to optimise the use of your time dealing with the current problem

Always take the path of least resistance. Test or check the components that are easiest to access first to prevent wasted time removing trim unnecessarily

Never overlook the obvious, never assume anything. Always check things for yourself. Assume everybody else is wrong and make your own checks to ensure that you always have the correct information during your investigation process

Always gather as much information as you can. If available, use manuals and wiring diagrams. Check them even if you think you know how the system works! If DTCs are available and accessible, use them to help point you in the right direction to start dealing with the problem

When dealing with intermittent problems take a strategic approach. Even though the systems can be complex there is no **magic**. If something does not work there is a reason. Also, problems do not fix themselves. Try to get to the root of the problem. If you do not, it will come back!

INDEX